ITALIAN IMMIGRATION IN THE AMERICAN WEST

ITALIAN IMMIGRATION IN THE AMERICAN WEST

1870–1940

Kenneth Scambray

UNIVERSITY OF NEVADA PRESS | *Reno & Las Vegas*

University of Nevada Press | Reno, Nevada 89557 USA
www.unpress.nevada.edu

Cover photograph courtesy of Galveston Photographic Subject Files:
Immigrants. Rosenberg Library, Galveston, TX.
Cover design by Iris Saltus

LIBRARY OF CONGRESS CATALOGING-IN-PUBLICATION DATA

Names: Scambray, Kenneth, author.
Title: Italian immigration in the American West : 1870–1940 / Kenneth Scambray.
Description: Reno : University of Nevada Press, [2021] | Includes bibliographical references and index. | Summary: "*Italian immigration in the American West: 1870–1940* is a study of Italian immigration in thirteen western states. In documenting the contributions of Italian men and women in the development of the American West and identifying the cooperative relationships between all immigrants in western enclaves before 1940, Scambray's study challenges today's assumptions about immigration, race, and gender"— Provided by publisher.
Identifiers: LCCN 2020051375 (print) | LCCN 2020051376 (ebook) |
ISBN 9781647790028 (trade paperback) | ISBN 9781647790035 (ebook)
Subjects: LCSH: Italian Americans—West (U.S.)—History—19th century. | Italian Americans—West (U.S.)—History—20th century. | Emigration and immigration—History. | West (U.S.)—Emigration and immigration—History—19th century. | West (U.S.)—Emigration and immigration—History—20th century.
Classification: LCC E184.I8 S435 2021 (print) | LCC E184.I8 (ebook) |
DDC 978/.0200451—dc23
LC record available at https://lccn.loc.gov/2020051375
LC ebook record available at https://lccn.loc.gov/2020051376
The paper used in this book meets the requirements of American National Standard for Information Sciences—Permanence of Paper for Printed Library Materials, ANSI/NISO Z39.48-1992 (R2002).

FIRST PRINTING

Manufactured in the United States of America

For

Carole Salisch Scambray

with love and respect

Contents

and Nancy Vezzuto. I relied on numerous interviews located in university archives. I also need to thank my parents, Marion (Schembri) and Josephine (Di Filippo) Scambray, for family documents located now in the Scambray Family Papers in my personal files and for their treasured oral histories of our family's origins in Italy, Texas, Utah, and Fresno's West Side immigrant community. If there is a fundamental source that predates all my academic research for this project, it must be located in their oral histories that began to raise questions about not just family origins but the very basis of the immigrant narrative in America.

Last but not least, I must extend a thanks to my wife, Carole, for her infinite patience and the incalculable hours she spent reading the scores of drafts of this manuscript. Wherever I resisted her suggestions on form and content, inevitably I found that she was correct, and my subsequent revisions of the manuscript reflect her thoughtful and careful analysis. Her patience with me is surpassed only by my respect and love for her as a person and as my life's partner. In honor of her tireless work and patience, I have dedicated this book to her.

Acknowledgments

A work of this scope was not possible without the aid of many institutions and people along the way to its completion. First and foremost, I would like to thank the Faculty Professional Support Committee at the University of La Verne for several faculty research grants and generous released time from my teaching responsibilities that allowed me to begin research on this work. Without the university's generous support, I would not have been able to launch this project. I would also like to thank colleagues in the Western Chapter of the American Italian Historical Association (now the Italian American Studies Association): Lawrence DiStasi, Laura Ruberto, and Teri Ann Bengiveno. Our collaboration in the early stages of this book gave me invaluable support and encouragement to continue with my research and writing. I would also like to thank Professor Andrew Rolle for his work over the years on Italians in the West, especially his early study, *The Immigrant Upraised*. It was an inspirational work for me that, as any good scholarly work, suggested yet many more avenues of research for a future study. I would also like to thank Professor Gloria Ricci Lothrop, who encouraged me in my research and whose works on California Italians served as models and valuable resources for further research. I would like to extend a special thank-you to Marianna Gatto, executive director of the Italian American Museum of Los Angeles. We both shared a common interest in identifying former Italian neighborhoods in Los Angeles and spent several mornings visiting locations that she had identified from her files as the curator of history and education at El Pueblo Historical Monument.

Oral history has also played an important role in my research. Where the documented historical record is blank, I often sought out personal friends and relatives for their recollections of events, people, and places. I would like to thank the following for their always generous time and patience with my questions and sometimes multiple phone calls: Sam Shiro, Reno Morra, Pete DeFendis, Leo La Mattina, Robert Scambray, Terry Scambray, Jo Ann Sorrenti, Diane Sorrenti, Sally Caglia, Al Cribari, John Cribari, James Jordan, Jo Meek, Marie Piccolo, Mauro Simone,

ITALIAN IMMIGRATION
IN THE AMERICAN WEST

INTRODUCTION

For my purpose I have defined the West as those states that are west of the 100th meridian. There is nothing sacrosanct about this line of demarcation. What constitutes the West has varied among historians over time, and the West's construction in the popular imagination has varied as well. The only qualification to my choice of states is Texas, which is a border state, both culturally and geographically. It is divided nearly in half by the 100th meridian. Its history of slavery links it with the South. But as Billington and Hardaway point out, its slave heritage does not necessarily distinguish it from other western states that also had slaves in their early histories.[1] What otherwise recommended Texas for my study was that it had in the post-1870s period a large settlement of Italians.

As a rule, Italian immigrants' migration pattern after settlement in the Southwest was more western than eastern oriented. This is why I begin with the three southwestern states. When farming proved to be too difficult or was unsuccessful in Texas, New Mexico, or Arizona, farmers migrated to more favorable western locations to farm or to find work. Likewise, when mines closed in New Mexico, miners traveled to mining centers such as Utah and Colorado. The same can be said for what I call the midsection of the West. If Italian workers in these four states sought other opportunities, their choices more often than not were other nearby western states where there were numerous Italian enclaves with available jobs and higher salaries than in the East. The same can be said of Montana and Alaska. Because of the cold climate in both regions, they provided fewer opportunities for Italian immigrants, especially in farming. As a result, migration to warmer states was the most desirable choice.

My work also intends to place Italians in the broader context of the immigrant narrative that includes all national groups that came to the United States between 1870 and 1940. A book of this scope raises many issues surrounding the history of gender, race, and privilege in America. The Chinese, Italians, Japanese, Jews, and Armenians did face xenophobia to varying degrees. However, all shared a similar immigrant experience distinct from Native American and African American experiences. This shared immigrant experience challenges the contemporary construction of race. All immigrants, no matter their individual struggles, were given access to America's economic resources, from jobs to land, either as owners or as leaseholders. The same cannot be said for African Americans and Native Americans at the time. As a result, I avoid the usual clichés that have characterized the immigrant experience such as "struggle and success." Such a simplistic notion devalues Native Americans' and African Americans' struggle not just to succeed but even to survive in the face of genocide and a segregated social order in America.

As Michael Rogin argues, land, especially in the West, was the major determiner of both political power and wealth. Native American lands had extraordinary value for the development of industrial America. But they were not given the opportunity to assimilate into the new economic and social order in the West. Native Americans were removed to reservations and segregated from thriving immigrant enclaves. It is impossible to extol immigrant hard work in developing western lands without acknowledging the genocide of Native Americans that preceded the mass arrival of immigrants after the 1870s. To expose this tragic history, I pause briefly at the beginning of the California chapter to document the extermination of Native Americans and the theft of their lands in California. At the risk of lengthening my manuscript beyond reason, I could have written a similar section in each of the other chapters. However, California was an appropriate place to qualify immigrant success in a state that provided all immigrant farmers with some of the cheapest and best farmland in the United States. While some groups such as the Chinese and Japanese were prohibited from owning land initially in some western states, in the long run it mattered little whether the immigrant farmer owned the land or leased it. In either case, the cheap cost of land was calculated accordingly, and the farmers were able to take their profits. They could also assume title under another name or a family member who was a citizen.[2]

Like Native Americans, African Americans did not share in the occupational opportunities afforded to immigrants. Nearly all immigrants were criminalized upon their arrival, Italians among them. But this was a stigma that they were able to overcome through the opportunities offered to them. However, as Khalil Gibran Muhammad has documented, at the time not only were African Americans stereotyped as criminals but laws were passed to further enforce this racist stigma. Furthermore, as

David M. Oshinsky explains, Black Codes were passed by states that made imprisonment for petty crimes mandatory for African American men. African American women suffered a similar fate in the West. By the 1930s, governmental housing policies segregated African Americans. Richard Rothstein reveals that African Americans were denied housing loans underwritten by the US government and were segregated in housing projects constructed on the outskirts of immigrant neighborhoods. Official federal government–sponsored segregation was not limited to the Jim Crow South. This legacy of criminalizing and segregation of African Americans has continued well into the post-1965 era, as Michele Alexander demonstrates.[3] Native Americans and African Americans faced permanent social, cultural, and institutional barriers to their success in the West that immigrants, regardless of the era's xenophobia, did not face. But my distinction among the narratives is not divisive. Rather, I am making distinctions in the interest of historical accuracy and social justice.

Immigrants had another advantage in the West. For decades, labor contractors were demonized for their exploitation of immigrant labor. Much of this criticism is justifiable. They often worked closely with management to break strikes, which resulted in violence and in one instance in Wyoming a bloody massacre of Chinese miners. Yet in the process of bringing large numbers of workers to the West, labor agents were laying the foundation for their own demise. As Gunther Peck illustrates, labor agents provided immigrants jobs. Most important, Peck points out that eventually those workers under contract with agents became free labor or at times simply broke their contracts and left for better-paying jobs. There was a chronic labor shortage in the West. However, African Americans and Native Americans did not share in the free-labor market to the same degree. Native Americans and African Americans were recruited by contractors only in rare instances, and sometimes only as strikebreakers.[4]

Adding to labor contractors' recruitment, nearly all western states launched official advertising campaigns to attract immigrant labor. Late-generation Americans (a term that I have adopted from Herbert Gans's article "The End of Late-Generation European Ethnicity in America?") migrated west to vacant western lands, either buying cheap land or availing themselves of free homestead lands ahead of the inevitable arrival of the railroads. Early biographical histories of California document these settlers. They either leased or sold their land to historically landless immigrants eager to invest in a piece of the American dream. Free-labor immigrants were able to leave their dangerous work in the mines, smelters, and mills with savings that they then invested in land or in enclave businesses.

At the same time that immigrants were making their way in America, according to John Higham, they were the target of xenophobic attacks from the highest levels of the federal government down to local citizens. The 1920s saw the revival of the Ku Klux Klan (KKK) in the West, especially in Colorado and Oregon, with its anti-Catholic and anti-Semitic platform. The Klan's platform found support from America's long-standing opposition to immigrants who brought with them to America that "whore of Rome," the Catholic Church. The KKK found context as well in the pseudoscientific movement of eugenics promoted by such widely read works as Madison Grant's *The Decline of the Great Race* (1916) and Lothrop Stoddard's *The Rising Tide of Color against White World-Supremacy* (1920). Grant wrote the introduction to Stoddard's work. As Daniel Okrent demonstrates, Grant "put the pieces together" of eugenics, and Stoddard defined America's bogus "Nordic inheritance." In the West the eugenics movement found support in Washington State's Representative Albert Johnson, who cosponsored the Johnson-Reed Act of 1924 and who was president of the Eugenics Research Association. In California he was joined on the national stage by Stanford University professor Edward Ross, who opposed the inclusion of masses of immigrants into the US population as "race suicide," a term that became widely used by anti-immigrant factions. The KKK's anti-Semitic platform found support in Ole Hanson's anti-Semitism. Former mayor of Seattle and founder of San Clemente, California, Hanson wrote that Bolshevism was in its international influence "as cosmopolitan as a Jew." Both *Bolshevism* and *cosmopolitan* were widely used anti-Semitic tropes at the time.[5]

In spite of the era's xenophobia and even the Klan's political influence in the 1920s, businessmen's associations and state immigration offices never relented in their recruitment of immigrant labor. In time, Italians and all immigrants won over skeptics and even earned praise for their productiveness. The era's nativism did finally result in the Johnson-Reed Act, which severely limited Italians and Jews. The Japanese and Chinese had previously been restricted. As Vincent Cannato reminds us, the Johnson-Reed Act, however, did not restrict immigration from America's neighbors, Canada and Mexico.[6] In addition, when the United States needed an ally in the Pacific at the beginning of World War II, the United States lifted the restriction on Chinese immigrants. Politics and economics nearly always trumped racial theory for immigrants.

But immigrants often paid a high price for their high wages and the abundance of jobs in the West. I document the injuries and lives lost in heavy industry, especially mining deaths. Before the rise of unions, the US government was slow and ineffective in establishing safety requirements, especially in mining. Many of even the most catastrophic accidents remained for decades forgotten and unrecorded in the history of the West. Deaths in industrial accidents also had a devastating effect on wives and children, including those families left behind in Italy. But those who survived or quit work in hazardous industries were able to find available jobs or to invest in businesses and farmland.

Equally important, the arriving unmarried male Italian immigrants found culturally accommodating circumstances in enclaves. Andrew Rolle challenged Oscar Handlin's characterization of America's immigrant masses toiling at low wages in eastern urban slums.[7] They were not totally "strangers in the land."

I open nearly every chapter with the documentation of the settlement of Italian Jesuits before 1870 in advance of Italian immigration. Their purpose was to bring Christianity to the native populations and to establish missions. But in the decades that followed, these missions became cultural and social centers for Catholic Italians, as well as for Germans, Irish, Mexicans, and other Catholic populations. In these early churches Italians were able to relocate familiar religious iconography from their villages, while enclaves provided some semblance of home, with festivals, folk traditions, food, and fraternal orders. Eventually, parishes built schools, and the Jesuits established Catholic colleges, which are now some of the oldest and most prestigious universities in the United States. These enclaves in the West provided a soft landing for Italians and other Catholic immigrants. Italians' mutual-aid societies and other cultural organizations in enclaves also aided in their assimilation into American life.

Although these western settlements were at least initially populated mostly by men, Italian immigrant women made a significant contribution to immigrant success. I address throughout the chapters their essential roles as farmwives, cannery workers, and enclave entrepreneurs. Defying their prescribed roles in the family, Italian women became entrepreneurs, often owning boardinghouses and hotels. These women applied their domestic skills, the cultural capital that they had brought with them from the Old World. In addition, Italian women provided the necessary recipes and culinary skills in the kitchen for scores of successful Italian restaurants in the West. Just as important, Italian women were responsible for keeping a well-organized home and rearing children, so important to immigrant success. But not all women were so successful in the West. I demonstrate that immigrant enclaves developed a vigorous prostitution trade that exploited and abused poor immigrant and late-generation women. These women did not share in the benefits of the immigrant narrative, that intersection of social and cultural capital that provided immigrant families and their children an opportunity to step up to America's middle class.

Unavoidably, in the post–World War II discourse over race, achieving success in America has too often revolved around the question of who became "white" in America. As Higham and Okrent argue, Italian Catholics were placed on the bottom of the racial hierarchy and were no less the target of degrading stereotypes than other immigrant groups. Their restriction under the Johnson-Reed Act placed a stringent quota on Italians, limiting their numbers to 3,845, or 1.3 percent of their previous annual immigration figure. From Italian immigrants' high of 222,496 in 1910, by 1925 fewer than 2,662 passed through Ellis Island.[8] The act focused on Italians because they were the largest single immigrant group entering the United States at the time. In Stoddard's words, they were a major contributor to the "rising tide of color," undermining "white world-supremacy."

But the xenophobic attitudes toward Italians and their exclusion from the United States did not limit their success in America. There was a shortage of labor in the West, and immigrant labor was too valuable a commodity to allow racial theorizing to stand in the way of America's industrial and agricultural development. The disparity between wages and the cost of living, including the cost of land, allowed even the day laborer in the West to invest in enclave businesses and farmland. Mining, millwork, and railroad work provided even higher wages. The social capital that circulated in what Donna Gabaccia calls "enclave markets" worked ultimately to the benefit of all immigrants.[9] If Italians were not initially able to capitalize the opening of a business, they either received a loan from a friend or relative or formed partnerships with other immigrants.

Cultural heritage was also a major factor in Italian success. Italians brought with them from Italy a variety of artisan skills that allowed them to find work or open businesses within enclaves. Formerly peasant farmers in Italy, they became farmers with dramatic results throughout the West, especially in California. I document how, from small farmers, many of the early Italian immigrants became some of the biggest growers and largest vintners of bulk wines in the United States. Many of the early family-owned wineries are still producers of some of California's finest wines. Italians' development of the wine industry and their eventual dominance in the industry were unchallenged by any other immigrant group. Italians colonized the Pacific Coast fishing industry as well, which provided a multiplicity of jobs for experienced Italian fishermen coming from fishing villages in Italy. In addition, scores of Italian immigrants entered America with college degrees that allowed them to further enhance the economic, social, and cultural development of their respective enclaves throughout the West. The exchange of social capital took a more official and obvious form in selected states where Tyrolean Italian bankers in Wyoming and Italian American A. P. Giannini in California funded thousands of farms, businesses, and other investments. In time, immigrants were able to receive bank loans from non-Italian late-generation bankers who even in the short term became convinced that Italians were reliable customers who could be trusted to pay their loans on time. But Italian immigrants' success does not distinguish them from any other immigrant group. Other immigrant groups shared to varying degrees the exercise of social and cultural capital in their farming enterprises, in their access to jobs, and in their businesses in western immigrant enclaves.

From the very outset of Italian settlement in the West, Italian success and their ready assimilation into American society before 1940 troubled many Italian community leaders, who warned their respective communities of the dangers of assimilation and the erasure of their heritage. Since the 1960s, Italian American scholars have been particularly concerned over the erasure of Italian immigrant history and have joined the labyrinthine discourse over "whiteness." Richard Alba was among the first Italian American scholars to signal a radical transformation in Italian identity in his influential book *Italian Americans: Into the Twilight of Ethnicity* (1985). Alba uses the term European Americans to describe all European immigrants and their late-generation offspring, which added yet another layer to the discourse over ethnicity. In an article, Rudolph Vecoli addresses the same issue. He was followed by Thomas A. Guglielmo. In response to this study, editors Jennifer Guglielmo and Salvatore Salerno published *Are Italians White? How Race Is Made in America* (2003). In his article, Gans concludes that identity is difficult to quantify and that it is impossible to predict with certainty the outcome of any social process. It is significant that three of the studies above pose the issue of ethnicity and Italian American "whiteness" in the interrogative. David Roediger is forced to admit, while tracking immigrant success from "Ellis Island to the Suburbs," that "whiteness" is impossible to define.[10] Left out of his subtitle are the roads from Angel Island in the San Francisco Bay where Asians entered the United States and the roads from the Canadian and Mexican borders where North, Central, and South Americans also began their journeys to the suburbs. Another interrogative comes to mind: Why were these journeys omitted in his subtitle?

None of the studies can offer a definitive answer to the question of identity, Italian American or otherwise. As Jacqueline Jones points out, Americans have held tenaciously onto the myth of race, in particular "whiteness." She contends that race has always been used and continues to be used as a pretext for the exercise of power and economic advantage. The role that race has played in the subjugation of African Americans is clearly different from the nuanced and sometimes difficult-to-define role that race has played in the immigrant narrative. However, as Cornel West successfully argues, whatever its problematic application to immigrants and late-generation Americans, race has always mattered and still does for African Americans and Native Americans.[11]

While Italian immigrant success did in fact lead them and their offspring to the suburbs, as I demonstrate in the conclusion of each chapter, post-1970s demographic statistics illustrate that Italian Americans' identification with their immigrant heritage has proved resilient to all theories of erasure. Both Andrew Greeley and Michael Novak documented the tenacity of the immigrant heritage and late-generation ethnic identity in American politics and culture. Although written more than a generation ago, Greeley's and Novak's prescient studies remain relevant today. Each of my chapters ends with what are always surprising numbers of the states' inhabitants that claim Italian immigrant heritage, numbers that are too often out of balance with the census records of Italian settlements in the states before 1940. As Greeley, Novak, and Gans have argued, the conventional notions of assimilation have proved ineffective in predicting and explaining the revival of Italian Americans' identification with their roots. While honoring their immigrant heritage, Italian Americans have also created a transnational identity in which they connect with modern Italy through cultural and business associations. The Internet and ease of international travel have shifted the locus of Italian identity. Francis Fukuyama validates the movement toward a transnational identity for all Americans who continue to identify with their immigrant heritage. Laura Ruberto and Joseph Sciorra demonstrate that a new generation of post-1990s immigrants from Italy has also enhanced this connection with contemporary Italian society.[12]

In the conclusion, I underscore how the exchange of social and cultural capital was at the basis of all immigrant communities' success. The exchange of social and cultural capital is dramatically illustrated in the banking career of Italian American A. P. Giannini. In his efforts to "democratize" banking, Giannini's initial success in his small bank in North Beach San Francisco was based on his Italian board members and Italian immigrant customers. Ultimately, he solicited business from all immigrants. Access to capital allowed Italians and all other immigrants within the context of the immigrant narrative to exploit the skills and aptitudes that their culture provided them. Before Giannini's Bank of Italy, the exchange of social and cultural capital within immigrant groups has a special history that predates their arrival in the United States. The Chinese have *hui*, the Japanese *tanomoshi*, Koreans *kye*, Mexican *tanda* or *cundina*, the Cambodians *tontine*, the Filipinos *paluwagan*, and Ethiopians *ekub*. All of these function as forms of savings-and-loan associations that funded and continue to fund today the establishment of enclave businesses and college educations.[13] From their investments and the success of their businesses, Italians created a legacy for future generations that allowed offspring to step up to the middle class and avail themselves of the opportunities in post–World War II America.

I

THE SOUTHWEST

CHAPTER 1

TEXAS

Railroads—Recruitment and Chain Migration

Similar to the other western territories and states at the close of the nineteenth century, the earliest Italians to come to Texas from the seventeenth to the early nineteenth centuries were explorers, missionaries, soldiers, and merchants. By 1870 there were 186 Italian immigrants in Texas. Thereafter, the extension of the railroad brought a significant number of Italians to the state. In the early construction of the rail lines, the Irish dominated the workforce but were soon followed by Italian, Chinese, Japanese, Romanian, and Mexican immigrants. An initial group of twelve hundred Italians, mainly from the region of Lombardy, worked on the extension of the railroad to Texas in 1882. While in time immigrants from southern Italy would outnumber those from the North, Italian immigrants initially came from northern Italy, the regions of Trentino–Alto Adige, Piedmont, Veneto, and Friuli-Venezia Giulia. Facing an agricultural crisis in southern Italy, southern Italians soon followed.[1]

Those who worked their way west often found the work on the railroads exploitative and dangerous. In 1889 approximately 1 worker out of 367 died on the job. The requirements for reporting industrial and mining accidents throughout the West were all but nonexistent before World War I. In 1907, pressured by eastern railroad workers, Congress passed legislation limiting work on the railroad to a sixteen-hour day. By any standard, such a limit still allowed for a long, grueling workday, already plagued by heavy lifting, strenuous pick-and-shovel roadwork, and dangerous explosives. How any regulations could be enforced in the remote railroad camps in the West is difficult to determine. While the more skilled railroad workers, including porters, mechanics, and engineers, began to organize in eastern urban centers, workers laying the tracks suffered a different fate.[2] Working for less than a dollar a day and crossing uninhabited lands, workers could not readily leave their jobs for other work or negotiate for better working conditions. Their housing consisted of little more than tents, and their diet was limited only to what railroad companies provided. However, they had little opportunity to spend their wages, meager as they were. As a result, when they reached the end of the line and were released from their contracts, they had some money in their pockets to begin life in Texas's remote but developing towns where relatives or friends from their native villages had informed them that there were jobs.

In addition to the railroads, local business associations advertised in European and Asian newspapers to attract immigrants to the state. Italian and American immigration officials also cooperated in recruiting Italians and placing them in regions that were compatible with their geographical origins. The landscape and climate in Sicily were similar to the South and Southwest, in particular Texas. Based on labor contracts or diplomatic agreements, Italians arriving in New Orleans sometimes boarded trains that took them directly to Texas. For those not under contract, New Orleans was often the first stop where free-labor Italians were able to find work in area sugarcane fields, on the docks, or at the local vegetable market, which was dominated by both Sicilian and French immigrants. The port at Galveston was a direct point of entry where a group of Waldensians from Tuscany settled Galveston in the 1890s.[3] Chain migration also became a factor in drawing others to the state. As a result, major Italian colonies formed in Bryan in Brazos County, Dickinson in Galveston County, and Montague in Montague County, with smaller enclaves in other parts of the state, including Jefferson County east of Houston.

By 1890 there were 2,107 Italians in Texas, but by 1920 that number grew to 8,024 out of a total of 363,832 foreign born, which was 7.8 percent of the state's population. Immigrants, Italians chief among them, were filling every possible labor and business category in the state, from small businesses, farm laborers, and tenant farmers to miners and family-owned truck farmers. At the time, Italians joined an already established and successful Mexican American and immigrant Mexican population. The community of Mexican immigrants was largely the work of three major Mexican labor contractors working out of El Paso to the north: Felix Martinez, the Zarate-Avina labor agency, and the most powerful Mexican labor contractor in the West, Roman Gonzalez, including three of Gonzalez's competitors in the labor market, Hanlin Supply Company, Holmes Supply Company, and the L. H. Manning Supply Company of El Paso.[4] The role of the labor contractor in locating jobs for all major immigrant groups cannot be undervalued, in spite of their often exploitative contracts.

Industry and the Enclave Economy—Jefferson County

The arrival of the railroad, including a spur of the Kansas City Southern Railway that was extended to Port Arthur on the Gulf, opened national markets for Texas's mining, timber, and agricultural products. An abundant source of immigrant labor was ready to fill the state's labor needs. It did not take long before Sicilians quickly outnumbered those original immigrants from Lombardy. Before 1920 more than 90 percent of the Italian immigrants who settled in Jefferson County came from villages in the provinces of Palermo, Trapani, Agrigento, and Caltanissetta. The Italian population grew fourfold between 1900 and 1910. In addition to establishing farms, immigrants worked for about a dollar a day in the area refineries and sawmills near Beaumont. They also opened new businesses, from grocery stores and confectioneries to tailor shops, barbershops, and shoe stores. By 1892 Beaumont, Jefferson's county seat, had the first rice mill in Texas. By the 1890s, it had a growing cattle industry and a number of small family-run farms. By the early 1900s, the Southern Pacific, Kansas City Southern, Missouri Pacific, and Atchison, Topeka, and Santa Fe Railroad all serviced the town. As a result, the population in Beaumont nearly tripled, from 3,296 in 1890 to 9,427 in 1900. In 1901 the "Spindletop oil gusher" created a boom that would allow Beaumont's population to more than double by 1910 to 20,640 residents. Immediately after the Spindletop discovery, three oil companies rushed into the town within a year: Texas Company (Texaco), Gulf Oil, and Humble (Exxon). The Magnolia Refinery soon became the town's largest employer. In the wake of the oil boom, the town's population grew again from 40,422 in 1920 to 57,732 by 1930.[5]

Just before the building of a new port and the extension of the southern terminus to Port Arthur, in 1899 immigrants were hired to dig a navigable canal at Sabine Lake that allowed oceangoing cargo ships access to the city docks. Italians in Jefferson County took advantage of the growing market in rice production and the developing coal, timber, and cattle industries. Farmers utilized the local bayous for the water-intensive rice fields in the area. Adding to the Sicilian immigrants who had already settled the region, additional Italians came from the North and South of Italy, Liguria, Trentino–Alto Adige, Campania, and Calabria.[6]

Just ahead of the oil boom in Beaumont, Italians had already established what Donna Gabaccia calls an "enclave market" containing several businesses. C. Angelo owned a fruit stand on Pearl Street, Frank Liberto opened the Crescent City Market on Houston Highway, and G. Fontana opened a shoe-repair shop on Pine Street. The men who owned these shops often moonlighted in the local mills or refineries while leaving their wives or older children to run their businesses. The family had the benefit of earning a double salary without the overhead of hiring additional labor. Because of their early success, Italians integrated quickly into Jefferson society. Fewer than 25 percent of them left for other regions of the United States or returned to Italy, while the national rate was more than double that percentage. Before 1920 Italians had one of the highest rates of return among the immigrant population. Between 1908 and 1916, 1,215,998 Italians returned to their homeland.[7]

Among the northern Italians and Sicilians who settled the state, by 1920 there were approximately four Tyroleans from Trentino occupying two colonies in San Antonio and Austin, where they worked mainly in cattle ranching and farming. They were unique among the many dialect groups that came from Italy. Because of their dual identity, both Italian and Austrian, as well as their German-influenced dialects, they tended to form homogeneous colonies and to limit membership in their churches and their mutual-aid societies only to other Tyroleans. As they developed businesses throughout the West, their retail partnerships and especially their banks were owned and operated largely by Tyroleans, though they did not limit their banking and retail businesses only to Tyrolean customers. They contributed greatly to the development of enclave economies for all immigrants in many regions of the West where they settled.[8]

At the time, San Antonio became well known as a center of the arts in Texas, as the home of an Italian-born sculptor, the colorful Pompeo Coppini. He opened an art school in San Antonio and sculpted public monuments throughout the state. Joined by at least eight other Italian and Italian American sculptors, he became the most renowned artist in Texas. Adding to the town's fame, it was also host to the theatrical arts and a nationally famous commercial brand. Joseph and Salvatore Lucchese arrived from Sicily at the Port of Galveston in 1882. They found work in a local boot factory, where they were able to apply the skills they had learned from their father, Gaetano Lucchese, a shoemaker in their hometown. Within a year the two brothers moved to San Antonio, where they opened a shop, Lucchese Bros., near Fort Sam Houston. They also signed a contract with the government and began making military boots for the troops stationed at the fort. With the combined sales from their government contract and their shop, their business flourished. Sharing much in common with the local Mexican Catholic community, the brothers learned Spanish and integrated well into the local culture. By 1912 Sam (as Salvatore was known), who had taken the leading role in the boot company, invested in San Antonio's Teatro Zaragoza, a venue that was the center of Mexican American entertainment and culture. He opened as well the Teatro Nacional. With frequent trips to Mexico, Sam brought some of the most famous acts to his theaters. Having been brought up in a theatrical environment in San Antonio, his daughter Josephine became an internationally known opera singer. Upon Sam's death in 1929, his son Cosimo assumed the reins of Lucchese Bros., which soon after became a nationally recognized brand. After Cosimo retired in 1961, the Lucchese shoemaking heritage extended to the third generation, when Cosimo's son Sam took over the company and modernized its production.[9]

In spite of their parochial allegiance to their dialect groups, Italian immigrants began to unify in Jefferson County. Living and working together among other dialect groups, they realized their common interest. By cooperating with other Italians, including other immigrants and the already settled late-generation Americans, they were taking that first step toward assimilation into American life. Italians began to fund benevolent societies and fraternal organizations. Originally, these mutual-aid societies attempted to limit their membership to a single dialect group. But in time, most began to diversify their membership. In Port Arthur, Italians formed the Vita Nuova Club and in Beaumont the San Salvadore Society. The oldest aid society on record was the Christopher Columbus Society, founded in 1918. These societies provided a safety net for immigrant families when a parent died or a member, especially the wage earner, was stricken with a debilitating illness.[10] The establishment and funding of mutual-aid societies and fraternal organizations were also a sign of the immigrant community's collective prosperity.

Enclave Businesses—Dallas County

As early as the 1880s, numerous Italians had established businesses along Main Street in Dallas in Dallas County. Among Dallas's early Italian arrivals, brothers Francesco and Achille De Stefano arrived in Texas in 1873. By 1884 they made their way to Dallas and established a produce business on Main Street as an outlet for the farm products Italians were producing in the surrounding area. In 1887 Nicola Negro arrived in Dallas and established a successful produce business as well. He had initially worked in the New Orleans Italian market before his move to Dallas. Drawing on both his experience and his connections with Italians in New Orleans, he pioneered in the refrigerated shipment of fruits from New Orleans, especially bananas.[11] With the expansion of the railroad, the developing enclave was not merely a local affair between farmers and the local greengrocers.

The De Stefano brothers were joined in the business enclave by George Sigari and Joseph Larcara with their two confectionery shops on Main; John Marini and Pascal Savone with their two grocery stores; Domenic Massa, who operated a fruit stand on Elm; and E. G. Fritta, who opened a saloon nearby. Based on the names in the local business directory, these early Italians were joined in the business district along Main and other cross streets by a variety of other immigrant businesses, Mexican, Jewish, and eastern European.[12]

Otherwise, immigrant businesses were mixed in with many long-established businesses. The names in the 1884 business directory suggest that the majority of the businesses in downtown Dallas were owned by late-generation European Americans who had begun arriving shortly after 1800. These Americans may have at first looked with some suspicion at their new neighbors. However, they had to admit finally, perhaps grudgingly, that the immigrants were, in Henry James's words, "affirming their vitality and value and playing their part" in the new social order in Dallas.[13]

Mining—Erath County

Italians settled in small communities as miners, farmers, merchants, and section hands on the railroad in Tarrant, Montague, McLennan, and Erath Counties. They had their most significant impact in Erath County, where they were "credited for helping Thurber change from a camp to a modern city." In the 1880s, the Texas Pacific Coal Company advertised for immigrant labor. Labor contractors and free-labor immigrant workers responded. The New York, Texas, and Mexican Railway also brought an additional twelve hundred Italians to build a line from Victoria to Rosenberg Junction, not far from Houston. The majority of these men came from northern Italy and settled in an area called Italian Hill. The men built brick ovens in which their wives baked upwards of fifteen loaves a week for their families. For Italians, food held a "symbolic value," a representation of their home and culture. Their traditional brick ovens allowed them to transfer their culinary traditions to their new home in an otherwise unfamiliar landscape. As one observer said, Italians were "unquestionably Thurber's most colorful citizens." But for many in the mining community, the work was far too dangerous. Many of the initial Italian miners began to leave the mines with their savings and establish businesses. A commercial enclave soon developed, with saloons and grocery stores run by several Italian families.[14]

Italians composed 52 percent of the miners, while all foreign born in the mines composed 84 percent of the workforce, about 35 percent of Thurber's population. Miners labored for $1 per ton for ten hours a day six days a week, earning approximately $35 a month. Thurber also established a secondary industry, the Thurber Brick Plant, which produced millions of bricks each month before World War I. Thurber thrived for more than three decades before its redbrick smokestacks stopped belching smoke and the site closed. Thurber's enclave declined, miners left, and immigrant businesses closed. As a result, there is little evidence left today of the Italian presence.[15]

Farming—Chambers, Harris, Dallas, Jefferson, Travis, and Val Verde Counties

By 1910 more than one hundred Italian families had farms surrounding the growing metropolitan centers of Houston (Harris County), Dallas (Dallas County), and Austin (Travis County). Most of these families owned their own farms. This suggests that the farmers had worked initially in New Orleans, at nearby industries, or possibly as tenant farmers in the area before they were able to purchase and finance their own farms. In the course of a year, for example, a tenant farmer could save upwards of $1,000 based on the $5 price of a rented acre and the market price of corn or cotton.[16] Whatever the source of their savings, free-labor Italians found plenty of work between New Orleans and the business-friendly environment in Texas before they were able to invest in farmland.

There was another settlement of Italians in the small town of Del Rio, the county seat of Val Verde County, 160 miles west of San Antonio. The town had the advantage of an abundant water supply provided by the nearby San Felipe Creek. As a result, the Southern Pacific Railroad made the town a site for its railroad headquarters in 1883. To aid in the development of agriculture, early settlers dug a series of irrigation canals. Nearly all of these families had come from northern Italy. They soon became known as the Italian Colony of Del Rio. Some had come with the railroad, while others had been attracted by the cheap land. Among the entrepreneurs in the community were G.B. Cassinelli and Gerolamo Taini, who settled in Del Rio in 1885 and together established a construction business. After initially working on the Val Verde County Courthouse, they went on to build many residential and commercial projects in the growing town. Cassinelli also owned a general store and opened the Cassinelli Gin House, while Taini also diversified and went into farming. The most well known among the early Italian immigrants in the town was Francesco Qualia (possibly Quaglia), who had settled in Del Rio in 1880. By 1883 he opened the Val Verde Winery, Texas's first commercial winery and one of the oldest wineries in the West. Part of the winery still occupies the original adobe building.[17]

East of Val Verde County, Harris County, where Houston is located, also became a major Italian farming settlement. Approximately 88 of the Italian farmers were from three Sicilian provinces, Palermo, Caltanissetta, and Agrigento. By 1920 there were 1,745 Italians in Houston, approximately 1 percent of Harris County's total population of 186,667. Surrounding Houston, Italians grew established crops and introduced new vegetables that had been staples in their diet in Italy. A small group settled in an area called Post Oak–San Felipe and sold their vegetables in Houston's Market Square in the center of town. Others formed a small colony in the center of town where other Italians opened businesses. There were several Catholic churches in the downtown area that became the Italian colony's social and religious centers: Church of the Annunciation (1869), St. Joseph's (1879), and Holy Rosary (1913). As the community prospered, Italians established mutual-aid societies, including the Queen Margherita Savoia Benefit Society and the St. Joseph's Society.[18]

There was an additional Sicilian settlement in adjacent Galveston County to the south as early as the 1890s. A major influx of Italian immigrants came from Bryan in Brazos County. In June and July 1899, the Brazos River flooded, inundating the surrounding farmland. The flooding caused dozens of deaths and left thousands homeless. Hundreds of cattle died, and thousands of acres of cotton, black-eyed peas, and sorghum crops were destroyed. At one point, the river surged to more than ten miles across.[19] It was not the first flood, nor would it be the last. Discouraged, many left the valley for other parts of Texas and the West.

In response to the devastation, the local Italian consular agent, Clemente Nicolini, became actively involved in the relocation effort and helped the flood victims resettle in Dickinson and Galveston. As early as 1906 in Galveston County, Italians owned 50 percent of the grocery stores and 25 percent of the fruit, confectionery, and shoe shops. By 1910 more than one thousand Italians resided near Dickinson where on their four- to ten-acre farms they grew berries and vegetables. Approximately one hundred families were originally from the province of Palermo. By 1912 land values had soared to between $100 and $200 an acre, a high price at the time for farm acreage in the West. When the Italian ambassador visited the area again in 1912, he reported similar successful Italian settlements in Hitchcock and Galveston. Francesco Termini was among these early immigrants to the area. He opened a small grocery store. When he saved enough capital, he bought land in Dickinson and Galveston and began a large farming operation. He became an influential figure in the development of the Dickinson business community and had a street named after him.[20]

By the 1920s, Galveston and the adjacent Chambers County developed a thriving fig industry. At the time, it had already become an established crop in California's San Joaquin Valley, which had created a national market for dried figs. In both Galveston and Chambers Counties by 1920, there were approximately eighteen thousand acres of figs, with seventeen fig plants for drying and packing. The dried-fig industry provided hundreds of seasonal and permanent jobs for men and women. At harvest time, unskilled women and men gathered the figs in the groves. In the plants, men composed the workforce that processed the dried figs, while women provided the labor required to pack the figs for shipment throughout the United States. The crop added to the image of the Gulf region of the state as a Mediterranean paradise, similar in climate and agricultural production to southern Italy.[21]

Jefferson County also attracted Italians. Between 1900 and 1910, the number of Italian immigrants increased fourfold, 90 percent of them from Sicily. Initially, they worked as day labor for $1 a day. It is important to point out that at that rate, a single male could earn about $6 a week or about $24 a month. If the worker had to pay room and board at a local rooming house, with few other expenses, especially if he controlled the time spent in the local saloon, he could save upwards of $10 to $12 a month.[22] If he lived with friends or relatives, his savings were considerably higher. With cash in his pocket and the always vibrant labor market, the free-labor immigrant was an independent agent, able to relocate himself wherever he could find higher wages.

Small farmers did not have the added expense of hiring workers. The family, especially wives, played a vital role in the farm's production and success. Not to be diminished or overlooked, wives had the arduous and dangerous task (before the widespread use of antibiotics) of giving birth, aided only by midwives at home. During pregnancy and shortly after delivery, they were on their feet throughout the long day of work at home attending to a variety of domestic family duties: supervising the children, cooking, and making domestic products, including canning spring and summer vegetables. Wives also worked on the farm, especially during harvest time, when all able-bodied members of the family had to help. However, they were relegated mainly to the home, where they were often isolated, a common problem for farmwives throughout rural America. Beyond the home and precincts of the farm, wives partnered with their husbands when the family opened roadside stands or took their farm products to local markets. Near Houston nearly a hundred families sold fruits and vegetables destined for both local and out-of-state markets.[23]

Farming and Enclave Businesses—Brazos County–Bryan

Located in the Brazos River valley about 150 miles north of Galveston, Bryan was among the most important immigrant farming settlements in Texas. The arrival of the railroad by 1867 greatly facilitated Italian immigration to Brazos County. Local Bryan businessmen who owned land and other interests, including mining and timber, advertised in European newspapers for workers and farmers. Landowners in the area who had purchased land in advance of the railroad especially wanted immigrant settlers to develop the local farming economy and increase the value of their land. A local association built houses for newly arriving immigrants until they could earn enough to locate their own dwellings and perhaps send for their families if they had not already arrived with them.[24]

By the 1880s, Sicilians began arriving in the Brazos River valley from New Orleans, where many had worked in the sugarcane fields and other jobs in Louisiana. Initially, the Louisiana Sugar Planters Association paid both the travel and the living expenses to attract immigrants. By the 1890s, Brazos County counted the greatest number of Italian farmers in the United States. By 1900 there were 553 Italian immigrants in the county. An additional 2,400 Sicilian railroad men moved to the valley when they lost work on the Houston and Texas railroad. Businessmen found southern Italian laborers "to be hard-working, thrifty, and content with few comforts." As a descendent of one local Bryan immigrant explained, "The Italians proved that they could, on their own, establish their independence through farming, industry and private enterprise.... The local bank soon found out that the average Italian's word was as good as a signed contract."[25]

Aiding in their settlement, by 1900 the Società di Colonizzazione Italiana del Texas purchased more than 25,000 acres for the incoming Italian immigrants. The society was not unique in immigrant history. As early as the 1820s, the Canadian Company subsidized settlers to develop its forest industry, and in the 1830s the British government subsidized English immigrants to settle the Ohio Valley. The society divided the land into 50-acre parcels and made the land available for sale or lease. The society also financed loans for building materials and farm equipment. The tenant farmers paid an average $5 per acre annually. Their program was so effective that in 1905, when the Italian ambassador visited Bryan, he was informed that Bryan had by one estimate more than 3,000 Sicilians. Further aiding the community, local Italians also established the Agricultural Benevolent Society, with J. M. Saladino as its first president. Out of Bryan's total population of 5,000 residents, Italians represented the highest concentration, 60 percent, in any town in the United States. By comparison to other towns in Texas, in 1900 Dallas had 107, Fort Worth 118, Galveston 866, and Houston 852. In fact, Sicilians were so effective in developing the land that local businessmen told the ambassador that they "wished that they had ten times that number."[26]

The Sicilians who settled Bryan came primarily from the central Sicilian villages of Poggioreale, Corleone, Salaparuta, and Bivona, all from a region that sent thousands of immigrants to the United States at the time. Following their tradition-bound sense of *campanilismo*, they settled in their respective communities, those from Corleone and Poggioreale on one side of the Brazos River and those from Bivona on the other. The early farmers grew mainly corn and cotton. Settlement and success came quickly for those early immigrants to the county as the enclave economy took root and began to develop.[27]

Typical among these Italian immigrants was first-generation Antonio Varisco, whose parents were from Poggioreale. After working in Houston, he moved to Bryan, worked as a day laborer for seventy-five cents a day, and soon was able to rent a 25-acre farm. By 1930 he and a son expanded their farm to more than 3,100 acres, most of it dedicated to raising cotton.

With his two sons, he opened a cotton gin in Bryan that produced more than two thousand cotton bales annually. Similarly, Sam Emola joined his covillagers from Corleone, and after working as a day laborer, he was able to purchase his own farm. Giovanni Cangelosi followed a similar pattern after his arrival in Bryan from Poggioreale. His brother had preceded him, and not long after his arrival, he was able to buy 250 acres of the less valuable Brazos river bottomland that was prone to flooding.[28] Although the record does not show it, the Società di Colonizzazione Italiana del Texas may well have had a hand in financing the purchase of the Emola and Cangelosi farms.

For the first time, Bryan's separate dialect groups were forced to live in close proximity. In their remote villages, they had been isolated in Sicily's interior. As a sense of common needs developed in Bryan, Italian immigrants were forced to make a greater effort at tolerating each other's differences and comprehending each other's dialects. They attended the same church and shopped in Bryan's growing enclave. Thrown together in their social and religious gatherings, young men and women met and began to intermarry. Settling in Bryan before 1910, farmer Vincenzo Schembri, who was from Bivona, married Maria Campisi from the Poggioreale settlement across the river. This "bicultural" union would have been next to impossible in Sicily.[29]

In time the Bryan Sicilians became a close-knit community that revolved around St. Anthony's Church, where all the families attended Mass and participated in the same feast days. In 1896 the first modest St. Anthony's Church was built on Polk Street. As a measure of their success, approximately ten years later the community raised more than $1,000 to build a new church with all of the appropriate religious accessories.[30]

In a pattern that would be repeated throughout the West, Italians got along well with the already established Mexican immigrant and Mexican American population. They shared the same parishes, had many cultural similarities, and readily learned each other's languages. Since they shared similar religious values and family structure, Italians and Mexicans often intermarried in Texas and other parts of the Southwest and West. Anthony "Tony" Lama, the son of Italian immigrants, became a successful entrepreneur in El Paso. He arrived in El Paso in 1911 and opened a boot and repair shop catering to the Italian and Mexican populations. He married first-generation Mexican American Esther Ojeda Hernandez, and together they had six children. His original boot shop eventually developed into the Tony Lama Company, a multimillion-dollar company.[31] It remains in operation today and, like the Lucchese label, is recognized as one of the finest brands in men's boots.

The investment that both the state and businessmen associations made in immigrant labor at the turn of the century paid off. Immigration had a dramatic effect on both farming and business development. By 1920 there were 436,033 farms in the state, with 232,395 as tenant farmers, a little more than 53 percent of the owner-operated farms. The farms covered 167,934,720 acres, 67 percent of the state's land. In Brazos County, the number of farms increased from 666 in 1870 to 3,023 in 1920, with 1,939 as tenant farmers.[32] Although the ratio of tenant farmers to owner-operated farms is higher than in some other states and counties at the time, the increase in the number of farms in Brazos County from 1870 to 1920 is an indication of the contribution that immigrants made to the state's farming industry.

Jim Crow and Southern Italians

Along with immigrant farmers, by 1920 African Americans owned 20 percent of the farms in and around Bryan. Under Jim Crow laws African American farmers were impeded in their efforts to organize their industry the way Italian, Japanese, and other immigrant farmers were able to do throughout the West. By the turn of the century in the Brazos River valley, there were more than 8,000 African Americans, the majority of whom were engaged in farming. To strengthen their position as both farmers and field workers in a state that banned them from the state's Farmers' Alliance, African Americans in 1886 formed the Colored Farmers' National Alliance and Cooperative Union in Houston County. They received a charter from the state of Texas in 1888 and merged with the fraternal organization the Colored Alliance and began a region-wide campaign to expand their membership, reaching more than 1 million members. However, they were met with strong opposition throughout the South, making it impossible for African American farmers to succeed on the same scale as their neighboring immigrant farmers.[33]

Sicilians and African Americans lived and worked in close proximity, as they had throughout the South before 1940. Initially, Italian children were sent to segregated African American schools. As a result, Sicilians' close relationships with local African Americans began to raise the ire of late-generation self-described "whites." Texans, as well as southerners in other states, soon discovered that Sicilians did not honor Jim Crow regulations and began to notice that Sicilians and African Americans often related on personal terms.[34] Their relationship with African Americans and their disregard of Jim Crow restrictions would not be ignored or go unpunished.

Southern Italians did not see "race" or "color" in the same way that Texans and southerners did. Southern Italians' cultural and religious iconography was radically different from the Protestant forms of worship. Many of the saints worshipped in their villages were originally either North African or Mediterranean cult figures carved and painted in various shades of brown to black. Many of the immigrant settlers in the Bivona colony worshipped the Black Madonna in their home village. It is little wonder that they shared such a close relationship with Mexican immigrants, who worshipped Our Lady of Guadalupe. The anti-immigrant faction in America often characterized southern Italians as pagans and "foreign Romanists" who blindly followed that "reactionary despot," the pope. Rumors of "Catholic political conspiracies" circulated among paranoid, xenophobic Protestants. The nativist sentiment against Italians erupted into violence in 1891 when eleven Italian immigrants were murdered and lynched in New Orleans. Although not the first lynching of Italians, neither would it be the last.[35]

Some Texans shared the same concern as southerners and believed that they had imported something of a political and cultural Trojan horse into their midst. Sicilians began to arouse suspicion when southerners overheard African Americans, who worked in tandem with Sicilians on southern plantations, address Sicilians by their first names. Italian immigrants' relationships with African Americans have been dramatized in two effective historical novels, Donna Jo Napoli's *Alligator Bayou* (2009) and Mary Bucci Bush's *Sweet Hope* (2011). Bush's novel treats the cooperative, working relationship between Italian immigrants and African Americans on a turn-of-the-century Arkansas cotton plantation, while Napoli's novel focuses on the friendly relationship between Sicilian immigrants and African Americans in Tallulah, Louisiana. Napoli portrays the 1899 Tallulah lynching of five Sicilians who refused to follow the dictates of the Jim Crow social order.[36]

In his article "The Italian: A Hindrance to White Solidarity in Louisiana, 1890–1898," George E. Cunningham reports that in the aftermath of the lynching of three Italians in Hahnville, St. Charles Parish, in 1896, "the Italians now had the sympathy of the Negroes, for a large number of Negroes and Italians were present at the burial, and went home from the scene almost terror-stricken." Some locals feared that with the support of African Americans, Italians would seek revenge. Sicilians' friendly relationships with African Americans was not limited to Texas or southern states. In the eastern and northeastern urban centers, particularly in Chicago's Near North Side, a similar relationship between Sicilians and African Americans existed. However, the friendly relationships between the two groups were at times fractured over their competition for jobs. Because of Sicilians' threat to African Americans' economic interests in the South, especially New Orleans, in one instance African American leaders launched an anti-Sicilian campaign that characterized Sicilians in the same xenophobic terms used by nativists at the time. Yet when two Italian immigrants were lynched in Tampa, Florida, in 1910, W.E.B. Du Bois came to their defense.[37]

Patrizia Salvetti demonstrates that the early lynchings of Sicilians in New Orleans became part of a larger pattern of not only Italian but other immigrant lynchings throughout the United States, including Mexican and Asian immigrants. Immigrant lynchings became so widespread that one lawyer, Charles H. Watson, in a 1916 article called for national legislation to stop the assault on immigrants.[38] He cited the most recent killings of two Italian immigrants in two southern Illinois towns. It must be emphasized that he said nothing in his article about the rampant lynchings of African Americans or Native Americans at the time.

What has been difficult to document in Texas is the role that the Klan played in less dramatic moments when it felt compelled to deliver threatening messages to immigrants who defied Jim Crow restrictions. By 1920 Texas joined such western states as Colorado and Oregon in the revival of the Ku Klux Klan. As just one example, shortly before or after World War I, three men from the Bryan community visited Vincenzo Schembri to inform him that he had to stop allowing African Americans to enter the front door of his house and stop allowing them to eat at the family dinner table. Whether they were official members of the revived KKK or just three self-appointed vigilantes bent on enforcing the Jim Crow social order in Bryan is not clear. Threatened, Vincenzo relented, but not totally. He avoided the more obvious Jim Crow violation: he did not allow his African American friends to enter the front door of the family's small house. However, he continued to host African Americans out back at the family table next to the barn, where the family more often than not took its evening meals. Whatever Vincenzo seemed to give up to the powerful and violent local men, in typical Sicilian fashion he surreptitiously took back in defiance of their demands.[39]

Perhaps Vincenzo's tactic was a response conditioned by Sicily's many centuries of hostile foreign domination, including a postunification government. In his view, the KKK was just another force, a foreign "imperium" that had always dominated Sicilians, from foreign colonists, the church, and the unification government to the Mafia. Feeling powerless to control their own destiny, in their self-deprecating folklore, Sicilians thought of their villages as merely "the footprints that God left on his way to better things."[40] Vincenzo resisted in the only way he could.

In spite of the xenophobia that they sometimes faced, Italians did not abandon their cultural traditions in Bryan or elsewhere in Texas. The West allowed Italian immigrants greater latitude to practice traditions and customs, which some observers believed were not in fact so at odds with Protestant American values. Italians were still able to transplant some of those festivals that their villages had celebrated for centuries. The Italians of Texas grew traditional crops for both the market and their own tables. Bringing their various folkways and horticultural traditions to America and merging and celebrating them with Catholics from other countries, they were becoming Italian Texans, as well as Americans.[41]

Late-Generation Revival

Although Italians in Texas were successful, their high numbers in such small towns as Bryan began to diminish in the post–World War II period. The first- and second-generation Italian Americans moved to the state's larger cities, where there were more economic and educational opportunities. However, by the 1970s Italian Americans began to organize cultural associations. In 1971 Andrew Greeley and Michael Novak documented a "rediscovered" European ethnicity at a time when it was believed to have disappeared in American society.[42] Italian Americans as well as ethnic Americans in general experienced a resurgence of interest in their immigrant forebears. The trend that Novak and Greeley identified nearly fifty years ago has continued into the twenty-first century.

There is little left of the original settlement of Sicilians in Bryan. Italians now represent little more than 3 percent of Bryan's population, down significantly from 60 percent of the population that Sicilians represented at the turn of the century. However, the descendants of those original

Italians in Bryan have organized recently. Since 2000 descendants from Poggioreale meet each August at St. Anthony's Church. As the recovery of the Bryan Italian community demonstrates, the families' search for their genealogical records has become a legitimate reclamation of the historical record. A complete list of all the families from Poggioreale is online, with names, marriages, and dates. It includes a history of Poggioreale, as well as a description of the devastating earthquake that destroyed the town in 1968 and left it uninhabitable.[43]

Although dispersed, the Italian population remains a demographic factor in Texas society. Still active are various Italian-language clubs, fraternal organizations, and national associations: the Italian Cultural Association of Greater Austin, the Italian Community Center in Houston, the Federation of Italian-American Organizations of Greater Houston, the Christopher Columbus Italian Society in San Antonio, the Italian Cultural Center of San Antonio, the Order Sons and Daughters of Italy, the Pompeo Coppini Lodge, La Famiglia di Southeast Texas in San Antonio and Beaumont, the Italian Club of Dallas, the Italian American Cultural Society of El Paso, and a branch of the influential National Italian American Foundation located in Houston. These organizations make charitable donations, advertise Italian American businesses, and promote Italian American activities. They also represent transnational Italian business and cultural events for both Italian Americans and the general population. Adding to this trend, recent studies have documented the continued post-1945 Italian immigration to the United States. Figures are difficult to establish, but approximately 490,000 Italians came to the United States between 1946 and 1975.[44] This new transnational emphasis in Italian American communities is also inclusive of that new post-1970s Italian immigrant to the United States.

The new organizations are supported by the 363,354 Texas Italian Americans, 1.7 percent of the state's current population. This is slightly larger than the percentage of Italian immigrants counted in the state in 1920. In Jefferson County, by 2000 the descendants of those early Italian immigrants numbered 6,974, about 3 percent of the county's population. The Dallas–Fort Worth metropolitan areas have 106,774, while the Houston-Galveston-Brazoria metropolitan areas have 105,645 Italian Americans. Houston's share of that figure stands at 31,899, approximately 1.6 percent of the city's current population.[45] The original Italian immigrant population and ethnic diversity that characterized early Texas continues to contribute to the multicultural mix in the Southwest's largest state.

CHAPTER 2

NEW MEXICO

Nuns and Priests

Much has been written about the religious orders, principally Jesuits, in their travels to western territories. But little has been written about the role that female religious orders played in the settlement of the western territories and states. Among the most famous was Ligurian nun Sister Blandina Segale, a member of the Sisters of Charity, a teaching and nursing order. Born in 1850 in the village of Cicagna in northern Italy near Genoa, Sister Blandina arrived in the United States as a child with her family in Cincinnati, Ohio. At the age of sixteen and against her father's wishes, Sister Blandina joined the Sisters of Charity. Adding to her father's consternation, she set off for the Wild West on the train alone without a chaperone. She wrote about her life in the West in *At the End of the Santa Fe Trial.*

In the many years of her service as a nun in the West, she started schools extending from Trinidad (Colorado) to Santa Fe and Albuquerque. In 1865 she moved to New Mexico. Her first assignment was in Santa Fe, where she taught school and where her order built an orphanage. Later in Albuquerque, she and the other nuns established churches, a hospital for railroad workers in New Mexico, and a trade school for the local Native American population. To build their schools and churches, her order opened a rock quarry, processed lime, and ran a brickyard and lumber mill. As a staunch supporter of Native American rights, she wrote, "Generations to come will blush for the deeds of this, toward the rightful possessors of the soil. Our government, which poses with upraised finger of scorn on any act which savors of tyranny, lowers that finger to crush out of existence a race whose right to land we call America is unquestioned." She also became active in efforts to reform lynch laws aimed at the Apache.[1]

Before Sister Blandina arrived, there was already a Catholic presence in New Mexico that dated back to the Spanish colonial period. By 1867 Father Donato Gasparri set out for New Mexico accompanied by Fathers Rafael Bianchi and Livio Vigilante and Brothers Rafael La Vezza and Prisco Caso. The four were later joined by at least seven other Italian priests. Together they established the parish Our Lady of Sorrows at Bernalillo and assumed responsibility for San Felipe de Neri Church in Albuquerque.

They established schools, colleges, and missions in the Rio Grande, Pecos, and Cimarron River valleys, including a college in Las Vegas, New Mexico. By the 1870s, the Jesuits had established a press and published a journal in Italian.[2] Both Sister Blandina in her memoir and Willa Cather in her novel *Death Comes for the Archbishop* wrote illuminating accounts of the influence and abuses of the Jesuits and religious groups during these early years of immigrant settlement in New Mexico.

When they arrived, Italian immigrants found already established Catholic communities and familiar rituals. They were not entirely strangers in the far-western landscape. There is a record of one unnamed tinsmith living in New Mexico as early as 1860, but the first significant number of Italian immigrants did not begin to arrive until after 1880. Between 1880 and 1900, the first wave of Italians settled in Bernalillo County, where Albuquerque is located. Initially, the majority of the early Italian immigrants who came to New Mexico were miners and railroad workers. Most of them originated from northern Italy, principally Tuscany. By 1900 there were 661 Italians in the territory, and by 1920 that number grew to 1,078 Italians in New Mexico, which became a state in 1912.[3]

Enclave Businesses—Bernalillo County

Seeking opportunity and cheap land in the developing territory, Italians fanned out across the state. Many began as day laborers and tenant farmers before they could afford to buy their own land and establish farms and ranches. In 1900 several Italian families settled in a largely Mexican community in Bernalillo County, just outside the Albuquerque city limits in Los Duranes, Los Griegos, and Sun Valley, where they ran truck farms. They sold their produce from roadside stands or outdoor farmers' markets. Where there were large concentrations of Mexican immigrants and Mexican Americans, Italians were able to integrate quickly into their new environment. With San Felipe de Neri Church as a natural bridge between the two cultures, they shared with Mexicans the same religious festivals and joined each other's cultural organizations. In addition to learning Spanish, they soon learned English and were able to communicate with all sectors of the population.[4]

By the early 1880s, several Italians appeared in business directories. P. H. Bianchi is listed as a mason and contractor, and Justiniano Castillo owned a butcher shop. In Rio Arriba County on the Colorado border, D. Boffa ran a music store.[5] Typical of southwestern settlements, these business zones were not homogeneous enclaves but composed of a mixture of immigrants and late-generation businesses.

Early in its settlement, Albuquerque was a rough western boomtown with a largely male immigrant population. In 1900 Albuquerque had about 100 newly settled Italian immigrants. By 1930 that number grew to 238 in Albuquerque. Backed by a willing and cooperative municipal government eager to see its business community grow, immigrants could begin businesses with minimal capital investment and red tape. The most common businesses that Italians owned were grocery stores, merchandise stores, and saloons. One immigrant newcomer began with a tent saloon and from that meager start built a large wholesale liquor-distribution business. About the same time, in the 1880s Alessandro Matteucci and his brother Giovanni opened the Porto Rico Saloon. By 1920 there were eight Italian-owned tailor shops employing at least ten Italian tailors. Among the most successful immigrant families in Albuquerque, the descendants of the famous composer Giacomo Puccini built Albuquerque's main theater, the Puccini Building, named after Luigi Puccini, the Italian composer's cousin. The building housed the El Rey Theater and Puccini's Golden West Saloon. Well into the twenty-first century, it continued to be owned and run by Luigi Puccini's granddaughter, a descendent of Oreste and Maria Bachechi, important entrepreneurs in Albuquerque's early-twentieth-century business community.[6]

In 1901 Bachechi partnered with Girolamo Giomi to open a wholesale liquor business. By 1907 they incorporated under the name Consolidated Liquor Company and took in more investment partners to expand their market. Bachechi also established the Bachechi Mercantile Company and became a distribution agent for beer, liquor, and olive oil. In 1901 the immigrant community in Albuquerque was served by at least four other Italian immigrant partnerships: Toti & Gradi, Morelli Brothers, Tartaglia & Ciddo, and Tomei & Brothers. In 1910 brothers Edward and Joseph Vaio opened a general merchandise store on North First Street. By 1910 there were eighteen Italian business partnerships in the city, and within a decade the number had grown to twenty-one, including the Luigi Del Frate and Pasqualino Sei partnership that opened the Pershing Café on South First Street. But by 1930, the number declined to fourteen. As a result of their success, partners separated and individuals struck out on their own with their newly acquired wealth.[7] Partnerships became a significant form of social capital that fueled success within enclaves.

Pompilio Matteucci followed his brothers to Albuquerque and brought with him shoemaking skills that he had learned in the army in Italy. After landing in Albuquerque in 1905, he opened a shoe-repair shop. His renown grew in town as a skilled shoemaker, which allowed him to open a small retail shoe store that he named the Paris Shoe Store. From this modest retail shop, he and his grandchildren expanded the Paris Shoe Store brand into one of the largest retail chain stores in the Southwest. Texas's Lucchese and Lama families and New Mexico's Matteucci family are iconic examples of how immigrants in a free-labor market were able to turn their Old World cultural capital into personal success.[8]

Enterprising women also established businesses in the booming Albuquerque immigrant economy. In America their Old World domestic skills found a public application in the immigrant marketplace. Maria Bachechi, wife of Oreste, was the proprietor of more than one Albuquerque hotel, including the Elms Hotel. She prepared lunches, cooked evening meals, cleaned rooms, and washed bedding. Later she partnered with Armida Bonaguidi in 1917 and opened a dry-goods business that stocked such products as beans, oats, fabric, clothing, shoes, and other household items. Such stores found a ready market, especially among an itinerant, largely male population that traveled with few personal belongings in search of work.[9]

In addition to other family businesses, in 1905 Oreste built the Savoy Hotel and later the KiMo Theater, which today remains on the state's Registry of Historic Properties. By 1920 he became the owner of the Pastime Theater Company and in 1922 the president of Anchor Milling Company, which included two other Italian managers. Not missing an opportunity, he also opened a saloon and a travel agency. As he grew older and less able, he turned his businesses over to his son, who conformed the family liquor enterprise to national Prohibition laws.[10]

While building his family's wealth, Oreste provided jobs for arriving immigrants, skilled and unskilled. Luigi Giacomelli worked initially as a servant for Oreste upon his arrival, while Ettore Franchini and Antonio Bandoni landed their first jobs in Oreste's businesses. Antonio Domenici and his partner and brother Cherubino Domenici, owners of the Montezuma Grocery Store, also supplied jobs for arriving Italians. The grocery store had a total of six Italians as employees, four as clerks and two as bartenders in the store.[11] These otherwise low-paying jobs provided the springboard for arriving Italians to open their own businesses in Albuquerque.

Like so many young men, Franchini was not content with the first job he landed. He began working in Albuquerque as a truck driver, then became a porter, and finally became a janitor in the Bachechi saloon. Inspired by his mentor, Oreste Bachechi, Franchini opened a travel agency. Because of his early success, Franchini was appointed later as the Italian consular agent in Albuquerque and knight of the Crown of Italy.[12] The free-labor population provided a lucrative market for Italian-speaking travel agents who could help immigrants relocate to find better jobs or to plan a route that would take them back to Italy.

Aladino Viviani is yet another example of the peripatetic worker who found work initially in a variety of jobs before he earned enough money to establish an enclave business. He did not stay with his high-paying job as a machinist with the Santa Fe Railroad. Such high-paying skilled jobs in industry often carried with them an equally high risk of injury. After a near-fatal accident, he moved to the Domenici brothers' Montezuma Grocery. From there he moved on to three other jobs before opening his own grocery store in 1928. His products, which he sold initially to the local Italian population, soon found a citywide customer base.[13] Like so many other food products that immigrants introduced in the West, his products began to influence the American diet. Inevitably, there was a certain reciprocity between immigrant culture and American customs.

As Viviani illustrates, free-labor immigrants did not need to rely solely on their imported artisan skills. Learning on the job, he became a railroad mechanic and then later a baker. If an immigrant did not bring artisan skills with him, he could begin with low-paying day labor and then follow the market. Julio and Amerigo Menicucci settled first in the Midwest, where they worked as miners. In an unusual occupational change, when they relocated to Albuquerque in 1922 they established the Safety First Tire Company in partnership with Astutillio Giannini. Having learned the skills needed, the two brothers left and opened the Super Service Station and Tire Company on North Fourth Street.[14]

But there was something more to the brothers' success. They were not strangers in Albuquerque when they arrived. Before the brothers opened their businesses, the Menicucci family was already established in town. The first of the Menicucci brothers, Alessandro, came to Albuquerque in 1899 and worked as a clerk in his uncle's Porto Rico saloon and grocery store. He then purchased the store from his uncle and partnered in 1905 with another Italian, Pio Lommori, and opened a grocery store.

When Lommori left, Alessandro partnered with his brother Amadeo and renamed the store the Champion Grocery and Meat Market. Amadeo soon took his profits from the business and started his own grocery store, while his brother continued as sole owner of the Champion until 1938.[15] The benefits of chain migration, having relatives already established in a region, and the exchange of social capital benefited all members of the Menicucci family.

The Italian family was an important element in the success of the small Italian business.[16] Often the exchange of social capital is obvious, as in the case of documented partnerships. At other times, the exchange of social capital that provided the initial investment in a successful business is not revealed in the historical record. The success of the Menicucci family in Albuquerque before Julio and Amerigo arrived suggests that perhaps family loans aided the two brothers in financing their businesses. Otherwise, the record implies that the family certainly provided them with free lodging and some type of work upon their arrival. They had few expenses and were able to save money from their otherwise meager wages. Immigrant social capital had many tentacles, and they were not always obvious. Chain migration provided the arriving immigrant with both a familiar cultural setting and, most important of all, immediate job opportunities.

While many Italian immigrants remained in their unskilled jobs for life, statistics show that before World War II those who were able to make the transition into business became successful. The western boomtown provided for a high rate of social mobility. Immigrants did not form businesses based solely on kinship relations. Language was an important factor in their success. These early Italian business partners, largely from northern Italy, were men who could communicate in standard Italian or, if they were from the same region, their shared dialect. For the next languages, they readily learned Spanish and in time English, which became their lingua franca used to communicate with other immigrants and their American customers. Italians' ability to speak English rose from 67 percent in 1900 to 86 percent by 1920 in Albuquerque.[17] Language proficiency in both Spanish and English was clearly a major factor in their success in the Southwest.

In fact, between 1900 and 1930 early Italian immigrants were among the most successful small-business owners in Albuquerque. By 1900 nineteen Italians, composing 35 percent of Italian immigrant males, owned an array of businesses: from hotels, saloons, wholesale liquor distributorships, and restaurants to grocery stores, shoe stores, and printing businesses. For the Italian in New Mexico, the ascent of the economic ladder was swift. As one measure of their success, as early as 1892 Italian immigrants formed mutual-aid societies, such as the Associazione Italiana di Mutua Protezione Cristoforo Colombo. Members were required to pay an annual fee dedicated to aiding widows and the less fortunate in their community. As further evidence of their accomplishments, by 1910 50 percent of Italian immigrants owned some type of business. In 1920 that percentage improved to 62 percent, and by 1930 that number jumped again to 83 percent. What is more, 88 percent of those with white-collar jobs maintained their success after 1930. Some of these immigrants became wealthy. With their good fortune, they built large homes and purchased large sections of land outside the city. The immigrant economy in Albuquerque allowed for a high rate of success with little downside.[18]

Among the most prominent members of the descendants of those early immigrants is the son of Cherubino Domenici, Pietro (Pete), born in Albuquerque in 1937. Pete worked in his father's grocery business in his youth and after high school attended the University of New Mexico. After teaching for a short period, he quit to attend law school in Denver. Upon completing his studies, he returned to Albuquerque to practice law. After winning local electoral positions, he ran for the US Senate in 1972 and held the seat until 2009, the longest term in the history of New Mexico. In spite of the era's anti-immigrant sentiment, Italians were busily making their worth known to late-generation Americans, who began to judge them by their contribution to the community and not by a pseudoscientific racial theory. Distrust dissolved into tolerance and in time acceptance. As Andrew Rolle wrote, "If discrimination occurred, they could wear it down." However, immigrant success did not deter Congress from passing the Johnson-Reed Act of 1924. In the years following the passage of the act, Canada became beneficiary of immigration to North America, especially in the post–World War II era.[19]

About sixty miles northeast of Albuquerque, Santa Fe also became the location of a settlement of Italian farmers that had farmed in Italy. Others brought valuable artisan skills that, like farming, found a ready market. Among them, three men, Gaetano Palladino, Michael Berardinelli, and Carlo Digneo, left a special legacy in Santa Fe. Palladino and Digneo, stonecutters from Abruzzo, had worked on the Jesuit college in Maryland and were later called to Santa Fe to help construct the town's Saint Francis

Cathedral. Digneo also worked on the construction of Hodgin Hall at the University of New Mexico in Albuquerque. Later Berardinelli and Palladino opened a construction business and were responsible for building many of the territory's early municipal buildings. Berardinelli's descendants went on to become prominent members of the Santa Fe community, where they held numerous political and public offices.[20]

Mining and Farming

Besides businesses, mining was perhaps the largest employer of Italians in New Mexico. Farming occupied only a minor place in Italians' lives and deserves only a brief mention. Unlike other western states, New Mexico did not attract large numbers of immigrant farmers. By 1920 it had 29,844 farms with only about 31 percent of the state's land dedicated to some form of agriculture. Compared to neighboring Texas, which had more than 200,000 tenant farmers and more than double the percentage of farmland, New Mexico had only 3,655 tenant farmers. In fact, between 1900 and 1930 more Italians were small-business owners than any other occupation in Albuquerque.[21]

However, by 1885 Italians composed more than 50 percent of the coal miners in Raton, Colfax County. By 1910 Italian immigrants settled in large numbers in Colfax County in the northeastern sector of the state and in McKinley County in the western region of New Mexico. Thereafter, over the next five decades, mining became one of New Mexico's principal industries, attracting a multinational workforce. But the jobs that mining and America's industrial development provided for immigrants came with a high price. Rebecca Harding Davis recounts the grueling and dangerous lives of Ohio ironworkers. Similarly, Pietro Di Donato dramatizes urban construction workers' life-threatening work building America's skyscrapers. Pascal D'Angelo offered an autobiographical account of the labor system and the grueling conditions under which immigrants worked in the 1920s.[22] The most influential novel of the era depicting immigrant life was Upton Sinclair's *The Jungle* (1906), which exposed the working conditions and exploitation of immigrant workers in the meatpacking industry. Safety standards were either nonexistent or ignored by both management and government. Like the horrific record of industrial accidents that maimed and killed immigrants throughout America, the West had its share of disasters.

New Mexico mining has a place in this tragic legacy. On September 14, 1903, a fire broke out in the Bernal Mine in Carthage. A total of twelve miners died in the explosion. Out of the twelve, it appears that three were Italians and six were Mexican, three from the Archuleta family. The others included the African American mine boss, C. L. Wilcox, and two others were probably from England and Eastern Europe.[23] If there was an investigation into the disaster, little was done to remedy what went wrong. The Carthage explosion and deaths would be nearly forgotten. Perhaps the reason is that the accident would soon be overshadowed by a larger and more deadly mine disaster. The now abandoned and nearly forgotten mining town of Dawson in the Vermejo Valley in Colfax County, northeast of Cimarron, is another example of the extreme danger that immigrants faced in America's mines.

Dawson's history began in 1869 when the town's founder, John Barkley Dawson, arrived in the Vermejo Valley looking for a plot of land to homestead. After finding a suitable piece of land along the Vermejo River upstream from the early settlement of Colfax, he purchased twenty thousand acres for $3,700. His investment in this barren stretch of land turned out to be a bonanza. He soon found coal near the surface of his property and began using it for fuel and selling it to his neighbors. He ranched the property until 1901, when he and a partner sold most of the land to the Dawson Fuel Company for $400,000. To exploit the rich vein of coal, the company constructed a 137-mile railroad track, and by 1901, its first year of production, the Dawson Fuel Company employed an initial crew of fifty miners. In its first year, the mine produced three hundred tons of coal.[24]

What happened next is an example of the extent to which industries in the West went to attract immigrants and house them in well-organized company towns. In 1906 the Phelps Dodge Corporation bought the mines with the intent of making Dawson a model company town. The company began by building houses for its miners. It also built a four-story brick Mercantile Department Store that stocked everything that families needed, from groceries, hardware items, home furnishings, and drugs to personal items such as jewelry. Phelps Dodge took the unprecedented step of building a hospital that included five permanent physicians who had access to surgery rooms, x-ray machines, and the latest in laboratory equipment. For the miners' leisure time, the company built a movie theater, swimming pool, parks, a pool hall, meeting halls, and an opera house. It also built a golf course, no doubt for the company's managers. In addition, it built two churches, Catholic and Protestant. Children could attend one of two nearby elementary schools, and later the company built a high school that employed forty teachers. The high school provided a full range of extracurricular activities, including competitive athletic teams. The company erected an electric power plant that supplied power for its own needs as well as for Dawson and Walsenburg, Colorado, to the north.[25]

Rows of miners' houses lined the ridge overlooking the coal-processing plant. There were as well ethnically homogeneous boardinghouses where workers could speak their own languages, eat traditional foods, and participate in traditional customs. In one boardinghouse dedicated to the Italian miners, the occupants prepared pasta and dined on local rabbit and pigeon along with copious amounts of red wine. For their wine, each fall the miners received large shipments by rail of wine grapes from California Italian growers. With the aid of their recruitment agents, Dawson drew miners from all over the world, including African Americans. Dawson's population swelled to more than nine thousand. By 1909 the Phelps Dodge operation was producing one million tons of coal a year and continued that yearly average until it shut the mines in 1950.[26]

Mine safety, however, was still in its infancy. There was the occasional accident during the first decade of its operation, but nothing that would have predicted what was to come. Furthermore, there seemed little that management could do about black lung disease caused by the accumulation of coal dust in the air. Phelps Dodge did appear to be concerned with mine safety and did make their mines as safe as technology allowed at the time. In fact, mine-safety experts felt that the company's Stag Canyon Mine No. 2 set the industry standard in mine safety. One safety expert said that Stag Canyon contained "the highest achievement in modern equipment and safety appliances that exist in the world." On October 20, 1913, the New Mexico inspector of mines completed two days of inspection and wrote in his report that the "Stag Canyon Mine No. 2 was totally free from traces of gas and in splendid general condition."[27]

However, within only forty-eight hours after the inspector released his report, on October 22, 1913, at 3:30 p.m. in the No. 2 mine, a massive explosion occurred that sent a flame out of the shaft one hundred feet in the air and shook buildings in Dawson two miles away. Out of the 284 workers who reported to work that day, 263 miners and 2 responders lost their lives. Phelps Dodge management brought in doctors, nurses, and medical supplies from as far away as El Paso, Texas. Even striking miners in Colorado left their picket lines to aid in the rescue.[28]

Inspectors concluded that the explosion "had been caused by an overcharged blast in a dusty pillar section of the mine." The original safety report of October 20 could have been a correct assessment of the mine's condition at the time. But in their investigation, safety experts found that Phelps Dodge had used dynamite, an illegal explosive that was prohibited by the Bureau of Mines. According to mine regulations, when blasting with approved explosives was allowed, the mine first had to be evacuated. Then water spray had to be employed to remove the coal dust from the air. The company had ignored these fundamental rules set by the bureau. After collective funerals were conducted, the bodies of the miners were taken to the nearby Dawson cemetery, which had to expand its borders to accommodate the extensive number of new graves. All were marked with a white cross.[29]

In the aftermath of the explosion, the company made a short silent film to demonstrate management's quick response to rescue and care for miners, including those who died. Some hooded with respirators, others without breathing gear, actors portray surviving miners removing purportedly dead miners on stretchers and in mule-drawn coal cars from the mine. One of the rescuers feigns being overcome by toxic fumes in the mine and has to be revived after reaching fresh air at the mouth of the mine.[30] At times the men in the film exhibit an odd sense of levity, smiling and even mugging for the camera, in spite of the purportedly grim task that they had been assigned to do.

The film, however, does not represent accurately the events in the immediate aftermath of the explosion. Based on one eyewitness account, grieving and distraught wives and relatives thronged the mine's opening and hampered rescue efforts. There are no family members surrounding the opening of the mine in the film. The film does not display any images of the scores of additional dead miners. One account reported that "rows of miners were brought to the surface."[31] If the film's intent was to demonstrate to the public the effort that Phelps Dodge took to rescue and remove the dead, it was a disingenuous piece of propaganda.

Phelps Dodge apparently did not learn any lessons from the 1913 tragedy. Fewer than ten years later, on the morning of February 8, 1923, 123 men reported to work, this time at the Stag Canyon Mine No. 1. At 2:00 p.m. another massive explosion occurred in No. 1, killing 121 men. A coal car derailed and smashed into the support timbers in the mine shaft, which ignited the excessive amount of coal dust in the mine. Wives and other relatives waited in vain for their loved ones to emerge from the stricken mine. Early the next morning, only a pair of miners who had been in another part of the mine walked out alive. Again the town went through the grieving process, and the Dawson cemetery was once again expanded to accommodate the new grave sites.[32] Within a decade, a total of 384 miners had lost their lives in the two mining accidents.

The tragic impact of both explosions is underscored by the list of the dead. The efficiency of the labor-contracting system and effectiveness of chain migration had a lethal and tragic result. Numerous brothers and fathers from single families lost their lives. Based on an examination of the cemetery, 4 members of the Montoya family and 3 members of the Pellegrini family died in the 1913 explosion. The registry of the dead lists as well several pairs of brothers, or perhaps sons and fathers. In the 1913 explosion 11 members of the Santi family lost their lives. Overall, Italian immigrants suffered the greatest number of deaths, approximately 130 (accounts vary up to nearly 160) of the total 263 who died in the 1913 explosion, with some additional Italians listed in the 1923 explosion. Approximately 30 (again as high as 63) Mexican immigrants lost their lives. At least 9 African Americans died in the explosion. The other deaths represented a cross-section of immigrant America.[33]

Neither the state of New Mexico nor the federal government was concerned enough about mine safety to act on behalf of the miners. The worst mine disaster in the United States had occurred previously on December 6, 1907, at Monongah, West Virginia, where 362 miners were killed. This tragedy forced Congress to establish the US Bureau of Mines in 1910. But the carnage in American mines would continue throughout the United States, including the West, where the toll would only increase, especially in Colorado.[34] It is significant that the value placed on miners' lives is reflected in the fact that the Dawson tragedy would go unnoticed for decades, seldom recorded in the history of the West.

After the accidents, Phelps Dodge continued to flourish for another three decades until April 30, 1950, when the mines were shut down. Dawson suffered the same fate as mining sites such as Thurber, Texas. The town was abandoned, and its cemetery, a grim reminder of the tragedy that had occurred, fell into neglect and disrepair, with weeds overgrowing the tilted and eroding crosses. Over the years, ranchers working on the Phelps Dodge Ranch occupied some of the buildings. Even the New Mexico Office of Cultural Affairs was unaware of the existence of the cemetery. The site was nearly forgotten until one day in 1991, when two brothers rediscovered the cemetery and successfully petitioned the state to place it on the National Register of Historic Places. Since its rediscovery, the friends and relatives of the deceased miners formed the Dawson New Mexico Association, which has held biannual Dawson Reunions for more than a decade at the cemetery. In 2003 the consul general of Los Angeles, Diego Brasioli, dedicated a plaque in a ceremony at the cemetery. There was as well a representative from the Greek Orthodox Church in Santa Fe and a memorial service in Japanese for all the miners.[35]

Late-Generation Revival

Today, New Mexico has approximately 43,218 residents who identify themselves as Italian American, about 2.4 percent of the state's total population.[36] The descendants of those early Italian immigrants who settled the state have participated in the post-1960s ethnic revival in the United States. The community that the immigrant generation created before World War II became the basis for the transnational Italian American culture that formed in the postwar era. Over the past forty years, Italian Americans have established cultural organizations and festivals in New Mexico: the Italian American Association of Rio Rancho, the Club Culturale Italiano in Albuquerque, and annual Italian film and cultural festivals held in Santa Fe and Albuquerque. Italian and Italian American interests in New Mexico are overseen by the Italian consul general's office located in Los Angeles. As miners, entrepreneurs, and professionals, those early immigrants made their impact on New Mexico's economy and in the process entered the mainstream of American society.

CHAPTER 3

ARIZONA

Settlement

Jesuits were among the first Italians to establish settlements in Arizona. Among the most influential of the early Jesuits was Jesuit Eusebio Francesco Chini (Kino), born in Trentino (1645–1711). Working in the service of the Spanish Empire, he was a skilled cartographer and is credited with proving once and for all that California is not an island. He mapped southern Arizona and Mexico and was responsible for the establishment of at least twenty southwestern towns and missions. Among his most important was San Xavier del Bac, near Tucson. His mapping, as well as the mapping of subsequent explorers, cannot be underestimated in what it meant for immigrants' possession of Native American lands.[1] These early Jesuits laid the foundation for Catholic immigrants that would follow and populate their missions.

Beginning in the 1890s, Italians were among the new arrivals in the Arizona Territory, but not nearly in the numbers of Texas and New Mexico. However, their low numbers in Arizona allow for some startling percentages. While the general population of Arizona grew about 60 percent from 1900 to 1910, the Italian immigrant population more than doubled from 699 to 1,531. During this period, Italians represented on average about 4 percent of the general population but 55 percent of the southern and eastern European immigrants in the area and 65 percent of the miners. They settled throughout Arizona, including Scottsdale and Phoenix, and established businesses, worked in the mines, and farmed.[2]

In the wake of Arizona's admission to the Union in 1912, business interests encouraged immigration to the state to develop its resources. The state's residents believed that the dusty desert town of Phoenix could do for the state what Los Angeles did for Southern California. By 1911 members of the Commercial Club for a Greater Phoenix envisioned that their town could become the "big city between LA and El Paso." Even so, some in the town felt that the immigrant class "did not meet with the high ideals" of the established residents. But they reasoned that as long as control of the city government remained in the hands of the "right people," a hardworking immigrant population could be relied upon to develop the new state's resources and grow its economy.[3]

Unfortunately for Native Americans, the original early immigrants and migrants who settled Arizona challenged Apache land rights, including mineral rights. Ultimately, the local Apache Nation would lose and be forced onto reservations. This became a common pattern in the undeveloped regions and territories of the West as developers and immigrants fought legal battles with Native Americans over land title and water rights. Immigrant success was often at the expense of Native American land rights.[4]

Mining

Initially, mining attracted immigrants to Arizona, which was a mineral-rich territory, principally copper, silver, and gold. Besides Scottsdale and Phoenix, there were small settlements of Italian immigrants in mining towns such as Globe and Wickenburg, where there were silver and gold mines, while Bisbee and Clifton provided jobs for immigrants and African Americans in the area copper mines. Bisbee became known as the Queen of the Copper Camps. African Americans, Mexicans, and Italians lived in an area called Brewery Gulch, where their children attended the same school and played together in the rubbish-filled streets of the Gulch. Italians did not form a distinct colony. Yet Italian saloons were a social venue for miners.[5]

There were other mining camps in the area. Metcalf was predominantly a Mexican town. In the nearby Morenci, the housing was spread out over a hilly landscape where housing units were allotted to newcomers without reference to their national origin. Probably arriving together under contract with a labor agent, a small group of Italians did reside at the base of one hill along with Chinese mine workers, while northern European miners lived higher up the hill. Additional Italian and Mexican neighborhoods were scattered in the surrounding terrain. To accommodate the sudden arrival of large numbers of men, mining companies built flimsy temporary housing with few amenities. In these culturally diverse circumstances, Italians as well as the other immigrant groups did not publicly practice their respective ethnic rituals. There was a small lodge of Italians in Morenci where Italians honored certain feast days, but under the circumstances Italian immigrants felt it best to remain anonymous in the copper-mining district. Spanish and French priests staffed the local

Catholic church, making it more a multicultural space not catering to any one immigrant group.[6]

Mines and quarries existed as well in Douglas, Jerome, Lowell, Miami, Oatman, Superior, Tiger, and Twin Buttes, locations in six of Arizona's fifteen counties. Although Arizona had fewer mining deaths, it was not because mine safety was a priority. It simply had fewer mines than other areas of the West. But Arizona had its share of mining accidents before 1940. Between 1914 and 1916, approximately 177 miners were killed and more than 2,600 were injured. There were many hazards in mining besides cave-ins, explosions, and fatal gas emissions. The largest number of miners killed in a single accident was in Clifton, where 9 were killed as a result of a failure of a drawbar on a car that was on an incline.[7] The establishment of the US Bureau of Mines in 1910 did not slow the pace of mine accidents. The number of mines, especially in the far reaches of the West, was far too many for any single federal agency to oversee.

By 1900 Italians formed a significant part of the mining labor force. In these areas, Italian miners aligned their interests with Mexican workers against management. Bisbee, in what became Greenlee County, was a so-called white man's camp, and Clifton-Morenci, just north in what is today Greenlee County on the state's eastern border, was a Mexican camp, largely to designate it as a location amenable to other immigrant groups, not just Mexicans. Many of the Italian miners in Clifton came from Calabria and shared aspects of their culture, especially Catholic iconography, with their Mexican cohorts. However, there were significant wage differences in all the camps. Because of their previous mining experiences, English, Cornish, and Irish miners received the highest wages and dominated the copper industry.[8]

As a rule, the racial hierarchy at the time guided management's policy that segregated immigrant and African American neighborhoods and placed them both, Italians included, at the bottom of the wage scale. However, it is unclear to what degree management was willing to compromise profits based on the constructed racial hierarchy at the time. While those at the top of the wage scale were certainly northern Europeans, they were also the most experienced and productive miners. Many had been miners in their native countries. But the shortage of labor in the West made hiring skilled workers difficult. When there were not sufficient northern European workers, the racial hierarchy was suspended, and management was forced to hire Italians, Asians, and others.[9]

While the underground jobs certainly paid a higher wage, they were also far more dangerous than work aboveground. The wages varied from $1.25 to $3.50 a day, depending on the workers' previous mining experience and the type of work the miners were assigned. In 1910 in Bisbee, for example, although Italians were allowed to work belowground in the mines, they were nevertheless placed on the so-called Mexican wage scale. As a result, Mexicans and Italians received $1.25 an hour, while experienced American and northern European immigrant miners received the $3.50 wage. There were a few instances, however, in which Italians and Mexicans earned higher wages. For example, in Morenci, Mexican immigrant Jesus Jurardo and Italian immigrant Domenico Oddonetto, who together operated jig cars, earned between $2.50 and $3.00 a day.[10] The otherwise lower wages that Italians and Mexicans earned in Arizona would be remedied in time throughout the West by the establishment of unions.

But even at the lowest end of the wage scale, weekly wages exceeded a miner's expenses, especially for unmarried men. No matter where they were on the scale, free-labor workers were in a position to quit work with savings from their work in the mines and to make lucrative business and land investments. Land was cheap, and start-up business expenses and taxes were low. Cities such as Scottsdale and Phoenix encouraged immigrant investment in their developing towns and made it as easy as possible to open a small business. Those early landowners who had migrated to the territory and invested in property ahead of the railroad were equally motivated to turn a quick profit by selling or leasing their land to immigrant farmers or entrepreneurs.

Class, Culture, and Race

The era's construction of race was a factor in the development of early Arizona society, in spite of business interests' efforts to attract immigrants to Arizona. In Clifton-Morenci, immigrants were viewed with suspicion by the dominant English-Scottish society that had formed in the wake of northern European immigration two or three generations earlier. In their dusty and remote frontier setting, those late-generation northern Europeans based their cultural and social life on an invented Victorian high society. In the promotion of their city in a 1920 directory, Phoenix business interests assured any future residents considering relocating to the city that it had a very small population of "Negroes, foreigners, or Mexicans." One historian wrote in 1925, "Its people are proud that it is an

American city in all the word 'American' means. The percentage of foreign population is relatively small, although the picturesque Mexican is much in evidence on all public occasions." Business leaders disparaged immigrants and African Americans in two ways: first by characterizing them as the subaltern "other" in their community and, in the case of Mexicans, then by caricaturing them as "picturesque," a nonthreatening image of them as merely an amusing aspect of the southwestern cultural landscape. When not characterized as anarchists or criminals, an Italian at the time was often caricatured in newspapers and journals as a "picturesque" street-corner organ grinder with his monkey. Chicago writer Henry Blake Fuller called one such "swarthy foreigner" a "music-cobbler." The city fathers were careful to gerrymander voting districts to ensure that the city government stayed in the hands of the "right people."[11] But such caricatures and efforts to limit the immigrants' political power were not enough to prohibit them from becoming an important part of Arizona's developing business community.

Although Arizonians expressed some of the same xenophobic attitudes prevalent throughout the United States at the time, they did not support the same rigid racial hierarchy enforced in Texas. Before 1920 there were no active members of the Ku Klux Klan in Arizona. During its national revival in the 1920s, the Klan, with its anti-immigrant platform, did make a feeble effort to establish a base in Prescott and Yuma. But its efforts fell on deaf ears. Because of its general lack of support among the local population, its membership was largely clandestine, rendering it ineffective in its political influence, which was much greater in Colorado and Oregon at the time. In one incident, a lynch mob did threaten an Italian immigrant who was accused of killing an "American boy" in a street brawl. This apparently was not the work of the Klan, but a spontaneous gathering as a result of the general suspicion of immigrants at the time.[12]

Hardworking immigrants were too far removed from the discourse over race in America to allow anti-immigrant sentiment to influence their struggle to succeed. Regardless of the attitude toward immigrants, Arizona's late-generation Americans did not establish any permanent barriers against immigrant success in Arizona. The same, however, cannot be said for more rigidly segregated African Americans, who were still forced to live under a long-standing racial code in America.

Italian and Mexican workers formed political alliances and in one instance successfully opposed a mining company's efforts to expropriate community land for a railroad. Immigrants banded together in several wildcat mining strikes in the area. In 1903 and again in 1915 in Clifton-Morenci, Italians united with Mexican, Spanish, and Chinese workers to go on strike. In Clifton-Morenci and Bisbee, Italians, Chinese, and Mexicans lived in the same settlement together.[13] National origin was insignificant next to their common interest in higher wages and better working and living conditions. However, such solidarity did not preclude violent attacks upon strikebreakers, regardless of their country of origin.

Early in Bisbee's settlement, at least three separate Italian dialect groups, the Piedmontese, Sicilians, and Tyroleans, populated the mining zone. Two hundred Tyroleans from Trentino formed two colonies in the Bisbee-Jerome area.[14] With their separate dialects and different cultural rituals, these three groups were unable to communicate and were for a time socially and culturally incompatible. However, thrown together in close quarters and sharing common economic and social concerns in their adopted home, over time northern and southern Italians overcame their differences and began to communicate with their new language, English.

But English was not the only lingua franca for Italians. As they did in New Mexico, Italians often became trilingual in English, Italian, and Spanish. They sometimes developed a form of "Italianized Spanish." In Arizona, Italians served on the boards of some Mexican community organizations. In 1924 in Bisbee, there was an Italian-Mexican social club. In Clifton, since they shared the same neighborhoods and churches, intermarriage became common between the two immigrant groups. As one woman with northern Italian roots explained, "My whole outlook is American with an Italian Mexican view." She went on to explain that having lived for so many years next to Mexican immigrants, she "felt more Mexican than Italian."[15]

Enclave Businesses—Phoenix

The first Italians to settle Phoenix, Maricopa County, were railroad workers after they and Mexican immigrants completed the rail line linking Ash Fork, Prescott, and Phoenix. However, there were not enough Italians to form a Little Italy. Where a significant number came from the same region, they did at times settle together in small neighborhoods. Most of the Italians in Globe, for example, came from the Piedmont region and managed to establish for a time a small Italian settlement. Otherwise, Italians were a part of the multinational mixture of immigrants in the area. Because of their small numbers, they joined already established cultural

Hispano organizations, such as the Alianza Hispano-American Lodge No. 9 in Phoenix. Francisco and Celestino Ceschetti served as officers in the lodge. This was also a Mexican-Italian mutual-aid society. Another Hispano organization that attracted Italians was the Yucatec Hose Company No. 2. Serving in this volunteer fire organization, Alexander Barsanti and the civic-minded brothers Francisco and Celestino Ceschetti volunteered their time and services along with Mexican immigrant Francisco Serrano.[16]

Following the same pattern throughout the United States at the time, males usually came alone to find a job. These free-labor immigrant men created another new market for enterprising immigrants, especially women. As early as the 1880s, Rebecca and Charles Salari opened the Phoenix Hotel. About the same time, in the *Phoenix City Directory*, Mr. and Mrs. Bardone also advertised rooms for rent in their Cottage Hotel. The wives played an important part in running the hotels. In 1899 the directory also lists Teresa Bianchi, who advertised furnished rooms on South Center Street. In the same year, Bianchi was joined by the Laziola sisters, who opened the Half-Way House. In the 1930s, another Italian established the Colombo Hotel. It is doubtful that these rooming houses and hotels served only Italian immigrants, but rather an international clientele. The cheapest rooms in town rented for about twenty-five cents a night, while the better hotels charged four dollars a week, or nine dollars a month.[17] Lodging was not expensive, especially considering that the weekly and monthly rates often included meals in many rooming houses.

Running boardinghouses and hotels required time-consuming labor. Aside from the daily grind of cleaning, the women who ran the boardinghouses usually had to be up before dawn to prepare breakfast, a lunch for the men to take with them to work, and then dinner. As one boardinghouse woman said, “The man who works hard must eat well.” Immigrant women’s domestic skills found a public place in the economic and social order.[18] In the process, these immigrant women began to redefine the role of women in both the family and society.

The Bianchi, Salari, and Bardone families, including the owner of the Columbo Hotel, all had to have start-up capital to lease, buy, or build their hotels and rooming houses. Mining was a rich source of capital for immigrant labor in Arizona, both within the state and even across the Mexican-US border. Italians, Mexicans, and other immigrants were known to travel to neighboring Mexico to work in the mines and then return with their wages to Phoenix. With a potential pay scale of up to $3.50 a day, it was an extremely lucrative job.[19] Their earnings were quickly transformed into the social capital that fueled the developing local enclave economy.

Arizona also attracted a professional class. Between 1892 and 1905, Phoenix directories list at least three Italian clerks: James and Elvezio Righetti and William Martini. All three brought with them to Arizona educational skills that their job required. It is reasonable to assume that they were from northern Italy. Even in postunification Italy, schools were all but nonexistent in southern Italy, especially Basilicata, Calabria, and Sicily. These regions experienced the highest illiteracy rates in the country, especially for women. Clerks, notaries, and lawyers prepared contracts, bills of sale, and other official documents. Even more important for immigrants thousands of miles from their villages, they could hire the literate among them to write letters in Italian or get help negotiating bank transfers in order to send money to aging parents or to cover expenses for their wives and children to join them. Letters home were an important means of maintaining contact with family members and friends left behind.[20]

The majority of the immigrants who came to Arizona were peasants from southern Italy. Although without formal schooling, they did bring artisan skills with them. Or lacking specific skills, after accumulating savings by working day labor or in the mines, they could partner with others more educated and open businesses. Francisco Ceschetti and Charles and Sam Donofrio are listed as greengrocers in Phoenix directories. Frank Gallardo and Frank Benenato opened barbershops, while J. Gatti opened a butcher shop. C. Farnese advertised vocal lessons in her home. No doubt Farnese was the product of an upper-class Italian family that could have afforded to educate her. In 1899 Frank Cavaliere began by shoeing horses for a farrier shop in Phoenix, but within five years he opened his own Pacific Horseshoeing business in Phoenix. His brother George became a blacksmith. He then used his iron-working skills to provide dredging equipment for irrigation canals. Two immigrants, L. Bonnani and R. Luchesi, teamed up to open a shop that served the general contracting needs of builders in the area and the home-decor needs of a wealthier clientele. They provided a variety of products for the construction of both private and municipal buildings, such as precast crown moldings, fireplace mantels, exterior moldings, lintels, and ornate classical capitals for columns, most made from plaster of paris.[21]

The Donofrio family, which became one of the most prominent names in Phoenix, is an excellent example of how social capital upraised the immigrant family. Before he opened his grocery store, Charles Donofrio sold cigars and tobacco from a sidewalk stand. Later, in his store he sold nuts, drinks, and candy. In 1887 Charles established in partnership the Donofrio-Zunkel Confectionery Company. Using the surrounding desert flora, it pioneered in the making of a unique product, cactus candy. Charles expanded his confectionery trade to include a bakery and an ice-cream distribution business. For the next sixty-eight years, the company remained in the family until it was dissolved in 1955.[22]

What is revealing about the litany of businesses in Phoenix is that each required a certain set of skills that were a part of the individual's heritage. Vocalist, barber, mason, butcher, and farrier all required specific skills or training. But it must be added that it was not always important whether the immigrant learned such skills in Italy. The majority of the artisan skills practiced were a part of the cultural heritage that Italians brought to the United States, including candy making. It is unknown if the Donofrio family, for example, had made candy in Italy before arriving in Arizona. But Italy has scores of famous centuries-old confectionery businesses, many of which have become international name brands.[23] The free-labor immigrant adapted.

Alessio Carraro is an example of the peripatetic immigrant male who was able to take advantage of the job and investment opportunities wherever he found them. From the northern Italian region of Lombardy, he immigrated to the United States in 1905 and worked as a shoemaker in Petaluma, California. His shoe-making skill, a part of his family heritage, was merely the beginning of a successful career in business and investments. He later moved to San Francisco, where he became a sheet-metal worker and opened four shops by 1919. By 1925 Carraro was able to retire. But he was not finished yet. With his new wealth, he moved to Phoenix and became a successful land developer in partnership with his son. In Phoenix, Carraro purchased a hill and built a three-story house that is now known as Tovrea Castle, named after a niece who lived on the property until 1969. The city of Phoenix purchased the property in 1993, spent millions in restoration, and opened it to the public. After Phoenix, Carraro settled in Yarnell, purchased another hill, and built a "castle," known as Carraro's Grotto, decorated with creative rock formations. He worked on his folk-art installation until his death in 1964. His grotto bears comparison to two other Italian immigrant folk sites, Baldassare Forestiere's Underground Gardens in Fresno and Simon Rodia's Watts Towers in Los Angeles. Such monuments are sites that recall the immigrants' nostalgic recollections of the homeland that they had left behind, as well as the creative spirit that many Italian immigrants brought to the United States before 1940.[24]

More commonly, partnerships and networking within the community became important vehicles for immigrant success in Phoenix. In 1883 the partnership of two Italians, J. P. Righetti and Stefano Daneri, sold a parcel of land to Stefano Purcella. Likewise, the partnership of John Belli, Burt Peirano, and Charles Donofrio purchased land from John Biaggiore in 1898. Biaggiore had apparently financed his land purchases from his work in the gold mines in Wickenburg, where he and other Italians had initially settled. Similarly, Felix Bertino worked in the Globe mines for ten years before settling in Phoenix in 1912. Networking with Biaggiore, who by that time had become a well-known businessman and investor in the Italian community, Bertino was able to purchase five acres of quality farmland and begin a small truck farm. As early as 1905, Lord, Trenor, and Borrows wrote, "The conditions in the smaller cities and towns are, as a rule, more favorable for the quick advance and independence of the immigrant colonists, for whom opportunities are open as artisans, small shopkeepers and cultivators of market gardens or outlying farms."[25] Fueling their entrepreneurship was the exchange of social capital, allowing individuals to invest in land and enclave businesses.

With a large customer base, the saloon business allowed Italians a quick entry into the enclave economy. In fact, one of the most important but certainly not the only factor that influenced the passage of the Eighteenth Amendment to the Constitution was the overwhelming immigrant involvement in the production, distribution, and sale of alcoholic beverages. At the same time that Germans controlled the beer trade, California Italians dominated the wine industry, and Jews presided over the distilling business. Prohibition was fueled by old-guard Protestants who were attempting to stave off the cultural and political influences of immigrants who brought with them to America not only different religious, social, and family values, but also different attitudes toward alcohol consumption. Among his famous photographs of urban immigrants, Jacob Riis depicted what he called Black and Tan pubs, unlicensed saloons where immigrants and African Americans drank and socialized. America's anti-immigrant faction feared that immigrants were forming a coalition with African Americans to rewrite the American racial code.[26] Immigrants' casual attitude toward alcohol was especially loathsome to those upper-class citizens who were a part of Clifton-Morenci's faux Victorian society.

In northeastern ethnic enclaves, German immigrants were especially influential in the brewery business and the growth of saloons. To promote sales of their beer, both Gustave Pabst and Anheuser-Busch paid for tenant improvements on all saloons as long as the proprietor sold their beer: "If Gustave Pabst's agents bankrolled a place on one corner, you could count on Aldophus Bush's men showing up to finance another one across the street." With Pabst and Busch behind them, and with a modest investment of approximately $200, immigrants could open a saloon. Supporting the development of businesses, municipalities were quick to grant business licenses. America's towns and cities contained thousands of hardworking but largely single young men. After ten or more hours on the job, these men were relegated to crowded, small rooming houses, where they often shared rooms and sometimes even beds with other immigrant men who worked different shifts. The saloon became a comfortable space, serving multiple functions as an unofficial post office, hiring hall, and social club.[27] Fueling the profits of distillers, distributors, and saloon owners, ethnic capital found yet another source for circulation in immigrant enclaves.

Before Congress passed the Eighteenth Amendment, the alcohol business thrived in America's cities and hamlets, and immigrants were quick to invest their capital in the burgeoning enterprise that had a thirsty clientele ready to support their investments. The West and Arizona in particular participated in the alcohol growth industry. Yet as the influence of the Prohibition movement grew, the United States Brewers Association realized that it might be undermining its own best interests by "financing ignorant foreigners who are not citizens" and allowing "brewery-controlled saloons." Phoenix had more than two thousand foreign born and more than fifteen thousand males, foreign and native born.[28] Saloons in the enclave did not cater only to the immigrant population. This wider influence in their communities is what prohibitionists feared most.

In Phoenix alone, "forty-percent of the Italians...established themselves...in the liquor business." As early as 1892, Italian immigrants opened the A. (Alexander) Barsanti and Company's saloon, and Charles Salari opened Salari's Place near the train depot. In 1896 the Donofrio family opened the Solid Comfort bar. The saloon business was bustling, as evidenced by the fact that saloon ownership kept changing as original partnerships dissolved and new investors bought them out. The Italian business community was a close-knit network, leading to the quick exchange of social capital in the funding of personal business loans. By 1897 Alexander Barsanti became the new owner of the Union Saloon, while John Biaggiore took his land-investment earnings and partnered with Prosper Bardone to launch the Board of Trade Saloon and the California Wine House, where he employed at least four other Italians. Giovanni Quadri and a Mr. Rolletto opened a saloon on South Seventh Street. Before the turn of the century, Guerino Bianchi owned and operated the Swiss Saloon, while Michael Marro opened a grocery store with a substantial wine cellar for his Italian clientele. Ethnic capital reached across nationalities when Oduardo Magnani partnered with Mr. Djonovich to open the Columbus Saloon. By 1898 Barsanti sold the Union Saloon to B. Poli, and Giovanni's brother, Peter Quadri, became the sole owner of the Depot Saloon, which he later sold to J. Vietti.[29]

Facilitating the exchange of social capital, the Italian network in Phoenix was tightly woven. An early arrival in Arizona, Paolo Perazzo was close friends with the Biaggiore, Donofrio, Barsanti, and Magnani families. Paolo had been preceded in Arizona by a brother, Carlo Perazzo. Stefano Purcella was encouraged to come to Arizona by his brother Frank, both of whom settled in Wickenburg to work in the gold mines. By 1889 Magnani and his partner, Djonovich, opened a new saloon with the suggestive name, the Red Light Saloon.[30]

As an early arrival in Phoenix, Perazzo was able to take advantage of the availability of cheap land. From his work in the Wickenburg mines, he had accumulated the capital reserves to purchase land in Phoenix and a ranch in Tempe. He also owned the Four Mile House. As a result of his many business interests in the Phoenix enclave, Perazzo became a well-known investor in the community. Set in his Old World ways, Perazzo refused to purchase an automobile, though he could well afford one, and instead continued to use a horse and buggy. He became so well known for his business acumen and reliability in Phoenix that the Phoenix National Bank and the W. K. James Real Estate Company placed iron rings set in the concrete sidewalks outside their offices to accommodate Perazzo's horse and carriage when he arrived to do business. His good friend Charles Donofrio also placed a ring outside his confectionery shop for Perazzo's carriage horses. He proved himself to be a trustworthy banking customer, making his loan payments on time and always having sufficient capital for down payments on real estate. He is an example of the trust that immigrants were able to develop first within the fabric of the ethnic network and then outside the enclave. At the very time that the Boston-based Immigration Restriction League and Senator Henry Cabot Lodge were influencing legislation to limit immigration to the United States, especially Italians and Jews, Italians had already established a valued place in the social and economic order in the West. As early as 1900, Italians were second only to Russian Jews in self-owned businesses. In 1907 Henry James wrote that the "foreign personality" was affirming its place in the economic and social order in America.[31]

Italian investment in Arizona's communities was not merely a local phenomenon. At times, for both the purchase and the sale of their products, businesses were linked to Italian communities in other states. G. H. Bardone's California Wine House, for example, included a list of wines and cordials made by California Italian vintners. By 1915 Andrea Sbarboro in Northern California and Secondo Guasti in Southern California owned two of the largest producing wineries in the United States. With their bulk wine sales and distribution, Italians were reshaping the American palate by making wine widely available, a product not important in the American diet before Italians arrived. Lunch at the California Wine House was served in the barroom, where the menu included an array of Italian, German, and French confections and pastries. In a concession to the cultural standards at the time, Bardone provided ladies with a private room separate from the bar where it was indecorous for "decent" ladies to be seen.[32]

It is safe to say that immigrant saloon owners Magnani and Djonovich did not provide private dining accommodations for respectable ladies in their Red Light Saloon. If the name of their establishment is any indication, they did not wish to attract them anyway. At the time, brothels and red-light districts had become an established part of nearly all immigrant communities. Cognizant of the economic value that the immigrant male brought to their town, the city fathers in Phoenix were tolerant of brothels, which were concentrated between Madison and Jackson Streets and Center Street in the immigrant section of the city. Their tolerance of brothels did not set them apart from any of the other western immigrant settlements. From time to time, in an effort to promote the image of law and order, if not moral order, law enforcement conducted raids. But the roundup of madams and their prostitutes was little more than an inconvenience for them, and the minimal fines judges assessed were just an added tax on the illicit establishments, which immediately reopened.[33] There was little concern voiced by the men running city governments over the exploitation and sexual violence that these poor women faced in their communities.

While the vast majority of Italian immigrant men and women ran legitimate business establishments, there were some within the community who attempted to skirt the law. In 1915, migrating from California, Louis Fasoni and A. Toledo settled in Phoenix and attempted to start a winery. Without pulling any municipal business permits, they built a crude palm-leaf hut on the edge of town and began making wine and serving the local immigrant population. When the sheriff got wind of what they were up to, he summarily shut down the illegal winery and bar. The sheriff arrested both men, but only after a brief unpleasant encounter with some of their customers.[34] There is no word in the literature about the quality of their wine.

But this seemingly insignificant and perhaps humorous incident inadvertently reveals a more significant aspect of the impact that immigrants were having in the West. Arizona did have a small number of vineyards at the time. So it is possible that the two men purchased their grapes from a local farmer. More likely, coming from California, the men must have been aware of the state's growing wine industry. By 1915 Andrea Sbarboro's Italian Swiss Colony in Northern California and Secondo Guasti's Italian Vineyard Company in Southern California were using a network of national brokers to ship their wine grapes throughout the country to Italian home winemakers. For their supply of wine grapes, the two would-be vintners in Phoenix had access to a local fruit and vegetable broker, Walter Hill Company. Hill had connections throughout the West, including California. By 1915 there was a well-established national fruit and vegetable brokerage system in place. The list of names of hundreds of brokers attending a Los Angeles convention in 1915 reveals that 98 percent of them were from northern European stock.[35] Initially, late-generation Americans provided the know-how and language skills to run national shipping brokerage companies to all parts of the United States. But in time, Italians and other immigrants and their offspring would become major brokers and distributors of all agricultural products.

Italians played only a small part in Arizona's agricultural industry. As one example, James Minotto, a latecomer to Phoenix in 1919, established a dairy farm in Yavapai County and the Salt River valley. Otherwise, Arizona farming was small compared with its neighboring states. By 1920 Arizona did have nearly ten thousand farms in operation, with nearly eight thousand owner-operators and more than eighteen hundred tenant farmers producing a variety of fruits and vegetables. Arizona farmers were producing about six hundred thousand pounds of grapes by 1920. However, there is no record of Italian growers. In the same year, neighboring New Mexico had 75 percent more farms, and Texas had 97 percent more farms in operation. California's number of farms was second only to Texas in the United States. With its burgeoning wine industry in the 1920s, California's grape production would dwarf grape production in all other western states.[36]

Late-Generation Arizonians

Although small in numbers, the original Italians who settled Arizona did leave a legacy in the state beyond 1940. Many Italian immigrants and their offspring found success in the professions and distinguished themselves in local and state politics. Evo DeConcini was the son of Tyrolean Italian immigrants who had settled in Michigan. In 1920 Evo migrated to Tucson, where he attended law school at the University of Arizona and graduated with a law degree. In 1932 he began a distinguished career in law and Arizona politics. In 1936 he became assistant attorney general, was elected judge of the Arizona Supreme Court (a position he held until 1946), and later served as the twice-elected attorney general of the state supreme court, a position he held until 1953. His son, Dennis, served as US senator from 1976 to 1995.[37]

At the time that Evo arrived in Arizona, the overall foreign-born population in Arizona had already begun to decline: 52 percent between 1920 and 1940. Because of the short-lived nature of mining operations, the Italian communities surrounding them dissolved, similar to the fate of mining towns such as Dawson, New Mexico, and Thurber, Texas. To maintain the community's identity in the face of an aging and declining demographic population, in 1939 Italians in Phoenix formed the Italo-American Club. By 1940 the Italian population of Arizona had dropped to 715, with a mere 84 residing in Phoenix.[38]

But ethnic identity is a slippery surface, where there is little agreement on what will constitute the future of ethnic identity in America. By 1950 the total Italian population in Arizona had more than doubled to 1,600, while Phoenix's population of those identifying themselves as Italian rose to 641. In 1970 the Italian numbers would surge again. Counting foreign born, native born, and native born of mixed parentage, there were 12,502 Italians living in Arizona, with 5,413 residing in Phoenix. Within twenty years, in 1990 Arizona counted 160,000 citizens identifying themselves as Italian, approximately 5 percent of the state's population, with more than 108,000 living in Phoenix. By 2000 Arizona's Italian American population soared to 224,795.[39]

Such an abrupt rise in numbers cannot be attributed solely to migration to the state. With migration from the East and Midwest, Arizona did become a destination for those looking for a more healthful climate and an affordable retirement venue. However, more likely, beginning in the 1960s, second- and third-generation ethnics, Italians included, suddenly found it acceptable in American society to claim their immigrant origins. The immigrant generation's success had catapulted the second and third generations into a comfortable middle-class status. The anti-immigrant sentiment of the previous generation that had shamed and stigmatized their immigrant grandparents and first-generation parents had dissipated. As a result, those of "mixed" parentage who had hidden under the cloak of their paternal surnames found it respectable to count themselves "Italian." For years scholars have wrestled unsuccessfully with the definition of what constitutes the Italian American identity, including all late-generation Americans who reclaim their families' foreign origins. Statistics cannot explain the psychological dimensions of this reclamation of roots.[40]

In 1960 Phoenix established its first Italian newspaper, *La Tribuna Italiana*, with a circulation of more than 20,000 readers. With at least one page in Italian, the paper covered news from Italy and community events. Although the paper ceased publication in 1971, many Italian American residents now receive the Southern California–based *L'Italo-Americano*.[41] Since the year 2000, with the newspaper's presence on the Internet, it now serves five western states, Arizona included.

In recent years, rather than diminishing, the number of Italian cultural associations in Arizona has grown. Facing a decline in its membership, the Italo-American Club of Phoenix in 1952 merged with the Arizona American-Italian Club, established in 1947. It exists today at its original location with approximately 11,000 members. The membership funded and built a center where they have monthly and annual events. In 1952 a largely professional group of Italian Americans formed the Amico Club, a service club that sponsors fund-raising for a variety of causes. There is also a chapter in Phoenix of the Order Sons of Italy, the oldest Italian association in the United States. It has additional lodges in Scottsdale, Sedona, Tucson, Prescott, and Yuma. Within the past decade, Italian Americans have established the Italian Association of Arizona, located in Scottsdale. Its goal is to promote the business interests of Italian Americans in Scottsdale and the surrounding region.[42] The National Italian American Foundation, located in Washington, DC, with local chapters and officers in all the states, established a chapter in Phoenix.

These new organizations are based on a model distinct from their predecessors. As Phylis Martinelli writes, these groups "point to a new ethnic dimension in the West."[43] They must be characterized as trans-Italian organizations that intend to connect local Italian businesses with Italian products, as well as with contemporary Italian culture. They are not modeled on the older fraternal organizations with an emphasis on helping Italian immigrants in their transition into American life. Instead, they are business organizations that link sponsors and participants with Italy through commerce. In Scottsdale's Old Town, the Italian Association now sponsors an annual festival where Italian business owners promote their businesses and sell Italian products. These new Italian organizations are driven less by nostalgia for the older generation of Italian immigrants than by their business interests. This serves to put a younger generation in closer touch with a modern commercial Italy than with the diminishing if not disappeared culture of their grandparents' or great-grandparents' Italy.

Pike Street Market. University of Washington Libraries, Special Collections, Pike Street Market, UW 1155.

Charcoal oven, Fish Creek, 1870s. Nevada Historical Society.

Workers, Italian Vineyard Company. Courtesy of Italian American Museum of Los Angeles.

Workers laying streetcar tracks on the Alameda Bridge, Denver. History Colorado—Denver.

Bertagnolli Mercantile Store. Collection of the Rock Springs Historical Museum, Rock Springs, Wyoming.

Utah miners. Scambray Family Papers, San Clemente, California.

Immigrants arriving on boat, Galveston. Galveston Photographic Subject Files: Immigrants. Rosenberg Library, Galveston, Texas.

Logging, Oregon. J.F. Ford Photographs, OSU Libraries Special Collections Research Center, Corvallis, Oregon.

Potlatch Corporation, Idaho. Lumber mill [03], 457_202_2_425, Potlatch Corporation Historical Archives, MG 475, Special Collections and Archives, University of Idaho, Moscow.

Phelps Dodge Co. Archives and Special Collections, New Mexico State University Library, Las Cruces.

II

THE MIDSECTION OF THE WEST

CHAPTER 4

COLORADO

Railroads—Arrival and Settlement

As early as the mid-1860s, the Colorado Territory had already established the Denver and Rio Grande Railroad, as well as other short lines that connected the territory and its mining activities to Wyoming and other regions of the West. In advance of the railroad, there were only four Italian prospectors, brothers who had settled in the region. Shortly after their arrival, Italian Jesuits established a mission in San Juan Valley in the southwest corner of the territory. These few Italians would soon be joined by a flood of Italian immigrants. By 1870, six years before Colorado would become a state, the territory's railroads connected with the transcontinental railroad, thus opening Colorado's vast mineral deposits to the rest of the United States. The first wave of immigrants followed in the 1880s. To oversee the needs and conditions of the growing Italian population, by 1880 the Italian government established a consular office in Denver headed by Angelo Capelli, who became a well-known and respected businessman in Denver. Immigrants followed in the upcoming decades. Labor contractors in Denver hired Italian agents who posted fliers in small villages throughout Italy with glowing descriptions of labor conditions in the Colorado mining districts. Initially, these first immigrants had to pay their own way with a deposit of three to ten dollars. They also signed contracts in which they agreed to pay their labor contractor 20 percent of their wages over the next three years. But the demand for labor was so great in Colorado that the Denver, South Park, and Pacific Railroad began paying for immigrants to travel to the West.[1]

In 1881 the railroad hired labor contractors in New York who rounded up a group of seventy Italian laborers and paid their passage to Denver. They found a town unlike any other they had experienced. In contrast to New York, at the time Denver's streets were unpaved, sidewalks were made of wood, and local housing consisted of log cabins and tents. Women drove wagons, and cowboys "wore furry western chaps." Adolfo Rossi was among those men from New York. Far from their native villages in Italy, Rossi and his fellow Italians suffered an even greater culture shock. Through a typical ruse that labor contractors used to lure workers to remote western settlements, a labor contractor promised Rossi that he would be hired as a railroad timekeeper and assured the other men that they would all be hired as carpenters, cooks, and blacksmiths. Instead, they were assigned work on a spur at an elevation of more than eleven thousand feet in the Rocky Mountains. Working alongside Irish and other immigrants, Rossi and the others labored in thin, frigid air clearing a roadbed over rocky terrain and through dense forest for an extension of a rail line over a mountain pass. To no avail, they complained to management about the food and the log-cabin accommodations without windows and fresh air. However, at two and a half dollars a day, including their room and board, they were well compensated for their pick-and-shovel labor.[2] This was nearly the equivalent of an experienced miner's wages by the 1910s.

Rossi and his companions made the best of their predicament. In time, the contract with his labor agent expired, and he became free labor. However, because of his experience and facility in Italian, management gave him a position in the Denver office. They then assigned him to travel to remote mountain camps, where he oversaw and directed railroad operations.[3]

Before Rossi and his crew of Italian laborers arrived, in 1870 there were just 16 Italians in Colorado. By 1880 their numbers grew to 335. Soon after, there was a dramatic increase of Italians in the state. In 1890 their number rose to 3,882, and by 1910 that number rose to 14,375, the highest before 1940. Italians represented 11 percent of Colorado's foreign-born population. Colorado became known at the time in European periodicals as the "Italy of the American West."[4]

With the coming of the railroad, all aspects of Colorado's economy and population grew. Colorado's vast mineral wealth had created a boom in such locations as Denver, whose population grew from 35,629 in 1880 to 133,859 in 1900. By 1920 Denver became home to the state's largest foreign-born population. In comparison to eastern cities, Denver's foreign-born population was nearly 15 percent, while Chicago's was 29.9 percent and Boston's 32.4 percent. At 2,871, Italians ranked sixth among the foreign born in Denver. In time, unskilled Italian immigrants soon supplanted the skilled English, Welsh, and Cornish miners in the area.[5]

Nuns—Education and Service to the Community

With the growth of the immigrant population in larger settlements such as Denver came the social problems associated with dislocation and poverty. The number of orphaned children as well began to rise with the influx of immigrant families. The first nun to enter the territory on missionary work was Sister Blandina Segale, who made a stop in Colorado on her way to Santa Fe, New Mexico. Following Sister Blandina, another nun, Mother Frances Xavier Cabrini, left a legacy with her work in Denver's Italian community. Born in 1850 in Lombardy, by the age of twenty-five she became well known for her service to the poor and sick in Italy. In 1880 she established the Missionary Sisters of the Sacred Heart. Her order soon became renowned, and Pope Leo XIII sent her and members of her order to America to begin establishing schools, hospitals, and orphanages to aid Italian immigrants. Arriving in New York in 1889, she and her order did a careful study to locate the largest Italian immigrant communities in the United States.[6]

Receiving a report of the "pitiable conditions" of the Italians in Denver's Italian community, Sister Cabrini and her contingent of sisters arrived in Denver in the summer of 1902. She immediately laid the foundation for a new school in the growing Italian settlement in North Denver. For their living quarters, the sisters rented a two-story building at the corner of Palmer Street and Thirty-Fourth Avenue for seventy-five dollars a month, a huge sum to the poor order of nuns. Many of the Italian parents, who came largely from Sicily, Calabria, and Campania, rallied around her and promised to pay twenty-five cents a month tuition to aid in the building of the school. The order opened the first floor of Our Lady of Mount Carmel Grade School in the fall of 1902. Cabrini had a keen business sense and continued to buy land surrounding the Mount Carmel School in order to give the children more space, including a site that became a summer camp. It still stands as the Queen of Heaven Mother Cabrini Memorial Institute.[7] Although the nuns' main objective was to educate the children in Catholic doctrine, they provided their pupils with a comprehensive education in the three R's. Catholic education for children must be counted among the major benefits that Italians and other Catholic children received on their path to assimilation in America.

During Sister Cabrini's tenure in Denver, the Italian community grew in both numbers and prosperity. When the first wave of Italian immigrants settled in Denver, they were forced to attend the already established Irish Catholic St. Patrick's Church. The Irish priest did not speak Italian or any Italian dialect. The church's iconography and liturgy as well were foreign to the largely southern Italian parishioners. This cultural divide between the Irish and Italians was not uncommon in the United States. Dissatisfied, these early immigrants established the Mount Carmel Society. By 1904 the North Denver Italian community was able to fund and build a new church, Our Lady of Mount Carmel on Navajo Street, not far from Sister Cabrini's school. The Italian parishioners placed a plaque to the right of the front door designating Our Lady of Mount Carmel as an "Italian Church" to distinguish it from the Irish and other Catholic parishes in Denver. The Italians contributed liberally to the church's construction. Ten of the twelve still existing nameplates below the stained-glass windows in the nave bear Italian names.[8]

Mining and Smelting— Labor Strife, Safety, and Disasters

Besides Denver, there were other important Italian immigrant settlements in Colorado. One hundred miles south of Denver in Pueblo County, there were few Italian immigrants in 1870. But by 1890 there were 474, and by 1920 the number of Italians in Pueblo County increased to 1,752. By then Colorado counted a total of 12,580 Italians, a decline from 1910. Located in central Colorado at the confluence of the Arkansas River and Fountain Creek, in 1870 Pueblo officially became a town in the Colorado Territory and soon after became an important mining and smelting center. The first immigrants who settled Pueblo arrived from Sicily, Calabria, and Campania. They settled in a neighborhood that became known as Goat Hill, located southeast of the city center. Reflecting the international nature of the workforce, there were settlements in and around Pueblo with colorful names such as Peppersauce, Bottoms, the Grove, Bojon Town, and Eilers.[9]

The major employers in the area were the Colorado Fuel and Iron Company (CF&I) and Pueblo Smelting and Refining Company. The sudden upsurge of immigrant numbers suggests that labor contractors were instrumental in bringing large groups of workers to Pueblo. Among the local labor contractors were the Tarabino brothers, saloon owners, and John Aiello, who owned a bank, general store, and saloon in Las Animas, Bent County, east of Pueblo. The three men had direct contacts in southern Italian villages. Small towns quickly developed around Pueblo's core: North Pueblo, South Pueblo, and Bessemer. The town of Bessemer, on the southern edge of Pueblo, was formed in 1880 when investors formed the CF&I. The Philadelphia Smelter was constructed near Goat Hill. In time all four settlements would be merged into modern-day Pueblo. Italians also formed small neighborhoods in Pueblo's downtown area, between First and Santa Fe Streets.[10]

The danger involved in mining operations is well documented. But little has been written about the dangers in the steel mills. The mills were places of unbearable heat with life-threatening hazards involved in nearly every aspect of the smelting operation at CF&I. Management did not provide workers with protective clothing to insulate them from the heat of the ovens. Instead, they had to wear two pairs of work trousers, two pairs of socks, and two pairs of gloves. One Italian immigrant, Jim Dilorio, recalls resorting to cutting lengths of old automobile tires and strapping them on his legs as a protective cover from the ovens' heat. The planks that they worked on were slippery and often burst into flames, engulfing the unsuspecting worker. Pueblo resident Louis Paglione recalls that his immigrant father was maimed for life when he lost an eye in the wire mill. Russell DiSalvo reported that his immigrant father was killed in a mill. Another worker, Tony Martellaro, explained that in the rod mill, he had to grab red-hot rods with tongs, but if he missed, the rod would bounce uncontrollably and injure or kill any worker unfortunate enough to be in its path. He added that one worker was impaled by a red-hot rod through the stomach. But after extensive surgery, he managed to survive and return to work. Federal or state standards were lax, and management showed little concern for improving worker safety. As Paul Palermo said, "It was a lot easier to replace a person than it was to replace a piece of machinery." One worker, Joe Genova, attempted to apply for a safer position as a crane operator, but was told by his supervisor, "As long as your name ends in a vowel you're gonna stay down in the cellar" working the blast furnace. "Before the war," as Ralph Montera said, "you didn't have a chance to go nowhere." Louis Paglione added, "I didn't know what discrimination was 'til I went to work in the mill." The statistics seem to bear out the racial hierarchy that plant managers maintained. By 1940, out of 125 crane operators, only 3 were Italian, 2 were Yugoslavian, and 2 were Mexican.[11]

In 1920 the coal-mining towns surrounding Pueblo, Brookside, Rockvale, and Berwind were almost exclusively Italian. In 1921 after the closure of the Pueblo Smelting and Refining Company, Italians moved to Bessemer in the current Lake Minnequa and Minnequa Park area. South of Pueblo County in Walsenburg, Huerfano County, there were approximately twenty mining camps. South of Walsenburg was Trinidad, Las Animas County, which contained at least sixteen mining camps, where Italians represented 40 percent of the miners. As a coke and mining center, by 1911 Trinidad had a population of 1,500 and was a bustling manufacturing and distribution center. The town was the juncture for the Denver and Rio Grande, Colorado & Southern, and Santa Fe Railroads. One commentator called it the Paris of the region. It had an opera house, a Carnegie library, schools, and an array of new municipal buildings.[12]

Italians in Trinidad were numerous enough to justify building a church and a parochial school, presided over for more than thirty years by a Jesuit, Father S. Personé, who was replaced in 1920 by Father Padre Telese. The community also boasted its own paper, *Il Corriere di Trinidad*, directed by Franchino Anselmo. By 1911 in Trinidad, Italians were well represented among the numerous downtown businesses also owned by Mexicans and late-generation Americans. Among those listed in the local business directory were brothers Emilio and John Aiello, who ran a merchandise store, while John doubled as president of the International State Bank in Trinidad. Their brother Charles ran one of the local saloons, and two other Italians ran the Pagliuso and Maio Saloon nearby. Mike Motto was a jeweler, and Louis Ferraro owned the Ferraro and Sons laundry. Carlo Basso was the local blacksmith, and Joe Bellino was a piano manufacturer. Two other Italians, Rossi and Segna, partnered to run the Trinidad Hotel. Mrs. M. D. Bonato ran the local cigar store.[13]

But the calm in enclave business centers and their surrounding neighborhoods was sometimes disrupted by local labor strife. Because of the unfair pay scale, as well as the unsafe conditions in the mills and mines, Italian immigrants supported unionization. Colorado and Utah became prime areas for labor organizing in the western states. Italians were quick to seize on the socialist ideals that offered a better, more equitable social order. In fact, many Italian miners and Italian women did bring with them experience in labor organizing. In 1904 the state called out the National Guard to evict and deport rabble-rousing immigrants and their supporters. Striking miners were often harassed by soldiers. In one instance, demonstrating miners were forced to board a train and were taken across state lines into New Mexico and told never to return to Colorado.[14]

The general distrust of foreigners, management's resistance to labor demands, and labor strife in mining districts made for a volatile mixture. The Colorado Fuel and Iron Company and the Victor Fuel Company were two of the largest mining interests in Utah and Colorado at the time. In the United Mine Works Association District 15, where the CF&I and the VFC had mines, there were 8,503 workers, including 2,976 Italians. District 15 overlapped with southern Colorado and Utah, which included mining camps in Sunnyside, Castle Gate, Helper, and Price in Carbon County. In 1903–4 the Italian miners in Carbon County, Utah, and southern Colorado called a strike. When the United Mine Workers had earlier staged a strike in 1903, the governor called out the National Guard in Utah. Italians were singled out for their role in organizing and supporting the strike. As evidence of the miners' subversive ideology, officials cited a broadside that had called for "Italian Comrades" to unite in the struggle.[15]

Martial law was instituted in Las Animas County and Carbon County in 1904. Law enforcement seized the presses and closed the offices of *Il Lavoratore Italiano*, published initially in Trinidad. The paper was founded by Charles Demolli, an organizer for the United Mine Workers Association (UMWA), and Adolfo Bartoli. Its correspondents were in both Utah and Colorado. Bartoli along with Joseph Poggiani, a newspaperman and also a labor organizer for the UMWA, were among 52 men deported and taken to the state line, where they were released. Law enforcement singled out Italian workers since officials concluded that at least 50 percent of the strikers were Italian. In another incident in Berwind, 80 striking Italians, members of the United Mine Workers, were detained and marched by a military escort eighteen miles out of Berwind to nearby Trinidad, Colorado, where they were put into pens, registered, and then turned loose. But this type of harassment did not deter Italians. Italians were also instrumental in the strikes at Cripple Creek, Teller County, in 1904 and became influential in organizing the Rockefeller Colorado Fuel and Iron Company Works at Trinidad and Pueblo. Similarly, in April 1904, in a halfway house between Castle Gate and Helper, 120 Italians were arrested, loaded into boxcars, and sent to Price, Utah, where they were again put in pens. After negotiations in Pueblo, with no tangible gains made for the workers, the UMWA decided to call off the strike in District 15. The Italian miners who had been singled out by the National Guard felt that the union had betrayed them, which then gave rise to a reaction from Italian anarchists, who advocated antiunion sentiments in both Colorado and Utah.[16]

The most tragic event of all the early-twentieth-century strikes occurred at Ludlow, Las Animas County, on April 20, 1914. Italian miners demanded better wages, hours, and working conditions from Rockefeller's Standard Oil Trust. By then the highest-paid miners were receiving about three and a half dollars a day for a six-day week. But not all miners were paid on that scale. During the demonstration, a conflict broke out among miners, and the governor called in the state militia. At nine on the morning of April 20, the militia raked with machine-gun fire the striking miners. In the process, the militia's rounds set the Ludlow miners' tent living quarters on fire, burning it to the ground. In the aftermath, it was discovered that 2 Italian women and 13 children had burned to death in the fire. President Wilson interceded and stopped the conflict. Ultimately, the state of Colorado accepted responsibility for the tragedy and did pay the Italian families for their losses.[17]

In the Ludlow Massacre, innocent women and children became the victims of management's intransigent position in the face of the union's demands. But women suffered in other ways, less visible or dramatic, in the West's mining towns. Living conditions were harsh in company housing, where miners and their families were forced to live. Only those wives who spoke the same or similar Italian dialects were able to socialize during the day when their husbands were at work. These tent cities did not always have churches where families could socialize and where women could serve in the various church societies. Living in these remote frontier settlements, women often experienced isolation and loneliness. Peasant women's lives in their native villages had been more public. Their domestic tasks had taken them to the village square, on outings in the fields to gather wild vegetables, or to the communal washing site.[18]

In his autobiographical novel, Jo Pagano describes what domestic life was like in Colorado mining camps. The house where his mother, the fictional Marietta, had to care for the children and prepare meals for the family was "a one-story frame shack with a sagging porch in front and a hen yard in the back." Pagano describes

> the great roaring in the pot-bellied stove in the wintertime, with the mist on the windows and the snow-covered mountains; the frosty cellar, with sacks of spidery potatoes and onions and the cans of spareribs and Italian pork-sausage preserved in lard; the sound of the wind whirling around the corners of the house, and the smell of my father's boots scorching before the fire; diapers cooking in pans of boiling water in the kitchen, and frosty washing hanging on stiff lines outside; the sound of her fretfully crying children and the feel of them against her breast; the great cauldrons of blood-red spaghetti, the pots of stews, the platters of fried potatoes and peppers, the redolent loaves of bread browning in the oven.[19]

The passage reveals the weight of the responsibilities that women shouldered in the family. It could also be assumed that Pagano's mother had her first two children without competent medical care or an extended family that could help in times of need.[20]

Pagano also describes the dangers that miners faced underground. As a skilled miner, Luigi Simone, Pagano's fictionalized father, "learned every trick of the mines: how to use pick and drill without time-wasting delays.... He learned the use of powder and of 'stick-giant,' as they called the dynamite, and his every sense was keenly attuned to the multiple dangers that lurked in the dark depths of the earth—gas-pockets, cracking beams, cave-ins, and so on." Unmarried at this point in his life in the novel and typical of those free-labor young men, Luigi does not work long in any mine, a few weeks to a maximum of six months, before he moves to another one.[21]

Mining families lived daily in the shadow of potential mine disasters. A deadly accident or death by black lung left wives and children destitute. Between 1884 and 1942, Colorado had fifteen mine explosions that killed 353 miners. While the number of dead in any single mine accident did not exceed those in Utah, New Mexico, and Wyoming, conditions were no safer in Colorado than in the rest of the West or the country at large. In spite of unions' efforts, little was done at either the state or the federal level to increase mine safety. If management had been forced by federal regulations at the time to report mine accidents, Colorado would have earned the dubious distinction of the mining-accident capital of the West. A list of the recurrence and number of the dead dramatizes the risks that Colorado miners faced: 1884, Gunnison, Crested Butte Mine (59); 1885, Custer, Bull-Domingo Mine (10); 1889, Jefferson, White Ash Mine (10); 1889, Newcastle, Santa Fe Mine (75); 1893, Park, Park Coal Co. (24); 1896, Victor, Anna Lee Mine (8); 1896, Garfield, Vulcan Mine (49); 1897, Garfield, Sunshine Mine (12); 1901, San Miguel, Smuggler-Union Mine (31); 1902, Las Animas, Bowen Mine (13); 1904, Las Animas, Tercio Mine (19); 1906, Huerfano, Maitland Mine (14); 1906, Las Animas, Cuatro Mine (19); 1913, New Castle, Vulcan Mine (38); 1942, Routt, Wadge Mine (34). Of those killed in the Tercio mine explosion, several were Mexican immigrants and 6 were Italians. The others are of unknown origin. In the 1913 explosion at New Castle, nearly all the dead are listed as American, with the exception of 6 Italians, half of them from a single family.[22]

The Ku Klux Klan

Before 1930 Colorado distinguished itself among most but not all of the other western states with the establishment of active, influential chapters of the Ku Klux Klan. In spite of its reliance on immigrant labor, the West was not immune to the general anti-immigrant sentiment and violence against immigrants in the United States. Decades before the rise of the Klan in Colorado, the state had been the site of violent anti-Italian and anti-immigrant sentiment. Throughout the period starting in the 1880s, the influx of Swiss Italians came into conflict with Cornish miners in Gilpin County, a gold and silver mining area. Stoking the anti-immigrant sentiment, mining companies, aided by labor contractors, brought to the state large numbers of miners that threatened to drive down wages. Because of the stereotype that Italians were prone to violence, they became a convenient target. In Denver in 1893, Daniele Arata, the owner of a saloon and hotel, killed a customer and a war veteran. He was arrested by the local sheriff. Soon after, a lynch mob formed that took him from the jail and hanged him from a nearby tree. In the process, they desecrated his body. Also in Denver in 1893, an Italian miner had an altercation with a contractor and shot and killed him. While he was incarcerated, at midnight an angry mob overcame the sole guard in the jailhouse and lynched him. Usually the local press in the United States took a supportive view of immigrant lynchings. However, in this case Denver's *Rocky Mountain News* condemned the local law enforcement for their incompetence and even complicity in the lynching. In the coal-mining camp of Walsenburg, about two hundred miles south of Denver, in 1895 five Italian immigrants purportedly killed a local brewer, Abner J. Dixon. One Italian miner, Lorenzo Andinino, allegedly confessed. Yet nine other miners were arrested in connection with the killing in spite of Andinino's confession. While four of the arrested were released, the local authorities held the others: Stanislao Vittone, Francesco Ronchietto, Antonio Gobbetto, and Pietro Giacobini. In the process of their transfer to Walsenburg for trial, the accused were ambushed by five or six men on horseback. They killed Vittone outright, while Ronchietto was wounded and taken to the Walsenburg jail with Andinino, who was not shot. The other two took flight. During the night, a mob of six or seven men stormed the jail, overcame the guards, and killed the two immigrant men. Their killers were never tried.[23]

In 1900 again in Walsenburg, four other Italian immigrants were murdered. In 1903 there were two other attempted lynchings in Minturn, about a hundred miles west of Denver in the Rockies, and one in the mining camp of Majestic in Las Animas County. However, Italian officials heard of the impending danger to both men, made official appeals for their safety, and saved them from being lynched.[24]

In the context of the state's anti-immigrant sentiment, the newly revived Klan found fertile ground. The resurgence of the Klan occurred in the same year that D. W. Griffith's *The Birth of a Nation* appeared, which idealized the old Klan. The newly revived Klan distinguished itself from its post–Civil War roots by describing itself as a "*patriotic* fraternal order." With its origins in Atlanta, by 1920 the Klan began a program of expansion. Established in 1921 in Denver, the Klan soon won widespread political power in Colorado with its racist and anti-immigrant platform. As Robert Goldberg argues, the Klan was not a group of fringe, psychopathic "white" men and women. Nor was its membership from the South. Rather, its Denver membership was composed of a majority of late-generation men and women originally from the East, Southwest, Northwest, and West. It was a resurgence of an earlier populist movement exploiting the anxiety over rapid industrial change and the presence of thousands of non-Protestant immigrants in the state. Nativism and general anti-immigrant sentiment at the time were voiced by both sides of the political spectrum, left and right, and the Klan exploited that sentiment in its recruiting.[25]

With the support of the Protestant population in Colorado, the Klan did target African Americans, but it focused largely on Roman Catholics, Jews, and immigrants in general, especially Italians for what the Klan called their pagan religious practices. The Klan concocted conspiracy theories surrounding the pope's purported control of his Catholic constituents and his plan for taking over American society. In its platform, "The Klan offered a program of Americanism, militant Protestantism, fraternity, order, religious intolerance, and racial purity." It also voiced a special warning about the rise of the "new Negro," who was "getting uppity" and demanding equal rights.[26] With the term *new Negro*, the Klan was responding to the African American cultural resurgence known as the Harlem Renaissance composed of African American professionals, musicians, writers, and artists.

In October 1923, five Denver Klansmen kidnapped Patrick Walker, a member of the Catholic organization the Knights of Columbus, and drove him to a remote spot outside the city and beat him. They boycotted immigrant businesses, burned crosses in front of Catholic churches and synagogues, and intimidated priests and rabbis on the streets of Denver. Also in 1923 the Klan lighted simultaneously eleven crosses across Denver. Because of the Klan's broad support, state and local officials were loath to charge the Klan with a crime.[27]

Pueblo was fertile ground for the Klan. Extending its power and influence, the Klan promoted itself as "an instrument of justice" in the face of what it called Italian criminality. Anti-immigrant sentiment fueled the lynching of two jailed Mexicans accused of murder. By 1920 immigrants accounted for 17 percent of Pueblo's population. Italians and Mexicans, both Catholic, were the town's largest groups. Also undermining the Klan's "100 percent American" movement, Italians resisted Prohibition's restrictions. It was an open secret that winemaking and bootlegging were rampant on Goat Hill. As a result, the Pueblo police conducted house-to-house searches for illegal booze. At times, Italians were their own worst enemies. A fraction of the community stigmatized the majority. Between 1922 and 1926, two factions of La Mano Nero (the Black Hand) gang killed ten men in their fight over control of the bootleg business. In 1923 La Mano Nero purportedly bombed two Italian homes. In *Golden Wedding* (1943), Jo Pagano recounts a factual incident from his family's history when Luigi Simone receives a threatening letter demanding money from La Mano Nero, which causes the Simone family to flee to Utah. La Mano Nero with impunity even threatened a local Italian judge, Henry Ruggieri of Price.[28]

By 1924, attempting to avoid its usual anti-Jewish and anti-Catholic rhetoric, the Klan based its platform in Pueblo on law and order. Because the Klan controlled the city government and the town's police force, in 1924 the city refused to issue a permit for the annual Columbus Day parade, which the defiant Italians held anyway. One resident reported, though there is no verification, that Italians had "shotguns poking out of the windows of all the cars." The Klan faced little resistance in Pueblo as well as in smaller communities in the state. In Bessemer it enjoyed the strong support of influential religious leaders such as the Reverend T. C. Collister of the North Avenue Methodist Church, the Reverend George Lowe of East Side Baptist Church, and the minister of the downtown Broadway Christian Church.[29]

Because it found fertile ground in the general population's reaction to the state's growing immigrant presence, the Klan was influential throughout the state, from Pueblo and Denver to Grand Junction, Cañon City, and Colorado Springs. It controlled the election of Republicans and some

Democrats to municipal and state offices. In 1924 Klan candidates "were elected to offices of lieutenant governor, secretary of state, attorney general, superintendent of public instruction and state supreme court justice." While its political influence was not uniform throughout the state, by 1924 the Klan achieved the zenith of its influence in the state when it controlled the state's house of representatives and elected Clarence Morley governor, a card-carrying, active member of the Klan. He supported immigrant-exclusion laws and laws prohibiting immigrants from owning property in Colorado.[30]

Nowhere are the effects of the role of Denver's Klan more dramatically represented than in John Fante's early stories set in the years before World War II. Fante was born in 1909 in Boulder and lived for a time in Denver. In his Colorado stories, Fante dramatically portrays the prejudice and even beatings he often took as the son of an Italian family. In later novels, he represents his marginalization as an Italian American among the established, wealthy citizens of Denver and California.[31]

Significantly, the policies that the Klan had attempted to implement in the state never established permanent insurmountable barriers to success for the immigrant population in the state. In the aftermath of the Johnson-Reed Act of 1924, which drastically cut the numbers of Italian and Jewish immigrants, by the late 1930s the Klan's influence waned in Colorado. It lost traction, began to lose members, and failed to stir up enough anti-immigrant xenophobia to attract new members. It burned its last cross in 1940.[32]

Enclave Businesses—Denver and Pueblo

Denver's population grew 275 percent between 1880 and 1900 and another 115 percent between 1900 and 1930. In 1868 professor of chemistry Nathaniel P. Hill and a group of investors opened the Boston and Colorado Smelting Company in Black Hawk, Gilpin County. In 1878 he renamed his company Argo and moved it just two miles northwest of Denver's commercial center. In the 1890s, the Globe Smelter Company built another one in the area. Both Argo and Globe created a diverse settlement of immigrants. The enclave economy thrived, as entrepreneurs opened bars, butcher shops, restaurants, grocery stores, and mercantile shops. The poorest of the groups, Italians began arriving in the area in the 1880s. Initially, they simply pitched tents along the South Platte River known as the Bottoms. Nearly four hundred Italians settled the area, where ditches with standing water became venues for the spread of diphtheria and typhoid among the Bottoms' residents. Families survived initially by growing their own vegetables and by children gathering coal dropped from nearby railcars or by stealing outright from the cars. They picked wild watercress along the banks of the river to sell in town and picked up cigar butts to sell in the Bottoms. These early Italian immigrants did not win the favor of established Denver residents, who viewed them with suspicion because of their Catholicism, wine consumption, and what they presumed to be their criminality.[33]

By the turn of the century, a Little Italy had formed in North Denver next to the already established Irish neighborhood along the northwestern bank of the South Platte River between Twenty-Sixth and West Fifty-Second Avenues. Just south of the Italian neighborhood, Jewish immigrants occupied an area known as Little Jerusalem. Italians purchased lots and began to build small brick and wood bungalows. Their children attended the nearby elementary school built in 1908 by Italian immigrant Frank Damascio. Italians opened enclave businesses alongside Jewish shop owners. Because of their close working relationship, Italians and Jews formed friendships. Italian women often attended Jewish functions and even went out with Jewish men, but with the understanding that they could never marry. By 1920 there were 2,872 Italian immigrants in Denver, with 61 percent of them living in Denver's Little Italy. Italians composed about 30 percent of the surrounding neighborhood. It was like many urban neighborhoods, with a mixture of all immigrants. In addition to Italians and Jews, the neighborhood contained Germans, Swedes, Scots, Hungarians, Irish, Slavs, and Mexicans. It also included African American families that were a part of the Great Migration out of the South during this period.[34]

Wages from smelting mills and the mines in Colorado supported the usual immigrant businesses in Denver, Pueblo, and other enclaves. Italian and Slavic single men lived in Pueblo's Schley Street neighborhood, which was located near the CF&I smelter. The majority of the Italians were from Lucca Sicula, Sicily. The Parlapiano and Bacino families established two grocery stores in the neighborhood. In nearby Bessemer, Joe and Marie Gagliano opened the Bessemer Mercantile store that sold a variety of domestic goods along with fruits, vegetables, and meat. Charles Conatore opened a small grocery store in Minnequa Heights, also in Bessemer. In the 1920s, E. F. Gobatti and his brother, John, from the northern Italian town of Bergantino, established a machine shop and foundry in Pueblo. One of the largest in the West, their shop manufactured centrifugal pumps and other specialized machinery for the area's factories.[35]

The enclave in North Denver provided Italians with an array of Italian businesses and services: markets, delicatessens, restaurants, importers, pasta factories, a mortuary, and banks. Funding many of the local businesses were the three Frazzini brothers, Cesare, Prospero, and Felicito, who owned the Italian-American Bank of Denver, where their brother Antonio worked as a cashier. Their partnership was joined in Denver by numerous other family partnerships, including the Iacino Bros., Bruno Bros., and Mapelli Bros., who all owned and operated grocery and meat markets. Giuseppe Mapelli codirected the Western Union Manufacturing Company with another Italian, and G. Mapelli also served as a public notary. There were many musicians, stonecutters, and sculptors as well servicing the community.[36] North Denver was a dynamic Italian enclave that offered numerous opportunities for the exchange of social and cultural capital among relatives and other enterprising immigrants.

Immigrants from Trentino, mostly from Altopiano di Piné and Val di Cembra, also settled Colorado. Nearly all the Trentino residents initially worked in the mines in other parts of Colorado before settling in Denver, where they established a close-knit community. By the late 1920s, the Denver area counted more than 170 families from Trentino. Leaving the mines with their savings, they were able to assimilate quickly into the growing economy. Dan Morganari and Oreste Rauzi, his brother-in-law, combined their savings and opened a tavern in Denver. Giuseppe Devigili moved from the mines in Russell Gulch and Telluride in 1923 and became a successful cattle rancher near Denver. Silvio Zucal bought land and began a small truck farm along with his sister Ida. Among the last to leave Trentino and arrive in Denver were three brothers from the Dallagiacoma family. They established the Dallagiacoma Brothers grinding factory, which made and repaired cutlery and industrial instruments. Nearly a century after the three brothers opened their business, it is still owned and operated by their descendants.[37]

Immigrants from Trentino also filled the ranks of all the professions. Davide Serafini became a professor at the University of Denver. Before his arrival in Denver, John Mattivi had studied at the Sorbonne, Stanford, and Mexico City University and then became a teacher of French, Spanish, and mathematics at East High School. Alexander Calliari, a lawyer, maintained three law offices in Denver. Banking was another of the professions in which Trentini excelled. Herman Zuech became a vice president at the local Security City Bank. Fausto Svaldi became an electrician for the US Mint in Denver. Women from Trentino followed the pattern of working immigrant women who broke from traditional roles and assumed important positions in the workplace. Lee Mattivi, John's sister, was the first Catholic to become a secretary in the state house of representatives. Flora Dalla was a US Air Force secretary and member of the Catholic Daughters of America. Mary Mancini, wife of editor Frank Mancini, though not from Trentino, worked as a private secretary for the secretary of state of Colorado. Denver numbered at least five sculptors and writers from Trentino before 1930, including the well-known sculptor Herman Casagrande. The Trentini organized and elected seven mayors and ten aldermen from their community before 1930.[38] With the social and cultural capital that they brought with them, the Trentini accomplishments in Denver were not unusual; they repeated their remarkable success throughout the West.

Among the first Italians to arrive in the Bottoms was Angelo Capelli. Before being appointed to the consulate office, he began modestly with a small produce stand. With his wife he opened the Highland House, a boardinghouse. Their initial investment grew into a business and real-estate empire. Angelo and his wife owned and operated several taverns, a macaroni factory, a confectionery shop, fruit stands, a butcher shop, and a real-estate business. After Siro Mangini married one of the Capelli daughters, he followed in Angelo's footsteps and opened the Christopher Columbus Saloon. He and his wife and their ten children lived above the saloon on Larimer Street where Mrs. Mangini cooked and dished out ravioli to local politicians, neighboring shopkeepers, and the policemen who walked the beat. In 1921 southern Italian Michael Aiello with his wife, Maggie, opened Aiello's Italian Kitchen on the north side. Their restaurant became an institution and survived for more than ninety-five years.[39]

Frank Mazza, Luigi Mosconi, Peter Albi, and Joseph Turre, like the Capelli family, joined an established and growing saloon business dominated by Denver's immigrant population. Each saloon became a second home to its respective immigrant clientele: a place to meet others who spoke the same dialect and to exchange valuable information regarding jobs and the best boardinghouses, stores, and restaurants. Some of the proprietors used their public exposure to enhance the cohesiveness of the community. Mosconi and Turre established the Unione Fratellanza and the Augustine Roncaglia societies. Mazza established the Unione e Fratellanza Italiana, the Bersaglieri society of Naples, and the Club Italo-Americano. Established in 1899, the Società Nativi di Potenza is the oldest of these societies. It is telling that these organizations formed by saloon owners spoke to the Italians' need to organize themselves as a defense against the Denver nativists. Stoking nativist resentment, Denver newspapers often published articles pointing to the rise of immigrant saloons in their midst, establishments that were undermining, so they claimed, the moral worth of their community.[40]

Farming

Immigrant farmers created Colorado's farming industry. Financed by their initial work in the mines, Italians purchased land and settled farmland along Clear Creek, west of downtown Denver. One family, Gerardo and Angelina Pergola, began a small truck farm and grew a variety of seasonal vegetables that they sold at the local Barth Market in Denver. The Barth Market would later be replaced by a more modern market, the Wazee Market, and later again in the late 1930s by the Denargo Market, which became the hub of the produce trade that was for nearly two decades dominated by Italians. Also among the early Italians was the Lossaso family that sold fruits and vegetables from the family's Bottoms farm from a horse-drawn cart. Son John would later establish a commission house in the market until he retired in the 1970s. In the late 1930s, Joe Giambrocco opened the Giambrocco Food Service in the Denargo Market. The Giambrocco Food Service warehouse still stands on Wazee Street and is a cultural landmark. The fourth generation of the family runs the business today. Other Italian families established farms along the South Platte River and Clear Creek near Welby, about ten miles north of Denver. In Welby they joined already established Slav, German, and Japanese farming families. Italians also established truck farms in such locations as St. Charles Mesa and on the outskirts of Goat Hill near Pueblo. Typical in farm families, wives worked alongside their husbands planting, cultivating, picking, and packing vegetables. Women also kept backyard gardens to supplement the family's diet and to cut food costs of produce not grown on their farms.[41]

By 1920 Colorado ranked fourth in the number of farms, approximately 60,000, behind Texas, California, and Washington. These new farmers increased Colorado's productive farmland from 20 percent in 1910 to nearly 37 percent by 1920. In spite of the shorter growing season, they produced a full range of fruits and vegetables, including grapes, which no doubt the local Italian immigrant population used for home winemaking. Another significant fact is that out of the nearly 60,000 farms, more than 45,000, 75 percent, were owner operated. This suggests that the majority of the immigrant farmers were able to purchase land out of wages earned in local mines and smelters or perhaps wages they had earned before they arrived in Colorado, possibly from the mines in Utah or Wyoming. In fact, out of the four leading farm-producing states, Colorado's owner-operator percentage was the highest in 1920. Italians owned 967 farms, fourth in the state behind Russians, Germans, and Swedes. Italians' total land assets were $7,963,500, ranking them fifth among other immigrant groups in the state.[42]

Women and the Italian Community

Women played a significant role in Colorado's booming economy before 1940. The Dillingham Commission report of 1920 stated that "all but one of the farmers are married and have their wives with them in the United States." They participated in the full range of farmwork, from the vegetable garden and cheese making to the harvest. Even when not working outside the farm or home, women were making a significant contribution to the economic well-being of the family. The Italian family was highly influential in the success of both small businesses and small truck farms throughout not just the West but the United States in general. In time, many of those families left the instability of their seasonal farming in the harsh Colorado climate to settle in North Denver, where factory work offered more opportunities for women. Denver's growing industrial base at the turn of the century offered greater job security than the more seasonal truck farming in the cold Colorado climate.[43]

In Denver and Pueblo, women worked in ironwork plants, macaroni factories, box factories, laundries, dry-goods stores, grocery stores, movie theaters, and restaurants, as well as self-owned businesses with their husbands. In restaurants, more often they were behind the scenes making fresh pasta and providing the recipes for the sauces and preparation of dishes. Some wives managed boardinghouses or even worked in taverns, not necessarily the work of choice for Italian women, married or not. Those who had a modicum of education worked in health care or as stenographers. These usually younger women had at least an eighth grade education, were first-generation Americans, and spoke fluent English. Second-generation women usually finished high school and were more socially mobile than their mothers and immigrant grandmothers. Ultimately, with their education and potential social and economic mobility, they and their daughters contributed to the transformation of North Denver, as well as to the Italian culture that had been transplanted in the West. They did not always conform to the stereotype of that eastern "urban ethnic model" based in the patriarchal nuclear Italian family.[44]

Marie Maffeo, for example, worked as a common laborer in a greenhouse in Denver. Others were able to work at home, such as Antoinette Denuzzi, who took in laundry since her husband could not work due to an industrial accident. Old World restrictions, out of necessity, were relaxed, and women became not only contributors to the family income but at times even the principal source of income. The Mauro and Nicoletti families owned two family-run laundries in Denver, while Lucy and Joseph Canino worked side by side in their neighborhood grocery on North Navajo Street in North Denver. As a professional, Elisa Palladino was one of four nurses in the 1920s. For patient care, she used a bedroom in the family home, where she delivered neighborhood women's babies and treated a variety of illnesses. In addition to licensed nurses, Teresa Severini, Assunta DeFeo, and Mrs. Rodolpho Albi, whose husband was a local physician, were all well-known midwives in the community. Severini took in laundry at her home.[45] Although women did not have the same freedom as men, they were no less resourceful in their ability to find work and contribute to the family income.

Those women who were not employed outside the home were never idle; they were at the center of North Denver's cultural development. They were instrumental in establishing those important benevolent societies that served as the only safety net that families had in times of crisis. The many diaries that immigrant women left indicate that they participated in these civic programs to break from the isolation they sometimes experienced in their new home. La Società Sant' Anna and La Società Santa Margherita in Denver were headed by Italian women. Women were also members of the Il Circolo Filodrammatico and the Dante Alighieri Society. In Pueblo they established the Principessa Yolanda and La Nuova Italia societies. The Principessa Yolanda lodge was founded largely by Sicilian women from Lucca Sicula and was established to provide medical and death benefits to members' families. Families received five dollars for each week that a member was in the hospital. In addition to their monthly dues, members were required to make home visits to the stricken families and to attend all funerals.[46]

With their charitable work, women contributed significantly to Italians' assimilation. The relationship between northern and southern Italians was not always easy. As one wife reported, her northern Italian husband "always felt that those people [southern Italians] were beneath him and needed help." Initially, regional prejudices were exacerbated in Colorado because men from northern Italy usually had the higher-paying jobs in the mines, while the southern Italian men worked in the lower-paying jobs in the coke ovens. The division between northern and southern Italy was also evident in the area businesses owned largely by more highly educated northern Italian families, while truck farms were owned by southern Italian families.[47]

While Principessa initially did allow non-Sicilians to join, there were some lodges in Pueblo that did not allow Sicilian women. In time this division would disappear. These women's lodges joined many others in Pueblo to bring about a greater solidarity in the community. Denver Italians established a variety of other fraternal organizations, among them the Società Protettiva (1897), the Fidelity Lodge (1898), the Sicilian Lodge (1899), later the St. Joseph's Lodge (1918), the Giuseppe Verdi Chapter of the Amici d'Italia, Società di Mutuo Soccorso Protettiva e di Beneficenza, and the Italian Federated Societies of Denver. Younger Italian immigrants joined the Ausonia Coro, a choral group, and the Gioventu Gaia, limited to young women, as well as the St. Theresa Sodality and St. Rita's Lodge for newly married women who attended the Mount Carmel Church. All of these groups overcame regional provincialism and assisted Italians in their assimilation into American life. They were also a part of that larger national trend at the time of women's organizations working for women's rights.[48]

Their work in secular and religious organizations helped break down social barriers, not just among Italian dialect groups but all other immigrant Catholics. Along with Jesuits, nuns were teachers in Catholic schools, and laywomen were teachers in area public schools and Protestant schools, as well as instructors in private conservatories. The increase of an immigrant population's literacy rested largely on their shoulders as elementary and secondary teachers.[49] What could be more important to an immigrant community's success in America than literacy?

Regardless of their regional differences, Italians began to exert a strong influence in places such as Pueblo. In 1905 the community came together to fund and erect only the second statue of Christopher Columbus in the United States. Also contributing to the unity of the community, between 1880 and 1947 Pueblo and Denver had numerous Italian papers, weeklies, and monthlies. *La Stella* was the first paper in Denver, established in 1885 by Angelo Noce. Others included *Roma*, the *Daily Vox Populi* (1881–82), *Vindice* (1896–1930), *Maschere* (1904–6), *Cooperatore* (1918–19), and *Abruzzo-Molise* (1924–26), which merged with the *Unione* and *Voce Del Popolo* (1926–37), edited by Vincenzo Massari. Among the Italian newspapers, the most successful were *Vindice* and the *Unione* (1897–1947). The *Unione*'s publisher, Hector Chiariglione, president of the Columbian Federation, was also instrumental in influencing the state to declare October 12 as Columbus Day. Frank Mancini from Campania settled in Denver in 1900 and became the publisher of the English-language *Colorado* and the Italian language *Il Risveglio*, a weekly. Under his direction in 1907 when he took control of the paper, Mancini wanted to make *Il Risveglio* a workers' paper. During the course of his publishing career, he bought four other Italian newspapers in Colorado. These early publications served to keep the Italian immigrant population in close touch with Italy and provided advertising for local Italian businesses.[50]

Late-Generation Revival

Like so many of the mining centers throughout the West, Colorado's mining districts emptied when the mines shut down in the postwar era. Nevertheless, turn-of-the-century Italian immigration made a significant contribution to Colorado's multicultural demographic makeup. Colorado counted 157,000 Italian Americans in 1990, and that number grew again by 2000 to 202,787, 4.7 percent of the state's population. About half of those lived in the Denver-Boulder metropolitan area with 123,553, a 4.7 percent share of the population.[51] Today, Denver hosts one of the most active Italian American communities in the United States. When it was time to restore the century-old Our Lady of Mount Carmel, Italian Americans helped to defray costs. In the foyer of the church are bronze plaques listing the names of those who helped fund the restoration. The majority of the plaques contain Italian names, many dedicated in memory of those immigrant family members who had funded the construction of the original church.

Italian Americans have established numerous organizations. Italian Americans in Denver continue to celebrate the now problematic Columbus

Day celebration with its annual parade and festival in honor of their roots. Established in 1905, the Order Sons of Italy still maintains chapters in Denver, Pueblo, Carson City, Colorado Springs, and Salida in central Colorado. Colorado Springs is also host to the American Italian Cultural Club. Italian Americans established the Louisville Italian American Society, which organizes a festival each year. The new generation has also established the Italian American Business Association of Colorado, located in Denver. In 2007 an Italian American and graduate of Colorado State University, Jenna Capra, established the monthly newspaper *Andiamo!* that is distributed statewide.[52]

Denver was once the hub of railroad transportation in the West. At the time, besides those immigrants who settled in Denver, millions more passed through Denver on their way to other parts of the West. Denver's downtown with its many historic buildings and its restored train station is an enduring reminder of Denver's and Colorado's immigrant heritage. Italians played a major role in that heritage, and their Italian American descendants are an important aspect of Colorado's contemporary multicultural population.

CHAPTER 5

UTAH

Settlement—Railroads and Labor Contractors

The development of the West was reliant on the expansion of the railroad to remote western lands. Utah was no exception. The coming of the railroad to Utah brought increased prosperity to a sparsely settled landscape occupied initially by Mormons. As early as 1849, Joseph Toronto from Sicily aided Brigham Young in the establishment of the Mormon mission in the region. In the 1850s, Protestant Waldensians, largely from Piedmont, the location of a Mormon mission in Italy, immigrated to the territory. In 1870 there were 74 Italians in the region. By the 1880s, the expansion of the Denver and Rio Grande (D&RG) Railroad made possible the development of Utah's coal-mining industry. As a result, those original northern Italian settlers would soon be followed by immigrants from Abruzzo, Calabria, and Sicily. Working for railroad and mining companies, labor contractors recruited the massive workforce needed to fill the jobs on the railroads and in the territory's mines.[1]

The major influx of workers to Utah began in 1882, when the D&RG brought foreign and domestic miners to Carbon County to work in the railroad's subsidiary company, the Utah Fuel Company, which had become by 1900 the state's largest coal supplier. The impact of the railroads and the labor-contracting system is apparent in the increase in Italian immigrants in the territory, which became a state in 1896. In 1890 there were only 347 Italians in the territory, but by 1900 that number more than tripled to 1,062 and nearly tripled again by 1910 to 3,117, the peak year for Italian settlement in Utah. At the time, Italians were about 1 percent of the state's population and just about 5 percent of the foreign-born population in the state. With the extension of the railroad into the region, six major coal-mining camps developed in Carbon County: Price, Helper, Clear Creek, Winter Quarters, Castle Gate, and Sunnyside. At the same time, three other counties became important mining centers: Salt Lake for copper and Summit and Juab for their silver and gold deposits.[2] These centers required a massive immigrant workforce to meet the growing demand for minerals in the United States.

Among the labor contractors was Japanese agent Edward Daigoro Hashimoto, who supplied Japanese laborers in Bingham, Salt Lake County. The Chinese labor agency Six Companies, founded in San Francisco and with connections in Hong Kong, Canton, and Shanghai, recruited more than 180,000 Chinese workers to the West between 1849 and 1882. They worked closely with many other Chinese agents throughout the West. The large number of workers that Six Companies brought into the labor market had the effect of lowering wages for all workers. As a result, miners and other workers supported the effort to exclude the Chinese altogether from the United States, which then passed the Chinese Exclusion Act in 1882. However, immigrant labor was in such demand that Chinese workers went to Canada aboard Canadian Pacific Railroad steamers and clandestinely crossed the border to work in the United States.[3]

The czar of the Greeks, Leon Skliris, working for the Utah Copper Company and the D&RG Railroad, provided Greek labor for the mines. But Skliris faced stiff competition from numerous other Greek agents operating throughout the West: William Caravelis, Pericles Skarlatos, Louis Skarlatos, Louis Cononelos, and Nicholas Meindaris. Caravelis recruited Greek workers for the Oregon Short Line Railroad that ran through Utah. Known as the king of laborers, Italian Antonio Cordasco, employed by the Canadian Pacific Railroad, supplied Italian workers for Utah as well as throughout Canada and other parts of the United States. Supplementing Cordasco's work, Moses Paggi provided Italian immigrants for the Utah Power and Light Company. To manage the large number of Italian immigrants brought in by labor agents, the D&RG hired foreman Joseph Bonnaci to oversee the Italian section-gang workers in Helper. For the Basque immigrants, Pedro Altube, stationed in Elko, Nevada, specialized in bringing shepherds to the West. At the end of their contracts with Altube, many Basques opted to leave herding to earn the higher wages offered in mining.[4]

Labor contracting was a lucrative business. In 1905 Skliris earned more than $50,000. Under his payment system, he earned more than Cordasco. Greek workers under contract with Skliris paid him approximately $10 to $25 for their jobs, whereas Cordasco's workers paid him about $3 for a job. Furthermore, all Greek workers under contract paid Skliris $1 a month, extracted from their pay by the employing railroad company. His contracts for mine workers were equally exploitative. His motto was "Jobs to the highest bidder with no refunds." Greek and Italian laborers came in large groups, 20 to 50 at a time.[5] Following the initial settlement of these first railroad workers and coal miners, chain migration later became a significant factor in bringing free-labor miners to Utah, particularly to Carbon County.

Price and Helper in Carbon County became the beneficiaries of the growth in the immigrant-labor population. By 1900 there were 374 Italians, and by 1920 that number grew to 1,215, making Italians the largest group among more than twenty-three other immigrant groups in Carbon County. As Notarianni has written, Carbon County became Utah's Ellis Island. The miners including African Americans were divided up largely among the state's six major camps.[6]

Among the coal camps, Price was a small but prosperous town populated largely by railroad men, freighters, farmers, and cattle ranchers. It had a small business district established as early as the 1880s. In 1920 Price had a population of 2,364 residents. Saloons grouped around the local train depot, while several blocks away its small business district was composed of a variety of businesses, including mercantile stores and banks. Among the first Italians to settle the area was building contractor Pietro Silvagni. Born in Cosenza, Italy, in 1873, he immigrated to Arabia, worked in construction, and in 1905 arrived in Price, where he established a construction business. Silvagni built commercial buildings, coke furnaces at Sunnyside, railroad bridges, and other projects. Among his other projects was a multistory building on the corner of Main Street and Carbon Avenue that housed a theater and a cinema. Silvagni later moved his construction company to Las Vegas, where in 1931 he built at least one large hotel.[7]

There was also a successful community of Italian immigrants in nearby Helper, about six miles northeast of Price. With the large number of workers in the area and the relatively high wages paid in the mines, a lucrative enclave business community developed in Helper. In 1900 there were only 44 Italian immigrants in Helper. However, after a 1903 strike in Castle Gate, many Italians moved to Helper and established businesses. By 1919 out of the town's sixty-three businesses, thirty-five were run by Italians, Greeks, Japanese, and Chinese. By 1923 Italians owned eighteen of the town's seventy-two businesses. Overall, Helper's enterprising immigrants owned 61 percent of the town's businesses. Italians lived in neighborhoods named Dugout and Wop Town, turf that Italians shared with Greeks, Japanese, and Chinese.[8] The enclave economy flourished as businesses provided services and products to all the immigrants in the community.

As the business district grew, Italian entrepreneurs opened new shops with loans from the Helper Central Bank, directed by Joseph Barboglio. From Lombardy, Barboglio arrived in Utah as a young man and worked in the Utah mines and later began buying real estate. He soon became an influential figure in the state. With his facility in Italian and English, he was able to help marginally literate Italians with loan applications and other banking services. The records of one local lodge, Stella d'America, indicate that these new businessmen in town were largely from northern Italy and had the advantage of having a higher degree of literacy than their southern Italian counterparts who worked in the mines. However, like so many enclaves in the West, the north-south divide that separated Italian regional and dialect groups began to diminish as they started to recognize their obvious common economic interests in the enclave business environment.[9]

The saloons and other businesses in both Price and Helper were frequented by miners and their families, who lived in nearby mining camps in company housing. The major coal companies, Pleasant Valley Coal and Utah Fuel, provided housing for both single men and families. However, the housing was far from adequate, consisting of little more than tents and railroad boxcars without running water. In Sunnyside miners built their own shacks and makeshift tents, which became known as Rag Town to local residents. As the Ludlow tragedy demonstrated, Rag Towns were not only inadequate against the weather but also fire hazards. Salt Lake County, mainly Bingham Canyon, also attracted Italian immigrants. Their town was known as Short Town, so named because of the small stature of the Piedmontese miners who lived in the settlement. There were other boomtowns, such as Magna, Garfield, and Murray. In Magna the diversity of immigrants created a Little Italy, Jap Town, and Greek Town. According to one observer, the Little Italy was a collection of shacks with sheet-iron roofs covered with tarpaper. These poor living conditions only reinforced nativists' stereotypes of immigrants, especially those from southern Europe. As one observer wrote in 1915, "The Greeks and Italians are perhaps the most careless and shiftless people found.... Comfort to them is unknown unless it is in the form of a smoke by the fire or a drink. Not only is this true of the hundreds of men who rent a house for themselves...but of the families as well.... The standard of living among them [Italians] is lower than of any other nationality." When Italian children went to school, they were bullied by schoolmates, who mirrored their parents' xenophobic attitudes.[10]

But such nativist sentiments would never become a permanent barrier to Italians' or other immigrants' success in Utah. Their work and businesses continued to fuel their dreams of success and the state's economy. Adjacent to Carbon County to the west, Tooele County, initially a Mormon farming district, soon developed both mining and smelting industries. Management cooperated with labor contractors to bring a large European and Asian labor force into an area that had a scarcity of workers. The largest settlement of Italians was in the mining town of Mercur, where in 1904 the community built a Catholic church. At the nearby Tooele smelter, southern European immigrants found work and eventually settled in the immigrant neighborhood named New Town. The community in New Town was large enough to organize a band that played at Italian functions. Italians celebrated traditional religious feast days, especially honoring the local saint, whose statue they removed from the church in the style of their old-country observance and paraded around the town. The number of Italians in the area was further enhanced by those who ran goat farms in the nearby countryside and came to town during these feast days.[11]

There were countercurrents that at times worked against the immigrant community's best efforts to succeed. There arose, as happened in Colorado, a faction of La Mano Nero, composed largely of southern Italians. Not to overstate their influence or their numbers, they no doubt were merely a loosely formed gang of thugs bent on exploiting the success of local businessmen and -women. They remained a threat, nevertheless, to those who were targeted for extortion. Besides the pernicious activities of La Mano Nero, there was as well a growing threat from the newly revived Ku Klux Klan.[12]

As it had in Colorado and Oregon during the same period, the Klan's influence grew in Utah and raised concern in the local immigrant population. Nativist assaults on Italians escalated. In the general population, immigrants had long been labeled "Bohunks," "Japs," "Wops," and "clannish" Greeks. As a result of the Carbon County strikes, it did not take much for a chapter of the Ku Klux Klan to form in Helper in the 1920s to offset what the Klan called the "Blatant Lawlessness Effrontry [*sic*] of South European Domination" in their community. Also targeting Mormons, the Klan burned a cross near a Mormon church in 1924 in Helper.

In its articles of incorporation submitted to the state in 1924, the Klan vowed "to uphold Americanism, advance Protestant Christianity, and eternally maintain white supremacy." Emboldened by its growing community support, the Klan's activities reached their zenith in 1925 when the Klan held its first state convention at Ensign Peak, north of Salt Lake City. They burned crosses in a dramatic display of their presence to the immigrant population as well as to African Americans. By that time, the Klan was active in Magna, Bingham, Provo, and other locations in Carbon County. In Magna, south of Helper, hooded members in their white sheets paraded down Main Street to the Gem Theater, where they held a meeting. Greeks, Italians, and other immigrants, some with their children, lined the streets. Although there were no lynchings of Italians in Utah, the locals must have known about the lynchings in nearby Colorado fifteen years before and perhaps elsewhere in the United States. As one Serbian miner said, "They call me everything but white man.... Yeah, sure I leave Carbon County. You could die down there and nobody care." The Klan's power and influence in Utah, as well as its intimidation of the local population, did in fact result in the lynching of Robert Marshall, a Carbon County African American "accused" of murder. The killers were never brought to justice. In addition, the East, Northeast, and West had become locations of numerous immigrant lynchings. The occurrence of these lawless acts was widely known and raised the concern of observers elsewhere in the country. In the East, masked Klansmen attacked Italian labor organizers and political activists.[13]

The Klan also targeted successful immigrant businesses in Helper, as La Mano Nero had. Not entirely intimidated by the town's criminal element, including the Klan, the immigrant community organized across national boundaries. When the Klan attempted to extort money from immigrant businesses, Irish, Italians, and Greeks successfully organized to confront the group and resist them. Where common interest prevailed, immigrants were able to overcome cultural differences and organize. Immigrants' social and family relationships were radically changed by the difficulties and responsibilities that they faced in industrial America.[14]

Mining—Unions and Italian Involvement

Immigrant unity was enhanced and at times challenged when the unionized workers clashed with management and powerful labor contractors. Labor agents worked for management, neither of which supported workers' rights or unionization. To secure jobs quickly for their workers and to get a return on their investment, agents negotiated wages below the union scale that union workers had either already established or demanded. It did not take long for miners to revolt against the collusion between management and their exploitative labor contractors. Forging ties across cultural boundaries, Italians became as significant a force in the labor movement in Utah as they were at the time in Colorado. In 1901 miners struck in the wake of the Winter Quarters Mine disaster. Italians led a strike in Carbon County in 1903 under the auspices of the United Mine Workers in sympathy with the strike in the mines in Colorado.[15]

Management feared the influence of the Italian miners more than all the other immigrant groups because of their high numbers and the influence that they had on other miners. In 1903 in Sunnyside there were 246 Italian miners, second behind the English and just ahead of a contingent of Austrian miners. In Castle Gate there were 356 Italians, the largest immigrant group. At Clear Creek, there were 172 Italians, the largest group ahead of the Finns and English, and at Winter Quarters there were 74 Italians, third behind the English and Finns. Overall, the Italians, 848, were the second-largest immigrant group behind the 1,245 Greeks in the four mining districts. Labor contractors for Italians, principally Moses Paggi and Antonio Cordasco, and for the Greeks Leon Skliris, had contributed the majority of the miners for the region. The Italians were largely from northern Italy. Another factor in management's distrust of Italians was that coming from northern Italy, especially those from Milan, many Italians already had some experience in labor politics. Such militancy was not limited to northern Italians, but also included the militant southern Italian peasant class as well. As one mining official said, he wanted to make Castle Gate an English-speaking mine because he feared, rightfully so, the radical politics of the Italian miners.[16]

But there were other times when labor agents and management were able to divide their immigrant labor force. To break the 1903 Castle Gate strike, the antiunion contractor, Leon Skliris, recruited Greek immigrants as strikebreakers. It is unknown what promises, wages, or other benefits he offered his new recruits, or even if he had informed his Greek-speaking crew that they would be engaging in the dangerous activity of breaking a strike. The condition of Skliris's Greek-speaking crew was no different from the Chinese workers recruited to break strikes in Wyoming. They were no doubt largely illiterate and unaware of the violence that they faced if they tried to break the strike. When the Greek workers attempted to cross the line, they were viciously attacked by striking miners. However, with the support of state officials and the Mormon Church, including help from Skliris, management broke the Castle Gate strike and expelled many of the Italians from the company-owned property.[17]

Undeterred, in 1907 in Bingham, 120 Italians continued with their support of union membership by swelling the Western Federation of Miners' local membership to 300. In one day they added more than 50 new members to the rolls. In spite of their labor contractors' opposition, Japanese and Greek workers joined with Italians and Serbians in a strike in Bingham. This time the workers won for themselves some of the highest wages in the West. The union scale paid from $3.00 to $4.50 a day, which included wages for timbermen, tool sharpeners, shaftmen, blacksmiths, pipemen, and mule drivers. The lowest-paid and unskilled miner received $1.75 a day, still a relatively high wage for unskilled day labor in the West.[18]

Mining—Accidents and Black Lung Disease

Labor organizing grew not just out of wage disputes but also out of the unsafe conditions in the mines. In spite of the success that unions had in raising wages, organized labor was unable to reform significantly safety and health conditions in the mines. Mining companies throughout the United States at the time did not have the technology at hand to eliminate the accumulation of gas and dust in mine shafts, the main cause of deadly explosions. There were some possible remedies, but management resisted implementing them because they were costly and were barriers to maximum production. If miners did not die from the initial explosion, those who were trapped in the caved-in shafts died a slow and horrifying death by suffocation. Utah had at least seven recorded fatal mine disasters between 1881 and 1945, including in 1902, Pleasant Valley explosion (1); 1924, Carbon Fuel Company Mine, Rains (5); 1928, Mammoth Mine Fire (?); 1930, Standard Oil Explosion, Standardville (30); and 1945, Utah Fuel Company, Sunnyside (23). In 1900 in Scofield at the Pleasant Valley Coal Company mine, the most devastating explosion occurred, known as the Winter Quarters Mine Explosion, where 201 miners died, more than 50 percent of the workforce of 400 miners. This number would be surpassed only by the death toll at Dawson, New Mexico, three years later. Multiple members from the same family lost their lives, including fathers, sons, and even grandchildren. Adding to the tragedies, toxic gasses formed in the shaft after the explosion and hampered rescue efforts. The explosion left more than 275 children without fathers and widowed 115 women. The married couples' settlement instantly became a widows' camp. Many of the surviving miners vowed never to work in the mines again and found other work. Descendants of the deceased miners placed a plaque at the site to commemorate this tragedy in 1987.[19]

In 1924 the second-greatest death toll in Utah mining accidents happened at the Utah Fuel Company, this time at Castle Gate, near the Helper-Price region, where 172 miners died: Greeks (49), Italians (22), Japanese (8), English (7), Austrians (6), Scots (2), "Negroes" (1), Belgians (1), and Americans (74). Fifty-seven of the dead were single men, and 114 were married. The rescue efforts of the dead miners reported in the papers at the time describe gruesome scenes as rescue teams reached the mutilated bodies. The force of the explosion propelled telephone poles, light standards, timber, and other debris across the valley floor. The Utah Fuel Company gave each family $150 for funeral expenses and $16 per week for six years, approximately $5,000. The state raised $132,445 in donations and distributed the funds to the families of the dead miners.[20]

However, the less dramatic but equally fatal black lung disease was largely overlooked or hidden altogether at the time. A 1914 study conducted in Butte, Montana, revealed that of the 1,000 miners examined, 40 percent had some form of pulmonary disease. Although miners went underground as early as the 1880s, the statistics show that the vast majority of the miners had arrived after 1900. In other words, the study indicated that miners did not have to spend a lifetime working in the mines to contract a pulmonary disorder. Many were afflicted after only a few years of breathing the contaminated air in the mines.

In one representative example of the impact that mining had on immigrant lives and families, Salvatore Di Filippo emigrated from a mountain village in Calabria. Salvatore and his wife, Rosa, owned a small one-acre farm, possibly the result of an earlier land-reform effort by the Italian government. But their small plot was not sufficient to sustain a family. So Salvatore answered the recruiting call from a labor contractor and left for Utah, where he settled in the mining district around Provo and Price. By 1911 Salvatore had earned enough to send for Rosa and their three-year-old daughter, Barbara Virginia. True to the prediction of the Montana study, by 1916 Salvatore contracted black lung disease and died. Salvatore's death certificate, however, lists "bronchitis" as the cause of death, with complications from "hypertrophic cirrhosis" disease. By the time of his death, Salvatore had left mining to become a section hand on the railroad in Price. But the damage had already been done. The physician did not list black lung disease as the determining cause of death, thus erasing an important statistic relevant to mine safety. Salvatore left Rosa with four daughters, ranging in age from six months to three, five, and nine years old. Destitute and without an income, she and her daughters left for Fresno, where she had relatives in the West Side immigrant community.[21]

Farming and Commerce

Since the states, the federal government, and the unions could do little to change the unsafe working conditions in the mines, the number of men dying from lung disease, serious injury, and mine explosions increased in the West before 1940. As a result of the dangerous conditions as well as the labor strife, many Italians left the mines and went into farming. In addition to mining companies' recruitment of foreign workers, by 1913 Utah was sending propaganda to Italy to entice Italians to come to Utah to develop the state's agricultural resources.

The state's efforts were successful. North of Salt Lake, Italians established truck farms and several dairies. Most were southern Italians, coming from the provinces of Cosenza and Catanzaro in Calabria. In Castle Gate, south of Salt Lake, one Italian rancher established a goat farm and took his cheese and goat meat to the immigrant community in Bingham to sell to Italians and Greeks. This early ranch soon influenced other Italians to establish goat ranches in Carbon, Tooele, and Salt Lake Counties, where numerous other Italians already had truck farms. Italians also began establishing farms along the Price River, near Helper and Price. In Carbon County, which attracted a large contingent of Calabrese, Italian farmers grew a variety of fruits and vegetables and trucked their produce to the Salt Lake City farmers' market on West Temple and Fifth South. Others raised sheep and goats, whose wool, milk, and meat products such as salami and sausage were sold to the surrounding Italian population. While raising of livestock was more easily managed in Utah's cold winter climate, Italian truck farmers utilized skills that allowed them to cope with Utah's harsh winters. To get a jump on Utah's short growing season, the Saccomanno family from Calabria started their seedlings as early as February in framed and covered "hot beds." When the weather turned, they transferred their seedlings to their fields.[22]

The West not only offered a higher standard of living when compared with the density of the population in eastern urban enclaves but also allowed Italians to continue many of their traditional folkways that would not have been possible in an urban tenement environment. On Utah farms, Italians built wood-burning ovens, butchered their farm animals for their own consumption, and planted gardens, including Italian herbs. They were able to make traditional cheese products as well for both home use and to sell to other Italians living in nearby towns.[23]

Contributing to the number of Italians in Utah was a secondary migration in 1910 to Ogden and its surrounding communities in Weber County. Tyroleans, mainly from the southern Alps valleys of Val di Non, the Val di Sole, and Borgo Valsugana, decided to leave the dangerous conditions in the Wyoming mines and settle in Ogden and in the small rural communities to the west of Ogden, such as Hooper, Kanesville, West Warren, Taylor, Plain City, and Wilson Lane, where they established farms. They were able to purchase land cheaply, from $10 to $20 an acre, depending on the quality of the soil and the availability of water.[24] Weber County is located in northern Utah, where winters are even colder than in other parts of the state. But coming from northern Italy, Tyroleans were accustomed to such winter conditions and were able to adapt quickly to their surroundings.

The Tyroleans' success was based on a number of important factors. They stepped into an already well-developed agricultural landscape and formed a tight-knit farming community. Wells dug by earlier farmers in the 1890s, dams on the Weber River, and irrigation canals made the otherwise barren landscape productive. By 1910 approximately fifty Tyrolean families had purchased farms in western Weber County, which became known as Little Tyrol. For those who did not have farming experience, their Tyrolean and even Mormon neighbors helped them develop their farms. During harvest time, the entire community pitched in. When they slaughtered their pigs, neighbors helped make sausage and other prepared meats. To pay for their farms, many of the Tyroleans had worked for years in the mines in Wyoming and had considerable savings when they arrived. As just one example, Luigi Degiorgio worked in the Superior mines and saved more than $13,000, a small fortune at the time, which he used to purchase a farm from a relative.[25] Their shared social and cultural capital uplifted them all.

Women played a significant role in farm and family life. They helped with the harvest, sold farm products on market days, and still shouldered all the household responsibilities, including the nearly exclusive care of the children. At the end of a day's work, the farmwife in west Weber County did not retire to a house with comforts. Farmwives did not have the convenience of indoor plumbing or electricity before 1930. Coal-oil lamps were the only source of light. A wood-burning stove and fireplace were the family's only sources for cooking and for heat during Utah's long winters. When tragedy stuck, widows became the sole support of the family. When Pietro Tremea died, he left his wife, Madalena, with six children and a farm to run. But the community and mutual-aid societies stepped in to help her.[26]

While farming may have provided a safer work environment, farm life also had its downside. Weather, pests, and market prices made life on a farm challenging and insecure. Farm prices declined in the 1920s and were hit even harder with the onslaught of the Great Depression. Yet Tyroleans managed to survive. By 1920 Utah had approximately 25,602 farms, ranking ninth in the West and ahead of Wyoming, Arizona, Nevada, and Alaska. Weber County had a total land acreage of 346,000 and by 1930 had 52,000 acres under cultivation. The average farm was 180 acres, while the smaller truck farms were about 29 acres. The family-run truck farms produced a wide variety of fruits and vegetables. Because of its Italian population and the demand for wine grapes, farmers harvested more than one million pounds of grapes from more than two hundred thousand vines.[27]

Significantly, Utah had a higher number of owner-operated farms, 22,597, compared with tenant farmers at a mere 2,787.[28] The 11 percent ratio of tenant farms to owner-operated farms in 1920 was smaller than the same percentage in larger, more productive agricultural states such as Texas and California. The high owner-operator number points to the profitability of mining as a capital resource that allowed immigrants to establish farms, especially for some of those Tyroleans who moved freely between the mines in Wyoming and farming in Utah. Mining wages far outpaced the cost of living, and the price of land gave immigrant men, willing to risk going underground, a significant economic advantage in the West, especially in Utah.

Enclave Businesses and Community Life

Investment in local businesses would also benefit from the relatively high mining wages and the stimulus that farming brought to Utah's economy. Salt Lake City was home to a vibrant immigrant settlement, including

Italians. By 1920 there were about five hundred Italians in Salt Lake City. Among those early arrivals attempting to capitalize on Salt Lake's growing population was Cesare Rinetti and his friend Francesco Capitolo, both from the Piedmont region of Italy. With years of experience behind them in the hospitality and restaurant business in Europe and the United States, when they arrived in Salt Lake they quickly acquired jobs in the upscale Newhouse Hotel. By 1933 Rinetti and Capitolo, fluent in English, combined their culinary and hospitality skills and opened the Rotisserie Inn, an Italian-French restaurant on 323 South Main. It was a cut above the usual Italian eateries established for the working class in enclaves. The Rotisserie was an elegant restaurant with well-designed décor, including white tablecloths and colorful table settings. It became an instant success and one of Salt Lake's and Utah's finest restaurants until 1957, when it closed. As well-known members of both the Italian and the Salt Lake communities in general, the two became members of the Knights of Columbus and the Cristoforo Colombo Society as well as members of the local Elks Lodge and the Salt Lake City Chamber of Commerce.[29] With their Italian and English fluency and their culinary skills, they are examples of how immigrants were able to move beyond the immigrant enclave and attract a customer base in the wider late-generation population in Salt Lake.

In a more representative route to success, Italians opened saloons, grocery stores, and tailor shops, businesses that more directly met the needs of the immigrant population in Salt Lake. Antonio Ferro, born in a small town in southern Italy, arrived in the United States in 1894. By 1905 he settled in Salt Lake and became owner and president of the Western Macaroni Company, which became one of the largest macaroni factories in the state by the 1930s. Among the most successful Italians in Utah, Francesco Mariani, born in northern Italy, arrived in 1910 with his mother in Carbon County to join his father, who had preceded them and was working as a miner. As a teenager, Francesco worked in the Carbon County mines but managed to attend Carbon County High School, where he learned English. He moved to Salt Lake in 1920 and opened a grocery store. Within five years, he expanded his grocery business to a region-wide distributorship. By 1932 he became the exclusive distribution agent for more than twenty-five companies, from manufacturers of machinery to distributors of beverage supplies and soft drinks for Utah, Wyoming, Montana, and Idaho. Still operating under the name Ernest F. Mariani Company, the company is now more than one hundred years old and is still family owned.[30]

Approximately forty miles north of Salt Lake, Ogden also became a cultural and commercial center, serving as an important outlet for Italians' farm products and for the establishment of immigrant businesses. In 1881 there were 150 Catholics in Ogden, but by 1884 their numbers had grown to more than 4,000. To meet the spiritual needs of both the urban and the rural families, in 1881 the Irish priest Father Patrick M. Cushnahan arrived in Ogden and organized the construction of a new and larger church, Saint Joseph Church, on Twenty-Fourth Street and Adams Avenue in Ogden, where it still stands today. By 1913 Salt Lake Catholics funded the building of two other churches. All of these parishes became community centers where Italians were able to attend funerals and celebrate weddings, baptisms, and traditional feast days, such as Saint Joseph's Day Tables. Many of the parishes remain active today. Tyroleans opened at least three hotels and a number of other businesses, from grocery stores to carpentry businesses, in Ogden. After her husband and a brother were killed in the 1923 Frontier, Wyoming, mine explosion, Lucy Andreatta and her sister, Ellen, owned and ran the Empire Hotel in downtown Ogden.[31]

Further solidifying the bonds within the community, Italians established the usual fraternal organizations throughout Utah: the Società Cristoforo Colombo (Salt Lake, 1897), Fratellanza Minatori (Sunnyside, 1902), Principe di Napoli (Castle Gate, 1902), Stella d'America (Castle Gate, 1908), Società di Beneficenza (Bingham Canyon and Mercur, 1907), Club Dante Alighieri (Salt Lake City, 1908), and Società Cristoforo Colombo (Castle Gate, 1910), with another chapter in Ogden (date unknown). Other clubs included the Italian-American Club (Salt Lake City, 1919), Figli d'Italia (Salt Lake City, 1915), and the Italian Freemasons.[32]

Italian journalists and entrepreneurs established many Italian-language newspapers. Former labor contractor and publisher Moses Paggi started *Il Minatore* (1908–9) in Salt Lake City, which focused on labor issues in the various mining camps in Utah and the surrounding Intermountain area. From 1911 to 1917, G. Milano published *La Gazzetta Italiana*, published by the Italian Publishing Company in Salt Lake. In 1926 Milano teamed up with Alfonso Russo to publish *La Scintilla*. By 1929 their paper merged with *America* to become *Il Corriere d'America*, published by Frank Niccoli and managed by Alfonso Russo. These papers were instrumental in bringing news of the Italian community from Italy, especially during the war years, where immigrants still had families.[33]

With the rise of Mussolini, his Ministry of Propaganda located all Italian newspapers in the West and used them to spread fascist propaganda. It did not matter whether editors were fascist sympathizers. Far from Italy, yet still connected by heritage, language, and family, they were largely defenseless against Mussolini's bloated claims of his revitalization of Italy's economy and his purported military success in foreign campaigns. As one Italian man opined in the aftermath of Mussolini's fall, "The radio has made fools of us all." In Italy the radio had become one of Mussolini's chief avenues of domestic propaganda, while he relied on North American Italian newspapers to rally support for his government abroad.[34] As the Utah Italian community aged and dispersed, few of these papers, however, survived much beyond World War II.

Late-Generation Revival

By the 1950s, the Utah mines closed, and many town centers were abandoned. The immigrants, including Italians, moved to either Utah's larger towns or other states. But the early Italian immigrants left their influence in the state wherever they settled. A younger generation runs the Italian American Civic League, the Italian Club, and the Italian American Meet Up Group, all located in Salt Lake but with outreach to other cities in the state. Each year the Italian American Civic League and the Italian Club host a street festival in the heart of Salt Lake. There is also the Italian Center of the West that promotes all aspects of Italian culture. Overseeing Italian interests, there is an Italian consulate office in Salt Lake City. While celebrating the Italian immigrant heritage in the state, these community and official organizations have also become transnational in their scope, emphasizing the Made in Italy brand and travel to Italy. The Italian Club offers a list of Italian-language courses. In the usual demographic mystery, by 1990, according to the National Italian American Foundation, there were 46,008 Italian Americans living in Utah. The 2000 US Census indicates that there were 57,212, about 2.6 percent of Utah's total population. The rise in the number of Italian Americans in one decade can be accounted for by the increased awareness of family roots over the past forty years. Being the descendants of immigrants no longer carries the stigma that it once did for first- and second-generation Americans. Today, Utah's Italian Americans represent 2.6 percent of the US population.[35]

CHAPTER 6

WYOMING

Settlement

Few associate the wide-open expanses of the Wyoming Territory with Italian immigrant settlement. But before 1940, Italian immigrants participated in all aspects of Wyoming's immigrant economy, from mining and farming to retail businesses and banking. Many of those Italians came from Trentino–Alto Adige, the province of South Tyrol. The numerical study of Italians in Wyoming is complicated by the fact that some listed themselves in the census as Tyroleans, while others listed themselves as Italian, even though they came from the same village and spoke the same dialect. In 1870 there were only 9 Italian immigrants living in the Wyoming Territory, which became a state in 1890. By 1900 there were 781 Italians in Wyoming, 4.5 percent of the total foreign-born population of the state.[1]

However, by 1910 the Italian foreign-born population, 1,961, nearly doubled to 7.7 percent of the state's foreign-born population. The Italians' rate of increase in the state was about the same as the rest of the United States. Most of those who came to the state initially worked in the mining industry. Accustomed to a cold climate, Italians from the northern regions were not deterred by Wyoming's climate. Few came from Basilicata, Calabria, or Sicily.[2]

For centuries the Tyroleans had a migratory tradition that sent workers throughout central Europe. Many had only two- to three-acre farms, which did not provide sufficient income. Making matters worse, the region had rocky and unproductive soil, and the Alpine climate did not allow for a long growing season. Life was difficult and was made more so during economic downturns and years of especially severe weather. As Mary Anselmi said when asked why she and the other Tyroleans left their villages, "When you are hungry you move."[3]

They were competent farmers and skilled artisans, which allowed them to integrate quickly into the immigrant economy in Sweetwater County in the southwestern corner of the state. Among their many skills, Tyroleans, like the southern Italians, had an extensive silkworm industry. Generally, they had a higher literacy rate that enabled them to open businesses, especially banks, and become active in state and local politics. Many of them regularly read *Il Progresso Italia*, published in New York City. Because of their exposure to unionization in Italy's industrial North, many Tyroleans became leaders in the union movement in Wyoming as well as throughout the West.[4]

Mining

Initially, the high wages paid in the mining industry attracted Tyroleans to the Wyoming Territory. When in 1868 the Union Pacific reached Wyoming, the railroad opened national markets for the shipment of trona and coal to the rest of the nation. There were also significant deposits of gas and oil, especially in an area known as Rock Springs Dome. In 1868 two brothers from Scotland, Archibald and Duncan Blair, found a vein of coal near the Rock Springs' stage depot. They had come to Rock Springs in Sweetwater County to manage the stage line. But like so many immigrant entrepreneurs in the West, they wisely anticipated the coming of the railroad, staked their claim, and began mining coal.[5]

With the discovery of the state's abundant natural resources, mine operators quickly hired labor contractors to recruit the needed labor. Chain migration as well contributed to the fast-growing immigrant population in Sweetwater County, where the Rock Springs mines were located. First among the arrivals were from Great Britain, the Irish included, who by 1870 took jobs as miners, while others became bankers and saloonkeepers. Native Americans and African Americans were also part of the labor force in Hartville in Platte County east of Rock Springs. By 1920 there were more than 130 mines in Sweetwater County surrounding Rock Springs. With the help of labor contractors, the workforce was soon composed of more than fifty-six nations.[6]

In Rock Springs, workers and their families formed small neighborhoods around their respective churches and temples: Protestant, Catholic, Orthodox, and Jewish. By 1885 the Chinese had a well-established Chinatown. Initially, mining companies provided the incoming European miners with company housing. Since housing was provided on a first-come, first-served basis, miners did not establish homogeneous neighborhoods. However, in one instance in Hartville, Italian miners did form a neighborhood for a period of time near the mine where they worked. As they saved their earnings, Italians were able to leave the mines and buy property in the north end of Hartville and establish a neighborhood next to Greek and Lebanese immigrants.[7]

By the mid-1890s, Tyrolean Italian miners joined the growing multinational community in Rock Springs. By one estimate, there were more than 100 Tyrolean families from Brez, a village in the far-northern region of Trentino-Alto Adige. The high number of families from Brez was the result of mine operators in Sweetwater County who had hired labor contractors to travel to the region to recruit workers. By 1912 there were more than 1,000 Tyroleans in Sweetwater County. They outnumbered all other groups in the Union Pacific Company. The Tyroleans quickly earned a reputation in the Union Pacific mines as hard workers and efficient miners. They lived frugally, and with their high wages, between $2.50 to $3.50 a day, they were able to capitalize their future business ventures. The low cost of living and cheap land aided in their transition out of the mines. Some of the best land in Wyoming cost little more than $10.00 per acre, low for western farmlands at the time.[8]

By 1920 about 60 percent of the nearly 2,000 Italians in Wyoming worked in Laramie, Sweetwater, and Uinta Counties. It appears that by 1912, Sunrise had about 350 Italian miners, first among all the immigrant groups and second behind late-generation Americans. Hartville's Italians came largely from northern Italy, with a small contingent from southern Italy. Italians and Greeks initially formed the majority of miners to reach Hartville, where the first miners lived in a shantytown of "dugouts" before management provided adequate housing. Others rented rooms in local boardinghouses for approximately $9.00 a month, including meals. Italian boardinghouses accommodated from a dozen to as many as 30 to 50 men. The boardinghouse owner sometimes worked in conjunction with labor contractors, who also took a percentage of the lodging fee.[9]

To aid immigrants in their assimilation, as early as 1901 the Union Pacific Company sponsored English-language classes for its workers, who began preparing themselves for permanent residence in the United States. Of all the immigrant groups in the Hartville area, Italian immigrants occupied the majority of the seats in class and "came night after night with commendable regularity, and in some instances requested that sessions be held every evening of the week."[10] This willingness to learn English might explain the ability of Italians to join local non-Italian business associations, where they felt comfortable and were able to communicate with the other English-speaking members. Their English-language ability also helped them to expand their grocery stores, saloons, and shoe-repair shops to service the local English-speaking population.

A contributing factor to the individual immigrant's success was that workers without a family in tow were able to move to higher-paying jobs. Even if they had signed a contract with a labor agent, at some point their contracts expired, or with impunity they simply broke the contract and left their work site. Italians, Greeks, and Mexicans routinely broke their contracts and left for better jobs. In the West it was difficult to enforce labor contracts on a peripatetic population of single males on the hunt for ever-higher wages. If they decided to break their contract, they could easily cross state and territory borders and take refuge with friends or family in their ethnic enclaves, where they could quickly find employment. Moreover, word spread through familial and friendship networks about higher-paying jobs. Miners routinely left northeastern mines, where they earned as little as $1.50 a day, for higher pay in western mines. Chain migration and hearsay within the Italian community were important elements in bringing free-labor miners to Hartville, outside the control of labor agents and their contractual abuses.[11] Free labor was one of the most important aspects of immigrant success.

To ensure a sufficient labor force, companies such as Union Pacific recruited their labor force through a system of official labor contractors and agents stationed in the East, the West, and Europe. For the non-English-speaking immigrant looking for a job in urban centers, the experience was often confusing. In addition to the official agents, the unofficial labor-contracting system included an assortment of unlicensed, self-appointed agents such as bankers, steamship agents, taxicab drivers, and hotel workers. These agents were often exploitative. They often misled desperate immigrants, who signed contracts without any guarantees of their salary or the type of work they would be required to do. At Hartville-Sunrise, Thomas Tucker, known as the "mine captain," was among the honest unofficial recruiters. He undertook an informal recruiting program through the mail by writing to friends and relatives in England to work in the Sunrise mines, while mining companies hired agents to recruit experienced English miners to the region.[12]

At the time, the labor contractor did not have a positive image in the United States. In 1911 the Dillingham Commission found that even official agents often promised immigrants higher wages or better jobs than was the reality. Under the system, farmers paid an Italian agent from about $1.50 to $3.00 per day for a crew of field workers and up to $3,000 for a season. Japanese labor contractor Kobo received upwards of $3.00 a month for each miner that he brought to Hartville-Sunrise mines. In Cheyenne one faux agent attempted to demand a fee for finding jobs for Italians, but local business owners saw through his scheme and rejected his request. The unofficial agent was a streetwise operator who scoured neighborhoods to "*fare gli uomini*," make the men. When he met his quota, he exacted a fee, a *bossatura*, from the workers. Since this freelance padrone was not usually licensed through an employment agency, his fee was illegal. In addition to the illegal *bossatura*, the agent was also paid by the company, from about $1.00 to $10.00 per worker, depending on the duration of the job. If the agent provided other services—writing letters or providing food, clothing, railroad tickets, and other services—he demanded as well a fee from the unsuspecting worker. Foreign agents hired by companies also charged fees from immigrants for tickets on steamships and railroads, including a fee for providing the outgoing emigrants with food and water for their two- to three-week journey across the ocean. Between 1880 and 1900, a steamship ticket cost from $15.00 to as high as $28.00. Left unexplained to the worker upon signing a contract, these hidden fees were actually a loan that the worker would have to pay off when he began work. He was bound by both the contract he had signed and the debt he owed the labor agent.[13]

The labor agents' exploitation of their contract workers led to one of the most tragic events in labor history. The powerful Chinese labor agents Six Companies likewise signed exploitative contracts with their workers. Faced with striking workers in Rock Springs, management hired Six Companies to bring in a group of Chinese miners to undermine unionized miners' demands for higher wages and safer mine conditions. By 1885 the miners in Rock Springs had joined a new union, the Knights of Labor. Tensions were already high among the workers over the unionization process. Adding to the labor unrest, Six Companies brought to Rock Springs Chinese workers whom management paid below the union scale, thus threatening to lower wages for all miners.[14]

The conflict instigated by Six Companies and management set the stage for a violent confrontation between the union miners and the Chinese workers. As a harbinger of what was to come, anonymous public threats had already been made against the Chinese in other surrounding mining towns. On the morning of September 2, 1885, a violent confrontation occurred between two Chinese miners and other mine workers in the No. 6 mine. The foreman stopped the attack, but only after two Chinese miners were seriously injured. Later that afternoon, between 100 and 150 armed miners, largely Welsh, Irish, Cornish, English, and Scandinavian, gathered near the No. 6 mine and attacked Chinatown. By the time the attack was over, they had killed 28 Chinese, wounded 15, and run out of town nearly 200 more men, women, and children. The miners burned and pillaged Chinatown in the process, resulting in more than $140,000 in property damage. Miners' wives purportedly joined in the murder and mayhem. The massacre drew the attention of President Grover Cleveland, who ordered federal troops into the territory to restore order. The Rock Springs Massacre is among the most disgraceful incidents in Wyoming and western history. Although escorted back by federal troops, the majority of Chinese workers gradually left Rock Springs by 1900 to settle in other parts of the West.[15]

In the wake of the killings, Union Pacific severed its relationship with Chinese labor contractors and began recruiting only European miners. However, the Chinese returned to Rock Springs before World War I to work in the mines. This time they joined the union, and the collective goals of higher wages and mine safety unified all the miners. By 1907 the union succeeded in organizing the majority of miners at Union Pacific sites in Sweetwater County. When the miners struck, the Union Pacific threatened to fire all participants. But all miners held their ground. Because of their solidarity, "scabs" did not cross the line, and the Union Pacific was forced to accept the union's demands. They agreed on a uniform contract in which miners were granted an eight-hour workday, a 20 percent wage increase, and a union representative in the mines to oversee working conditions.[16]

Realizing that its own interests were at stake, the Union Pacific even took some measures to unify its multicultural community. By 1920 Rock Springs began to honor its workforce with an "International Night," a festival featuring traditional costumes, food, songs, and folk dance. There were other events, including the annual August Turnfest, the Scots' Caledonian Club festival celebrating the birthday of poet Robert Burns, and a Saint Patrick's Day celebration, as well as numerous feast days celebrated by the Italian colonies in Sweetwater and other counties. All of these public festivals were supported enthusiastically by local officials, who were eager to accommodate immigrant workers in their towns. Management organized town bands, which included Italians, and in Rock Springs sponsored lawn and garden contests. The names of Italian miners, with their carefully designed gardens and lawns, often appeared along with the names of

Greek and Japanese winners. One resident said that he could remember a time when on a single street he could find "a Greek baker, a Chinese restaurant, and a Jewish market."[17]

Management also opened lines of communication with the union to better manage the workforce. Scots and English workers, the first to arrive in Wyoming, held the upper-management positions in the union. Italians, who arrived later, in time developed English skills and were appointed to lower-level positions to bridge the language gap between management, the union hierarchy, and Italian miners. The inability to communicate with such a multilingual workforce was a common-enough problem in all the mines. In Cheyenne, for example, the Union Pacific Railroad employed so many Italians that they hired a community leader and interpreter, Paul Milatzo, to help management communicate with the Italian workers.[18]

By 1920, in addition to their settlement in Laramie, Sweetwater, and Uinta, Italians were attracted to Platte County, where they worked in the iron mines and limestone quarries. Hanna, Rock Springs, and Carbon were also major mining centers where the Union Pacific mines were located. In Rock Springs by 1920, the Japanese were the largest immigrant group, thanks to the work of three Japanese labor contractors, Kondo Chikai, Suzuki Rokuhiko, and Ueda Heitaro. To protect their interests and their workers' jobs in the mines, the three labor contractors were instrumental in obtaining membership for seven hundred of their Japanese workers in the United Mine Workers of America.[19] The Rock Springs Massacre and the growing labor strife in general had reformed out of necessity, at least in Wyoming, labor contractors' bias against unions.

As the war approached, by 1914 coal prices skyrocketed as the government demanded more coal for the war effort. In one year, between 1917 and 1918, coal production in the United States increased by almost one million tons. By 1917 Wyoming was producing ten thousand tons of coal a day. The population of Sweetwater in 1910 grew from 8,455 to 13,640 by 1920. Wages also increased. Unskilled Italian miners working on top of the mines worked for about $1.50 for a ten-hour day. However, if a miner were able to move underground, even after deductions for waste, tools, oil, explosives, and sundry other items, the miner could make $75.00 to $85.00 a month. By 1916, because of the demand for coal and a labor shortage, wages jumped from $3.25 per day to $5.42. In comparison, by 1918 railroad engineers earned $8.50 a day. Women's wages also rose from $1.50 a day for stenographers to $5.80 a day.[20]

The relatively high pay that miners received did not come without risks. With more than 40 percent of its landmass containing coal, Wyoming at the time was among the nation's leading coal producers, all of which were supplying fuel for America's industrial appetite at breakneck speed with little regard to mine safety. Workers were exposed to injury and death on a daily basis in less dramatic incidents that were, nevertheless, deadly or permanently debilitating. By one worker's account, there were countless ways a miner could be injured or killed: "Cave-ins, coal-dust explosions, gas explosions, burns, sprains, back injuries, and falls were commonplace." A miner could as well "drown in a sump, get scalded by steam, hit by a runaway ore car, or break his neck in a hoist frame. Moreover, new accidents were constantly happening, the likes of which were never before heard of." As one miner frequently said to his family, "It was a dangerous day today...in the mines."[21]

For the Hanna mine, the worst did in fact occur. Ten years before the catastrophic Dawson, New Mexico, mine disaster where 263 miners lost their lives, on June 30, 1903, the Union Pacific's Hanna No. 1 mine exploded, killing more than 169 miners. Because of the difficulty of the recovery operation at the time, the exact number of the dead will never be known. The Hanna explosion left hundreds of children fatherless. Five years later, two explosions in the Hanna mine left 59 miners dead. Many of the miners' bodies were never recovered. The list of the dead in the 1903 explosion exposes the tragic results of chain migration and the labor-contracting system, both of which brought multiple members from the same family into a single mine. At least 17 families lost 2 members, and 4 families lost 3 members. The Longi family lost 4 members, and the worst among the miners, the Matson family, probably Swedish, lost 5 members. There were more than 20 Japanese killed. African Americans are also listed among the dead. In a typical payoff to families, in the wake of the 1903 Hanna explosion, widows received $800, and their children under the age of fifteen each received $50. The men were buried in a nearby cemetery that remained abandoned and forgotten until only recently.[22]

This disaster was not the first in Wyoming or the last. Before Hanna, in 1895, 60 were killed at Red Canyon, and in 1886, at Almy No. 4, 13 died. In 1901 at Diamondville, there were two disasters, February 15, when 26 were killed, and again on October 26, when 22 more died. Little was done in Hanna to improve safety conditions. In addition to the 1908 deadly accident, in 1912 in Kemmerer 6 died, and in 1923 at Cumberland 5 were killed. Again in 1923 at the Frontier No. 1 Mine near Kemmerer, 99 died, marking the largest death toll of the year. In the following year, 1924, 39 died in Sublette, Lincoln County. Accidents in Wyoming mines continued with the Centennial Gold Mine Fire in 1931 and the Rock Springs explosion in 1942.[23] Unions attempted to bargain for greater mine safety. But given the accidents and the rate of pulmonary disease among miners that continued well into the 1940s, they were not successful in their efforts to reform the unsafe conditions in the mines.

Farming

Because of the harsh Wyoming winters and short growing season, farming was one option, though not the most lucrative, for those immigrants who wished to avoid the dangers of mining. Dairies and ranching were the most practical enterprises, given the long, severe winters. Those few who did begin ranches were able to participate in the rising state and national demand for wool, mutton, and beef. Among the farmers, Sicilian Sam Adragna arrived in Cheyenne in 1907 and began work on the railroads. Taking advantage of the Homestead Act, Adragna found a plot of free land and started a dairy farm on the outskirts of Cheyenne. Similarly, Romano Dapra, a Tyrolean, began work in Sunrise in the mines until one day he discovered a fertile piece of unclaimed land about a mile and a half from the mine in a nearby valley. He filed a homestead claim and began a livestock business. However, Dapra continued working in mining while his wife, Theresia, and their several children managed the daily chores on the ranch. The family also produced cheese and sold it at the local market.[24]

Although the Dapra family left no details about the family's farm life, it is not difficult to read into the few details available of their daily life. While Romano left the farm each day to work in the mine, Theresia assumed responsibility for running the farm, caring for the children, and managing the cheese business. In farm families, there was a certain "gendering of ranch work" where women played an essential role. As did those other farmwives in the West, Theresia challenged the boundaries of the otherwise patriarchal family system. Her economic value to the family cannot be exaggerated, given her husband's absence from the day-to-day running of the farm.[25]

But there was a downside for women on remote farms. The most dramatic representations of farm life for women during this period of rural settlement are in Willa Cather's *My Antonia* (1918), about eastern European immigrant life on the plains of Nebraska, and in O.E. Rölvaag's saga *Giants in the Earth* (1924), about immigrant Norwegian settlements in the Dakota Territory. As these novels demonstrate, in rural areas women had little opportunity for "communal work and socializing."[26] Rölvaag's and Cather's female protagonists were far from the bustle of daily life in town. Although they were respected for their work, especially Cather's Antonia, the women in the two novels paid a high price. Because of her profound isolation and dislocation from her native village, Rölvaag's Beret Hansa descends into mental illness.

By 1920 Wyoming ranked ahead of only Montana and Alaska in agricultural production. Between 1900 and 1910, the cost of land had doubled under the pressure from increased immigration and settlement. Nevertheless, in 1920 the cost of land still remained low, about $20 an acre. Compared with other western states, Wyoming had a high percentage of owner-operated farms, 13,463, next to the small number of tenant farms, 1,968. Also contributing to the settlement of the state, in addition to the low cost of land, the Homestead Act offered settlers free land. From their mining wages or business ventures, they had enough capital either to purchase land or to do the required improvements on the free land within the allotted time that the government required under the Homestead Act's provisions. In the two years leading up to US entry into the war, 1915–17, approximately 4,180 claims were filed. In the wake of the war, by 1921 the number of homestead claims rose to more than 10,000. In 1920 Wyoming ranchers had more than eight hundred thousand head of cattle. In addition to cattle production, farmers also produced limited crops of grains and fruits.[27]

Commerce and the Enclave Economy

With the dangerous conditions in the mines and with farming as a secondary option, many Italians chose to open enclave businesses servicing the immigrant population in mining towns. Tyrolean Henry Bertagnolli left the mines and purchased a local livery stable. He left mining because he became disillusioned over the labor politics that had led to the Chinese massacre in Rock Springs in 1885. He supplied hay, grain, and feed to area ranchers. As the enclave economy grew around him, in 1893 he expanded his business and took in partners, his brother Alexander and several other Tyroleans who left mining to join him. He renamed his company the Union Mercantile and Supply Company and expanded his original line of products to groceries and personal items such as clothing, shoes, and hardware. The name of his business was a clever marketing maneuver to lure customers away from the Union Pacific company store. But Bertagnolli was not done yet. In 1905 he expanded his company to Superior, about twenty-five miles from Rock Springs, where the Bertagnolli partnership had enough capital to purchase 160 acres of federal land next to the Union Pacific Coal Company. He and his partners found a lucrative market in Superior. By 1900 Superior, in Sweetwater County, became an important coal-mining center. There were six mines in Superior, where the D. O. Clark Mine was by far the most productive, producing more coal in a day than all the others combined. After opening his new store, Bertagnolli reorganized the Superior location and sold stock. The original six Tyroleans held stock in the business, and the rest was sold to miners, most likely to those who spoke Bertagnolli's dialect and felt that they could trust him. He added to his customer base by doing business in both English and Tyrolean.[28]

In 1912 Henry's younger brother, Joseph, immigrated to Superior to work in the mines. By 1920 he left the mines and began work as a clerk in his brother's company, where he was promoted to vice president by 1926. Joseph was soon able to purchase land and start a sheep ranch. Becoming a well-known and successful businessman, he was elected mayor of Superior in 1924. With the support of his family, especially his brother Joseph and other Tyroleans, Henry's companies continued to grow over the next thirty years, until he sold the Superior location in 1955. However, the original Rock Springs location, owned and managed by his family and other Tyroleans, continued to do business for ninety-four years.[29]

As they did on the farm, women played an equally important role in enclave centers. Unmarried, single Tyrolean men's first stop in Sweetwater County was often the home of Tyrolean Rachela Anselmi. Like so many other immigrant women in boardinghouse and hotel businesses in the West, she saw an opportunity, and for a price Anselmi provided room and board to her conationals. She provided that "infrastructure of support," kinship and a familiar cultural ambience, for the uprooted men far from their families and villages. The men ate at the family dinner table, spoke their familiar dialect, and were treated like family members. To borrow terms from Oscar Handlin's and John Higham's works, immigrant men may well have been "uprooted," but they were not always "strangers in the land."[30]

Before the Tyroleans, northern Europeans had initially settled the region and opened businesses in downtown centers just before the mining boom. Among the first Italians to settle in Hartville, about three hundred miles east of Superior, was the Louis Bacchieri family. Louis had previously worked in the Colorado mines before moving to Hartville, where northern Italian Attilio Testolin married Louis Bacchieri's daughter. Family ties became a significant factor in his success in Hartville. Leaving the mines, he began speculating in real estate. From there he went into construction and employed a number of Italian carpenters. With a loan from his father-in-law, Louis, he then opened a large hardware and grocery store as well as a saloon. Both Louis and Attilio went on to become important members of the Hartville business community and are listed in the directory of the Hartville Commercial Club.[31]

John Boschetto emigrated from the town of Salorno, Trentino, in 1901 with his two boys, Louis and Ben. They worked in the Cumberland mines south of Kemmerer, Lincoln County. But after narrowly escaping death in a cave-in, in 1911 he returned with his family to Italy. Louis returned to Kemmerer in 1921. But he avoided the dangerous work in the mines and began peddling scrap metal and other recyclable materials that were the detritus of the mining and smelting industries. In 1922 he moved to Rock Springs, where, with the profits from his refuse-collection business, he opened two clothing businesses and later began investing in real estate. Boschetto's brother, a butcher, followed him and opened his own shop by 1930 under the name Foodliner. Today, after more than eighty-five years, the business is run by the third and fourth generations of the Boschetto family under its new name, Boschetto's European Market and Deli.[32] The enterprising immigrant found opportunity, sometimes in unlikely places in the enclave, but that opportunity was nearly always buttressed by the social and cultural capital that the community and family provided immigrant entrepreneurs, men and women.

With its growing post-1880s immigrant population, Wyoming was staunchly anti-Prohibition. The city fathers in all the mining centers were well aware of how much the liquor trade contributed to the local business economy. To service the large number of immigrants that the Union Pacific Company brought to Rock Springs, each nationality had its own bar. Italians were no exception. The well-known Rock Springs Fountain Club, located right across the street from the rail station, attracted a largely Tyrolean clientele.[33]

In Hartville saloons were among the most affordable businesses to finance. In 1906 in Hartville a saloon proprietor could open a new saloon with a $1,000 licensing fee. Making it even easier for the potential immigrant saloon owner, in the Wyoming anti-Prohibition and business-friendly environment, that fee dropped the next year to $700. In spite of the growing anti-immigrant furor that was gaining ground in the rest of the United States at the time, the town council was willing to accommodate the newly arrived population. The members of the town council also declared prostitution legal in Hartville, which already had established brothels. Rock Springs also had a red-light district. While some members of the town council did object to prostitution on moral grounds, the council did not want to eliminate it. Rather than allowing for the expansion of brothels, the council decided that saloons could more efficiently be used as a venue for "Lewd Women." This added another level of revenue for tavern owners. It seemed to help that some council members also owned saloons in town. There were few rules regarding who could get a license, other than the ability of prospective owners to pay the fee. By 1907 in Hartville, several Greek immigrants and only one Italian were in the saloon business.[34] But Italians' small number in the saloon business would soon change.

The male members of the council in Hartville did not express any consideration for the exploitation of the prostitutes in their town. Given the illicit and marginal nature of prostitution, it would be easy to ignore the exploitation of women. However, poor, unmarried women had few opportunities anywhere in the United States at the time, including small western boomtowns. In a patriarchal social order, women could not own property and had no access to those higher-paying mining, railroad, and timber jobs available to men. In studies conducted in 1900 and 1910, 11 percent of the prostitutes questioned said they were coerced into the sex trade. Another 28 percent said they went into the trade because of the money they could earn. An average working-class woman could earn about $6.67 a week, while a prostitute could earn upwards of $30 to $50 a week. In one case, the prostitutes in Virginia City, Nevada, were reported to be among the town's wealthiest citizens at $233 a week. Some madams at the top of the prostitution hierarchy in the West became wealthy: "Diamond Jessie" Hayman of San Francisco; Denver's Jessie Rodgers, the "Queen of the Colorado Underworld"; Josephine "Chicago Joe" Airey of Helena,

Montana; Lou Graham of Seattle; and Mattie Silks and Eleanor Dumont of the Sierra Nevada Gold Country.[35]

These famous, or perhaps infamous, madams and those higher-earning prostitutes represented only a fraction of the large number of female prostitutes in the West. Whatever a prostitute's earning capacity, her life expectancy as a prostitute was short for many reasons, health among them. They were abused physically and emotionally. Whatever the earning capacity of madams, the earnings of those women forced by their poverty to work in brothels did not underwrite businesses or endow a family legacy. They remained a marginal group within business enclaves that were otherwise uplifting all other immigrants and late-generation citizens.

Along with the nearby red-light districts, the saloon business thrived in spite of Prohibition. When Prohibition passed, the OK Saloon on K Street reopened the next day as a coffee bar. Other saloon owners closed their doors and reopened the next day as soft-drink parlors. In 1915 Tony Jordinelli arrived in Riverton, Freemont County. He began as a bartender in Frank Lamar's tavern. A year later, he and a partner opened their own saloon. When Prohibition intervened in 1919, Tony and his partner closed their saloon. However, the ever-resourceful Tony would not be defeated by what he saw as merely a temporary amendment to the Constitution. He opened what he called a "drugstore." He merely continued doing what others were doing, only in a slightly altered form. He was still in the liquor business, and legally. "Drugstores" could legally dispense a "medicinal liquor" with a high alcohol content. When Prohibition ended, with his profits, ill-gained or not, he opened another bar in Riverton. In time, he became a successful businessman and was reportedly worth millions. Such success was not unusual. Charles Walgreen Jr., whose Swedish immigrant father established Walgreens Pharmacy, revealed that the pharmacy stores always had a plentiful supply of liquor on hand in their back rooms. The faux liquor trade was so successful that Walgreens expanded its locations from 20 to 525 during the 1920s. Walgreens continues today as a major nationwide pharmacy.[36]

While some aspects of the liquor trade were legal, or at least marginally legal, Kemmerer moonshine soon became a sought-after beverage by miners in the region. Under the cover of darkness, immigrant men drove trucks and distributed the moonshine throughout the region and even across state lines. To service the new trade in illegal booze, stills dotted the area, while home winemaking as well fueled the underground market. Private homes, the miners' form of a speakeasy, also became drinking parlors that attracted a regular clientele.[37]

The most infamous of the bootleg-whiskey businessmen was Joe Colletti, who lived in the small town of Diamondville, the location of the Diamond Coal and Coke Company, not far from Kemmerer. Probably from central Sicily, Colletti, a former saloon owner, ran a well-organized bootleg-whiskey business. In fact, the local moonshine became so famous among the whiskey-drinking men of the area that it became known as "Kemmerer Moon." Colletti did so well that he paid his still operators and truck drivers market wages. His drivers distributed his "moon" to all the surrounding mining towns, including towns in Utah and Colorado. When his workers were arrested, Colletti stepped in to pay lawyers' fees and court costs. It is rumored that he also paid jurors a fee, as well as the living expenses of any witness who might testify against him and his workers.[38] Among an immigrant population that viewed alcoholic beverages, especially wine, as an aspect of their cultural heritage, Prohibition did more to damage the rule of law than it did to discourage immigrants, as well as all Americans, from drinking.

In addition to the production of illegal alcohol, as many as a hundred truckloads of wine grapes a year arrived in Rock Springs from California, many from the vineyards of Secondo Guasti and Andrea Sbarboro. Prohibition did not prohibit wineries from selling grapes or from making "sacramental" wines. In fact, during Prohibition, in a pattern that virtually kept Italian California winemakers in business, Hartville imported hundreds of boxes of wine grapes for homemade wine, which was legal to a limit and as long as it was consumed at home and not sold. It was estimated that Italians made enough wine each year in Rock Springs, Superior, and other locations to supply each family with twenty gallons. The Tyroleans were no exception and were active in supplementing their mining wages and business profits by making homemade beer, wine, and other spirits for sale.[39]

Federal officials conducted more than one hundred raids on soft-drink parlors, private homes, and stills. On one night in December 1921, federal officials arrested more than sixty people in Rock Springs, Green River, and Superior, the settlement of Tyrolean immigrants. While there is no documentation of exactly how many Italian homes or establishments were raided, officials did report that they destroyed more than three thousand gallons of what they described as "dago red" and more than one thousand gallons of other alcoholic beverages. However, the trade in illegal booze continued. There is no escaping the judgment of many that Prohibition's intent was to curtail what Protestant America saw as immigrants' unsavory cultural influence on American culture. As Clarence Darrow said in 1924, "The father and mother of the Ku Klux is the Anti-Saloon League. I would not say every Anti-Saloon Leaguer is a Ku Kluxer, but every Ku Kluxer is an Anti-Saloon Leaguer." The Women's Christian Temperance Union also had roots in the Klan.[40]

The potential profit in the liquor business made the risk of arrest worth the trouble and expense for the accused. Although busts and prosecutions became common in the area, federal prosecutors soon discovered that convictions were hard to come by. Part of the reason was that immigrants were not the only sector of the population undermining the Eighteenth Amendment. Resistance was widespread. On May 18, 1930, thirteen Rock Springs city officials, including thirty-eight others, were arrested for bootlegging. Those officials arrested included the Rock Springs mayor, three councilmen, the city attorney, the chief of police, the city treasurer, the deputy sheriff, four city policemen, and a judge. Yet at the end of the federal trial in Cheyenne, all were acquitted. Colletti was not the only one influencing juries and witnesses. The degree to which resistance to the law reached into the very political infrastructure of Sweetwater County is testimony to the general opposition to Prohibition in Wyoming. It is commonly accepted that "in almost every respect imaginable, Prohibition was a failure." The amendment "encouraged criminality" and "fostered a culture of bribery, blackmail, and official corruption."[41]

Besides saloon owners, other Italian immigrants established more acceptable retail businesses in Wyoming. Worth noting, the aforementioned Sicilian Paul Milatzo arrived in the United States at the age of twenty in 1893. Before his job as interpreter for the railroad, he had opened a shoe store soon after arriving in Cheyenne's Little Italy. Other Italians soon followed his example in the shoe business in Cheyenne. His cousin Vincent, as well as other Sicilian immigrants, Nunzio Pippitone and brothers Carl and Peter Rizzuto, all opened shoe businesses. Owned and operated by the family, Milatzo's shoe store continued until the 1990s. He distinguished himself as an Italian community leader. While working on the railroad, he also served as a liaison between management and labor to help settle labor disputes. For 30 years, he served as Italian deputy council.

For his service to the immigrant community and the state in general, he received letters of commendation from Presidents Roosevelt and Taft as well as other dignitaries.[42]

During Wyoming's boom years before 1940, construction was also an industry that attracted immigrants, especially for those with masonry skills. The DiTullio and DeBernardi families became successful contractors. Dino DiTullio's father was a mason and worked on monuments in Utah and Montana. Dino, who came with his father from Molise, later opened a successful construction business in Rock Springs in 1929. George DeBernardi from Piedmont established a cement business in Rock Springs before 1910 and was joined in the business by his sons in the 1940s. It became the DeBernardi Brothers Construction Company and has continued as a family business for more than 105 years and counting. Rocco Costantino was a policeman in Piedmont, but when he arrived, there was no work for an immigrant policeman in the town, so he opened a bakery in Rock Springs. His sons did not follow in his footsteps and chose in later years to open a construction company, the Costantino Brothers Construction Company.[43] The construction industry was one of those ever-growing sectors where men in all towns of the West, regardless of previous experience, were able to find a job, learn the rudimentary skills needed, and then establish their own companies.

Professions and Politics

As Italians in Wyoming succeeded in their various jobs and businesses, they ascended the economic and social ladder and were quick to assimilate into Wyoming professional life. Tyroleans Lino Menghini and Olivo Bertagnolli became bankers, Rinaldo Menghini a dentist, Frank French a high school principal, and Fred Magagna a real-estate salesman. Celeste Roncalio's father was a miner and on the side a junk dealer. As a boy, Celeste had two jobs, one as a pushcart operator and the other as a shoe-shine boy on the streets of Rock Springs. He managed to graduate from high school, became a reporter for the *Rock Springs Rocket*, and later graduated from college as a journalism major. He went on to earn a law degree and became active in politics. In 1957 he was chairman of the Democratic State Central Committee. He was an avid supporter of Irish American John Kennedy. When Kennedy was elected president, he appointed Roncalio chairman of the United States Section of the International Commission. But Roncalio's political activism predated his official positions. In 1954, while having lunch in Cheyenne's Plains Hotel, Roncalio watched as an African American serviceman and his wife entered the café and seated themselves. To his disgust and that of his colleague, they observed the waitress as she snatched the menus from their hands and as the manager ushered the two African Americans out of the restaurant.[44]

The injustice infuriated Roncalio and his colleague Dr. Francis Barrett, son of Republican senator Frank A. Barrett. Both were appalled that an African American who had served his country could not sit peacefully and have lunch in a restaurant. Their appeals to the management of the restaurant fell on deaf ears. Undaunted, Roncalio took the matter to the Wyoming Democratic Party. He and a coalition that included his father wrote and passed the Wyoming Civil Rights Act of 1957. In the process, Roncalio linked the discrimination against African Americans to the treatment historically of Native Americans in Wyoming. In the midst of the African American civil rights movement at the time, Roncalio's 1957 state law was a significant step toward federal legislation that would one day override state discrimination. While building on the Supreme Court's 1954 *Brown v. Board of Education*, the Wyoming act was as well a significant step toward the Civil Rights Act of 1964 passed by the Johnson administration.[45]

E. D. (Ted) Crippa became another distinguished politician and businessman in Wyoming. Born in Rock Springs in 1889, he was the son of immigrant parents from the Tyrol region. He owned the Ford-Lincoln automobile dealership in Sweetwater County and served as president in 1926 of the Union Mercantile Company and as secretary and manager of the Rock Springs branch of the company from 1921 to 1934. He was also director of the North Side Bank and director of the Rock Springs Fuel Company, a coal mine. His political career began at the age of twenty-one, when he was elected to the local precinct committee. Thereafter, he served sixteen years as chair of the Republican Party in Sweetwater County. Active all his life in Republican politics, he served as a US senator in 1954 when Governor C. J. Rogers appointed him to complete the term of L. C. Hunt.[46]

Other Tyroleans distinguished themselves in Wyoming politics. Rudolph Anselmi, son of Joe Anselmi and Mary Menghini Anselmi, served as a Wyoming state senator from 1937 to 1950. Active in Democratic politics all his life, Rudolph was also manager of the North Side Bank in Rock Springs. Born in 1888, Victor Facinelli, a graduate of the University of Wyoming, had a distinguished career in banking in Rock Springs.

Edwin Magagna graduated from Creighton University Law School in 1931 and served as city attorney for Cheyenne, Rock Springs, and Superior. Giovanni Rizzi, born in 1884, served as mayor, councilman, and trustee of the school district in Kemmerer.[47]

The Tyroleans' political success was not coincidental. The Tyroleans maintained a tight grip on the social capital generated within their community. Not only did they own and operate such businesses as the North Side Bank and the Union Mercantile Company, they were careful to hire only Tyrolean directors and managers. Crippa, Facinelli, Anselmi, and other Tyroleans were among their many directors and presidents. They protected their business interests, which allowed them to expand their economic and political influence through the election of Tyroleans to municipal, state, and federal positions. Tyroleans became members and officers of the Lions, Moose, Elks, and Knights of Columbus organizations in Sweetwater County. Some, like Facinelli, remained close to their Italian heritage by being inducted into such Italian-based organizations as the Order of the Crown of Italy. Like A. P. Giannini in California, the Tyroleans in Wyoming financed not only other Tyrolean businesses but other Italian and immigrant businesses in the state as well. Although they would never succeed in banking to the degree that Giannini did with the Bank of America, with their success they burnished the public image of all Italians and other immigrants in Wyoming.

Mutual-Aid Societies and Churches

Mutual-aid and cultural societies cannot be underestimated in their contributions to immigrant communities. They provided a safety net for their members, while cultural organizations provided much-needed community cohesion for immigrants far from their homeland. Regional societies often reflected not only individuals' celebration of their identity but also the members' nostalgia for that irretrievable Old World culture that they had left behind. In Rock Springs, the Tyroleans established the Andrea Hoffer Society, admitting only Tyroleans. However, by 1906 the Sunrise-Hartville Italian community established the Dante Alighieri Society, which promoted Italian culture and social networking for the community at large.[48]

In addition to the Dante Alighieri and Andrea Hoffer associations, Rock Springs had numerous aid societies: the Rock Springs Italo-American Society, Alphonso Lamarmora Society, Cristoforo Colombo Society,

Giorgio Washington Society, Italian Legion, and Francesco Giuseppe Society. Typically, these mutual-aid societies provided the affected families one dollar a day for six months and then fifty cents a day for the remainder of the year. Although assistance usually ended the first year, desperate families could apply for an extension of benefits. Societies also provided a hundred dollars for funeral expenses. The need for these societies began to decline by the 1930s, as unions pressured mining management to provide a wider slate of benefits for the miners. By 1931 three of the societies with declining membership—the Cristoforo Colombo, Giorgio Washington, and Francesco Giuseppe Societies—merged to form the Italo-American Benevolent Society in Rock Springs. By this time, Italian men, because of their success, had other options and were beginning to be accepted into the local late-generation clubs such as the Elks, the Moose, and other civic organizations.[49]

Churches also provided immigrant settlements with a sense of community and solidarity. Often, urban churches catered to homogeneous groups, such as Irish, Italian, and other Catholic groups. Also, small homogeneous immigrant communities could not support parishes. As a result, the two Catholic churches in Rock Springs were a mixture of Irish, Mexican, Italian, and eastern European. Italians attended both the Southern Side and the North Side Catholic churches. Only once in Rock Springs, from 1905 to 1907, did the Italians have an Italian priest. This multicultural mix helped all groups to assimilate more comfortably into American culture. However, the tight-knit Tyroleans rebelled against the church's insensitivity to their dialect group and formed a Masonic lodge.[50] They were determined not to allow their heritage to be so easily erased.

Late-Generation Revival

Once the mines closed, that multinational mining population dispersed to other parts of the state and other regions of the West. By 1938 most of the mining activity in Rock Springs stopped, and by the 1970s Superior had become a ghost town. In Rock Springs, however, descendants remain of that earlier immigrant community. With Rock Springs' current population of more than 23,000 residents, Italians are fourth, at 6 percent of the total population, behind the English (16 percent), Germans (15 percent), and Irish (10 percent). Otherwise, among the approximately fourteen cities in Wyoming with populations of more than 10,000, Italians represent nearly 3 percent of the total population. Overall, Wyoming's Italian American population, 15,286, is about the same as other southwestern and western states. Those claiming Italian heritage support the Italian American Benevolent Society of Rock Springs and at least one chapter of the Order Sons of Italy. The immigrant legacy can be seen in those still family-owned businesses DeBernardi Brothers Construction and Boschetto's European Market and Deli. As Gans argues, it is impossible to quantify what has not yet happened. If history is any indication, the descendants of those original immigrants who settled the state will not easily forget their forebears' contributions to Wyoming.[51]

CHAPTER 7

IDAHO

Black Robes and Native Americans

Idaho's contemporary image as a bastion of intolerance of ethnic diversity obscures the territory's and state's multicultural immigrant heritage. Idaho was no less a settlement ground for the new immigrants than any other state in the Union before 1940. Among the first was a small group of English fur traders who settled the region in the 1850s. At about the same time, government soldiers, composed largely of Irish and German immigrants stationed at Fort Boise before 1860, remained in the territory after their service. The discovery of gold brought an additional wave of British islanders, who by the 1880s composed half of the miners in Wood River, known today as Blaine County. During the following decades up to 1920, a workforce of Italians, Greeks, Portuguese, Scandinavians, Chinese, Syrians, Lebanese, Japanese, French Canadians, Basques, and others settled the state.[1]

Before the initial wave of European and Mexican settlers, Italian Jesuits had arrived in the territory in 1842. By 1850 Jesuit Anthony Ravalli from Ferrara arrived at the Coeur d'Alene Mission in the Idaho Territory, where he built, with Native American labor, the Sacred Heart Mission Church and surrounding buildings, today the oldest buildings in Idaho. Included among the early priests to settle the area were Italian Jesuits Joseph M. Cataldo, Alexander Diomedi, Joseph Giorda, and Joseph Caruana from Malta. The black robes proselytized, no doubt their official mission as Jesuits, but they also befriended the Native American population. One Jesuit priest who visited the Nez Perce and Ponca people in 1879 quoted Chief Joseph of the Nez Perce as saying, "Cataldo is my friend, he is a good man, all my people love him and I would wish very much to see him once more." Their work in the region often crossed what is now the contemporary boundaries of the surrounding states, Washington, Oregon, Montana, and Idaho. While it is difficult to define precise boundaries for each nation, at least six Native American nations occupied the Idaho Territory, which became a state in 1890.[2]

Although the Jesuits tried to bridge the cultural gap between the indigenous people and immigrants, their efforts were doomed to failure. In the midst of the growing conflict, the Italian Jesuits saw themselves as religious men who believed that they had the best interests of the Native people at heart. Father Diomedi, for example, who lived and worked in the Upper Columbia River and Coeur d'Alene regions, wrote *Sketches of Modern Indian Life*, published in 1894. In retrospect, however, they intervened in Native American culture in ways that inflicted more damage on them than the Jesuits had realized. They convinced parents to send their children to the local Sisters of Charity Boarding School at De Smet on the Coeur d'Alene Reservation in what is now Benewah County in northern Idaho. At the school, they were "properly" dressed and forbidden to speak their native languages. Their Catholic education disparaged their oral traditions and the Native American family structure. Church officials confiscated Native American sacred religious objects and replaced them with traditional Catholic iconography. Furthering their proselytizing, the Jesuits translated sections of the Bible into Native American languages.[3]

Italian Jesuits played a pivotal role during the critical years of the Indian Wars (1855–58). Recognizing the potential for conflict and violence between the incoming settlers and the Native people of the area, the Jesuits counseled the various nations to remain peaceful and to accept treaties, even though the terms of the treaties were unfair to Native Americans. As a result, Native people felt that the Jesuits were pressuring them to agree to treaties that only compromised their bargaining positions. Two infamous massacres—Wounded Knee on December 29, 1890, in South Dakota, where 146 Oglala Sioux died, and the 1864 Sand Creek Massacre, where 130 Cheyenne and Arapaho died—have overshadowed Idaho's equally tragic Battle of Bear River, where in 1863 government troops killed more than 368 Native Americans, including women and children. By the turn of the century, a decade after the territory became a state in 1890, Native Americans' original ancestral lands of more than 60 million acres had been reduced to little more than 3.2 million acres of restricted reservation land.[4]

Railroads and Mining

Adding to the Jesuits' doomed peace efforts and Native American removal, gold fever brought thousands of miners to Boise between 1863 and 1886. Those original miners then sold out their nearly exhausted claims to Chinese immigrants, who had developed labor-intensive techniques to extract the remaining gold. By 1870 two Chinese labor-contracting agencies, part of the network of Six Companies, brought 4,274 Chinese workers to the territory. They composed 33 percent of the territory's total population and 60 percent of the miners. By 1892 there were more than 3,500 Japanese in Idaho. Few were in mining; instead, Japanese labor contractors recruited them for railroad and agricultural work, mainly the state's sugar-beet fields, where they were paid from $1.10 to $1.50 a day, the standard wage for unskilled agricultural labor at the time. The majority of the jobs for immigrants were in the timber industry, mining, and railroad work. At $1.30 a day, workers dynamited for roadways, laid tracks, and repaired existing lines. As one Greek immigrant explained, "It was hard work. There was no machinery.... It was all hand work and it required lots of men...to build a road. We had to work with pick and shovel and whatever they had. And if they wanted it against the mountain or something, they had to blast with the dynamite and then level it off with the pick and shovel."[5]

The Boise Basin in Boise County began as a mining region as early as 1860, when a workforce of French Canadians came to work in the mines. The region had a plethora of mines: silver, coal, gold, lead, and quartz. Between 1870 and 1880, most of the miners drawn to Idaho's mining camps were Irish. From 1880 until 1906, the Welsh dominated the mining camps around Wardner and Kellogg, Shoshone County. They were joined by a contingent of Cornish miners working in the mines at Gibbonsville in Lemhi County. In Loon Creek, Idaho County, Mexican immigrants, who had settled the territory as early as the 1860s during the gold rush, worked in quartz mines located along the Salmon River. A small number of African Americans worked in the northern Idaho mines.[6]

By 1900 there were 779 Italians in Idaho. By 1910 this number grew to 2,627 Italians, 6 percent of the state's foreign born. In 1910 the largest concentrations of Italians were in the far-northern counties of Bonner (113), Nez Perce (202), and Shoshone (373) and to the south in Lincoln (216). These counties were mining (gold, silver, and coal) and railroad centers. Arriving late after the mining boom in the state, only a small number of Italians worked in area mines between 1890 and 1920. In certain mining areas, however, Italians were a noticeable presence. By 1890 Kellogg and Wallace, for example, both in Shoshone County, represented 8 percent of the miners, which accounts for Shoshone's high number of Italians by 1910. Otherwise, the majority of Italians established farms, ranches, and businesses, in addition to working on the railroad.[7] If Italians had worked in mining in other states such as Colorado or Utah, that was reason enough for them to avoid the dangerous conditions in the mines and to seek other means of employment.

Commerce and Enclaves

While mining and railroad companies in cooperation with labor agents might have been the chief labor source for the initial population of Italians in the territory, secondary and chain migration soon became important factors in drawing additional free-labor Italians to Idaho. Frank Sala, for example, worked in the Michigan and Wisconsin mines before his father influenced him to move to Burke, Idaho, in Shoshone County, where his uncle was a blacksmith in the Poorman Mine. One group of Italian immigrants migrated from the Pennsylvania coalfields, while another group entered Idaho illegally from Canada after working in the Canadian mining and timber industries.[8]

Italians began farming and opening businesses in the enclave centers that serviced the immigrant population. By 1910 Wallace in northern Shoshone County was the settlement of a significant Italian population. By the mid-1920s the Italian community was large enough to fund the building of the St. Alphonsus Catholic Church and to establish the Knights of Columbus fraternal organization. The northern end of the town was largely Italian and where George and Dan Albertini established a grocery business. Both brothers began as miners before beginning their grocery store and later investing in commercial real estate in Wallace. For their produce the Albertini brothers relied on Charles Pastori and Mr. Zunino, both of whom had small truck farms in the area. Pastori and Zunino did masonry on the side to supplement their incomes.[9]

Another settlement was in Pocatello, the county seat of Bannock County. In 1910 the county had a population of 9,242, and by 1920 it had grown to 27,532 residents, with a foreign-born population of 1,837 immigrants, 6.6 percent of its population. Pocatello attracted the highest number of Italians, 284, more than 15 percent of the foreign born and a little more than 1 percent of the county's total population. In addition to mining, the town benefited from the junction of two rail lines, the Montana and Idaho legs of the Oregon Short Line, which provided jobs for the skilled and unskilled labor market, Italians included. Besides Pocatello, by 1920 Italian immigrants had spread throughout the state, from Bonners Ferry, Naples, Kellogg, Wallace, Priest River, and Mullan Village in the northern counties to Lava Hot Springs and Roston on the southern border of the state. Wherever they settled, they were numerous enough to form identifiable enclaves labeled Dago Point or Dago Peak by the established late-generation population.[10]

Like so many other towns in Idaho, Pocatello became a roaring boomtown. Nearly every town had at least one saloon, and Pocatello had more than its share of them. Saloons owned by immigrants became social centers for men after a hard day's work in the mines or railroads. There were few regulations on the liquor industry, though that would soon change. Many of the liquor products, either locally produced or imported from adjoining states, indicated the quality of the product the men consumed: "extract of scorpions," "forty-rod," "panther sweat," "tonsil paint," "stagger soup," and "milk of the wild cow." One mining boomtown, Sawtooth, only a year after its founding, had twenty saloons out of only forty-one retail establishments. But public drunkenness and other problems associated with saloons would soon rile the conservative, established residents of the state. In November 1916, the voters officially declared Idaho a dry state. The state law effectively cut off a chief source of revenue for the local immigrant population. Idaho's self-imposed dry status and later the Eighteenth Amendment had the usual results. As soon as Idaho declared itself dry, a thriving bootleg business developed to service the thirsty immigrant population.[11]

Because of what observers believed was Italians' cultural inclination toward strong drink, locals often singled them out as the most resistant to the state law and Prohibition. As one commentator at the time wrote, "People of this type [Italians], who are otherwise law-abiding and patriotic and well-intentioned, protect bootleggers and otherwise violate the Volstead Act with the same faith in the justice of their actions that a group of Middle Western Americans would have in evading a law that prohibited them from planting corn."[12] The writer was correct in his assumption that wine and other spirits were an integral part of Catholic Italians' cultural heritage, which Prohibitionists and nativists feared would influence and transform American culture for the worse.

Reinforcing locals' image of Italians, in Wallace each year a produce agent imported sixty tons of grapes from the Pacific Fruit Company in California to meet the winemaking needs of the area's Italian population. Each family made about 150 gallons for its annual consumption. To avoid detection, Wallace Italians picked up their grapes at midnight or later. There were small distributors in the state as well. Adelmo Colaianni began work in the Colorado Springs mines before moving in 1918 to Pocatello, where he worked for his uncle Tony Colaianni in his grocery store. During Prohibition he and his uncle imported wine grapes from California and clandestinely sold them to local Italians.[13]

In spite of the state's restrictions on liquor, the dynamic nature of the enclave economy allowed legitimate businesses to flourish. In addition to Colaianni in Pocatello, Sam Guido, Vito Cuoio, husband and wife Ferdinand and Maria Lombardi, and Gaetano Valentine owned grocery stores. For their chiefly Italian clientele, the grocery-store owners imported Italian products such as olive oil, pasta, canned tomatoes, olives, and meat. But immigrant labor did not always follow what had become predictable retail occupations. Mike Bosco, for example, earned a living by collecting the town's garbage and selling it to Italian farmers for their pigs. This work sustained him until he found a job as the gardener for the university. In honor of his service to the community, Pocatello named Bosco Park after him.[14]

During this period, the local St. Joseph's Church in Pocatello became the center of the Italian settlement. They honored St. Anthony with an annual festival on June 10 of each year. The Italian parishioners also established a Cristobal Columbus Lodge and raised funds to build a center for their meetings and activities. The fact that they were able to fund construction of the lodge is a sign of the quick success of the Italian community in their work as farmers, entrepreneurs, railroad workers, and miners. The Italians lived in the neighborhood on the east side of the town, referred to by the local nonimmigrant population as the "League of Nations," an ethnically diverse neighborhood that included African Americans.[15]

The railroad attracted many Italian workers to Priest River, Bonner County, north of Pocatello. In the early 1890s, six Calabrese brothers from the Naccarato family settled near Priest River to work on the Great Northern Railway. In typical fashion, one brother came first and then sent for the other five. In addition to providing jobs on the railroad, Priest River was a center for the production of railroad ties. Many of the Italians were former sawmill workers and brought with them to Priest River their milling expertise. The Italians concentrated on the south side of the town, an area known as "the Italian settlement" by the 1890s. Leaving railroad work, one brother, Tony Naccarato, opened a general store, while other Italians established ranches and farms on the outskirts of the small settlement. Numbering about fifty Italians, in 1915 the community funded the building of St. Anthony's Mission Church, presided over by an Italian Jesuit.

The community built as well an adjoining school where nuns came in the summer to help prepare the community's children for communion and confirmation. St. Anthony's became the cultural focal point for Italians, while the schoolhouse doubled as a location for weddings, social events, and feast-day celebrations. It was a close-knit community that, according to one resident, "was just like being back home in Italy."[16]

Farming

Before the arrival of immigrants, Native Americans had planted fruit trees in adjacent Whitman County in Washington. Building on what Native Americans had demonstrated was possible in the Idaho climate and soil, immigrants established fruit and vegetable farms. By 1920 Italians were spread out in small numbers throughout Idaho's forty-four counties. Boundary, Benewah, and Latah Counties had approximately fifty Italian settlers each. Kootenai and Bonner Counties each contained about one hundred Italians. These northern counties were the location of numerous far-flung small towns that initially provided Italians with a limited market for their farm products. Aiding their settlement in the region, some Italians acquired land from the Great Northern Railway. A community of Italians also settled south, near Lewiston, Nez Perce County, along the Washington and Oregon borders, where they established farms along the Clearwater River. In Lewiston, Frank Speno and his parents and John and Phoebe Paffile ran vegetable and fruit farms. Initially, farmers in the counties north of Nez Perce were forced to truck much of their produce to Moscow, Idaho, and across the state line to Pullman, Washington. However, when the region's production in both neighboring Washington and in the northern counties in Idaho grew large enough, growers lobbied railroad companies to bring a line into the area to transport their products to eastern markets. The Oregon Railway and the Northern Pacific won the rights to the area, and railroad management recruited Italian and Greek immigrants to lay the tracks.[17]

While farming provided some with a reasonable income, the state's farms did not excel in agricultural production. Farmers harvested only a fraction of the grape tonnage that California produced annually. Farmers had an equally low harvest of fruits and vegetables. Idaho ranked seventh among western states in number of farms and in farm production, ahead of Alaska, Wyoming, and New Mexico. By 1920 the state had little more than forty-two thousand farms covering only about 16 percent of its land.

It had a high rate of tenant farmers to farm ownership, nearly 50 percent. Compatible with the climate, cattle ranching and dairy farms were the state's main agricultural enterprises.[18] Italians were able to find a more favorable agricultural industry in other states.

Potlatch Lumber Company

Among the most important industries for Italians in Idaho was the Potlatch Lumber Company, located in Latah County in northwestern Idaho. Established in 1903, within a year the lumber company completed the building of the "largest white pine mill in the world." In the mining town of Dawson, New Mexico, the Phelps Dodge Company had set out to build a model company town for its workers. Likewise, Potlatch's intent was to make a contribution to the community by creating an orderly social environment in its company town and by paying workers a decent wage. To help the company enforce appropriate social and moral behavior, manager William Deary considered the best workers to be either American or northern European, specifically Norwegians, Danes, and Swedes. To that end, the company hired employment agencies in Spokane that specialized in recruiting "white men," a term that did not apply to Greeks, Italians, or Japanese. One agency, the All Nations Employment Agency, placed a coded message on its letterhead: "Scandinavian Labor is our Specialty." The company's manager wrote to Potlatch supervisor Mark Seymour, "As you are aware, this class of men are [*sic*] appreciated all over the continent for their ability, willingness and steady work." But when the Northwestern Employment Agency could not provide enough northern Europeans, supervisor Seymour conceded, "If you cannot get White men for Common Labor you may send five or six good Greeks or Italians." Unable to hire sufficient numbers of northern Europeans, by 1908 the company began to hire Japanese, Italians, and Greeks to meet the number of workers needed in the mill and to harvest the eastern Palouse's white-pine forests.[19]

To fulfill its commitment to create a well-organized company town, by 1906 the company built 128 workers' houses, two boardinghouses, two schools, a hotel, a store, a bank, a post office, and an opera house. It also built two churches, one Protestant and one Catholic. The town soon became a multinational settlement. Greek, Italian, Scandinavian, and Japanese neighborhoods developed on the north side of town, which also had an interfaith Union Church. Saloons were disallowed and gambling forbidden in the rooming and bunkhouses. Management did not want company housing to become bachelor quarters where in their idle time young single men hung out, caroused in the company-owned neighborhood, and drank illegal beverages.[20]

In spite of the company's best efforts to create a satisfied workforce, Italians and other workers staged a work slowdown for higher wages in 1907. Successfully resisting their demands, managers told supervisors to "get rid of as many single men as possible and replace them with familied [*sic*] men...men who would be apt to be with you when you have...need for them." Thereafter, bachelors were the first to be fired and the last to be hired.[21]

In the company housing, Greeks, Italians, and Japanese were segregated from northern European families. As one local resident explained, "There weren't any of the Greeks or Italians or the Japs that lived in the town itself." They lived in housing at the bottom of the hill in neighborhoods known as Greek Town, Jap Town, and Dago Town. The top of the hill was known as Nob Hill, the higher-rent neighborhood reserved for the better class of people in Potlatch. The company insisted that the various ethnic groups preferred to live in their segregated quarters. As one resident said, reflecting the town's general attitude toward immigrants, "In those unself-conscious days we thought they preferred to stay down there." When immigrant families ventured out of their neighborhoods, they were not always welcomed at the company's Catholic church, where "snooty women that went to church there...didn't want to mingle with" the immigrant families. In their neighborhoods, immigrants maintained many of their traditional folkways. Against company rules, Italians surreptitiously made wine. Most important, the rents were lower in the immigrant section of the company town. To aid in creating a unified, stable workforce, the company sponsored evening Americanization and English classes, including naturalization classes for its workers. Management was in step with the national policy of assimilation of America's immigrant workforce.[22]

The lumber company also built an Elk River location in Clearwater County, where the company directed some of its Italian and Yugoslavian applicants. By 1920 Elk River had attracted 847 residents, all reliant in some form on the lumber company. However, the availability of jobs in the lumber industry did not last. By 1932 and the height of the Great Depression, both the Potlatch and the Elk River locations were closed.[23] By then, the immigrants had long since benefited from the jobs created by Potlatch, and the free-labor workers took their savings and moved to other regions of the West with their families.

Approximately three hundred miles south of Potlatch, Boise, the state capital, became an important immigrant center. Because of early Chinese settlement in the territory, Boise already had a well-established and thriving Chinatown by 1890. However, Boise had few Italian immigrants during their peak years of settlement in the state. Ada County, where Boise is located, counted 2,927 foreign born, with only 25 Italians in 1920. Boise had only 10 Italians at the time, down from 20 in 1910. Jobs in the rail industry, mining, timber, and mills had taken Italians to other regions of the state. In 1906 Bishop Alphonse J. Glorieux, bishop of the Diocese of Boise, began the construction of the Cathedral of St. John the Evangelist. With so few Italians in Boise, the cathedral was built to accommodate a broad range of immigrant Catholics, German and Irish among them. It took builders a decade to complete the stately Romanesque cathedral, which is still standing on Eighth Street. The architects were of French and German descent, while the stone setter for the cathedral's marble was Italian, Enrico Tonegatti. Little is known about Tonegatti other than that he likely came from northern Italy.[24]

Even though Idaho's foreign-born population more than doubled between 1890 and 1910, from to 17,456 to 42,578, by 1920 there was a sudden reversal. Adding to Italians' exodus from the state, in 1922 workers struck, this time with disastrous consequences, in several construction and mining sites. Italians not only supported the strikes, but were often portrayed as leaders in many of the local union chapters. When the workers lost the strikes, many, especially those perceived to be the leaders, were summarily blacklisted and unable to regain their jobs. By one account, in the wake of the nationwide railroad strike in Pocatello, many were blacklisted and forced to leave Idaho. As a result, many Italians moved to Oakland, California, where there was a large Italian settlement.[25]

But Italians, Greeks, and Chinese had already begun to leave the state even before the failed strikes. The beginning of World War I, the closing of the Potlatch Mill, and the Great Depression were all factors contributing to the decline of the immigrant population in the state. In addition, the construction of the major rail lines servicing the state had also been completed. From 1920 to 1940, the foreign-born population dropped from 40,747 to 24,712. By the 1930s and the beginning of the Great Depression, the number of Italians fell to 1,153.[26] The immigrant exodus from the state eventually gave rise to the incorrect belief after 1945 that Idaho had always been an ethnically homogeneous population, composed largely of late-generation northern Europeans.

Other parts of the West provided immigrants with a plethora of job opportunities. Free-labor immigrants took their savings and skills and moved on to more promising regions. Between 1914 and 1917, as the US involvement in World War I approached, coal-mining wages in Colorado and Utah rose to nearly eight dollars a day for experienced miners. Like the West's many Chinatowns, thriving Little Italys from Seattle and Portland to San Francisco, Oakland, San Jose, Fresno, Los Angeles, and San Diego provided an abundance of farming and enclave opportunities for the Italian immigrant. There remained available cheap land in Washington, Oregon, Nevada, and California. Jobs in agricultural field work, canneries, and packinghouses were abundant, from Walla Walla and Seattle to the Sacramento, San Joaquin, and Salinas Valleys. By 1920 Italians dominated the California fishing industry, from San Francisco, Monterey, and Santa Cruz to San Pedro and San Diego, all surrounded by thriving Italian communities.

Late-Generation Revival

Although few Italians remained in Idaho, the Italian families that did remain left a legacy. Today Idaho has 34,553 Italian Americans, roughly 2.7 percent of its population, and ranks thirty-ninth among the states in total population of Italian Americans. In spite of the small number of Italian immigrants who originally settled Boise, the Italian American population in Boise is approximately 6,300, about 3 percent of the total population. Otherwise, a review of the distribution of the Italian American population throughout Idaho today demonstrates relatively the same pattern that existed before World War I. Italian Americans are spread out across the state in small numbers, never much exceeding the statewide 3 percent, except in some smaller hamlets. Priest River, for example, with a population of 6,283, has 5.6 percent, about 350 Italian Americans. That early settlement Coeur d'Alene has a 3 percent Italian American population out of a total population of 44,777. Pocatello and Lewiston, once important Italian immigrant settlements, today have 2.8 percent and 2.3 percent Italian Americans, respectively.[27]

The state has an active chapter of the Order Sons of Italy, called the North Idaho American Italian Lodge, established in 2004 and located in

Post Falls in Kootenai County. It is a part of an umbrella Order Sons of Italy group called the Grand Lodge of the North West that has nineteen chapters in Idaho, Washington, and Oregon. In 1920 Post Falls Village had 576 Italian immigrants. Today, with a population of 27,385, Post Falls has one of the largest percentages, 4.6 percent, or 1,267 residents who now identify themselves as Italian Americans. Established in 1975, the Italian American Club of Boise sponsors a variety of activities, including Italian-language classes. The recent establishment of Italian cultural organizations is evidence of how ethnic consciousness has evolved over the past fifty years for Italian Americans. It is impossible to say when or how a new ethnic organization will form, especially those transnational business associations seeking to establish trade relationships with Italian businesses in Italy. In addition, with high unemployment for Italian youth under thirty-five in Italy, Italians with technical skills continue to come to the United States. This new immigration does open further opportunities for transnational business associations.[28] These new arrivals often serve as the nucleus of new organizations. Whatever the cause, Italian immigration to early Idaho remains for these cultural and business organizations the origin of their Italian heritage.

III

THE NORTH OF THE WEST

CHAPTER 8

MONTANA

Jesuits and Native Americans

The Italian settlement of Montana was much like the settlement of neighboring Idaho. It began with the migration of a phalanx of Jesuit priests whose mission was to bring Christianity to the Native populations and to convert as many as possible to Catholicism. But in the process, many Jesuits became assimilated into Native American culture and came to understand and respect many of their traditional beliefs and practices. Between 1840 and 1900, approximately seventy priests and lay brothers came to the Northwest region, including Montana. Distinguished among these early Jesuits was twenty-nine-year-old linguist Gregorio Mengarini, who wrote *A Selish or Flat-Head Grammar* in 1861 and followed that work in 1877 with a dictionary, *A Kalispel or Flat-Head Indian Language.* While he had knowledge of European medicine, he also became a well-informed practitioner of Native American medicine and herbalism.[1]

Following in Father Mengarini's footsteps was Father Anthony Ravalli, Montana's first pharmacist and medical authority. An accomplished craftsman, painter, and musician, he arrived in Montana in 1845 and later served at St. Mary's Church at Fort Colville in present-day Ravalli County and then became president of California's Santa Clara College in California. He brought with him to the West an extraordinary set of skills. For St. Mary's Church, he built "an unlikely baroque structure ninety feet long and sixty feet high...of hewn timber, completely without nails." Three distinguished linguists followed Father Ravalli. While he ministered to the spiritual needs of some of Montana's wildest mining towns known for their violence, lawlessness, and prostitution, Father Giuseppe Giorda delivered his sermons in six languages, including Nez Perce, Flathead, and Blackfoot. Father Philip Canestrelli wrote *A Kootenai Grammar* in 1894, and Father Anthony Morvillo published *A Dictionary of the Numípu or Nez Perce Language* in 1895. Without these works, Native American languages would have been lost to future generations of Native Americans as well as to linguistic scholars. Adding to their influence, because of the trust that Giorda was able to build with the indigenous population, Native American leaders asked him to act as a negotiator during the Nez Perce War of 1877.[2]

Other priests left informative historical accounts of life in the Montana Territory. Father Philip Rappagliosi's published letters provide a detailed description of Flathead daily life in the Bitterroot Valley. Father Lawrence Palladino wrote an account of the interaction between European settlers and the Native American population. In his academic career, he was professor of Latin and Greek at St. Ignatius College in San Francisco and the University of Santa Clara as well as president of Gonzaga University in Spokane. In many cases, the first wave of Catholic immigrants began to form around the early churches that the Jesuits built. These seemingly inconsequential settlements provided an important link for new immigrants between their Old World culture and their transition into a new way of life in the West.[3]

Mining and Industry

In the wake of these black robes, in the 1870s Italian immigrants began settling Montana. To attract immigrants, in 1872 Montana established the Montana Immigration Society, which advertised for northern European workers. While Chinese labor contractors brought in a nominal number of Chinese to work in Butte's gold mines as early as the 1870s, Butte's Anaconda Copper Mining Company located in Silver Bow County also drew several thousand immigrants to the Montana Territory before it became a state in 1889. By the 1880s, the Great Western Labor Bureau began recruiting hundreds of laborers from Mexico for the Montana sugar-beet industry. About the same time, labor contractor Christian Yegen brought the first Italian Swiss into the county to work the coal mines in Billings and Red Lodge. But there were not many Italians in these remote mining centers. By 1920 Billings, Missoula, Anaconda, and Great Falls attracted 11,459 foreign born but fewer than 400 Italians, with Anaconda at 163 and the others with fewer than 100 Italians.[4]

By 1910 the state had the greatest number of immigrants among the mountain states. By 1916 there were more than 14,500 miners working in the interconnected honeycomb of mines under Butte. The Irish composed the largest foreign born in the mines. They were aided in their efforts by Irishman Marcus Daly, an influential mine owner and operator who preferred to hire only Irish miners to work in his copper mines in Butte. After the settlement of the first wave of Irish immigrants, chain migration then became the principal means of attracting a fresh supply of Irish labor to Butte, which became one of the most prosperous mining regions in the West. Once settled, Irish sent train and steamship tickets home to relatives in Ireland when jobs opened up at the Anaconda copper mine. At $3.50 per day, the wages were high relative to the cost of living. Mining wages were on average more than 30 percent higher than industrial work at the time in eastern and northeastern cities, where the cost of living was considerably higher.[5]

By the turn of the century, there were only 188 Italian immigrants in Butte out of a population of about 10,000. By 1920 immigrant workers and their children made up more than 70 percent of Butte's residents. In 1920 the total foreign-born European population in Silver Bow County, which included Butte, stood at 17,343. Initially, Italians arrived in Butte as linemen for the railroad and later found work in the mines. By 1920 Italians, numbering 3,842, were eighth in foreign born in Montana. They were more than 4 percent of the state's immigrant population, 93,620, which represented 17 percent of the state's total population. Italians spread out across Montana's mining counties, with the largest numbers in Silver Bow County (964), Carbon County (450), and Cascade County (455).[6]

Montana shared in the labor strife that afflicted other western mining states, but in a slightly different way. In 1878 management attempted to lower wages in the Alice and Lexington silver mines from $3.50 to $3.00 a day. Using the Nevada Comstock Lode union bylaws, miners formed the Butte Workingmen's Union in 1878. Because of their small number, Italians did not assume a leadership role in the union movement, but rather remained supporters among the rank and file. At the time, there was only one nonunion mine, Bluebird. But in what became known as the Bluebird incident, on June 13 on Miners' Day, a group of union members threatened to shut down the mine. Management relented, and Butte became effectively a closed shop. By 1893 Butte miners were influential in forming the Western Federation of Miners, with Butte's designation as Local No. 1. Butte soon earned the reputation in the West as the "Gibraltar of unionism." Aside from internal union politics and some conflicts with management, there was little strife among the multicultural assortment of unionized workers.[7]

However, the mining companies continued to resist unionization. In the wake of the union's success, mining interests began to consolidate their power to resist workers' demands. In 1899 Marcus Daly joined forces with William Rockefeller, Henry Rogers, and Thomas Lawson to form the Amalgamated Copper Mining Company, which soon after changed its name to the Anaconda Mining Company. Anaconda was the fourth-largest corporation in the United States. The four men controlled local, state, and federal legislators whose job it was to oversee mining regulations. As a result of the company's power, the union in the Anaconda mines fragmented and was not able to sustain a united front. Adding to the resistance to union demands, when Standard Oil bought the mining company, the owners began a concerted effort at union busting. In 1912 the company hired the infamous Pinkerton and Thiel agency to infiltrate the union and single out its leaders and foment violence within the union's ranks. In 1912 Standard Oil fired five hundred miners whom they designated socialists and created a blacklist. Their efforts paid dividends. By 1914, frustrated by stagnant wages and their union's inaction, union members stormed their union hall. When the acting mayor of the town appeared at the hall to calm the workers, they threw him out the second-story window. With no agreement in sight, in order to negotiate a settlement, Charles Moyer, president of the Western Federation of Miners, came to town. At a meeting on June 23, 1914, one man was shot and killed by an unknown assailant and the hall dynamited. But the violence did not end there. Three years later, when Frank Little, an organizer for the International Workers of the World, came to town to help quell the labor chaos, one dark night he was brutally beaten and lynched.[8]

The workers continued to demand better working conditions, but the Company, as Anaconda was known locally, refused. In 1920 the workers walked out at the Neversweat Mine owned by the Company. The strike lasted for more than seven months. Events turned violent when the Company again hired the notorious Pinkerton agency, whose guards shot fifteen miners, killing two. This event was labeled Bloody Wednesday on the Anaconda Road. The labor strife did not end in Butte. During a later 1920 strike, President Woodrow Wilson sent in federal troops, and the miners were forced to return to the mines at gunpoint. In the end, the Company exploited the division among the union ranks and refused to recognize the Western Federation of Miners. In Butte, once known as the Gibraltar of unionism, the "era of the closed shop had ended."[9]

With their power and control reestablished, management was more concerned with productivity than safety. To distinguish one mine from the other in the massive honeycomb of shafts under the area, some of the mines were known by such felicitous names as Bell Diamond, Anselma Mountain View, Moonlight, and others. But these names could not mask the harsh reality that work underground was perilous and unpredictable. Deaths in mine explosions increased dramatically when management made the premature decision to begin using explosives in mine operations before operators had established adequate safety measures and training for men assigned to place and detonate the charges. In the hands of inexperienced and untrained miners, explosives were responsible for countless deaths. Making matters worse, unskilled miners were sometimes given the most dangerous jobs. Management's policy was "rock first safety second."[10] Management's calloused view of mine safety was that immigrant miners could always be replaced.

Among the many other ways in which a miner could be injured or killed, because of the instability of Montana's unique geography, falling rocks in the mines became the leading cause of death for miners. Miners were often crushed when they worked hastily in a shaft that was not properly secured with timber supports. The miners called these falling rocks "Duggans," named after a local funeral parlor, Duggan Dolan Mortuary. Even though management was aware of the area's perilous geography in the silver, gold, and copper mines, it did not take any extra measures to guard against falling rocks or cave-ins.[11]

Even if a miner were to escape sudden death or injury by a Duggan, he still might succumb to the more common black lung disease or another respiratory ailment unique to Montana mining. Following the influx of miners into area mines beginning in 1900, a 1914 study of 1,000 miners in Butte found that 40 percent of the miners had chronic respiratory problems. Again, Montana's unique geography played another role in miners' health in the mines. Montana copper, gold, and silver miners suffered from a special lung disease known as "miner's con," which was contracted from the inhalation of quartz dust. It did not take long, working ten-hour shifts six days a week, for miners to begin having respiratory problems that led ultimately to chronic illness and death.[12]

Adding to the dangers in the mines, electricity was introduced into the mines in 1915 to increase miners' productivity and to bring some degree of ventilation to quell the heat and humidity in the shafts. However, management did little to train the inexperienced miners in the safe use of electricity in the gas- and soot-filled shafts. As a result, 5 men were electrocuted in the first year. On June 8, 1917, a crew descended the Granite Mountain shaft to inspect another of the electrical systems. When a careless assistant foreman allowed his lamp to touch a frayed wire, an explosion occurred that swept through the shaft and into the Speculator Mine, ultimately taking the lives of 168 miners, the worst disaster in Montana mining history. Italian miners accounted for approximately 7 of the dead, 2 from one family. Overall, 8 families lost 2 family members, while 1 family lost 3.[13]

As a result, Montana holds a prominent place in the list of states with multiple mine disasters before 1945. Between 1906 and 1925, in Butte alone at least 685 miners were killed and scores more injured or permanently disabled. On April 21, 1893, 9 miners were killed at Silver Bow No. 2. Between 1896 and 1900, there were an additional five major fatal mine disasters in Montana: Neihart, Broadwater Mine Explosion, April 1896 (7); Butte, St. Lawrence and Anaconda Mine fire, November 1889 (6); Aldridge, Montana Coal and Coke Company Accident, August 1900 (1); Butte, Bell Mine Explosion, August 1900 (1); and Anaconda, Stewart Mine Explosion, September 1900 (2). At the Cora Mine on May 12, 1905, an explosion killed 7 miners. At Butte Superior mine on September 3, 1911, 6 miners died in a cage accident, and on April 13, 1913, 5 miners died in a similar accident. Sixteen miners died on October 19, 1915, at the Granite Mountain mine when workers inadvertently discharged dynamite aboveground. In one of the worst disasters, 21 miners died at the Pennsylvania mine in Butte. Mortuary records show that more than 65 miners died in 1916 alone.[14] The recurrence of disasters, especially electrical and equipment malfunctions such as cage accidents (the cage used to lower and lift miners out of the shafts), points to management's general disregard for miners' safety.

Butte and Meaderville—The Enclave Economy

Because of the high wages in the mines, immigrants, including Italians, were willing to take the risk of working underground, at least in the short term. As a result, it did not take long for Italians and other immigrants to create a thriving enclave economy in the mining districts. Workers and entrepreneurs bent on exploiting the rise of the new economy in the mining zone flooded into Butte and Meaderville. In 1874 there were 3,360 residents in Butte, but by 1900 that number had soared to 47,000. The Irish were the largest group in the boom town. By 1915 Butte had about 100,000 residents, including a small community of 192 Italians. At the time, there were more than thirty different nationalities in Butte.[15]

The majority of Italians lived in nearby Meaderville and adjoining neighborhoods surrounding the Berkeley Pit, which were approximately two miles from Butte and its commercial district. The 14,000 to 16,000 miners (the number varies) toiling in the pit in 1920 generated conservatively $1 million a month in earned wages, an astonishing amount of money for a small town. By 1920, 78 percent of Butte's population was under forty-five with little more than 2 percent over sixty-five. Most were single men. As one female resident said, Butte was "typically a man's world." Its streets teemed with a variety of types: men in blue overalls and businessmen in three-piece suits. Flashy gamblers and other men adorned with a rich array of jewelry frequented the town's cafés, dance halls, barbershops, and businesses. Celebrities such as Mark Twain, Sarah Bernhardt, Clark Gable, and Charlie Chaplin performed in Butte's local theater, where they found an enthusiastic audience.[16] It was Montana's version of the Wild West.

Many of the young men arrived in town after working on the railroad or after traveling west on the train from elsewhere in the United States to work in the mines. Without a home or family, these young miners immediately began spending their wages in area businesses. Their sudden arrival also caused a housing shortage and a subsequent housing boom of new construction, further fueling the local economy with more jobs. In fact, Butte became the largest city between Spokane and Minneapolis and Salt Lake City to the south. Not only was the area the copper empire in the Northwest but it also became the most important regional commercial center.[17]

On the west side of the mines were neighborhoods such as Dublin Gulch, Cork Town, Finn Town, Centerville, and Walkerville, populated largely by the English. McQueen became the settlement of a mixture of Austrians, Slovenians, and Croatians. In this multilingual mix, to guard against explosions, companies posted no-smoking signs in sixteen languages in the mines. The zone called Cabbage Patch, on the southeast side of the mines closer to Butte's central business district, was a settlement composed of more than two hundred shacks with no electricity, no running water, and a fetid open sewer that ran through the neighborhood. It became the home of criminals, bootleggers, prostitutes, and new arrivals who lived in twelve-by-twelve single-room shacks. Usually three to a shack, the miners shared beds based on their shifts in the mines. Because of the neighborhood's criminal reputation, respectable residents of Butte and the other mining neighborhoods avoided the area.[18]

With most of Butte's Italian workforce settled in Meaderville, it became known as Little Italy. By the 1920s Meaderville had a lively commercial center, with restaurants, bakeries, cafés, grocery stores, saloons, and even nightclubs. Italians dominated the businesses. The Guidi family and Mike Ciabatarri owned two of the town's five grocery stores. With eight saloons, the downtown area was so lively on Saturday nights that it was called "Little Monte Carlo." Between Butte and Meaderville by 1916, there were fifty-three boardinghouses, run mostly by women. Among them, Mrs. Rippi ran the Broadway Dining Room, while presumably an Italian owned and operated the Florence, which had three hundred beds. Italian Swiss immigrants opened dairies in the countryside surrounding Meaderville. As their numbers increased in Meaderville, Italians demanded their own parish. By 1920 the community funded the building of St. Helena Catholic Church, where Mass was served only in Italian. Holy Savior Church was nearby and serviced the non-Italian population in the area. Children in Butte and Meaderville attended the Holy Savior parochial school or the public Franklin Elementary. Meaderville Italians established a Società Cristoforo Colombo, the first Italian organization in Montana, and later an Italian-American Club. Although working in the mines was dangerous and arduous work, the families lived relatively comfortably compared with other mining centers in the West. Each of these families had space enough around their homes for a garden. Each fall a trainload of grapes came from California, and Italians made their own wine and grappa.[19]

Among the most successful Italians in the area was Dominic Bertoglio. Born in northern Italy in 1871, he arrived in Butte in 1892. Having worked in the mines in Wisconsin and Arizona, he established in 1894 the Bertoglio Mercantile Co., which soon grew into one of the largest merchandise companies in Montana. By 1910 Bertoglio employed more than a dozen members of his family in his widespread business interests. By 1924 he expanded his company and became vice president of Bertoglio and McTaggart, a wholesale distribution business of liquor, wine, and beer as well as domestic supplies. It had sales of more than $750,000 a year. Bertoglio did not limit his business interests to Montana. In addition to acquiring mining property in the state, he was among the founders of the Spokane Telephone Company and was involved in the Tivoli Brewing Company of Butte, the Marconi Wireless Company, and the Patent Plow Point Company of Detroit, Michigan. Civic minded, Bertoglio was also the founder and president of the Meaderville Società Cristoforo Colombo.[20]

In other less populated Montana towns, Italians brought their artisan skills, made a modest living, and often left a legacy of their presence. Before

1920 Michael Jacobucci settled in Columbus, the county seat of Stillwater County, approximately forty miles from Billings. In 1920 Stillwater County had a mere thirty-one Italian immigrants. Jacobucci, who simplified his name to Jacobs, was the principal owner of the Montana Sandstone Company. He and his crew of workers became the most renowned masons in Montana. Before 1930 he and his associate Pasquale Petosa built many private residences and commercial buildings, all still standing and a testimony to Jacobucci's craftsmanship. He became well known throughout the state and was hired to construct buildings in Billings and Butte. His most recognized is the Montana state capitol in Helena. Many of his buildings are on the state's National Register of Historic Places, including Columbus's New Atlas Bar, which Jacobucci built in 1915. His masonry home still stands, and many of the tombstones in the local cemetery are attributed to his company, probably carved by his associate Petosa.[21] From mining to commerce, Italians played a central role in the developing economy throughout Montana.

Women in a Man's Town

Butte's prosperity had its downside. As one evangelist described it, Butte "became the lowest sinkhole in the West." After the young, unmarried miners arrived, so did the prostitutes. Butte's sex trade is another unsavory chapter in the exploitation of women in a male-dominated western boomtown. By the 1890s, Butte's red-light district quickly established a social pecking order, from expensive and moderately priced brothels to the inexpensive "cribs." The Dumas Hotel and the Victoria were two of the higher-priced establishments. The Blue Range was one of the district's "cribs." No matter the clientele that the houses attracted, they were all built by some of Butte's most well-established and wealthiest late-generation citizens. Harry Adams, who managed the Nadeau Investment Company, was known in town as "the 'czar' of the red-light district." The zone was initially located along Mercury and Galena Streets, where it was far too visible for some of Butte's more respectable residents. Alarmed by the growth of this new enterprise in their midst and by Butte's sleazy reputation, the city fathers moved the red-light quarter to a less conspicuous zone, tagged with such sugarcoated names as Pleasant Alley, Fashion Terrace, and Model Terrace. The names and the district's new location did little to curb Butte's reputation. After playing in Butte, Charlie Chaplin in his autobiography callously raved about Butte's beautiful prostitutes and was quick to note with impunity that they ranged in age from teenagers to older women. As another insensitive writer reported at the time, while many were well dressed and pretty in the fancier houses, in the less expensive brothels there were some "tough-looking blisters."[22] Like waste material from the mining process, women in the sex trade became the offal of immigrant success.

Poverty was the engine that fueled the sex trade. These unfortunate women were not challenging the role of women in society or in the tradition-bound Italian family, as did immigrant farmwives, boarding-house owners, shop owners, restaurateurs, and those intrepid frontier nuns. Rather, their role as prostitutes speaks not to women's role in the development of the West but to the patriarchal hierarchy that relegated anonymous, poor women to the margins of enclaves. Chaplin's repellent and insensitive remark about Butte's prostitutes struck at the core of a national problem for poor immigrant and late-generation women at the time. No degree of idealization of the sex trade, especially of some of the prostitutes' and their madams' high earnings, can mitigate the fact that they were marginal, exploited women in the otherwise dynamic immigrant economy around them.[23]

Anti-immigrant factions at the time attempted to gain additional support for their cause by stoking fear over the purportedly large number of "immoral" women entering the United States. Many believed that there was even a well-organized network of procurers who were luring unsuspecting immigrant women into "white slavery." Before World War I, publishers issued more than twenty-two "white slavery" narratives. It is unclear, however, what percentage of the narratives were mere urban folktales or were documented accounts. One government official claimed that there were more than fifty thousand immigrant prostitutes in America from New York to San Francisco and Seattle. However, the more scientific Dillingham Commission, published in 1911, concluded that it was impossible to place a precise figure on the number of immigrant women coerced into the sex trade. The closest that the commission could come was that in an examination of two thousand prostitutes in New York City before 1909, only about 25 percent were foreign born and that perhaps 10 percent of America's prostitutes were victims of some form of "white slavery." The commission concluded that the vast majority of prostitutes were not captured and sold into slavery but were in fact products of impoverished American and immigrant families. The commission reported that many were exploited by unscrupulous men who became their overseers, otherwise known as pimps.[24]

Those women who had fallen on hard times in the West sought prostitution as a way out of their poverty. Although it is difficult to document because of their anonymity, some no doubt were immigrants, possibly Italian. In Pocatello, Idaho, for example, the town's largest brothel, the Sisters Hotel, was managed by Greek immigrant Stella Poulos, who oversaw a group of French and American prostitutes. But the citizenship status of women was less significant than their exploitation. Every evening and well into the morning hours, with disposable cash, Butte's young men patrolled the narrow alleyways of the red-light district, which soon became the venue of choice for pickpockets, thieves, and drug addicts.[25] While Butte earned a special reputation in the West, in reality its red-light district differed little from those in other western states.

Butte's middle class, American and immigrant, however, played a respectable and important role in the town's social and economic development. By 1920 there were nearly 148 men to every 100 women in Butte, about 40 percent of whom were single women. The first- and second-generation women were on the whole well educated, but generally did not find work outside the family. Following the national trend of women's rights and their growing place in American public life, they joined the local charitable associations, became active in the League of Women Voters, and organized theater and other cultural events. Immigrant Serbian women began, for example, the Circle of Serbian Sisters, who sponsored plays and taught Serbian folk songs to a younger generation of unmarried girls. The Order of Vasa worked to pass on Swedish traditions to the younger generation. The first convention of the Montana Federation of Negro Women's Clubs met in Butte in 1921. Most of the names that appear in Butte's social registry were northern European, with few Italian, Mexican, Chinese, or Japanese women involved by the 1920s.[26]

Farming

Besides mining and business opportunities in Montana's boomtowns, Italians in smaller numbers were drawn to the state to farm. To entice immigrants, the Northern Pacific Railroad offered round-trip "excursion tickets" for as little as $49.50 to attract settlers. In the 1880s, the railroad offered land for as little as $2.60 an acre, an extremely low price for western farmlands. Because of the low cost of land, 87 percent of the farms were owner operated, a high percentage in the West. It was equal to Washington's percentage, but much higher than California's owner-occupied farms at 74 percent. However, Italian peasants, even those from northern Italy, were not accustomed to the long, snowbound Montana winters. Some tried farming, but only for a short period before they were drawn to the state's urban centers. The limited growing season and critical lack of irrigation made farming difficult and much less profitable compared with other regions of the West. With the increase in the immigrant population, farmers and ranchers had at least a local market for their produce and meat. By 1920 Montana had 57,647 farms and 35,070,656 acres dedicated to agriculture. While the number of Montana's farms and acres under production was about average for western states such as Colorado, Idaho, Washington, and Oregon, it was dwarfed by California's production, which had more than double the number of farms and more than triple the number of acres under production. Owing to the climate, the largest production in Montana came from dairy farming and ranching, primarily raising swine and cattle, with more than one million cattle on the hoof by 1920.[27]

Late-Generation Revival

As historical sites of the early immigrant communities, two of the oldest early Catholic churches still remain, St. Patrick's, established in 1879, and St. John's, built just before the onset of World War I. In the 1950s, the Anaconda Mining Company began open-pit mining, resulting in the destruction of the Meaderville neighborhood. St. Helena Church was moved to the World Museum of Mining, where it remains as testimony to those early Italians who settled Butte and Meaderville. By 1983 Anaconda closed all operations in Butte.[28]

Nevertheless, many of the original families remained in Montana. Once the dominant immigrant group in the 1920s, Butte's Irish today continue to have a visible social and cultural presence with annual Irish festivals, including Saint Patrick's Day festivities, all supported by active Irish cultural associations. Not all of Meaderville's Italian population moved out of the state. By 1985 those Italian Americans living in the area began to organize luncheons. Determined not to allow their heritage to be erased, organizers did research and created lists of former residents of Meaderville and nearby McQueen and East Butte, and by 2000 they began having reunions.[29]

With increased interest in their Italian heritage, the Montana Italian American population rose from 21,461 in 1990 to 28,000 in 2000, about 3 percent of the state's total population, which is commensurate with percentages in other western states. Montana's population is not immune to the late-generation revival of ethnic identity. While Montana does not have the same dynamic Italian American community as other western states, its percentage of Italian Americans is equal to or more than twenty-three other states in the United States.[30]

CHAPTER 9

ALASKA

Exploration and Settlement

The place of Italians in the history of Alaska begins with explorer Alessandro Malaspina from the Duchy of Parma, which in the late eighteenth century was under the control of Spain. Before sailing west, Malaspina had considerable experience in the Spanish Navy. In 1789 he was dispatched by Spain to undertake a scientific expedition to find another version of the mythical Northwest Passage, this one named the Strait of Anián that would connect the Pacific and Atlantic Oceans. If Spain could make this discovery, it would challenge the hegemony of other countries, namely, the French, English, and Russians.[1]

On July 30, 1789, Malaspina departed from Cadiz in southwestern Spain, and in late spring of 1791 he arrived in Acapulco, Mexico, where he took on board the Reverend Fabio Aliponzoni, an Italian missionary who served as his chaplain. He left Acapulco on May 1 on his journey north to Alaska. Malaspina's mission was successful in dispelling any further speculation about the existence of the Anián passage. Another outcome of the journey was that a Spanish explorer and artist among Malaspina's crew, Tomas de Suria, wrote a detailed description of the local Tlingit people and made the first drawings of the Alaskan coastline. Malaspina's accurate charts and geographical mapping of the coast up to what is today called Prince Albert Sound opened the region for further exploration. Malaspina made an estimate of Mount St. Elias at 5,040 meters. Modern calculations show that he was off by only about 50 meters. He returned to Acapulco and continued with his scientific research while circumnavigating the globe.[2]

Approximately ninety years later, Mount St. Elias attracted Italian alpinist Prince Luigi Amedeo (1873–1933), Duke of Abruzzi and cousin of the king of Italy. In the late eighteenth century, Amedeo led an expedition of eight climbers and scaled Mount St. Elias. They reached the summit in just thirty days on July 31, 1897. European journals, newspapers, and books recounted Amedeo's achievement. Both Malaspina and Amedeo were responsible for exposing the newly explored region to a wider European audience, which ultimately led to the settlement of the region. It was designated at the time as the District of Alaska before it became a territory of the United States in 1912.[3] Alaska would not become a state until 1959.

Amedeo's accomplishment and his celebrity in Europe may well have drawn the attention of many in Europe to the far-northeastern region. However, it was Malaspina's navigational charts that allowed the Jesuit order to be among the first Europeans to arrive and settle Alaska. By 1886 the superior of the Rocky Mountain Province assigned Bishop Charles J. Seghers, the bishop of Victoria, British Columbia, and two Italian Jesuits, Paschal Tosi and Louis Robaut, to the Yukon Basin. Not only were the elements life-threatening in Alaska, it was also a lawless territory that attracted an unsavory assortment of men. The three priests stayed for the winter at Forty Mile, nearly four hundred miles inland from Anchorage. After the spring thaw, Bishop Seghers decided to travel south down the Yukon River with a guide. Unfortunately, the mentally disturbed guide murdered Bishop Seghers somewhere near Nulato, about five hundred miles from Forty Mile. Tosi and Robaut remained and established a mission to continue their work. Soon after, other Jesuits followed and established missions: Holy Cross on the Yukon River, St. Peter Claver at Nulato, and St. Alphonse Rodriguez at Cape Vancouver on Nelson Island.[4]

Some of these early Italian Jesuits became legendary figures for their stamina and love of the outdoors. Among them were Jesuits Father Giovanni L. Lucchesi and Father Joseph Treca, who settled in the region in 1889. Both priests traveled regularly by dogsled between the missions in Akulurak and Nelson Island, more than eighty miles apart. In order to communicate with their potential converts, they learned native languages and compiled dictionaries and grammars of the local native people. Among the skilled linguists was Brother Carmelo Giordano, who arrived in Nulato in 1887. Not a Jesuit, Giordano spoke only his local Italian dialect and had never learned to read or write standard Italian. However, he soon became fluent in the Nulato language. In time, his assimilation into Nulato culture was so complete that he alarmed his superiors, who sent him back to the United States. Within two years, he returned to Alaska, where he spent the rest of his life in service to the indigenous people. Other Jesuits who remained in the wilderness built hospitals and schools for the native population.[5]

Gold and the Immigrant Workforce

In 1880 Joe Juneau and Richard Harris discovered gold in the vicinity of what would become known as Juneau. With the discovery of gold in the Klondike, the rush was on. Northern Europeans formed the majority of the initial wave of immigrants. As occurred elsewhere in North America, the population of native people in Alaska would decline with the settlement of immigrants. At that time, the nonnative population was only 430 settlers, while the native population was 32,996. By 1890, with immigration spurred by both the discovery of gold and the growing commercial fishing industry, the nonnative population grew to 4,298, with a corresponding decline of the native population to 25,354. By 1900 the immigrant and American population stood at 30,450, outnumbering the indigenous population of 29,542. In 1900 there were 438 Italians in Alaska, and by 1910 that number rose to 804, the high point of Italian settlement in the district. The majority were miners who had left jobs in other parts of the Northeast and West. Few had traveled to Alaska directly from Italy.[6]

By 1914 Italian labor contractors hired by owners of Alaskan canneries recruited seasonal fishermen and cannery workers. There was also a network of Asian labor contractors that supplied workers for the canning industry in Alaska and the Northwest. By 1900 there were 7,167 Chinese and Japanese workers employed, more than half of the shore workforce, in salmon canneries from Alaska to Puget Sound and the Columbia River. Over the next three decades, they would make up about one-third of the labor force in Alaskan and northwestern canneries. Those Italians who initially joined the workforce in Alaska were concentrated in the gold-mining camps surrounding "Circle, Council, Eagle, and Fairbanks, as well as along the tributaries of the Chena River, Forty Mile District, Iditarod, and Nome."[7]

Among the first settlers was northern Italian Felice Pedroni, known as Felix Pedro in Alaska. After working in mining in several other western states, he traveled to the Yukon Territory and then finally to Alaska in 1880. With Italian partners, he prospected for gold and explored the Yukon. In 1889 he and his group were the first Europeans to reach the Tanana River in eastern Alaska. While still in the wilderness, Pedroni and his crew of miners were visited by the regional director of the US Geological Survey, Alfred H. Brooks. Brooks gave Pedroni and his group additional maps that allowed them to explore other parts of the district.

By 1901 Pedroni reached the Chena River farther to the north, near the headwaters of the Tanana River. Their explorations were instrumental in providing more complete maps of the region. They did find some gold and did stake a claim on Pedro Creek in central Alaska just northeast of Fairbanks. Pedroni's claim to fame in Alaska was his role in 1902 in establishing and naming Fairbanks as a permanent settlement in the district. While continuing to work on his various claims in the area, Pedroni lived the rest of his life in Fairbanks. At the time of his death in 1910, he was honored by the community as the founder of Fairbanks.[8]

Railroads and Mining

Like Pedroni, few if any Italians ever struck it rich in the Klondike or elsewhere in Alaska. Rather, Italians and other immigrants soon found that work on the railroad and in other industries was more financially rewarding than the pipe dream of sudden riches in Alaska's goldfields. Alaska relied on the railroad to bring cheap labor to the region and to open markets in the United States for its resources, principally fisheries, minerals, and timber. In 1887 Congress passed a bill that allowed the building of railroads in the district. The Yukon Railway and Alaska Railroad became the two largest systems that serviced both the major mining zones and the ports of the district. The Copper River and Northwestern Railway was shorter and serviced mainly mining sites. Further extending the railroad system, the Chamber of Commerce in Valdez, about eight hundred miles north of Juneau on Port Valdez, lobbied business interests in 1903 to build a railroad line from the Valdez port to interior copper claims. A small number of Italians worked on the Valdez line. In 1905 eastern moneymen J. P. Morgan and the Guggenheim brothers organized the Alaska Syndicate. The syndicate was already involved in the Alaska Steamship Company and had investments in Alaskan canneries, gold mines, and other mining operations.[9]

The Copper River and Northwestern Railway began service in 1906 after nearly two hundred miles of tracks were laid from Cordova to copper mines in Kennicott, about three hundred miles west of Anchorage. By 1910 railroad officials and labor agents recruited a workforce of 384 immigrants from at least ten countries, including a small number of Italians. In 1915 the federal government began the Alaska Railroad, and by 1917 Italians worked on the new White Pass and Yukon Railway along with more than 4,500 other foreign laborers.[10]

Work in a section gang laying new lines was arduous and dangerous in any area of the United States at the time. By 1900 railroad work and coal mining accounted for half of all worker deaths. Railroad work in the remote Alaska tundra was even more difficult and exploitative for workers than in other parts of the West. In other regions of the West, the railroad worker at least had options to quit or to break his contract and find a job in nearby immigrant enclaves. In Alaska's frigid climate, workers labored on rail lines far from any civilized settlements until they reached the end of the line. Line workers were forced to live in unheated tents or windowless boxcars under unsanitary conditions. Beds were well-used bags of straw that were the homes of vermin and mold. Their clothing could not be properly laundered. They had to purchase their food from the company and prepare their own meals on inadequate wood- or coal-burning stoves. The men were at the mercy of the section bosses, who without regard to labor laws determined how many hours a day they worked. After blasting with dynamite, workers with picks and shovels cleared timber and rocks from the roadway. They then leveled the ground with horse-drawn road graders. Earning approximately ten dollars a week, they were paid a fixed price based on the amount of ground that they cleared, about a half mile a day. Often the railroad company forced the workers to buy or rent company tools, handcarts, graders, and blasting powder. Along with the high cost of food at the company store, their tool costs further eroded their take-home pay. The workers' labor contractor took his cut of their pay as well. As a result, few Italian workers were attracted to railroad work in Alaska, and when they were, they did not stay long. Yet when the Alaska Railroad was finally completed in 1923, a few Italians did stay on as foremen, positions that paid more and offered better working conditions.[11]

Reaching the end of the railroad line and freed from their labor contracts, workers became free labor and some found jobs as miners in towns such as Juneau, Kayak, and Latouche. Beginning in 1900, eighteen Italians found work at the Alaska Treadwell Gold Mining Company near Juneau and a few others at the Alaska Juneau Gold Mining Company, McDonald's Coal Mine Company in Kayak, and Alaska Gastineau Mining Company in Perseverance, near Juneau. By 1915 a larger number of Italians were employed at the Beatson Copper Company on Latouche Island, Chenega Bay. In 1917 records show that fifty-three Italian immigrants worked at the Alaska Gastineau Mining company at Thane, about thirteen miles south of the growing Juneau. Small numbers of Italians took jobs as loggers and in lumber mills at the Juneau Lumber Company and Northern Lumber Company in Juneau and at the Ketchikan Spruce Mills, about three hundred miles south of Juneau. As elsewhere in the Northwest, with unguarded belts and large power-driven saw blades, mills were dangerous work environments that often resulted in debilitating injuries or death. Adding to the dangers was the immigrant's inexperience around such power-driven machinery.[12]

Fishing and Canning Industries

More suitable to Italian skills was the lucrative fishing and canning industry. Even though the fishing season in Alaska was short, immigrants could still make a decent wage. Among the earliest Italian gill-net fishermen in Alaska were four brothers from the Aiello and Bruno families from Pittsburg, in Northern California. The brothers left their home port and traveled to Alaska in May 1886 to fish for the season. As word spread to ports along the Pacific Coast, chain migration sent other Italian fishermen north for the season to exploit the opportunities in the developing Alaskan fishing industry. However, as the Alaska fishing industry grew and with it the demand for workers, management soon hired labor agents. In 1914 at least six Italian labor contractors in San Francisco, Seattle, and Astoria loaded more than eighteen steamships and fifty sailing vessels with workers and supplies, including food and tin cans for canning, all bound for Alaska. They were paid a commission by the salmon companies that hired them and a fee by the individual fishermen whom they recruited. Though only seasonal, the labor-contracting business in Alaska was as lucrative as it was in other parts of the United States. The labor agents provided the fishermen with contracts covering their wages, food allowance, and ticket. The usual contract stipulated a term of one to two months, beginning in April. However, labor contractors were not always honest with the men. Once unscrupulous agents had their recruits in Alaska, they sometimes did not pay them their food allowance. By 1915 the fishing industry with the assistance of labor agents employed more than three thousand men, two thousand of whom came from San Francisco, while the remaining approximately one thousand came from Portland, Astoria, and Seattle. At the end of the Alaska season, most Italian fishermen returned to their home ports. Only a few remained in Alaska to work in other industries.[13]

Upon arrival the men were provided bunkhouses near canneries and ports and equipped fishing boats. During the summer run, the ports were a frenzied jumble of men, equipment, and boxes of fresh fish that had to be rushed to the area's canneries. As one observer wrote in 1915: "Fish, fish everywhere. Boats, scows, wharves and canneries are filled with fish; the machinery grinds, men work with nervous haste, and the finest crops of salmon ever seen in the waters of the world is [*sic*] caught and canned. Day and night the harvest goes on." In addition to salmon, they fished for herring, halibut, crab, and shrimp. The summer run accounted for about 60 percent of the year's catch. The fishermen's pay varied depending on their location. In 1914 in Nushagak and Ugashik, located along Bristol Bay in southwest Alaska, fishermen were paid 3 to 4 cents per salmon, while in Koggiuk and Naknek they earned 3.5 cents per head. The companies paid an additional $100 in what was termed "run money" to entice the men to Alaska, and family men were paid an extra $75. During a good season, a family man could bring home about $650 for two months of work. In comparison, a miner at the low end of the mining scale in 1915 earned about $3.50 a day, only about $85 a month. But fishermen took a risk leaving their home ports. Their pay was subject to the catch. In 1923, for example, fishermen earned only $150 for the season.[14]

In addition to the uncertainties of the catch, the fishermen faced serious, life-threatening hazards while on the Bering Sea with its unpredictable weather pattern and its always frigid waters. There was no early warning system for inclement weather, including dense fog and severe rainstorms that suddenly engulfed and battered the Alaskan coast. Especially frightening, a fall into the cold waters, even during the summer months, usually ended in fatality.[15]

Given the brevity of the season, there was no time to train fishermen. The Italian labor force that companies brought to Alaska consisted of fishermen with years of experience in Italy and in the fishing ports along the Pacific Coast. Many hailed originally from Sicilian fishing colonies in Tunisia, Syracuse, Palermo, Bari, and ports located in the province of Le Marche, where many used a lantern-rigged fishing craft called a *felucca*. Initially, before the design and development of more advanced fishing boats, they built and used a version of this original craft in California. Although they were forced to use company-provided boats in the Alaskan waters, they did bring with them special nets, the *paranzella*, a small mesh net used for bottom fishing, and the *lampara*, used for sardine fishing in California. They were also skilled with a larger mesh net called the trammel, used closer to shore.[16]

In good years and flush with cash, the men returned home on the company boats with the same agents that brought them to Alaska. Some of the unscrupulous agents plied the fishermen with liquor and encouraged gambling on board to separate them from their hard-earned wages. When Italian consul general Ferdinando Daneo in San Francisco heard of labor contractors' exploitation of the fishermen, he complained to the companies and published warnings about fishermen's potential exploitation. To protect fishermen's rights, as early as 1902 fishermen organized the San Francisco–based Fishermen's Protective Union of the Pacific Coast and Alaska. By 1904 it had a membership of thirty-four hundred. There were so many Italians at the meetings that union officials had to hire translators. The union equalized wages and demanded better food, living conditions, and medical services.[17]

A lucrative canning industry grew simultaneously with the rapid growth of the fishing industry. Since salmon was especially susceptible to spoilage and could not be shipped fresh, it soon became the gold standard in the Alaskan canning industry. In 1883 investors established the first cannery, the Arctic Packing Company, in Nushagak. By 1878 canneries produced more than 8,000 cases, each containing forty-eight one-pound cans of salmon. That number by 1900 grew to more than 1.5 million cases. Even that output was destined to grow rapidly. In 1900 there were 30 fishing and canning companies incorporated under the name of Alaska Packers Association. By 1910 the industry had grown to more than 42 salmon canneries producing 2.5 million cases. By 1915 several other large companies were fishing the waters off the Alaska coast: the Bristol Bay Packing Company, Alaska Salmon Company, North Alaska Company, and Naknek Bay Packing Company. In 1917 there were 118 canneries in operation in Alaska. In 1920 they averaged 4.8 million cases of salmon a year, and by 1930 that average rose again to 6,905,843. At their peak of production, Alaskan canneries produced more than 50 percent of the world's canned salmon at a value of $46 million.[18] While partnerships and corporations bankrolled the establishment of the canneries, the West Coast immigrant labor force was the beneficiary of the thousands of jobs that the industry created.

By 1890 more than ten thousand nonresident and native seasonal workers were employed in the canning industry. Labor contractors recruited Italian, Chinese, Japanese, Mexican, and Filipino workers. Beginning in 1915, Italians worked mainly in the Purse Food Fish Company and the

New England Fish Company, located at Ketchikan. Most of the canneries were owned by businessmen from San Francisco, Portland, and Seattle.[19]

However, in spite of their early success, the fishing and canning industries could not maintain their level of production. They inevitably came into conflict with native Alaskans who relied on the salmon run each year for the sustenance of their people. As early as 1899, native people, particularly the Tlingit and Haida, appealed to Congress to protect the salmon run from overfishing. The salmon canning industry had expanded north and west and had impacted the Eskimos and Aleuts as well. Adding to the conflict, many of the new canneries were built on the former fishing sites of the native population.[20] But the native people's protests were largely ignored.

As the fishing industry continued to expand, it became the victim of its own careless, unsustainable policies. Between 1917 and 1919, the industry added an additional 16 canneries. In the aftermath of World War I, the number of Alaskan canneries fell dramatically to 76 from a total of 135 in 1919. While production stabilized for the next two decades, by the late 1930s overfishing irreparably damaged the salmon run, and fishermen were forced to fish for other species. By the 1950s, the average number of cases dropped dramatically again, to 2,787,600. The industry was no longer able to attract seasonal workers in the same numbers. Congress became involved and tried several reforms aimed at regulating the industry, from limiting the fishing season to restrictions on the different types of nets and other gear, all of which were resisted by fishing companies. As a result, the Pacific Coast ports, with their large number of Italian fishermen, continued to be the locus of the fishing industry before and after World War II.[21]

Farming and Enclave Businesses

Because of the climate, agriculture never became an important attraction for immigrants, especially for Italians. In 1897 in the aftermath of the gold rush, when the Alaskan population was growing, the federal government sent agents to explore the development of farming and the possibility of making Alaska a self-sustaining region on the model of Washington or California. Their best recommendation was to encourage immigrant families to establish small farms. In the wake of the agents' recommendations, in 1898 the federal government established several agricultural experimental stations at Kenai, Kodiak, Rampart, Sitka, Copper Center, Fairbanks, and later in 1917 at Matanuska. These remote sites did not attract immigrants in sufficient numbers.[22]

By 1920 there were a mere 364 farms in the territory. Because of the low cost of land and the possibility of homesteading federal property, 345 of these farms were owner operated, the highest percentage of owner-operated farms in the West. Congress extended the Homestead Act to the District of Alaska in 1898. But it appears that few Italians availed themselves of the free federal land. Among those farmers who appear in the record, G. Codiga, possibly from Ticino, Switzerland, owned and operated the Valdez Dairy in 1902. By 1927 Alaska registered only seventy-nine dairy cows, more than eight thousand sheep, and approximately eight hundred cattle. Because of its distance to customers out of the region, cattle ranching was not profitable, though wool did find a market.[23]

In another federal program, in the 1930s under the auspices of the New Deal, President Roosevelt set aside some eighty thousand acres in the Matanuska Valley for farmers. The Federal Emergency Relief Administration and the Department of the Interior chose to attract farmers from Minnesota, Wisconsin, and Michigan, areas where farmers already had experience in harsh winter climates. Most of the farmers listed appear to be of English, Scottish, German, and Scandinavian descent, immigrant groups that had originally settled that northeastern region. Since there were few Italian farmers in those states, only about three or four Italian families migrated to the Matanuska Valley. They did not last long.[24]

There were also few Italian business owners in Alaska. Work in the fishing industry was only seasonal, mostly composed of transient single men and few families. Among the notable exceptions were George Rapuzzi and his wife, Teresa Maria, who traveled to America from Genoa in the 1880s. They settled first in Minnesota and later Seattle, where they opened a mercantile business. From there they followed the gold rush to Alaska before the turn of the century and settled in Skagway, about one hundred miles north of Juneau on the Taiya Inlet. In 1899 they started the Washington Fruit and Candy Store and later expanded to a cigar and grocery store and a wine shop, the California Wine House. The nascent wine industry in California found a ready market in Alaska, where there was no grape industry. They were joined by another Italian, D. Lucci, who opened a general merchandise store in 1901. Lucci later moved to Nome in 1909, where he opened the California Grocery.[25] Other than these few, Italians did not settle or stay long in the region.

Late-Generation Revival and the Italian Heritage

What distinguishes Alaska from the other western states is that its Italian population never took root in its early settlement to establish Little Italys or Catholic churches. Climate, seasonal work, and the eventual closure of mining districts were not conducive to long-term residence. When the fishing season ended, fishermen and cannery workers returned home and took their savings with them. They did not invest in the local community or fund the building of local churches. Nor did they establish the usual contingent of mutual-aid societies and community newspapers. One of the earliest Catholic parishes dates back to the 1880s in Silverbow Basin, near Juneau, where the original parish is still serving a Catholic population today. But Silverbow was composed largely of miners who departed with their earnings for other parts of the West. The parishes never served an established community that left a legacy of Italian immigrant presence, as Italians had in so many western Little Italys.[26] As a result, those churches do not serve today as locations for Italian Americans where they can honor their immigrant forebears and celebrate their immigrant heritage.

Nevertheless, Italians left their mark on various geographical locations that honor those early Italian explorers, settlers, and government officials. Bucareli Bay is named after a Mexican viceroy who was born in Florence. Malaspina Glacier on the Yakutat Bay honors the Italian explorer, as well as two other glaciers named for Columbus and Quintino Sella (1827–84), an Italian scientist, statesman, and alpinist. There is also Mount Bona, named after Prince Amedeo's yacht, and Mount Lucania, which Amedeo named after the liner he used to cross the Atlantic. Italian miners also left their names on the landscape: Pedro Creek, named after Felice Pedroni, and the town of Usibelli, named after Emil Usibelli, who developed the coal mines in the region in the 1940s.[27]

In spite of the small number of immigrants to settle the region, 8,678 Italians claimed Italian ancestry in 1980. According to the 2000 census, that number more than doubled to 17,944, approximately 2.9 percent of the state's overall population of 626,982. There are no statistics yet on whether this sudden rise in the number of Italian Americans is the result of postwar immigration from Italy or migration from other parts of the United States. The number may well represent the same resurgence of ethnic identity that appears to have influenced the number of Italian Americans in all other western states. Even so, Alaska is not last, ranking ninth among the thirteen western states in total percentage of Italian Americans.[28]

CHAPTER 10

WASHINGTON

Italian Jesuits and Early Settlement

Among the states where the immigrant narrative was all but forgotten for nearly a half century, Washington ranks high on the list. In 1978 David Nicandri published a groundbreaking study that documented Italian immigrants' contribution to the development of Washington before 1940. Census records reveal that in 1920, Washington had the second-highest foreign-born population in the West at 265,292, second only to California's 757,625. (These figures vary slightly based on the inclusion or exclusion of Asian foreign born in census figures.) By 1920 immigrants were 19.6 percent (a slight decline from 1910 at 21.1 percent) of the state's population. Between 1900 and 1920, Washington's immigrant population increased 138 percent. By 1920 more than 37 percent of Italian immigrants in Washington had chosen to settle in rural settings to avail themselves of the state's cheap, fertile land.[1] Italians joined a large multinational workforce that created a thriving immigrant economy in enclaves throughout the state.

Before the arrival of the great wave of immigrants to what was called Oregon Country, in 1844 Father John Nobili was probably the first Italian to reach present-day Washington, which would not become a territory until 1853 and a state until 1889. Born in Rome, Nobili lived among the Native people and learned their languages. Like so many of the Jesuits in the remote regions of the West, Father Nobili intervened culturally in the Nisqually Nation to stop them from their ancient traditions of cremating their dead, polygamy, and the practice of torturing surviving spouses of their enemies. By 1849 his superiors ordered him to travel to California, where he established Santa Clara College.[2]

Father Nobili laid the foundation for nearly two generations of Jesuits that followed his work in the Northwest. By 1900, out of more than seventy seminarians, lay brothers, and Jesuits in the region, over a dozen were Italian Jesuits. They established missions throughout present-day Washington. The most influential of those early Jesuits was the polylingual Sicilian Father Joseph Cataldo, who established mission schools and Gonzaga College in Spokane in 1887. Originally planned as a college for Native Americans, under pressure from donors Native Americans were disallowed and relegated to the area mission schools.[3] The Italian Jesuits left their influence in every quarter of the state.

About the same time that the Jesuits were establishing missions, a small number of Italians and other immigrants began migrating to the northwestern territory. By 1860 there were eleven Italian immigrants in the territory where German, Irish, and English immigrants had already settled. By 1870 the census records show that there were twenty Italian immigrants in the region who occupied positions as clergymen, laborers, fishermen, shop owners, and at least one farmer.[4]

Railroads

As in many other western states, the railroad brought an influx of immigrants whose labor and entrepreneurship opened the state's resources to the rest of the United States. In fact, the railroad was "the great engine of Italian immigration to Washington." In 1893 the Great Northern Railway completed a line from St. Paul, Minnesota, to Everett, about thirty miles north of Seattle. At the same time, the Northern Pacific Railroad also reached the Pacific Ocean. During this period, the Union Pacific and Atchison, Topeka, and Santa Fe were laying an extensive network of tracks in the West. Railroad tycoon Jay Gould sent labor contractors to Italy to recruit a workforce. His agents in Italy offered workers not only free passage to the West but also free land that his corporation had secured from the US government. By the 1890s, other Italians already in the United States that were recruited by in-country labor contractors from Chicago could take a variety of rail lines to the western states. Often employment agencies paid for the workers' transportation costs, which were later deducted by the railroad from their pay, usually about two to seven dollars, depending on the distance. To locate potential workers in the United States, western railroads dealt directly with eastern and northeastern employment agencies, took out ads in newspapers, or used labor contractors. Usually an Italian-speaking agent was hired as a foreman or section-gang boss for the Italian workers.[5] There was no shortage of resources to help immigrants find jobs.

By 1910 Italians, numbering 13,114, were sixth in the foreign-born population behind Canadians (39,263), Swedes (32,195), Germans (29,382), Norwegians (28,363), and English (19,413). At the time there were 7,497 Japanese and 1,186 Chinese in the state. The largest concentrations of these groups resided in Seattle. There were also settlements of Austrians,

Russians, Irish, and about 80,000 other immigrants from throughout the world. Italians in small numbers were spread out across the state in smaller communities, such as Aberdeen (135), North Yakima (128), Bellingham (128), Everett (67), and Walla Walla (61). As the major settlement in the state, Seattle was in the lead with 3,454 Italians.[6]

In King County, where Seattle is located, in 1910 there were 5,003 Italians, while in Pierce County Italians numbered 1,700. In Walla Walla County, there were 259 Italians, nearly a 9 percent share of the immigrant farming community. In the Inland Empire, Spokane County's Italians numbered 1,772. In the smaller but important mining area of Kittitas County, there were 1,170 Italians. These five counties accounted for more than 75 percent of the Italian population in the state. By 1910 Washington had become a multicultural landscape, with immigrant farming communities and neighborhoods in every region of the state. As was the case throughout the West, the numbers of Italian immigrants in four of the counties above, excluding Walla Walla, would decline after World War I.[7]

Most of the Italians hired by railroad companies were from southern Italy. They worked in section gangs laying new tracks or repairing roadbeds damaged by inclement weather. In 1880 Spokane was the gathering point for the section gangs that were then dispersed throughout Montana, Idaho, and eastern Washington. The coming of the Northern Pacific Railroad changed Spokane's fortunes. By 1900 Spokane County had the second-largest Italian population in the state. After 1900 Italian gangs dug gravel for the railbed near Spokane for the Great Northern at Edwall, about thirty miles southwest of Spokane. Seventy miles north of Spokane out of Colville, another crew of thirty Italians worked on the Spokane Falls and Northern Railway laying a new line. Its surrounding small towns had few amenities for the immigrant men. These pick-and-shovel workers earned about $1.25 a day for a grueling ten- to twelve-hour day. The living conditions for line workers were as bad as they were in other parts of the West. Six to twelve men slept in unventilated boxcars, whose overnight stench was unbearable. They cooked over makeshift stoves. Their bread grew moldy, and their staples, such as salami, sardines, and macaroni, were all the cheapest varieties.[8]

Those Italian immigrants who were able to land work as mechanics, car cleaners, or boiler workers could earn up to $2.25 a day, while flagmen, telegraph operators, and signalmen could earn $2.75 a day for a six-day week. Other jobs requiring more experience paid $3.00 to $4.00 a day for firemen, engineers, or brakemen. Most of the higher-paying jobs, including management positions, required some facility in English.[9] But even those who worked at the lower end of the pay scale managed to save enough money for investments in enclave businesses or to purchase farmland when their contracts expired. Because of their higher pay scale, managers were more likely to remain in their positions for longer periods of time. Some worked long enough to make an entire career out of railroad work.

Logging and Timber Industry

The growth of railroads in the state created a need for railroad ties. With the demand for wood, the timber industry boomed. By 1910 unions raised the pay for loggers from $2.25 to $3.00 a day, while the least-skilled millworkers earned about $2.00 a day. But Italians were not drawn to work in the timber industry, either logging or millwork. By the turn of the century, there were only about fourteen Italian loggers and only eleven working in lumber mills. Many of these workers, especially in Spokane, were from southern Italy. In the mills, the Japanese outnumbered Italians. Adding to job opportunities in the region, one of the largest timber and wood products companies in the United States at the time, Weyerhaeuser Timber Company, established by German immigrant Frederick Weyerhaeuser, opened an office in Tacoma in 1900.[10]

Unionization had raised millworkers' salaries to $4.50 a day, the equivalent of the highly paid mining jobs in the West. But the high-paying jobs often came with risks. In 1906 alone, thirty-six men were killed in mill accidents in Everett. In 1915 Robert Frost wrote "The Self-Seeker," a poem about a man whose feet had been mutilated in a mill. He says to a friend that the buzz saw's whine is "all music. / One ought as a good villager to like it. / No doubt it has a sort of prosperous sound, / and it's our life." His friend answers, "Yes, when it's not our death." Losing fingers in the mill's saws was a common accident, especially for workers not used to power-driven machines and saws. One particular job, shingle weaving, was extremely perilous and required a long apprenticeship at a lower pay, which Italian workers were often unwilling to accept. In their remote logging camps, loggers were charged 75 cents a day for room and board for their windowless and overcrowded boxcar dormitory furnished with straw mattresses and double-deck beds. However, food was both good and plentiful, with at least two types of meat for dinner.[11]

The timber industry provided a plethora of jobs for both the contract and free-labor worker in the state. With the high salaries, the timber industry contributed significantly to immigrant enclave economies and farming. Saved wages could be invested in cheap land or businesses. Among those few Italians who risked work in the timber industry, Dominick Cavalero began logging in the 1880s. He worked first in San Francisco before arriving in Snohomish County in 1884, where he began logging. Later he opened his own shingle mill near Everett just north of Seattle. With earnings from his profitable shingle mill, in 1911 he moved to Everett, where over time he purchased 2,150 acres dedicated to both farming and timber. His son would follow him into farming and contribute significantly to the development of agriculture in Snohomish County. Likewise, the lumber industry similarly provided a lucrative business for Italian American Dominick Contratto and his brother. When they inherited their father's land in upper Kittitas County, southeast of Seattle, they cleared the land and developed it for farming. To add to his income, Dominick also worked for the Cascade Lumber Company.[12]

Fishing—Puget Sound

Chief among the other resources in the Northwest, fishing provided some jobs for Italians in Seattle, especially for those who brought fishing skills with them from Italy. But the state's fishing industry would never equal California's level of production. Immigrants from Sicily, Genoa, and Naples fished out of Seattle, Tacoma, Aberdeen, Bellingham, and Everett. But Italians did not dominate the industry as they did in California ports. By 1900 there were seventy-seven Italians listed as fishermen in Seattle's port, where they joined both established and itinerant fishermen: Japanese, Greeks, Slavs, Portuguese, and Spaniards, some of whom came only for the salmon run. The fishing fleet also brought in halibut, crab, clams, and oysters. Among the larger established communities were the Norwegians and the Croatians, who established a fishing colony at Gig Harbor, across from the southern tip of Vashon Island. In addition to their fishing skills, the Croatians also brought to the Northwest their shipbuilding skills. One family became the main shipbuilders for the fishing colony. Fishing also gave rise to a canning industry, largely populated by Japanese and Chinese workers. By 1920, with the combined efforts of all immigrant fishermen, Seattle fishermen brought in 14,355,450 pounds of fish worth $1,992,759. Nevertheless, Seattle's catch was only a fraction of California's at 212,635,075 pounds.[13]

Mining

With the growth of the railroad, Washington could begin to capitalize on its mineral resources. By 1900 there were 370 Italian miners in the state. But with the high wages paid in the mines, that number would grow over the next two decades. In Black Diamond, King County, in 1896, miners began working for as little as $1.50 for a ten-hour day. After 1900 miners' wages rose to $3.50 a day. But the pay could be lower or higher depending on the worker's experience and the location of the mine. Greasers worked for $1.45 a day, while boys under eighteen worked unskilled jobs as trappers for $1.60. In an abuse of child-labor laws, children below the age of eighteen were given, with tragic consequences, the important job as trappers, opening and closing trapdoors to prevent the flow of air and noxious gases as coal cars moved through the mine shaft. Management felt that the trapdoors helped to prevent explosions. From 1909 to 1917, working approximately 144 to 300 days a year in Pierce County, a miner could earn from $3.80 for inside mine work to $3.95 a day for the extremely dangerous job of shot lighter (dynamite lighter). Experienced carpenters earned $3.70 a day. With the beginning of US involvement in World War I, in 1917 wages shot up to $5.89 per day. But as the war put more strain on the nation's coal supply and as the labor pool began to shrink, miners' wages rose to $6.95 and hit their peak in 1921 at $8.25 a day. After the war, with the diminishing demand for coal and the growing labor pool as soldiers returned home, wages declined. Miners were able to rent company-owned houses for as little as $5.00 to $6.00 a month. If the miner did not have a family, he could presumably share the rental cost with other single miners, thus lowering his living expenses.[14]

Even with expenses such as housing, tools, and union dues of about $1.25 a month, including medical coverage, the highest-paid miners could still manage to save money at the end of the month. In fact, coal miners in the West, even at the lowest belowground wage, made more in two days than garment pieceworkers in New York City earned in a week. As one of the state's major mining areas, Black Diamond was another example of a western company-run town that attempted to provide immigrant workers with adequate housing and access to cheap goods. Morgan Morgan, who was Welsh and the mine superintendent, ran the mines and just about everything else in the town, which was settled originally by Italians and Welsh. Because the Welsh were more experienced, they were given the higher-paying jobs in the mine, while the Italians were given the lower-paying jobs aboveground. Morgan leased company land to miners at a dollar a month. They were allowed at their own expense to build houses on company property. At the company store where the workers shopped, the cost of their supplies and food was deducted from their weekly pay. As the workforce grew, the housing soon partitioned off into areas known as Swede Town, Welsh Town, and Dago Town, as well as other neighborhoods. Morgan decided that the town needed only one church, a Congregational church, in spite of the multinational workforce that the mines attracted. The various services were simply held at different hours on Sunday to accommodate the different faiths of the workers.[15]

In 1904 the Pacific Coast Company, based in New York, bought the Black Diamond mine and the town. By 1907 workers formed the Local 6481 of the United Mine Workers of America. After the war, the company tried to lower wages to $7.00, down from the prewar high of $8.25. However, in 1921 the miners struck. The company quickly contracted with labor agents to import a crew of strikebreakers, cordoned off the mining area with barbed wire, and hired thirty-five security guards to provide safety for the strikebreaking workers. Since it still owned the leases on the housing property, the company revoked all leases and forced the striking miners and their families to leave. With its complete control over the town, the company prevailed. Some of the striking miners gave in and went back to work under the company's conditions, while others, blackballed for life in Black Diamond, left town for other jobs.[16]

Mining in Washington was as perilous as it was in other states in the United States. Between 1892 and 1930, Washington had at least fourteen recorded mine disasters, about one disaster every three years. Kittitas County, the region surrounding Roslyn, was the largest coal-mining area in the state. By 1910, 85 percent of the miners were foreign born, with Italians composing 22 percent of the total. Northern Italians outnumbered southern Italians by twelve to one in the mines. On May 10, 1892, in the North Pacific Company's No. 1 mine in Roslyn, an explosion occurred, killing forty-five miners. It was the worst coal-mining disaster in the state at the time. Mine officials theorized that a controlled blast opened a fissure in the rock that let gas into a chamber where a miner's lamp set off the explosion. One Italian and several African Americans were among the deceased. All the others were of northern European heritage, mainly from the British Isles. All forty-five bodies of the miners were recovered and buried, one cemetery for the immigrant miners and another for African Americans.[17]

In another of the state's worst mine disasters, on Sunday morning, November 6, 1910, an explosion rocked the Lawson Coal Mine in Black Diamond, southeast of Seattle. The explosion killed sixteen miners, all immigrants, including nine Italians, four Belgians, and one each from Finland, Poland, and Austria. The deceased miners left ten widows and seven children. After two days, the search of the collapsed mine was abandoned. Of the sixteen killed, five bodies were never recovered. Management did little to improve safety in the mines. As a result, the Lawson explosion was surpassed little more than five years later by the second-largest mine disaster in the state. On November 16, 1915, an explosion in the Ravensdale mine killed thirty-five miners, including eleven Italians. Among those killed were the mine's foreman, a city councilman, and the director of the local school district. Twenty-three of the men were married with children. The deaths of the Italian miners this time came to the attention of the Italian consul general, who paid a visit to the area to inspect the conditions of the mines. However, he was powerless to influence management to implement costly safety measures to prevent such tragedies in the future.[18]

There were countless other mine explosions and cave-ins that received only passing mention because fewer men died: Franklin, 1894 and 1914; New Whatcom, 1895; Carbonado, 1899 and 1930; Black Diamond, 1902, 1907, and 1910; Pittsburg, 1903, 1904; Burnett, 1904; and Milan, 1910. Only one coal-mining town, Elk Coal, in King County near Sugarloaf Mountain just east of Ravensdale, operated for more than thirty years without a major accident.[19] Mine disasters, strikes, and the general decline in coal production in the region slowly eroded jobs and made mining less attractive to immigrants.

Workers, Professionals, and Entrepreneurs—Seattle, King County

The loss of a mining job in Washington was not a devastating blow for the free-labor immigrant. By 1900 Italians could easily find jobs, both skilled and unskilled. The largest concentration of Italian immigrants was in King County at 5,003, more than 38 percent of the Italians in the state. Of those 3,454 Italians residing in Seattle at the time, many began as pick-and-shovel laborers building the city's infrastructure, while others were hired to drive garbage wagons, which many of them owned. In 1915 the city took over the service and hired the men as municipal garbage workers. Italians also held jobs building the local rail system as well as working on the railroads servicing Seattle, the county seat of King County.[20]

As the Italian working-class population grew and its enclave economy developed, Italians began to occupy the spectrum of jobs, such as masons, bakers, blacksmiths, boat builders, carpenters, printers, toolmakers, and tailors. Among the early entrepreneurs, Italians owned fifty-eight retail stores in the state. The largest number had jobs in trade and transportation, which included grocery-store owners, teamsters, and railroad workers. They began as well to fill the ranks of meatpackers, fish-cannery workers, agricultural laborers, loggers, millworkers, and other factory jobs. At the bottom of the laboring class, there was also a significant number of street peddlers. A small number of women also joined the laboring class in positions such as waitresses, seamstresses, laundresses, and dressmakers.[21]

At the same time that Italian workers were contributing to Seattle's and the state's economic development, by the 1920s a more educated class of Italian immigrants also contributed to the region's cultural growth. With the establishment of the University of Washington, Seattle became a dynamic cultural center. The professional class comprised approximately 20 percent of the Italians in Seattle. By 1900 there were doctors, editors, music teachers, lawyers, and college professors. Notable among them were Drs. Xavier DeDonato and August J. Ghiglione and newspaper editors Federico Bassetti and Nick Paolella. Attilio Sbedico, professor of literature at the University of Washington, was later joined by Angelo Pellegrini, who became a widely published and well-known professor of English in the post–World War II years. Father Giuseppe Chianale was a distinguished professor of philosophy at Gonzaga University in Spokane. There were as well numerous pharmacists, engineers, bankers, and lawyers. New York–born Italian American Dr. Ghiglione, in addition to his medical practice, was president of the Seattle Academy of Surgery, an agent of the Royal Italian Consulate, and president of the local Dante Alighieri Society.[22]

Italians also made an important contribution to the arts. With an opera and symphony by 1920, Seattle was staking its claim as the cultural center of the Northwest. Among those Italian artists attracted to Seattle's arts community were Giuseppe Inzerillo, from Palermo, and Silvio Risegari, from Genoa. Both singers had distinguished musical careers before settling in Seattle prior to World War I. Educated at the University of Naples,

Risegari opened his studio in Seattle and taught voice for years. A child prodigy, Risegari, who studied in La Spezia, gave his first concert at the age of eleven and played throughout Europe and the United States before settling in Seattle by the 1920s. An accomplished composer, he became a soloist for the Seattle Symphony Orchestra. He also directed the Seattle Grand Opera Chorus, Seattle Music Festival, and North Pacific Saengerbund Festival, organized by Washington's German community.[23]

As early as 1915, Italians in Seattle and in the region established a number of fraternal organizations: the Mazzini Society, Società Italiana Indipendente, Knights of Columbus, Foresters of America, and Italian Commercial Club. In the decades that followed, Italians added to the list of fraternal organizations with the Order Sons of Italy, Dante Alighieri Society, Italian Club, Società Stella d'Italia, Circolo Italiano of Auburn, Circolo Italiano of Yakima, and the Italian Council. For first-generation Americans, there was also the Sons and Daughters of Italy. Many of the more prominent Italians in Seattle also joined non-Italian businessman organizations such as the local Elks lodge.[24] This was considered the ultimate step of acceptance as a new American for successful immigrant Italian businessmen and professionals.

To create a more cohesive Italian community, Italians established many community newspapers. Educated at the University of Naples, Dr. Bonaventura De Rosa started *La Patria* (1907–10) in Spokane and later another one, *Lavoro e Commercio*, in Seattle (1910–15). In the wake of the closure of De Rosa's paper, three other papers competed for readership in Seattle: *La Gazzetta Italiana*, with a circulation of twelve hundred; *Il Messaggero Italo-Americano*, with a circulation of five hundred; and *La Rivista del Ovest*. *La Gazzetta Italiana*, published by Nicola Paolella, was edited by Federico Bassetti, educated in Turin. Bassetti arrived in the United States in 1907. Both men became influential members of the Italian community in Washington. Bassetti claimed membership in at least eight Italian organizations, from Seattle to Auburn and Yakima. Paolella, who arrived in the United States in 1905, was educated in Italy and was a pharmacist by trade. From his small pharmacy in Rainier Valley, Paolella embarked on a notable career in the Northwest. He became president of Seattle's Italian Commercial Club and an influential member of the Chamber of Commerce. Like Bassetti, he was a radio broadcaster and hosted an Italian radio program for more than twenty-six years. In recognition of his contribution to Italian culture in the Northwest, the Italian government gave him the Order of Merit, Italy's highest civilian honor.[25] By 1930 Italians played a role in every level of Seattle society.

Unfortunately, the downside of nearly all North American Italian newspapers was that with the rise of Mussolini, these papers became instruments for the spread of fascist propaganda. Beginning in the early 1920s, Mussolini sought the support of Italian communities, especially in North America. In an appeal to immigrants' nostalgic recollection of their homeland, he urged them and their offspring to "celebrate their *Italianità*." With the propaganda articles that his ministry sent abroad, "he took every opportunity to remind Italian Americans that they remained Italian to the seventh generation." It is difficult to assess Mussolini's effectiveness in the Italian diaspora. However, some Italians began to construct an imaginary nationalism and even sought ways that "they might serve the nation that they left behind."[26] This might explain why so many Italian newspapers in America, if the editors did not overtly support the Italian fascist movement, at least allowed their newspapers to become instruments of Mussolini's propaganda.

There were numerous immigrant settlements in the surrounding neighborhoods outside Seattle's downtown. Southeast of downtown, Beacon Hill became a Japanese and Italian settlement that supported many Italian businesses. Just north of Beacon Hill in the Central Area, Giglio and Cecilia Gai from Calabria established their New Home Bakery. After more than thirty years in business and after their father's death in 1953, his two sons took over the operation under the new name Northwest Bakeries before the two brothers sold it. Another of the long-established firms, south of the city center on South King Street, the Oberto Sausage Company was established by Constantino Oberto in 1919. Now more than a century old, it employs over nine hundred people in its relocated and larger factory.[27]

The success of Italians in wholesale distribution and import companies relied almost exclusively on the purchasing power in their various enclaves. In obscure warehouses on the fringes of retail centers, companies sold an array of imported and locally produced Italian products, all destined for the Italian immigrant table: from cheeses, olives, olive oil, and rice to salt cod, garlic, salame, prosciutto, and provolone, as well as fifty-gallon barrels of wine from California. They also imported tins of smoked herring, anchovies, sardines, and tomato products. For those who were working ten- to twelve-hour days, six and seven days a week in mines and mills, eating was one of the men's few comforts. Having access to Italian products was another way to feel at home in an otherwise new environment.[28]

Among the most successful businesses was the A. Magnano Co. After working in other regions of the United States, Antonio Magnano arrived in Seattle in 1903. Soon after his arrival, he established the A. Magnano Company, a wholesale food-distribution business on First Avenue. Over the next twenty-five years, he continued to expand his distribution of grocery products, including olive oil from Italy. After their father's death in 1951, Antonio's three sons took over the business, reorganized it under A. Magnano & Sons, and began a new import and distribution company, Napoleon, specializing in importing quality foods from around the world. The Napoleon brand is still in existence today and controlled by Antonio's grandchildren.[29]

Three families, all with the last name Rosellini, distinguished themselves in Washington. The saga of the Rosellini families began with their fathers, Giovanni Rosellini, Vittorio Rosellini, and Primo Rosellini, who was not related to the other two. The three men emigrated from Tuscany at the turn of the century, worked as section hands on the railroad, and settled initially in Tacoma. Vittorio's son Leo became a surgeon, and his other son Victor became a famous restaurateur, opening four Seattle restaurants that hosted governors and presidents. Giovanni's son Albert became governor, albeit a controversial one, from 1957 to 1965. Primo's son Hugh was elected to the state supreme court. Shortly after their arrival in Tacoma, Vittorio married Fine Gasperetti, whose family owned a restaurant in Seattle. The Rosellini-Gasperetti family expanded their business and opened additional restaurants in Cle Elum, Yakima, Tacoma, and one in San Francisco.[30]

The growing Italian population in Seattle was not lost on Catholic interests, either in Rome or in the United States. The community of Italian Catholics in Seattle soon came to the attention of that ardent, dedicated Italian nun Frances Xavier Cabrini. Prior to her work in Colorado, Cabrini went to Seattle in 1903. Upon her arrival, she wrote of the city, "Here we are, not far from the North Pole. This city is charmingly situated, and is growing so rapidly.... The town of Seattle spreads over two hills.... In the valleys between the hills, there are about five thousand Italians who follow us like chicks follow the hen. We hope to help them and they will help us." With indefatigable energy, within a year she had established the Mount Carmel Mission on Beacon Hill, containing a school, orphanage, kindergarten, chapel, and convent for her order. She left Seattle only to return in 1909. By then the settlement on Beacon Hill had grown considerably, and the orphanage, with eighty-five children, was overcrowded. She expanded the site and opened the Columbus Sanitarium. Upon her canonization in 1946, she was designated patron saint of immigrants. Her relics are interred in Seattle's St. James Cathedral on Ninth Street, which contains a statue of her in a chapel in the cathedral's west nave.[31]

Her mission in Seattle was quickly followed by the establishment of several new parishes for the growing Catholic population: the Immaculate Conception Church built in 1904, St. James Cathedral in 1907, the Blessed Sacrament in 1908, and Our Lady of Mount Virgin in 1911, directed by Italian priest Father Louis Caramello. All the churches are still functioning today as parishes.[32]

In the midst of its economic and cultural development, Seattle was not immune to one of the major problems that accompanied immigrant success nearly everywhere in the West. With scores of single common laborers, loggers, millworkers, itinerant Alaskan miners, and sailors, a vigorous prostitution trade developed composed of late-generation and immigrant women, mainly Asian. The inexpensive "crib houses" drew the laboring class, while "parlor houses" attracted an affluent clientele. As prostitution grew in the city and became more visible, in the 1880s reformists and pro-prostitution advocates battled over whether to ban the sex trade. But in 1916, with a mayor who had investments in brothels, the pro-prostitution faction won. As usual, the winning faction voiced little concern for the poor women trapped in the sex trade. The only limitation passed was a law against public solicitation on the streets and the removal of the brothels to a different quarter of the city out of view of the city's more respectable residents.[33]

Angelo Pellegrini's American Dream

Amid Seattle's development as the Northwest's economic and cultural center, the Pellegrini family arrived in Washington. Years later as a retired professor of English at the University of Washington, Angelo Pellegrini wrote about the sudden transformation of his family's life upon its settlement in McCleary, about eighty miles southwest of Seattle in Grays Harbor County. Logging and fishing were the two main occupations in the region. His autobiography is a revealing account of the quality of life that the majority of immigrants experienced in Washington. His description of life in the West differed radically from those of early American sociologists such as Oscar Handlin, who focused only on the toiling immigrant masses inhabiting overcrowded eastern urban neighborhoods before World War II.[34]

In 1913, after weeks of travel from the village of Casabianca in Tuscany, Pellegrini with his mother and four siblings landed in McCleary, where his father had settled two years earlier. In 1910 Grays Harbor already had a substantial Italian population of 273, the seventh-largest community of Italian immigrants in the state. As a young boy only weeks from a life of deprivation and poverty in his native village, Pellegrini suddenly found a different world before him:

> In less than a year after our arrival we were rich. The land we needed was ours for the asking. Firewood littered the landscape. There was game in the hills and fish in the waters. The internal organs of the beef cattle—liver, heart, kidney, tripe—were given freely to us who were barbarians enough to eat them. Father had a job. Mother, with the aid of the children, took in boarders. We had cows in the barn, pigs in the sty, rabbits in the hutches, chickens in the henhouse. On rich land that had never been cultivated we grew all our vegetables and some of our fruits. The resources were ours at no cost other than the sweat of our brows.

Pellegrini also describes the opportunities that awaited him as a young boy, from his success at school to earning his PhD at the University of Washington, where he became a professor of English until his retirement in 1967.[35]

Growing up speaking his regional dialect, Pellegrini wrote about his desire to learn English and about the quality of the education he received from competent and inspiring teachers in the public school system. He wrote that by the time he had reached fifth grade, "I could now read and write and speak well enough to continue learning with my peers." But adjusting to American culture was not easy for the young Pellegrini. Years later in another work, he wrote that at times in school among his peers he felt profoundly isolated. Adding to his problem, he was unable to explain to his parents the new American values and culture he was experiencing at school. However, one of his many influential teachers explained to him one day how education would be the means of escaping his family's parochial background. Pellegrini wrote, "The course was set. There were no alternatives."[36]

His desire to learn English is revealing. Seattle's early Italian immigrants realized that English was the lingua franca needed for success in America. As early as 1915, one English night-school class at a local elementary school had 150 adults, 30 of whom were Italian men. For children and adults, part of that educational process was designed to teach them values that "transcended family" and their cultural values and to prepare them all for entrance into American culture.[37]

The emphasis on English education at the time for children and adults was what John Higham described as the national "crusade for assimilation." That crusade was motivated by both nativists' fear of the new immigrants' influence on American culture and a legitimate concern for their well-being and success in America. Italian immigrant Constantine M. Panunzio supported the "crusade for assimilation" at the time. Panunzio (1884–1964), born in southern Italy, explains that his autobiography "traces the liberation of a mind from the conceptions it brought from the Old World and pictures its development into the American consciousness." Earning his PhD in 1925, he would succeed as Pellegrini did. After his education in the East, he became a professor of sociology at Whittier College and later the University of California, Los Angeles.[38] Pellegrini's writing contrasts with Panunzio's autobiography. While Pellegrini may have struggled at times with the conflict between his immigrant family and the American culture around him, judging from his lifelong focus on his Italian heritage in his many works, his public school education did not erase his immigrant past.

Yet in his positive depiction of life in Washington, Pellegrini was careful not to idealize the immigrant Italian. Always the realist with a sharp eye for detail, he wrote too about the "charlatans" and "slackers," those *sfruttatori* (exploiters) who took advantage of the illiterate and unsophisticated Italian peasants who settled America. These opportunistic *sfruttatori* did not honor the values of thrift and family that characterized the majority of Italian immigrants. Many of these immigrants had not traveled far from their native villages.[39] For immigrants who were not accustomed to the vagaries of the modern marketplace and above all the tenacity of American law enforcement, their quest for success sometimes blinded them to the risks they were taking.

Early immigrants were thrust into an environment that contained more than just occupational hazards. Pellegrini tells the story of Don Cicciarello, a fictional name, who came to McCleary one winter in 1917, convinced his father and his neighbors to invest in the production of a chain pipe wrench, and absconded with all their money. Likewise, immigrant Guido Sella became a successful entrepreneur. By 1916 he was married, had four children, and was worth an estimated $50,000. But he became involved in bootlegging, made an unwise investment in a brothel, and had a lascivious affair with a prostitute, all of which resulted in his arrest, imprisonment, and ruination. Armando, an old friend, said of him after his release from prison, "We were made to understand and to endure pain and poverty; but we were not made to understand and to endure pleasure and riches."[40]

Although he benefited from his education, as an adult Pellegrini viewed with a critical eye that Americanization policy implemented in the public schools at the time. As a boy he was fascinated by his American history classes, but as an adult he became disillusioned with the official version of American history that he had learned in his childhood textbooks. When he realized that America's history of social injustice was left out of his Americanization process in the schools, at one point he joined the American Communist Party, before disillusionment set in and he resigned from its ranks.[41] As a university student before World War II, he was not swayed by Mussolini's propaganda published in Seattle's local Italian newspapers. All of his works are insightful and balanced representations of the Italian immigrant experience and culture that surrounded him in Washington during his long and distinguished career.

Farming—King County and Pierce County

With the arrival of the railroad in the 1890s, Washington's already well-established agricultural industry was able to expand to regional and national markets. In 1900 Washington had 47,505 farms. With the influx of the new immigrants to the state, by 1900 that number grew to 56,192. By 1900 there were 1,692 Italian males in the state, with 211 involved in some form of agriculture and another 125 doing common labor on farms. Out of the 211, there were 60 farmers and an additional 2 ranchers, 2 dairymen, and 2 nurserymen. Several Italian truck farmers were also connected to the wholesale distribution of agricultural products. Although Italians made up only a small fraction of the already established farms in the state, that would soon change.[42]

By 1915 Italians had settled Rainier Valley, about four miles south of Seattle. At the time, the enclave was bordered by nearby truck farms in the surrounding rural areas. These farms extended throughout King County and farther south to Pierce County, which includes Tacoma. These two counties contained the two largest concentrations of Italians in the state. In addition to the cheap land, the climate provided sufficient rainfall. Immigrants were able to purchase small leftover parcels from government and railroad land promotions available in the area that were suitable for family-run farms. Italians were among the earliest arrivals in the area and managed to lease or purchase the most valuable land. The acreage of Italian farms ranged from 5 to 160 acres. Among the earliest Italians, George Colello settled initially south of downtown Seattle in 1875 and began farming. Later he moved his farming operation to a larger plot along the Duwamish River in the South Park area in King County. With his new plot, he joined a growing number of immigrant farmers, mainly Japanese and Italian, who purchased or leased small plots along the fertile banks of the Duwamish.[43]

Joining Colello, by 1910 there were eighteen Italian farmers who owned a total of 900 acres. They had been preceded by the Germans, Scandinavians, and English. By 1915 there were more than two hundred Italian farmers, mainly Tuscan and Genovese in King County. Initially, Italian farmers cultivated more land than did all the other immigrants. The Japanese by state law were barred from owning property, but not from leasing it. But where there was a motivated seller, the law was easily circumvented. The majority of the plots of land in the area leased from $200 for the least desirable land to $5,000 a year for the most desirable. In an interesting division of products, the various ethnic groups did not all grow the same crops. While a small number of Italians established dairy farms, the majority grew vegetables, while the Japanese diversified their crops to include strawberries, blackberries, and potatoes. They also opened a small number of dairy farms. Scandinavians, the most diverse group, did poultry, dairies, vegetables, and fruits.[44]

In 1910 the Immigration Commission interviewed thirty-six King and Pierce County Italian truck farmers. The results of the interviews revealed how immigrant farmers were able to enter into farming with minimal resources, yet become successful in a short time. Of the men interviewed, the majority were under thirty years of age. Before going into farming, many had worked their way across the country as section hands on the railroad or as miners. For a down payment on parcels of farmland, they needed only $75, less than a month's wages on the railroad or in the mines at the time and about two months' wages for a farmworker. Others settled for leasing land at an average of about $1,000 annually. The Italians with the largest farms, upwards of 160 acres, sold produce valued at $60,000, while smaller truck farmers sold their produce at a respectable $5,000 annually. The margin between the low cost of establishing a farm and the gross sale of their produce allowed for the immediate success of the small farmer.[45]

In the early 1900s, Seattle had an unusual ordinance that prevented farmers from selling directly to customers. Yet within the enclaves where small farmers sold from their horse-drawn wagons or from the backs of their trucks, this was an ordinance honored more in the breach than in the observance. Farmers also set up roadside stalls on country roads. Otherwise, for farmers who had larger farms and higher production, this restrictive ordinance forced them to sell their produce to wholesalers, who sometimes resorted to price gouging and other devious practices. When the farmers complained, the city rescinded the ordinance and established an outdoor farmers' market at Pike Place downtown, where the now famous market still stands. On its opening day, August 17, 1907, only a few farmers showed up with their wagons, but they quickly sold out and had to turn away many disappointed customers. One farmer said, "The people come a runnin' and I give some things without a paper bag. And they was glad to get it. And now I think in an hour there, I make seven, eight dollars." Word soon spread, and within a week more than seventy wagons were parked along the street. Frank Goodwin, a real-estate investor, recognized the potential and put a group of investors together to build a permanent structure that became Pike Place Market. In time, Japanese farmers operated about 75 percent of the stalls and Italians the remaining 25 percent.[46]

Before 1910 Germans, Chinese, Japanese, and Filipinos owned or at least worked about half the farms in the region. However, no single group dominated the market in King and Pierce Counties. The various ethnic groups, Italians included, were fierce competitors. For obvious reasons of language and culture, each group hired only within its own ethnic group. Both the Italian and the Japanese farmers paid their workers $1.35 a day, about $30 to $35 a month, which included food and lodging if the owners lodged the workers on the farm. However, the average wage paid by other farmers was about $50 per month. With lower labor costs, the Japanese and Italians had an edge at Pike Place since they were able to sell their produce at a price below their competitors' farm products. The smaller

Italian truck farmers sometimes complained that the larger Japanese farms overproduced, thus lowering the price of produce for everyone. Although they competed, their competition never descended to the level of open conflict.[47]

An Italian farmer named Giuseppe "Joe" Desimone was among those original farmers in the region who sold produce at Pike Place Market. He came from the small town of Avellino, east of Naples, in 1897. He made his way to the Northwest, where he became a truck farmer in South Park and Tukwila, near Seattle, and in Kent Valley, near the Green River. In addition to being a successful farmer, he was also an astute investor. He purchased what appeared to be a useless parcel of swampland south of Seattle along the Duwamish River. He apparently saw an opportunity that other land investors did not see. He must have studied carefully the swamp's terrain and knew what he could do to drain the otherwise worthless, sodden property. After he purchased the parcel, no doubt at a low price, he drained the swamp and turned it into valuable farmland. As his investments grew, he accumulated a fortune and managed to buy a small interest in Pike Place Market in 1925. By 1941 he became president of Pike Place and its majority stockholder. A clever businessman, he kept costs to a minimum in the market and his lease rates low. Desimone rented stalls to Japanese and Italian farmers with nothing more than a handshake and their mutual verbal agreement on terms. The market was a lucrative venue for the small farmers, who could sell upwards of $5,000 worth of produce and vegetables annually from their small spaces.[48]

After Joe retired in 1946, his son Richard became the manager of the market. But little changed in the way Richard did business. To keep the stalls full and the market solvent, he continued to offer all the farmers a fair rental price so that they too could make a profit. In typical fashion, they settled all rental agreements with the usual handshake. In 1974 the family sold the market to the city. A sign of the Desimone heritage in Seattle is the market's Desimone Bridge.[49] Pike Place remains today one of Seattle's major attractions and a monument to the city's early immigrant history.

Rainier Valley and Tacoma—Enclave Businesses

South of Seattle was the vibrant Rainier Valley enclave where many of the area farmers lived and also sold their produce. Contributing to the valley's development, in 1890 the Rainier Valley Electric Railway connected the valley to Seattle, about five miles north. After 1900 the Rainier Valley was virtually transformed from a wilderness area into a thriving immigrant enclave. In 1910, out of 3,454 Italians in Seattle, 1,519 were located in the Rainier Valley, known locally as Garlic Gulch.[50]

By 1915 there were 215 Italian families living in the neighborhood occupying about two hundred houses. These were two- to five-room wood-frame houses on small plots, some large enough to accommodate a garden. The neighborhood was home to professionals, laborers, and small-business owners. Several Italians, including Nicola Marucca, George Colella, and C. Vacca, as well as Norwegian immigrant Charles Malmo, purchased property along Rainier Avenue and opened Malmo's Nursery, which would later become the Ernst/Malmo hardware store in Seattle. For the Italian population, Angelo Merlino opened Merlino & Sons, selling cheese, olive oil, and pasta. After 120 years, Merlino & Sons is still in business. Nick Paolella ran his small drugstore on Rainier Avenue. Other Italian businesses included the Casal Grocery, Maletta and Violi barbershops, Three Monks Macaroni Factory, and Tony La Salle's Atlantic Street Shoe Repair. The Traverso family opened the Fiore d'Italia café on Fifth Avenue to compete with the already established New Italian Café. They joined a number of other Italian businesses in the area: Gavasto's Torino sausage market, John DiJulio's butcher shop, A. Dominick Mastro's Italian restaurant, Gil's Restaurant, and the A. Magnano Co. The Borracchini family established the Borracchini's Bakery in 1922 on Rainier Avenue. After nearly a century, it is still run by the same family.[51]

Supporting the businesses in the enclave, jobs in the mines south of Rainier Valley at Renton, Newcastle, and Black Diamond brought additional wage-earning Italians to the neighborhood. The area also offered numerous other job opportunities in steel and lumber mills as well as in manufacturing plants. One clothing manufacturer, Black Bear Manufacturing, employed largely Chinese and Italian immigrants. Farmers surrounding Garlic Gulch sold their produce from the backs of their wagons or trucks on neighborhood streets. Although city hall did not consider the immigrant settlement Seattle's best neighborhood, by 1907 Seattle annexed the area. Because of the large concentration of Italians in the neighborhood, their children were segregated initially in classes that emphasized the rudiments of English grammar and conversation before they were allowed into mainstream classes. The Colman School that serviced the area was 33 percent Italian. By 1913 the neighborhood established the

Mount Virgin Roman Catholic Church and School, as well as Protestant denominational churches and schools.[52]

Italians settled a variety of locations north and south of Rainier Valley in neighborhoods such as Georgetown, Youngstown, South Park, and First Hill. About twenty-five miles south of Rainier Valley is the town of Tacoma in Pierce County, which also shared in the prosperity of the region's Italian population. There were enough Italians in Pierce County to justify a consulate, run by southern Italian Angelo Cerminara. Professionals such as Italian-born Salvi Gagliardi opened a law office to address the Italians' legal and immigration needs. In 1903 Frank Paravati, at the age of nineteen, left Calabria for America. He opened tailor shops first in New Jersey and later in Tacoma before he moved to Los Angeles, where he opened another shop in fashionable Beverly Hills. About the same time as Paravati's arrival in America, in 1905 twenty-one-year-old Domenico Lenzi arrived in Chicago and later with the encouragement of friends traveled to Tacoma to run their grocery store with its line of Italian products. In 1916 he left the grocery business and opened a Tuscan-style restaurant, the Toscano Café, in the heart of the Italian community in Tacoma, where it became a popular meeting place for both Italians and the non-Italian community. By 1921 the Italian population in Tacoma, at 1,150, was large enough to justify building the Church of Santa Rita, directed by Father Achille Bruno, SJ.[53]

The restaurateurs in the Tacoma Italian community relied on what they knew, the home cooking they were exposed to in their mothers' kitchens. It is improbable that any of them had run restaurants in their native villages or had ever had any experience preparing dishes from outside their regions. In a seemingly insignificant but illuminating passage, Angelo Pellegrini wrote that when he left his parents' home in McCleary to attend the University of Washington, he "set up bachelor quarters and learned to cook. It really wasn't all that difficult, as the saying goes these days. With the aid of Mother Pellegrini, and by picking the culinary brains of certain Italian ladies in the city who were excellent cooks and who were flattered by my interest in their craft, I soon learned how to do certain basic dishes rather well—pastas, soups, roasts, stews." Pellegrini would go on to write his own cookbook.[54]

Pellegrini reveals more than he realized. It is significant that he was unable to find Italian cookbooks in Seattle and instead had to rely on his mother's and other Italian women's recipes. By the turn of the century, there were many international cookbooks in print in English, but not many Italian cookbooks. Part of the reason was that Italy still did not have a "codified Italian cuisine." At the time, cooking in Italy was regional. By the turn of the nineteenth century, Pellegrino Artusi in his classic *La scienza in cucina e l'arte di mangiar bene* (1891) attempted to bring some unity to Italian cuisine. But it is doubtful that his book was read or consulted widely in the West. Italian cuisine was unpopular in the United States at the time. Americans believed that fruits and vegetables, important in the Italian diet, had little nutritional value because they "contain too much water." As a result, there was a lack of interest outside the Italian community in Italian cuisine. But that would soon change. At the basis of the Italian restaurateurs' success, as Donna Gabaccia wrote, "much of what remained of regional and immigrant cooking was in the unwritten form of female art." For Italian restaurateurs in America, the origins of recipes emanated largely from kitchens managed by immigrant women. Adding authenticity to Italian cooking, Italian truck farmers were making Italian herbs and vegetables widely available, eggplant and artichoke among them.[55]

Originally, those early enclave restaurants in Seattle and Tacoma catered to the immigrant working class. A meal could be purchased for just pennies. It almost always included spaghetti (in some dialects referred to as macaroni), bread, a cheap cut of meat, and potatoes. Olives or dried fruits were sometimes served as dessert.[56] But in time, Italian restaurant owners were able to expand to the non-Italian middle class.

Many of the restaurants opened by northern Italians promoted a distinctly southern Italian dish: spaghetti. It soon became combined with the Italian meatball (*polpetta*) to form the very un-Italian dish spaghetti with meatballs. Although restaurant owners such as Lenzi chose to tag their restaurants Tuscan, they were serving a mostly southern Italian immigrant population. In his march up the Italian peninsula from Sicily through Naples to the north in his campaign to unify Italy, Giuseppe Garibaldi is said to have quipped, "It will be spaghetti, I swear to you, that unifies Italy." In the nineteenth century, spaghetti was a Neapolitan street food, sold by street venders and eaten with the hands by Naples's hordes of impoverished, homeless *lazzaroni*. These spaghetti-eating vagabonds were described, with a large degree of disgust, by those Grand Tour British travelers throughout the eighteenth and nineteenth centuries in the British travel literature as filthy, lazy, good-for-nothing beggars who defiled their noble Roman past. In spite of its ignoble history, this southern Italian dish became the staple of the Italian American culinary tradition. Spaghetti even became a canned product that was distributed nationally under the label Chef Boyardee, created by an Italian immigrant. By the 1920s, every town in the state with a sizable Italian population had Italian restaurants that served spaghetti.[57] Spaghetti not only helped to unify Italy but unified Italian American cuisine as well.

Spokane—Railroad Hub and Enclave

While Seattle and King County were the destinations of most immigrant settlers, the coming of the railroad to Spokane County on the eastern side of the Cascades seeded another lesser-known settlement of Italians. By 1910 there were 1,544 Italian immigrants in the city of Spokane, more than 87 percent of the county's Italian population. Italians quickly established a presence in both the business and the civic life of the small town. As a measure of the immigrants' impact, in 1900 Spokane's population stood at 36,848. Within ten years, in 1910 the population grew to 104,102. By 1920 it leaped again to 141,289.[58]

The most successful Italian in Spokane at the time was civic leader and businessman Garibaldi Albi, born in Italy in 1861. He immigrated to Denver, where he worked on the railroad, and in 1889 he settled in Spokane, where he worked on the railroad and began investing. By the turn of the century, he opened a saloon and by 1907 invested in an office building on Washington Street in the center of the enclave. He then opened a steamship agency catering to the travel needs of the enclave's population. He married, and one of his seven sons, Joseph, became a prominent lawyer and served for twelve years as the Italian consul general for eastern Washington.[59]

Albi's success mirrors the upward mobility of the Italian community in general in Spokane. In their efforts to establish a place in Spokane society, in 1915 Italians formed the Fratellanza Marconi-Colombo society. These societies created among Italians not only a sense of security but also what they hoped was legitimacy in the eyes of the larger community. Composed largely of southern Italians, the society launched fund drives for the Red Cross, provided death benefits for widows, and held festivals and dinners for members. As a public display of their place and role in Spokane society, they began an annual Columbus Day celebration, complete with speeches from local leaders.[60]

Yet despite their success and their show of civic responsibility, Italians faced considerable opposition to their integration into Spokane society. Adding to the general anti-immigrant sentiment in the state and Spokane in particular, Washington representative Albert Johnson (1869–1957) sponsored the Immigration Act in 1924 (Johnson-Reed Act) and was president of the Eugenics Research Association. Eugenic "science" at the time placed southern Italians at the low end of the genetic hierarchy. Italian immigrants bore the additional stigma of being criminals and of importing the notorious La Mano Nero. Mayor of Seattle from 1918 to 1919, Ole Hanson also stoked anti-immigrant sentiment in his opposition to what he described as the "anarchist" International Workers of the World and union organizing in Seattle. In his anti-Semitic work *Americanism versus Bolshevism* (1920), Hanson used two popular tropes for anti-Semitism, "Bolshevism" and "cosmopolitanism." Nativists employed both words to support the myth of Jewish communism and to stoke anti-immigrant sentiment at the time.[61]

Adding to Italians' negative image, labor leaders resisted hiring them on road construction because they felt that Italians were prone to work for wages below those paid to American workers. During the labor strife that hit Spokane between 1890 and 1917, Italians were not as visible in the union movement as they were in other parts of the West. As one labor leader pointed out in the local press, Italian immigrants were most often itinerant, unreliable workers who lived on subsistence wages. Union bosses also characterized Italians as strikebreakers. Contrary to Albi's success, some labor leaders continued to believe that what little they did earn, Italians did not invest in the community but instead sent all their savings to relatives in Italy. Adding to their problems in Spokane, in 1896 the American Protective Association, with the mayor's support, convinced the city not to hire Catholics. In 1908 union leaders tried but failed to influence the city to pass an ordinance that prohibited immigrants from holding municipal jobs. Instrumental in the ordinance's failure, Joseph Plastino, the Italian consul general in Spokane, inspired 744 Italians to form a protest group to oppose the ordinance.[62]

Yet such anti-Italian and anti-Catholic rhetoric never became a permanent barrier to Italian success. In remote Spokane, there were miles of tracks to be laid and a scarcity of laborers. There was as well a fast-growing enclave business economy that not only created profits for enterprising immigrants but, equally important, created new tax revenue as well. In spite of those who opposed their presence in the state, immigrants found support among state, county, and city officials, as well as business interests that were well aware of their contribution to the region's economy. In fact, as Congress debated the passage of immigrant exclusion acts in the 1920s, culminating in the passage of the 1924 Immigration Act, the North German Lloyd steamship line asked their two hundred western agents to write to their congressmen to vote against immigration restriction.[63]

Walla Walla—Italians and Onions

Besides King, Pierce, and Spokane Counties, Italians settled another major farming region in the state, Walla Walla County. At the turn of the nineteenth century, it was a sparsely populated region that offered cheap but fertile land. As a result, it became a destination for Italians seeking a quick foothold in the state's economy. Among the very first Italians to reach the Washington Territory was Frank Orselli, born in Lucca in 1833. He was the first recorded Italian immigrant to settle the Washington Territory. As an infantryman stationed at Fort Walla Walla in 1857, upon his discharge he remained in the town. By 1865 he owned 180 acres of land just north of Main Street, where he planted vines, vegetables, and an orchard. He also opened the California Bakery, a general merchandise store selling not only baked goods but supplies, liquor, and his own produce and wine as well. Winemaking soon became Orselli's main occupation. In 1875 he crushed six thousand pounds of grapes and produced more than three hundred gallons of white wine. He increased production the following year to more than twenty-five hundred gallons, nearly all the grapes coming from his own vineyard. Before his death in 1894, Orselli was credited with being a visionary in large-capacity wine production in advance of even the many successful bulk wine producers in California.[64]

Other early arrivals in Walla Walla included Pasquale Saturno, who left the island of Ischia off the coast of Naples and settled in Walla Walla in 1876. In 1888 he sent for his wife and children. He was the first commercial farmer in Walla Walla. On his 80-acre farm, in addition to his fruit and vegetable crops, he planted a vineyard and imported two to four tons of Zinfandel grapes each year from California to make his own wine. Before he died in 1919, he was a well-known citizen active in Republican politics.[65]

At about the same time that Saturno arrived, Joseph Tachi, from Lombardy, landed in Walla Walla. Saturno and Tachi began what would soon become an established, well-organized community of Italian truck farmers that remains even today. They were followed in Walla Walla in 1886 by Louis Rizzuti from Calabria and Tony Locati from Lombardy. Also from Lombardy, John Arbini arrived in Walla Walla in 1890. Chain migration and the railroads soon brought scores of new arrivals from northern and southern Italy, mainly Lombardy and Calabria. Most of those from Lombardy, largely from Milan, settled in a northern neighborhood, while the Calabrese bought cheaper land and began farming in the southern part of town. At one point before 1940, so many Italian children attended the Branden School in town that it became known as "the Italian school." By 1910 there were 259 Italians in Walla Walla County. They were fifth in order behind the Germans (665), Canadians (508), English (331), and Irish (307). When most Italian numbers decreased in western enclaves, the increase to 301 Italians in the county by 1920 testifies to the county's attractiveness to the immigrant farmer.[66]

Italians in Walla Walla established an Italian Workingmen's Association and a newspaper. However, as a result of the cultural divide between the northern and southern Italians in the valley, the association did not survive. The Italian community did contribute funds for the building of the Catholic school and St. Patrick's Church, which they shared with other Catholic groups. But differing religious observances were still an issue for immigrant Catholics, and Italians began to lobby for their own parish. In 1913 Father G. R. Balducci arrived to aid in funding the new Italian parish. In 1915 St. Francis of Assisi Church opened its doors to the Italian families in the valley. The original church was replaced in 1939 by a new church. As a measure of the cultural differences that had once separated the northern and southern Italians, the new church still has the original pews, which are labeled "Donated by the Northern Colony" and "Donated by the Southern Colony." It appears that church attendance may well have been segregated.[67] It is doubtful that the next generation of Italian Americans would have honored such a division.

While their regional identities distinguished the parish community, outside the church they eventually discovered their common interests. Many were farmers whose economic interests and success were linked. Italian families formed work parties to harvest their carrots, beets, and other vegetables. As they did in King and Pierce Counties, Italians soon dominated the truck-farming business in Walla Walla. They became aware, if slowly, that cooperation was their best strategy in the marketplace. As a result, by 1916 the Italian community formed the Walla Walla Gardeners Association (WWGA) in order to ensure a fair price for their produce. It also served as a marketing cooperative, a packinghouse for their produce, and a credit union. It sold groceries to its membership at cost, and was the only source in the Walla Walla Valley for Italian products. The association also purchased grapes from California and made its own wine for sale to its membership.[68] This association lasted and is now more than one hundred years old.

While the early Italian farmers in Walla Walla shipped a variety of produce, they specialized in a product that soon became the iconic symbol of the Italian community in Walla Walla: a savory, sweet onion. As early as 1863, the Chinese had planted the first onions in the valley. However, some believed that Italian immigrant Pete Pieri brought the first seeds of the Walla Walla sweet onion from Corsica around the turn of the century. This particular species of onion matured early and did well in Walla Walla winters. The seeds and plantings soon spread to other Italian farmers. A local newspaper spread the word that Italian gardeners were planting French onions in Walla Walla. By 1915, because of its origins in French-controlled Corsica, it became known in the Milanese dialect as *la cipulla francaisa.* Because of the market that the French onion had created, soon Italian gardeners were planting other varietals that did well in Walla Walla's climate and soil.[69]

Walla Walla Italians were an important piece of Washington State's agricultural production that they shared with Chinese farmers. As one monthly publication reported, "In the vegetable industry, John Chinaman and the sons of Italy cut considerable figures. As gardeners, these two classes have few superiors." By 1920 Washington's agricultural development placed the state third in the West, behind Texas and California. Washington had 66,288 farms with more than thirteen million acres under production. In fact, it had a larger percentage of the state's land, 31 percent, under production than California's 29.5 percent. Always an interesting and telling agricultural statistic, the state boasted more than 52,700 owner-operated farms, with only 12,419 tenant farmers. This high ratio of owner-occupied farms to tenant farmers is a testimony to both the affordability of land in Washington and the immigrant's ability to capitalize a farming enterprise with savings from wages earned elsewhere. In grape production in 1920, California led Washington, which had approximately five hundred thousand vines planted. Little did he realize it, but Frank Orselli, a pioneer in wine production, left a legacy in the state. Walla Walla, which became an officially designated American Viticultural Area (AVAS) in 1984, now has more than one hundred wineries. These wineries are counted among Washington's total of more than nine hundred wineries. In addition to Walla Walla, the Columbia Valley and the Yakima Valley are now AVAS-designated areas.[70]

Late-Generation Revival

The story of Washington's Italian immigrants does not end with the peak years of immigration. Typical of the post-1960s ethnic revival, from the original immigrant population of fewer than 4,000, Washington now has 191,442 Italian Americans, ranking sixth in the West, with 3.2 percent of the state's population. Out of fifty major cities, Seattle ranks twenty-fifth in the United States and eighth among western cities, with 21,754 Italian Americans, 3.8 percent of its population. There are more than a dozen active Italian American clubs in the metropolitan area of Seattle, including the Italian Club of Seattle, founded in 1919 as the Italian Commercial Club.[71]

Seattle now has three annual Italian festivals: a Little Italy Festival in Pioneer Square, a San Gennaro Festival in South Seattle, and Festa Italiana held in the Seattle Center. While these festivals recall the city's immigrant roots, they also reflect the transnational theme in Italian American communities in the West. To encourage contemporary business and trade, in 1992 Seattle created a sister city with Perugia, Italy. In addition to its annual festivals, Walla Walla also created a sister city with the town of Cannara, appropriately Italy's onion capital. Overall, there are at least eighteen Italian cultural organizations between Seattle and Tacoma alone. There are five chapters of the Order Sons of Italy and one Seattle Trentino Club. In addition, Seattle has a Dante Alighieri Society that holds language classes for all ages and in general promotes Italian culture in the city. Adding to the transnational theme in Italian organizations, Seattle hosts an annual Italian film festival, Cinema Italian Style. In 1966 Italian Americans established the Italian American Club of Spokane that sponsors an annual summer Italian Festival that raises funds for a variety of causes. In 2016 Spokane formed a sister-city relationship with Cagli in the Le Marche region of Italy. This was the fourth sister-city relationship in Washington, including the town of Auburn with Mola di Bari.[72]

Third-generation Italian American farmers continue today to farm Walla Walla onions. In 1986 Walla Walla Italian Americans established the Italian Heritage Association. Still guided by its 1916 charter, the Walla Walla Gardeners Association is the oldest cooperative in the West. It remains active in the area's newly formed Italian Heritage Association. In 1980 the original Saturno house in Walla Walla was placed on the National Register of Historic Places, and it remains today owned by the Saturno family. With the support of such groups as the WWGA, the Walla Walla community celebrates both Italian Heritage Festa and the Sweet Onion Festival each year.[73] Whether local or transnational in scope, Italians helped to transform Washington from a far-northwestern territory to a state that shares in America's immigrant heritage.

IV

THE FAR WEST

CHAPTER 11

OREGON

Oregon's Checkered History—The Ku Klux Klan and Immigration

Although seldom recognized in the literature on immigration, Oregon was a destination for Italians and other immigrant groups. In spite of its liberal image today, Oregon has a checkered history. Before 1920 its state and business interests began a concerted effort to recruit immigrants to develop the state's resources. However, Linda Gordon argues that Oregon was once "arguably the most racist place outside the southern states, possibly even all the states." To balance the record, the newly revived Klan had a similar influence during the 1920s in Colorado. In Oregon the Klan was equally successful in promoting its anti-Catholic, anti-Semitic, anti-immigrant, and anti–African American platform. The Klan's influence lasted for a decade, from 1922 to 1932, when it elected the majority of state and local officials. While attracting the highest number of immigrants in the state, Portland became the epicenter of the Klan's activities. During its approximately ten-year reign in Oregon, the Klan was influential in passing laws that were designed to limit the settlement of African Americans and the "wrong kind" of immigrants. The laws also included the restriction of property ownership and the prohibition of "interracial marriages." The Klan influenced the Oregon Legislature to pass a law that did not require a unanimous jury decision, thus allowing courts to easily convict immigrants of crimes and incarcerate them. Oregon joined Louisiana, at the time the only two states that passed the Jim Crow–era law, which Louisiana had passed to mitigate African Americans' influence on juries' decisions against African American defendants. Based on its 100 percent American campaign, the Klan attacked with impunity all institutions that it thought were undermining American culture, including parochial schools and official state and business agencies that were actively recruiting immigrants.[1]

Despite the Klan's political influence in the state, its policies and the laws they managed to pass never became a permanent barrier to immigrant success. However, the same cannot be said for African Americans and Native Americans, who labored under broader restrictions of their rights throughout the United States. The economic needs of the state, the official sponsorship of immigrant labor, the power of labor contractors, and industries' ever-growing need for labor all militated against the Klan's efforts to create a uniform composition of Oregon's population. In spite of the Klan's policies and influence, immigrants achieved success and in the process helped develop the state's considerable resources.

Jesuits and First Settlers

Before 1830 there were no Italians registered in the Oregon Territory. By the 1850s, the usual contingent of Jesuits began to establish missions in the region that would become the state of Oregon in 1859. Among the first six who entered the territory, three were Italian, including Father John Nobili, who had worked previously in the state of Washington. Upon settling in the territory, he began his work among the Native populations, which included baptisms and other sacraments. He was followed in the region by Father Michael Accolti, who helped found St. Francis Xavier Mission on the Willamette River.[2]

By the late 1850s, one Italian of note did settle the territory. From Milan, S. N. Arrigoni arrived with his Irish wife and established a roughly furnished hostel, the Pioneer, located on the banks of the Willamette River. He soon expanded his hostel to a three-hundred-bed hotel. At this remote and unlikely location, the hotel soon became well known and hosted many famous people, among them Giuseppe Garibaldi, General Ulysses S. Grant, and William Tecumseh Sherman. Arrigoni's influence in early Portland grew with his fame as a successful hotelier. He was instrumental in organizing Portland's Arlington Club and the town's first Masonic lodge. He introduced the first streetlamps in Portland, which were erected outside his hotel. Upon his death in 1869, he was remembered in the town as one of Portland's most important settlers.[3]

Immigrant Settlement

With immigrants still only sparsely represented in the state, by the mid-1870s Oregon officials felt that they were not getting their fair share of those "substantial, industrious people" who were beginning to arrive in surrounding western states. In 1874 the state legislature established the Board of Immigration Commission, composed of state officials, local businessmen, and representatives of transportation companies. The commission distributed fliers and pamphlets aimed at the immigrant population in the East. The commission also went so far as to set up twenty-two special commissions, one each in New Zealand and Canada and ten in Europe and the United States.[4]

Commission members were well aware of the anti-immigrant sentiment in the state. As a result, the commission was ordered to recruit only the most "'desirable' foreigners," mainly Germans and Scandinavians. However, the northern European immigrant labor pool was not sufficient to meet their needs. As a result, with the need for a large workforce, including farmers, labor agents were forced to recruit southern Europeans and Asians. By 1880 Oregon had 30,503 foreign born; by 1890 Oregon's foreign-born population rose again to 57,817. As a result of the commission's efforts, by 1920 Oregon's foreign-born population swelled to 107,644, nearly 14 percent of the total population. The state's population jumped from 413,536 in 1900 to more than 783,389 by 1920, when immigration leveled off. Among the foreign born in 1890, Italians numbered only 589. But by 1910, the peak year for Italian settlement in Oregon, that number grew to 5,535 before the number declined to 4,324 in 1920.[5]

Although the state's numbers declined, there was a higher concentration of Italians in both Multnomah County and in Portland, the county seat. By 1920 Multnomah County had 3,052 Italians. Portland had the lion's share of the county's population at 2,847, an increase of 290 over the city's Italian population in 1910. There was a similar increase in the number of Italians in the county. The increase in the number suggests that Portland provided better than average opportunities for Italians and other immigrants. In 1920 Italians ranked seventh in Portland behind, in order, Canadians, Germans, Russians, Swedes, English, and Norwegians. The Willamette Valley, where Portland is located, was by far the most populated area of Oregon and the largest farm-producing region in the state. By 1920 immigrant farmers in the Willamette Valley produced enough products for export from the state. Fifty-one percent of the state's population resided in its towns, while Portland contained 31 percent of the state's urban population. Italians not residing in Portland were widely dispersed in the state's small towns, where they did not establish enclave settlements as large or as productive as Portland's Italian community. Out of Oregon's thirty-six counties at the time, only four had more than 100 Italians, and none, with the exception of Multnomah, had more than 200 Italians. Otherwise, Italians ranked seventh in the county behind Canadians, Germans, Swedes, Russians, English, and Norwegians. Although their numbers declined, especially the Chinese, from the 1910 census there were also smaller numbers of Chinese and Japanese in the county and in Portland by 1920. Additionally, in 1857 just before statehood, Oregonians voted against slavery in the territory but also voted to deny residency to freed blacks. However, the law was rescinded, and by 1920 there were 2,144 African Americans in the state.[6]

In a pattern that was similar throughout the Far West, the state commission, railroads, and labor agents brought thousands of single men to Oregon. Out of the total Oregon population of Italians in 1910, only 771 were women counted against 4,767 men, leaving about 618 males per 100 women. If they were previously married, they then sent to Italy for their wives. It was not uncommon for single men to make the arduous and time-consuming voyage back to their native villages to marry and bring their wives west. Because of its distance from Italy, the West posed a special problem for those who wished to return periodically to their native villages. As a result, there were few birds of passage in the Far West. For the Eastern Seaboard, however, in one four-year period before World War I, for every 100 Italian immigrants who arrived, 75 returned home. Although set in the postwar period in Quebec, *Beyond the Ruins*, a play by Toronto resident Marco Micone, dramatizes the social and psychological bifurcation that workers experienced while trying to live between two cultures.[7]

There is an aspect of the Italian women's narrative that is often obscured, because it is not directly a part of the immigrant historical record in the United States. But it is no less significant in immigration's impact on women, especially in the remote western states. Wives left behind in their native villages had to endure months of uncertainty, not knowing if their husbands had arrived or were even alive. Married but without her husband in the house, she became stigmatized by the term *vedova bianca* (white widow). The *vedova bianca* was often disrespected and feared by the married women in the village for her potential competition for married men's attention. Worse, a pregnant wife left behind had to endure the added humiliation of the village gossips' sharp tongues. If she were not taken in by her parents or other relatives, she had to work in the surrounding fields to survive or until money arrived from her husband. When that letter arrived asking her to join her husband in the West, she had to undertake the odyssey alone, sometimes bringing children with her for the monthlong journey to the West. There were times that some wives simply refused to join their husbands. They feared, justifiably, that they would never see their parents again. In one instance, a husband returned to Italy three times before, after fifteen years, he was able to convince his wife to move to Portland in 1927. Life was worse if her immigrant husband was killed, thus leaving her destitute. What wives and widows had to endure in the immigrant process on both sides of the Atlantic is often buried in family oral history and is unrecorded in official historical documents.[8]

In addition to chain migration and the state's official efforts to attract immigrants, labor contractors played a significant role in Oregon's settlement. More than twelve Italian labor contractors lived in Portland's eastside neighborhood where Italians and other immigrants settled. Many of these Italian labor contractors were self-appointed, while others were in the employ of railroads, mining companies, and other industries in the region. The relatively high number of Japanese immigrants in Oregon at the time can be attributed to the Japanese-born Ban Shinzaburo. By the 1920s, Shinzaburo was based in Portland and supplied Japanese labor to several railroads, mining companies, and large farming enterprises throughout the West.[9]

If Italians and other immigrants did not have a job upon arrival, they could purchase a job for three dollars at one of several employment agencies in Portland. Otherwise, the highest percentage of Italians in the state, 27.4 percent, were employed by the railroad, while the next highest was farming at 20.2 percent, followed by merchants at 13.1 percent and logging at 11.9 percent. The remainder, working in construction, ranching, and mining, constituted 1.9 percent of the workforce. In Portland's enclave, Italians held a variety of jobs. About 13 percent of the Italians in Portland were shopkeepers, third behind railroad workers and farmers, while nearly 12 percent worked in the lumber industry. The rest worked in construction, 2.4 percent, and stonemasonry, 2.4 percent. By 1916 there were approximately 200 Italian families in Portland representing numerous regions from north to south: Calabria, 62; Abruzzo, 35; Liguria, 29; Sicily, 27; Puglia, 11; Piedmont, 9; and Tuscany, 7.[10]

In the state, southern Italians composed more than 60 percent of the Italian immigrants. The largest concentration, 33 percent, came from Calabria, while the next-largest group was from Sicily at 14.8 percent, followed by those from Abruzzo at 8.6 percent and Puglia at 6.2 percent. In the North, 21 percent came from Liguria, followed by Piedmont with 6.2 percent and Tuscany with nearly 5 percent. By the 1930s, Genovese immigrants (from Liguria) established farms from north to south Portland. There were as well about 135 Tyrolean Italian families who settled in Portland by 1920. They had immigrated to the state to work in the gold and copper mines.[11] The high concentration of southern Italians suggests that the state's efforts at recruiting immigrants no doubt concentrated on southern Italy.

The shortage of labor in the Portland area provided higher wages for even the unskilled laborer. Oregon shared with other western states in the imbalance between high wages and low cost of living, including cheap land. In other parts of the United States, the Italian worker was often placed on the lowest rung of the racial and economic ladder. In New York City, for example, in the racialized lexicon of the era, the "Common laborer, white" earned between $1.30 and $1.50 a day; the "Common laborer, colored" earned between $1.25 and $1.40; and the "Common laborer, Italian" earned between $1.15 and $1.25. But because of the shortage of labor in the West, the economic needs of the region trumped race, at least for the immigrant class. In Portland the average day laborer could earn as much as $1.50 a day. The lumber industry paid from $2.00 to $3.00 a day. Railroad workers worked for as high as $3.00 to $4.00 a day, while mining wages ranged from $2.50 a day to as high as $8.00 at the outbreak of US involvement in World War I.[12] All these wages were commensurate with the wage scale throughout the West at the time. The arrival of the railroad allowed for the growth of logging, mining, and farming, all of which contributed to the development of a lucrative business environment in Portland's immigrant enclave.

Enclave Entrepreneurs—Portland

As loggers or section-hand workers on the railroad in the wilderness, Italian men had little on which to spend their money besides their living expenses. With their excess cash, some sent money to their families in Italy. There were no Italian banks in Portland. A. P. Giannini had not yet begun his banking empire, which would extend to Oregon by the 1920s. Otherwise, Italians used the First National Bank with its two Italian translators to wire money to their relatives in their home villages. In time, many were able to afford small bungalows in Portland's enclave, open a business, or make a down payment on one of the inexpensive pieces of land near the city, where they joined other Italian truck farmers.[13]

Portland's Italians were scattered throughout the city, with concentrations along certain avenues, east and south. The first Italian colony in Portland was established near the city dump. By the late 1880s, Italians settled in two neighborhoods near rail yards, Italian Row in East Portland and Italian Gardeners' Garden that was located near the Willamette River. In the general area of the east side, there were approximately 1,300 Italian immigrants. Other groups settled in similar patterns. There was a large settlement of Jewish immigrants that numbered 2,220 in the enclave. Southwest Portland was the settlement of southern Italians, mainly from Calabria, Basilicata, Abruzzo, and Sicily. Proximity to their jobs was also a factor in where they settled. Genovese farm laborers lived mainly in an area known as Penrose Park in northeast Portland, while Italians working on the Southern Pacific Railroad or the Southern Pacific Electric light rail lived in southwest Portland near their job sites.[14]

With the growing Italian presence in Portland's enclave, there was plenty of room in the grocery and import market. Italian food products such as olive oil were in high demand. Frank Amato emigrated from a small town near Palermo when he was fourteen. After landing first in Canada and working on the railroad, in 1887 he settled in Portland, where he began a wholesale produce business. He soon became one of Portland's chief produce distributors. After he felt financially secure, he returned to Italy, married, and brought his entire family to Portland, including three brothers and three sisters. The Amato family was joined in the enclave by Vito Vitti, who was the owner of the Garibaldi Grocery and who also worked as a labor agent. From 1910 through the 1920s, he found jobs for men as far away as Idaho on the railroads, in construction, and in the timber industry. In addition to his labor services, because of his imported Italian products, he attracted a dedicated Italian clientele.[15]

The free-labor worker was able to move quickly in the Oregon labor market. Sam Simonatti, originally a carpenter, came from Tuscany. However, the mechanized, machine-driven wood industry was alien to Simonatti's skills. As a result, he felt that there was no place for his artisan skills in carpentry. He purportedly complained, "In Italy everything was done by hand—here machines." He took his first job in 1914 in Tacoma, where he worked on the railroad and later in the lumber industry and finally on road construction. However, when he reached Portland, he did in fact find a market for his carpentry skills. Combining their money, he and two other Italians opened a building company. To upgrade his skills, he attended trade school in Portland in 1918.[16]

To accommodate Portland's Italian population, grocery stores, saloons, restaurants, private homes, boardinghouses, and hotels provided familiar food and social meeting places for single men and families in the enclave. Among the earliest boardinghouses, two were owned and operated by Michele Del Conte on Gibbs Street and Abramo Cereghino on Front Street. For a more exclusive clientele, Angiolo Aletro owned and ran the Italian Hotel on the corner of Fifth and Pine Streets. The enterprising Campi family from northern Italy owned not only Campi's Hotel at 86 First Street but also a saloon and a restaurant with a menu that included "Macaroni, Ravioli, Taglierini, Lasagne, Spaghetti, and Risotto." Sammy Amato ran a popular barbershop in town, while the enclave also had, besides Vitti's Garibaldi Grocery, Quilici's Italian Delicatessen and Grocery and the Colombo Tomato Paste Company. There was an Italian information bureau for new arrivals in the enclave and an Italian Hall for community events.[17] Italian-owned hotels, familiar food, and community meeting places for arriving Italians provided them all with a sense of belonging in their new home in the far-western settlement.

With the growth of the Italian population in the Italian Row district, in 1894 Portland's Catholic archdiocese turned over control of a small chapel on the corner of Southwest Fourth Avenue and Mill Street to Italian priest Father Titus Piacentini. After an initial renovation of the building, Father Piacentini began having regular Sunday Masses for the Italian community under the new name, St. Michael's Parish. The church's cornerstone bears the inscription "Chiesa Italiana di San Michele Arcangelo, Fabbricata Della Colonia Italiana di Portland, Oregon, A 1901 D." In 1899 Rome declared the church an Italian National Parish. Following Father Piacentini's work at St. Michael's, Father Alexander Cestelli arrived in 1901 and decided that the parish needed a larger church. Within six weeks, he raised from his immigrant parishioners more than $7,000, and within another three months Cestelli more than doubled the donations to $15,000, the amount needed to begin building the new church. When it was finished in June 1902, the 4,275-square-foot church, with a 35-foot vault, became the center of community and family events. By 1912 Italians had become so numerous on the east side of the Willamette River that they funded the construction of another church, St. Philip Neri, on Southeast Sixteenth Avenue. The arriving priests that came directly from Rome resided at the Graziano family home on Division Street until the completion of the rectory and church. The community celebrated the first Mass on Christmas Day 1913. The parish also included a school run by an order of nuns.[18]

Although Italians lived in neighborhoods composed largely of *paesani* from their dialect groups, they did not dominate any single area. Rather, all the immigrants, including late-generation American workers, lived among each other and worked together. There was the usual tension between northern and southern Italians. By living in close proximity, attending the same parish, and working together, they eventually overcame the cultural barriers that had separated them for centuries in Italy.[19] Life in Portland's Catholic churches also brought Catholics from other national groups together since they shared the same Latin liturgy and often participated in the same church societies.

Women—The Italian Family and Portland Social Life

As it was in other states, women, mothers, and daughters worked for the support and maintenance of their families. Even though they did essential work on the farm or in the home, their labor too often came under the category of "domestic" work. Their contribution was seldom defined as essential, family-sustaining work. Figures are hard to come by, but oral history indicates that women sometimes took excess produce from the family garden and sold it at Portland's downtown markets. In addition to their home gardens, many Italian families lowered food costs by planting a garden in a large area known as Ladd's Addition in southeast Portland. Producing more than the family could consume, wives also added to the family income by transporting their extra produce from their Ladd's plot to area markets. Sometimes older daughters in a household took in laundry to add additional income.[20] With the responsibilities that came with running a well-organized household, raising a family, and having enough food on the table, wives and daughters did not have idle time, whether they lived in the enclave or on a farm.

Among the most important public images of the immigrant in America at the time was a well-kept and orderly home, especially its outside appearance visible to passersby. In the early-twentieth-century discourse over immigration, pro-immigrant supporters such as Lord, Eliot, and Trenor as well as Antonio Mangano promoted the social and religious suitability of the Catholic Italian family in American society. Much of what they had to say in their books focused on the compatibility of Italian and American values and Italians' willingness to assimilate into American culture. Mangano wrote about the important religious and educational role that Italian women played in the support of the family. Lord, Eliot, and Trenor focused on Italians' economic contribution to the United States and, above all, their social and cultural compatibility with American values, especially the high value that Italians placed on the family managed by women. They reported that "Italians like to have their homes neat and attractive, and Italian women as a body are excellent housewives." As Richard Gambino wrote, "The home was the site and the source of all that gave meaning to life" within Italian culture. He added, "A well-kept home was the symbol of a sound family."[21]

Immigrant women played an important role not only in the quality of family life but also in the assimilation of the next generation into American life. As Gambino explained, echoing Mangano's view of the Italian mother, she was "the 'center' of the family" and "in a critical way the center of the culture." Too often in a patriarchal social order, her role within the home has been stereotyped as the stay-at-home "Italian mama" who contributes little to the successful public persona of the Italian immigrant. However, women were important in creating a positive image of the Italian family in America in the face of the stereotypes of the Italian immigrant at the time.[22] Beyond the home, women also participated in the much-needed and important church societies and cultural associations. They contributed to a more cohesive social order in the community.

As they organized and came together as a community, Italians became more visible in Portland's social life and business community. The Italian Ranchers and Gardeners Association started a produce market on Clay Street similar to Pike Place Market in Seattle. Because the wood pilings of the building were sunk into the banks of the Willamette River, the market's foundation soon decayed. In 1906 the association moved the market east of the river, where it was more accessible to Italian growers, who dominated the new market. The cost of a five-foot-square stall for the farmer was a mere fifteen cents a day. Families such as Fazio, DeBenedetti, Rossi, Garbarino, Spada, Cereghino, and other farmers sold their fruits and vegetables in the market each day. If there was no room in the market on any given day, other farmers sold their produce from their wagons in the streets. The market manager hired young boys before and after school to clean the stalls. As the number of Italian truck farmers grew, in 1908 Italians established the Unione dei Rivenditori di Frutta ed Erbaggi, a cooperative of fruit and vegetable vendors.[23]

Portland did not have a Little Italy. Rather, the town center was a bustling multicultural immigrant enclave. By 1910, among more than twenty-three other immigrant groups living in Portland, Italians ranked ninth behind, in order, Germans, Canadians, Swedes, Russians, English, Norwegians, Austrians, and Irish. Before 1900 Jews had also begun to move to Portland, and by 1910 they established a settlement in south Portland. By 1920 Jewish children were 40 percent while Italian children were 17 percent of the enrollment of the Failing Elementary school in south Portland. The school was especially attentive to immigrant pupils' needs and established "Opportunity Classes" for those children who were not working up to grade level. In line with the federal government's "crusade for assimilation," education officials provided funds to ensure children's success at school.[24]

Jews in the commercial sector of the city specialized in kosher products, secondhand clothing, and dental clinics, while Italians filled in with saloons, barbershops, grocery stores, and merchandise shops. Jews established about six small congregations, which by the mid-1920s had merged into three large synagogues. They established free-loan societies, mutual-benefit societies, and a Neighborhood House for cooking and language lessons and other services. Unlike Butte, Montana, the enclave was less a western boomtown than a family-sustaining business district. The neighborhood was relatively stable, with most businesses remaining in place for more than a decade and with more than 80 percent of the families remaining in the city throughout the 1920s and later.[25]

Because of the high percentage of southern Italians in Portland, there was only a small professional class of Italian immigrants in the city, approximately 1 percent. The reason for this was that between 1900 and 1910, immigration officials calculated that approximately 57 percent of the incoming Italians were illiterate. Figures for the same period indicated that more than 70 percent of southern Italians were illiterate, in spite of the fact that in the 1870s Italy passed the Coppino Law, mandating that all Italians between the ages of six and nine attend school. Italian educators in Italy had concluded that these three years of education would give children the basics they needed to be responsible citizens in the new republic: basic math skills and the ability to read and write standard Italian. But the new law did not radically change educational standards in southern Italy. As Pino Aprile wrote in *Terroni*, southern Italian schools, even today, have inferior teachers and lower-achieving students. In 1911, 37.6 percent of the Italian population over six years old was illiterate. In four southern regions—Abruzzo, Basilicata, Calabria, and Sicily—the average rate of illiteracy was 67.7 percent. Calabria's illiteracy rate, at 70 percent, was the highest among the four. Accordingly, approximately 37 percent of the Italians in Portland had no education at all, and only about 27 percent had achieved the requisite three years of schooling in Italy before coming to the United States. Northern Italians were far more likely to have completed the three years of education. As a result, being educationally ahead of southern Italians, these northern Italians raised the first generation of Italian Americans who went to school and then on to the professional class.[26]

But there were notable exceptions from southern Italy. Active in Italian American affairs, entrepreneur Joseph Lemma, born in Bari, began as a laborer in a local sawmill before he was able to open a winery and what later became the largest department store in Linnton, minutes north of Portland. Bonaventura De Rosa, born in Cosenza, was a distinguished doctor in Portland, where he later became a community leader and founded a newspaper. Editor Joseph De Santis, also born in Cosenza, directed many of Portland's Italian organizations and was active in local politics as well. Also among the city's accomplished Italians, Raffaele Colonna, born in Bari, was a pharmacist in Portland after World War I. He began his distinguished career at Bari's Regio Istituto Tecnico Pitagora, where he graduated in physics and mathematics. He later attended the Royal University of Rome, where he took another degree in engineering. After arriving in Oregon in 1922, he attended Reed College in Portland, the University of Oregon, the University of Oregon Medical School, and North Pacific College in Portland, where he graduated with a degree in pharmacy and a bachelor of science in 1925. He was president of the Italian School Committee in Oregon, founded the Italian School of the Dante Society in 1933, and was influential in having Italian taught in the public schools in Portland. He was a charter member of the Portland Lodge, a chapter of the Order Sons of Italy. He wrote articles for numerous newspapers and periodicals. There were at least two other medical doctors in Portland, Dr. Visetta from Calabria and Dr. Candiani from northern Italy. Among Portland's most prominent Italians was Roberto Corruccini, who served as the director of Portland's Civic Opera Association and the American Grand Opera Company. Among the professional and business class, Mrs. Jerome Colosuonno was a public notary who moonlighted in the family grocery store. Mary DeMartini and a Mr. Gregorio worked at the First National Bank and conducted all the business for the bank's Italian customers.[27]

Farming

As a measure of the value that immigrant farmers brought to the land in Oregon, in 1900 the average cost of an acre in Willamette Valley was $25. By 1910 an acre of farmland rose to $75, before prices peaked in 1920 at $100 an acre, after which they gradually began to fall. Because of the quality of the land, prices in the Willamette Valley were double the cost of an acre compared to the rest of Oregon at $50 an acre. The best acreage in Oregon on average was about 30 percent higher than the average cost of an acre at $75 in other parts of the United States. However, in one notable exception, land prices in Iowa and the nation's Corn Belt states were as high as $225 an acre in 1920, before prices began a steep decline. To the immigrant's advantage, wages in the surrounding industries in Oregon were commensurate with the cost of the most expensive farmland in the state. Because of the climate and the confluence of the Columbia and Willamette Rivers in the Willamette Valley, water was less a concern than it was in other western states such as Nevada. As a result of the availability of water, more than half of Oregon's 64,862 farms in the 1920s were located in the Willamette Valley.[28]

By 1910 Italian immigrants had already purchased land in the outskirts of the growing city. In their settlement in Parkrose, the Genovese established ten- to fifteen-acre truck farms along the Columbia River. As Italians continued to buy land in the area, by 1930 there was a line of Italian truck farmers that ran from north Portland to the town of Milwaukie, eighteen miles south of the city. Sicilians also established farms in Beaverton, about ten miles west of downtown Portland. Many also had truck farms along Sandy Boulevard in northeast Portland and in Ladd's Addition southeast of the downtown district. These farmers started an open-air market in Portland at Union and Madison Streets. Only a small number of Italians went into ranching, 1.2 percent.[29]

By 1920 Oregon was sixth in the number of farms in the West behind Texas, California, Washington, Colorado, and Montana. Farmers produced a variety of grains, fruits, and vegetables, including wine grapes. The state had approximately thirteen million acres under production, slightly more than neighboring Washington's acreage, but only about 13 percent of California's farm acreage. Over 76 percent of the farms were owner occupied. By one estimate, Genovese immigrants composed the majority of the farmers. Twenty percent of the Italian immigrant workforce owned farms.

The Italians' and other immigrants' ability to purchase their farms was a measure of their rapid success in the immigrant economy in Oregon.[30]

Mutual-Aid Societies and Newspapers

Settlement and success in Italian communities were always followed by the establishment of mutual-aid societies. In 1889 early Portland Italians founded the Christopher Columbus Society, probably the first fraternal organization in the city. Established in New York City in 1905, the Order Sons of Italy had three chapters in Portland by 1922. In 1908 the Mazzini Society was organized by those who shared Mazzini's radical Republican political interests that had formed the basis of the new Italian state. There was also a Bersaglieri Society, composed of those who had served in the Piedmontese Bersaglieri unit in the Italian Army. Organizations such as the American Foresters, the Peddlers Union, and the Gardeners and Ranchers Association focused on employment. The Peddlers Union was composed of about 80 percent Sicilians, while the remaining 20 percent was composed of Calabrese and other southern Italians. The Gardeners and Ranchers Association, however, was a cross-section of the dialect groups, northern and southern. There was also the United Ancient Order of the Druids, which had more than one location in Portland. It provided insurance for widows and orphans as well as other community services aimed at the general Italian population. St. Michael's and St. Philip of Neri Church hosted the Daughters of Pompeii. Other women's organizations included the Italian Federation Hall and the Daughters of Italy as well as the Italian Red Cross staffed during World War I by women. These organizations were especially important to Italian women. They allowed them to create networks that addressed their particular concerns. Aware of their subaltern status as immigrants, made obvious by nativist sentiments and the revival of the KKK, in 1916 the locals established the Italian-American Republican Club, which had up to five hundred members. The club's hyphenated name is a sign of the Italian community's quest for assimilation into American culture. Its dual purpose was to aid in the naturalization of Italian immigrants and to encourage them to vote Republican.[31]

By the turn of the century, Portland established Italian magazines and newspapers, providing news from Italy, notices for community events, and advertising. As the official voice of the Catholic Church, the *Catholic Sentinel*, begun in 1870, continued to reach an English-reading audience well after the turn of the century. Printed in both English and Italian, the *Italian*

Tribune, established in 1889 in Seattle but edited in Portland by Albert Ferrera, was distributed throughout the Northwest.[32] Italian consular official in Portland, Dr. Carlo Visetti, in 1917 started the Italian-language *L'Asino* (the Donkey), which served as an official propaganda voice for the Italian government.

After closing his Spokane and Seattle newspapers, Dr. Bonaventura De Rosa moved his medical office to Portland, where he founded *La Stella.* All three newspapers competed for the Italian and Italian American readership in the city and at times disagreed in their editorial policies. Before De Rosa's paper came on the scene, Visetti and Ferrera had shared a long-standing animosity. Visetti's editorials were often at odds with Ferrara's more Americanized viewpoint in his *Tribune.* Raphael E. Romano edited a weekly magazine of lighter reading, *L'Italico*, an agricultural and literary publication.[33]

In 1930 Joseph De Santis began publishing the *Columbus Record.* Born in the province of Cosenza in southern Italy, De Santis immigrated to the United States in 1906 and became a US citizen in 1934. But De Santis's assimilation was not at the expense of his Italian heritage. A Republican and staunch Catholic, he became an indefatigable promoter of Italian culture in Portland. He persuaded the city council to name a city boulevard after the early Portland pioneer S. N. Arrigoni and was instrumental in placing four Italian Catholics on Portland's motion-picture Censor Board Committee. Along with Colonna, he influenced the local school board to place the Italian language in the curriculum. He established the original Portland Lodge, Order Sons of Italy, and served on numerous Italian American organizations, as well as being active in Republican politics in the city.[34] With the inclusion of the Italian language in the schools and with their social activism in other areas of Portland life, Italians had a significant impact on Oregon culture. By the 1940s, Italian influence would reach its zenith before its decline in the post–World War II years.

Late-Generation Revival

The Order Sons of Italy remains the only fraternal organization to survive from before 1940. After 1945 freeways, suburban growth, and relocation of families from central Portland scattered that once tight-knit community that had surrounded Portland's original immigrant churches, especially St. Michael's. World War II and Mussolini's joining the Axis powers also played a destructive role in the public identity of Italian Americans in the postwar era. As a result, Portland's Italian Americans lost touch with each other, but apparently did not forget their immigrant forebears. Since the 1960s, Italian Americans have reorganized. Designated a historical landmark in 1971, St. Michael's is currently undergoing restoration and retrofitting.[35] As a reminder of Portland's immigrant history, it is especially important for Italian Americans whose ancestors funded the construction of the church. Besides the Order Sons of Italy, before 1991 there was little in the way of public Italian American identity in Portland. However, in 1991 several Italian American organizations joined forces and set out to remedy their lack of visibility in the state.

Italian Americans established the Festa Italiana Association, which sponsors an annual weeklong community festival in August held in Portland's Pioneer Courthouse Square. In addition, the community began the annual Italian Film Festival USA of Portland, sponsored by the Italian Cultural Association of Portland. In 1996 Carlo Mannocci, who emigrated from Lucca, established the Tuscan Association of Oregon. For more than twenty years, the organization has sponsored an annual Festa della Befana as well as numerous concerts, lectures, films, and other events for the Italian and non-Italian community.[36] The festival focuses on modern Italy and Portland's history of Italian immigration.

The original 5,535 Italian immigrants who settled Oregon in 1910 now number 111,462 Italian Americans, 3.3 percent of the state's population, with a ranking of fifth out of the thirteen southwestern and western states. The Portland-Salem metropolitan district has 76,540 Italian Americans, a 3.3 percent share of the region's total population. Portland's Italian American community numbers 19,810, 3.7 percent of the city's population, with a ranking of tenth among western cities with the largest number of Italian Americans. Today there are seven Italian American organizations and at least three Italian-language groups. As Charles Gould wrote, "Portland has an easily identifiable population of Italian-Americans that still retain a touch of the old country in their habits of mind, social and domestic customs, and in their incredibly mellifluous names." The revival of Italian organizations and the establishment of annual festivals run by Italian Americans who have reclaimed their Italian heritage are further evidence of the perdurability of America's multicultural heritage. As Gans wrote, American identity remains fluid and unpredictable.[37]

CHAPTER 12

NEVADA

Settlement

Popular culture in the post–World War II era has too often erroneously identified the Las Vegas gaming industry as the locus of Italian influence in the state of Nevada. This inaccurate image has all but erased the importance that Italian immigrants played in the development of the state's resources before 1940. Italian immigrants settled Nevada before World War I in disproportionate numbers compared to the majority of western states. Those who arrived in Nevada before 1880 were largely northern Italians. As a measure of their early success, by 1880 these early arrivals in northern Nevada owned more than 7 percent of the taxable property in Eureka County, while representing just over 15 percent of the population, a little more than 1,000 Italian residents. By 1920 the state boasted a population of nearly 20 percent foreign born out of its sparse 77,407 inhabitants. By then there were 2,841 Italian immigrants in the state. They were first among all immigrants and composed the unusually high 17.7 percent of the foreign-born population. Overall, they were more than 3 percent of the state's total population.[1] These Italian immigrants arrived long before the gaming industry in Nevada became what it is today.

As early as the 1850s, northern Italians had come to Nevada, which became a state in 1864. In 1856 Chinese labor contractors brought in 200 Chinese workers to dig a water canal west of the town of Gold Canyon in what is now Lyon County in western Nevada. These Chinese immigrants established Nevada's first Chinatown in Dayton alongside the Italian enclave. In the 1860s, Italians came to Nevada to work on the transcontinental railroad. Initially, they settled in Truckee Meadows in Washoe County in western Nevada near the Reno-Sparks area. Truckee provided the arriving immigrants cheap farmland. Although many were from the North of Italy, a region with high rainfall, they quickly adapted to the farming techniques required in the desert climate. After 1870 and the completion of the railroad, Italians continued to arrive in the area to work on the growing number of ranches and to establish businesses in the nearby Reno-Sparks metropolitan area. By 1892 Italians established truck farms near Reno and had already opened some businesses thirty miles south in Carson City, Nevada's capital. There were enough Italians in Carson to establish the Società di Beneficenza Italiana and in 1902 the Ordine Internazionale dei Druidi.[2]

As the population grew in Washoe County, Italians began to establish enclaves in central Sparks on Prater Way in north Reno on Washington Street and another south of downtown Reno along the Truckee River. These early settlements soon became the basis of a larger Little Italy in the Reno-Sparks area. In addition, by 1900 Italians established a presence in Dayton in Lyon County, the far-western side of the state near the bend of the Carson River in Eureka County. By 1910 Washoe County had the highest number of Italian immigrants, 913, of any other county. In the larger urban settlements, Italians were concentrated in the Reno–Virginia City–Carson City region. Several of these original Italians opened restaurants and saloons in Reno.[3]

Mining

After the turn of the century, the eastern Nevada towns of Treasure, Ruth, Kimberly, Ely, and McGill in White Pine County on the eastern border of Utah became important mining centers. In Treasure City, Italians had settled the area as early as the 1870s to work in the mines. It seems that word was out concerning the hazards of mining. One Italian immigrant told a visitor to the state, "If you wish to sell coffee, or sugar or almost anything else, that is fine, but stay away from mining." Not all Italians would follow his advice. The Nevada Consolidated Copper Company, the Utah Copper Company, and the Cumberland-Ely Company had mines in the county that attracted Asians and European immigrants. Italians were fourth (203), behind Greeks (702), Austrians (250), and English (224). A vigorous labor market developed in the zone. In and around the now-abandoned Treasure, immigrants diversified and found well-paying jobs as smelter workers, mule packers, and charcoal burners. According to one report, they all made and saved substantial money, $200 to $300, before they left the mining industry.[4]

The larger number of Greek miners was the work of Greek labor contractor Louis Cononelos, who recruited more than 600 Greeks to work in the county's copper mines. By 1909 the new immigrants joined the local union. In 1909, led by the large faction of Greek miners, Japanese, Italian, Serbian, and Mexican miners struck and shut down the Cumberland-Ely Veteran Mine for more than two years in their successful demand for a

$3.50 daily pay scale. They struck again in 1912, putting more than 3,000 miners out of work. The miners, especially the Greeks, also rebelled against the excessive control that Cononelos and other labor contractors exercised over their work crews. They demanded that the labor-contractor system be abolished. Opposing the rebellious Greek workers, the antiunion Leon Skliris and his subordinate Greek agents met to form a plan to break the strike. Attempting to exploit the xenophobia of the local population and to turn public opinion against the striking miners, the unscrupulous labor contractors crafted press releases stating that the strike was organized by alien "nonwhite miners," Greeks, Mexicans, Japanese, Serbs, and Italians, against "white" American miners. Their plan failed.[5] As they had in other states in the West, the miners demonstrated how a multinational workforce could organize and work together when their economic interests were aligned.

The Eureka and Comstock mining booms in Virginia City, Storey County, also drew some of the initial Italian immigrants, mainly from Genoa and the Italian region of Switzerland. There were approximately 400 Tyroleans who worked in the copper, silver, and coal mines located near Virginia City. Italians had settled Virginia City as early as the 1860s. By 1861 M. Crosetta owned and operated the Virginia Saloon. To accommodate the influx of those early miners, in the same year an Italian owned and operated the Molinelli Hotel. There were enough Italians that by 1865 the Catholic hierarchy sent Father Dominic Monteverdi to minister to the Italian colony. Curiously, even in the sparsely settled Far West with few newspapers, in October 1870 the Italian community in Virginia City held a dinner to celebrate the unification of Italy. Their knowledge and approval of political events in distant Italy are revealing. In the first place, they must have been a literate group to be so well informed about the unification process in their homeland. That they approved and celebrated Italy's unification suggests also that they were from northern Italy, where support for unification was the strongest.[6]

Before the 1870s in Virginia City, the few Italians in the region worked in the mines. Typically, living cheaply and saving their money, they left the dangerous work in the mines and established ranches, farms, and small businesses. In 1874 a group of Italian investors took advantage of federal law, pooled their capital, and purchased fifty acres of land at little more than ten dollars an acre to establish the Roman Capital Gold and Silver Mining Company near Virginia City. The original investors were a diverse group that made up the board of trustees, composed of both northern and southern Italians. They issued six thousand shares that were initially divided among the various investors based on their investment. But their experiment in social capital did not last long. The investors quickly descended into litigation over control of the mine. Antonio Pitagna, Thomas Pettineli, Nicola Soffia, and Antonio Sitaro were the first elected officers and trustees. However, they were soon challenged and unseated, returning only Pitagna and Sitaro as trustees. The officers, trustees, and stockholders were so divided that by the mid-1880s, they were forced to dissolve the partnership.[7]

The investors seem to have divided along regional lines: four of the trustees were from the South, Lazio, Puglia, and Campania, while others were from Veneto in the North.[8] This squabble is worth the telling because it is another example of how quickly these types of divisions along regional lines disappeared among Italian immigrants. While they would continue to identify with their villages or regions, that familiar *campanilismo*, economic and social concerns would soon overcome their provincialism. In the short term, Italians learned what constituted their common interests with not only other Italians but other immigrants as well: joining unions, participating in strikes, and doing business together in their enclaves.

By the turn of the century, Italian settlements were located in two areas of the state: the Reno–Virginia City–Carson City zone and farther east in Eureka. At the time, Italians also made up the largest Catholic population in the state.[9] Railroad work and labor in the mines were the first steps of upward mobility for Italians. With wages high relative to the cost of living in the remote state, these early immigrants soon found both economic and social success beyond their expectations.

Enclaves and Commerce

An important step in the unification of the Italian community was the establishment of community and statewide newspapers. Linguistically, they were signs of a common culture and an indication of a common interest among the dialect groups that could read standard Italian. To service this diversely settled population throughout the state, the Reno-Sparks area on the western border of the state supported three Italian newspapers: *Bollettino del Nevada*, the paper with the largest circulation; *Corriere di Nevada*; and one publication in English, the *Italian French Colony News*. There were approximately six hundred French-speaking immigrants in

Nevada by 1920. With the decline of the immigrant population in the wake of the Johnson-Reed Act of 1924, the last of these Italian papers stopped publication by 1944.[10]

Before 1900, Austin in Lander County, east of Reno, also became home to Italian settlements. Samuel Crescenzo from Naples lived in Austin for four decades and owned and operated the International Hotel and a general store. His story exemplifies the mobility of the free-labor immigrant's ability to find opportunity in western enclaves. Born in 1833, he sailed to New York in the late 1840s and worked on steamships for twelve years before moving to San Francisco. He later opened a dry-goods store in Calaveras County and sold merchandise at Angels Camp. Settling in Washington for two years, he established another merchandise business before he arrived in Austin in 1864. Having saved enough money from his previous investments, he purchased commercial real estate, including the International Hotel, which he owned for thirty-seven years before his death in 1913.[11]

About 150 miles northeast of Austin in Elko, Elko County, Swiss Italian Emilio Dotta started as a common laborer hauling freight but soon owned and operated the largest milk- and dairy-supply company in the area. In 1875 Frank Pastorino from northern Italy arrived in Eureka, Eureka County; worked in the mines; and later bought the Hay Ranch, which became one of the most successful ranches in the area. He sold the ranch by 1937, purchased the Eureka Theatre, and became the town's assessor.[12]

In Paradise Valley, a small enclave in Humboldt County northwest of Eureka, Batista Recanzone and Angelo Forgnone became two of the wealthiest entrepreneurs in northern Nevada. As young men, they left Italy and traveled first to North Africa, where they worked in masonry. When they arrived in Paradise Valley in 1864, they began working common labor on the Winnemucca canals and later were hired as masons at Fort Scott. In a short time, they were able to parlay their savings into the purchase of numerous ranches and commercial buildings as well as the Silver State Flour Mill in 1890. Operating until 1945, the mill won prizes at the St. Louis Exposition in 1904 and the San Francisco Exposition in 1915.[13]

While many Italian immigrants were earning a living in smaller remote Italian settlements throughout the state, Reno, the county seat of Washoe County, still remained the location of choice for the majority of Italian entrepreneurs. Although Italians entered the United States at the bottom of the era's racial hierarchy, they were earning a place in Reno. In 1926

John Gottardi, a community member of Italian descent, wrote, "Speaking particularly of the Italians in Reno; the community is well organized with an excellent element. The people are daring, have initiative, [are] honest, good, and respected by the American population." A non-Italian resident said, "Our Italian people have become such fine citizens, and in two generations they have become complete Americans." Americanization was the era's litmus test for the acceptance of immigrants, especially Italian Catholics.[14]

But the national impetus to assimilate immigrants would not go unchallenged in Nevada. John Granata, the editor and publisher of the *Bollettino del Nevada*, concerned about the ease with which Italians were assimilating into Reno society, became the self-appointed conscience of the Italian community. Born and educated in Torre, Italy, he opened an insurance and travel office on Lake Street, and by 1911 he opened one of the city's most innovative businesses, a car wash. He began publishing the *Bollettino del Nevada* in 1915, which remained in publication until 1944. In editorials he urged his readership to remember their Italian heritage and not be too readily assimilated into the values of Protestant American life. In one editorial, he wrote, "The majority of Italians cannot think like Anglo-Saxons (those who try do not realize the consequences). Our ideal should not be the dollar; one does not live by bread alone. Do not forget Italy. Therefore, read Italian books, Italian magazines, and play Italian sports." In all immigrant communities, there was a tug-of-war between a sentimental attachment to their villages, in spite of the poverty that they had escaped and their desire to become real Americans. Jerre Mangione famously dramatized this conflict in his memoir about growing up in a Sicilian community in Rochester, New York, before 1945. Many Italians in Reno reflected Granata's concerns. Adding to their earlier fraternal organizations, they established the Dante Club to promote Italian culture. In 1904 Italians also established a chapter of the Figli d'Italia. These organizations actually served as a bridge, allowing them to feel more comfortable as Italian Catholics in the West while easing their assimilation into American society.[15] They were becoming Italian American.

In their ascent of the social ladder, they were challenging their image as semiliterate peasants. They were as well overcoming the suspicion espoused by the anti-Catholic element in the United States, which was not limited only to such groups as the revitalized KKK. They were also eroding the stereotype of them as criminals and as bootleggers generated by Prohibition. They were proving that they were not a "menace" to the American way of life and could be trusted. Given Italians' economic success in Nevada, local banks had a motive to hire Italian-speaking workers. To attract immigrant money, in 1929 the Reno National Bank advertised that "Italian is spoken." Italian American Edward Questa, born in Reno, worked his way up the ranks in the First National Bank of Nevada and by the 1940s became president. Because of his distinguished career in banking, Italy awarded him the title of vice consul of Italy in Nevada. Reno resident Hugo Quilici and Harry Menante of Las Vegas later became the bank's vice presidents, while William Cassinella became manager of the Carson City branch. The willingness of local banks to hire Italian-speaking workers in order to attract Italian clients suggests perhaps that management had learned from California's A. P. Giannini, who a decade before had established a fully staffed Italian Department in the Bank of Italy, as well as several other departments aimed at other immigrant communities. It seems that Giannini had democratized banking well beyond the precincts of his own banking empire.[16]

In Reno Italians established a Little Italy along Lake Street, Second, and Commercial Row. By 1910 there were 372 Italians residing in Reno, the town with the largest settlement of Italians in the state. In 1908 Lake Street had the Grosseria [*sic*] Italiana di Zolezzi. *Grosseria* does not exist in Italian. The word is an example of one of the adjustments that Italians made in their efforts to assimilate into their new environment. In adapting their version of Italian to English, they created what Frank La Sorte calls an "immigrant idiom," which "became an effective medium of communication among Italians and between Italians and Americans." It became a utilitarian, everyday idiom that was an important part of their cultural and "linguistic assimilation" in America. La Sorte explains that this "Italglish" was commonly used in both professional and personal relationships. Others simply used English in the names of their stores. Joe Brunetti named his store Lake Street Grocery. In the 1930s, the Italian Chain Store Company opened on Fifth and Virginia, which advertised to its immigrant clientele that the store stocked foreign products. It did not take long for Italian entrepreneurs to attract a clientele outside the boundaries of their communities. Like so many western immigrant settlements, Reno's Little Italy was not a homogeneous grouping of Italians, but rather a multicultural mix of all the immigrant groups, including Chinese, French, and Basque.[17] Immigrant social capital became an exchange among all the groups in the quarter.

Early Italian settlers opened at least fourteen hotels in Reno. The Pincolini family immigrated to Reno from Palma near Naples in the 1890s. Working initially in western Nevada, Aldevado Pincolini finally settled with his family in Reno and built a first-class hotel. In 1927, ever the supporter of all things Italian, Granata wrote in his *Bollettino del Nevada* that "the Pincolini Hotel was 'the most unique modern hotel in the state of Nevada.'" The family stayed in the hotel business for decades. Among other hotel families, northern Italians Leopold and Teresa Saturno accumulated a fortune with their purchase of large farming and ranching properties in Truckee Meadows and Mason Valley. They later invested in similar properties in Northern California. With their considerable wealth, they built the Senator Hotel on the corner of Second and West Streets in Little Italy. All the hotel owners competed for Reno's immigrant clientele, yet differentiated the quality of their services. The Tuscano boasted of an Italian restaurant, fine wines, cigars, beer, and "the maximum in cleanliness." Likewise, the Colombo billed itself as a "first-class" hotel with an excellent restaurant. For the working class, the Dormio family that owned the Depot Hotel aimed lower and advertised only "modest rooms." It seems that C. Ramelli's Swiss American House aimed a little lower yet, renting rooms for a mere twenty-five cents a night. In nearby Sparks, Italians established two more hotels, the Europa and the Piedmont. The fourteen hotels in the area serviced a wide range of visitors, from just-arrived immigrants and farmers to wealthy ranchers, railroad men, and businessmen from outlying communities.[18]

Besides mining and railroad work, Eureka, approximately 240 miles east of Reno, also provided arriving men, Italians especially, a unique job opportunity in which they could apply their Old World artisan skills to a modern industry. Many Italian immigrants came to the district of Eureka in the late 1860s through the 1890s to find jobs in the charcoal industry. Following the pattern of a Wild West boomtown, in 1860 Eureka had a population of about 100 people. By May 1870, the population had grown to 1,000. By August of the same year, it doubled and by 1873 doubled again to 4,000. By 1880 the population reached 6,116. In the 1880s Italians had become the largest immigrant group in Eureka. In 1875 there were 242 Italians and 94 Swiss Italians in Eureka County, composing 8 percent of the county's population. However, by 1880 the total Italian population, Swiss Italians included, increased to 1,070, 15 percent of the county's population and the largest immigrant group in the county at the time. (There may be some question about statistics since changes in county boundaries altered these numbers in previous and succeeding census records.) Italians were dispersed in twenty-one locations throughout the county in and around Eureka. Besides Eureka, none of these settlements, however, appears to have been large enough to form a Little Italy.[19]

Throughout the 1880s in the town of Eureka, many Italians opened businesses. The list of those early Italian families includes names such as Biale, Damele, Pastorino, de Paoli, Ratazzi, and Rogantini. Among the most successful was northern Italian Lambert Molinelli, a real-estate and insurance agent and owner of a mine in partnership with W.A. Barsanti. Molinelli wrote a self-promotional work, *Eureka and Its Resources*, designed to bring additional settlers to Eureka to enhance his business interests. Joseph Vanina owned and operated the Railroad Saloon and Store, a general merchandise business. Ferdinando Bonetti partnered with Gabriel Morgantini to open the Stone Saloon on Main Street. Bonetti and Vanina would become two of the town's wealthiest citizens when they entered the charcoal-brokerage business. Joining them in the charcoal business, Joseph Torre owned the Garibaldi Hotel on Main Street and was also a vendor of cigars, liquors, wines, and general merchandise. P. Roberti and W.M. Sholderer were partners in the Capitol Market on Main Street. On South Main, Louis Monaco ran a photographic studio not far from Celso Tatti's saloon. Nearby was the Tognini and Company Building, built in 1877 on North Monroe Street. The building was the home of one of Eureka's most successful charcoal-brokerage businesses, owned by partners Joseph Tognini, Gabriele Zonali, and Ferdinando Bonetti.[20]

The three partners were numbered among the community of Swiss Italians who became some of the most successful entrepreneurs in Eureka. Fueling Italian Swiss immigration to Nevada, Montreal labor contractor Antonio Cordasco formed a close relationship with Frank Ludwig, a labor contractor in northern Italy. A shady character, Ludwig ran afoul of Italian labor law and fled to Chiasso, Switzerland, just on the other side of the Italian-Swiss border. Working outside Italian immigration regulations, Ludwig continued to recruit Swiss Italian workers for Cordasco to work on Canadian railroads and in the Canadian timber industry. Ludwig also sent workers to Cordasco's agent in New York, Anthony Aiello, who under

Cordasco's instructions sent them to Canada. Cordasco was particularly skilled at circumventing Canadian and US immigration laws. In 1884 US immigration officials estimated that forty-nine thousand undocumented workers had entered through Port Huron or Detroit. By 1890 it was estimated that more than a million persons of Canadian birth resided in the United States. The border was porous and left largely unregulated for any immigrant to cross at will. It soon became known among US immigration officials as the "Canadian back door" to the United States. Adding to the problem, the completion of the Canadian Pacific Railroad, for which Cordasco was its chief labor agent, made long-distance travel to the West possible. The problem came to a head in 1893 when a joint effort by both Canadian and US immigration officials made an unsuccessful effort to stanch the flow of undocumented immigrants.[21] Whether undocumented or not, the large number of Swiss Italians in Nevada, including Virginia City and Eureka mining operations, was initially the work of labor contractors before chain migration attracted additional friends and family members.

As legal residents or not, in Eureka Italians moved quickly up the economic ladder. In addition to Italians, Jews also settled Eureka and quickly ascended the social ladder. Numbering only about one hundred in 1880, Jews soon played a prominent role in the business and civic life in the town. Italian and Jewish entrepreneurs formed partnerships. In one example in Eureka, Lambert Molinelli and W.A. Barsanti partnered with Sol Ashim and Joseph Hausman when the two Italians sold them a quarter interest in their mine.[22]

Carbonari and the Fish Creek Massacre

While mining was an important aspect of the county's economy, charcoal production was also one of the area's major industries. Charcoal was used for fuel in the district's smelters. There is little information on Tognini and his two partners, Zonali and Bonetti, all three of whom probably came from the Swiss Italian region Trentino. What is known is that they arrived in the United States in the 1850s or early 1860s before settling finally in Eureka. Shortly after their arrival, the three men established their charcoal-brokerage business. Fellow Swiss Italians Joseph Vanina and Joseph Torre joined Tognini and his partners in the charcoal-hauling business and set up their offices on North Monroe Street. As middlemen they purchased charcoal produced by Italian burners working in the area forests and sold it to Eureka's six smelters, which were operating a total of sixteen furnaces. While other immigrants rushed to the goldfields in the West, these men struck it rich in a matter of years with their form of black gold, charcoal. Taking control of the market, they were able to make their fortunes in large part because they could dictate the price of charcoal to the burners, who were powerless, at least in the short run, to challenge the brokers. They soon became prominent members of Eureka's high society. They and their wives regularly attended charity balls and other social functions.[23]

The Italian brokers no doubt knew something about the industry in which they invested. Charcoal burning was a long-established trade in northern and southern Italy. Ninety percent of the early Italian immigrants in the 1870s in Eureka came from northern Italy and were joined by English, Irish, and French immigrants. Charcoal burning allowed the Italian workers to apply their skill to the mining industry in Eureka. Calabrese novelist Saverio Strati wrote about the impoverished charcoal burners of Calabria in his novel. As Strati explains, felling the trees and carrying the wood to the burner was dangerous and grueling work. If workers were not careful and trees were not cut properly, men could be crushed. The workers also had to lug the cut wood up or down the steep slopes of the mountain. In addition to knowing how to fell trees, they had to know how to cut them into the required size and stack them properly in stone kilns, which they also had to know how to build. Archaeological studies have found that most of the charcoal ovens in Eureka were circular pits, approximately twenty feet in diameter, while others were circular cone-shaped stone ovens approximately thirty-five feet high. Some of these stone ovens still dot the Nevada landscape north of Eureka, close to where the timber once stood.[24]

Working under dangerous conditions and low wages, the workers unionized in 1879 under the banner of the Charcoal Burners Protective Association, led by Italian Severino Strozzi. By 1880 there were about eight hundred foreign *carbonari* working in the Eureka district, where Italians composed the largest foreign-born group and the majority of the charcoal burners. Italians fiercely guarded their interests as charcoal burners. In the event that management in cooperation with labor agents attempted to recruit workers at lower wages, Italians made it clear that all groups, including Native Americans, "were taking a considerable risk" if they attempted to get jobs in the industry at lower wages. Labor agents sometimes recruited Yuma Native Americans from Colorado and the Yaqui from Mexico.[25]

Averting any potential divisions within their ranks, workers focused on their conflict with the Italian charcoal brokers. In addition to their demand for higher wages, workers also began to complain about the means brokers used to weigh their charcoal, thus lowering unfairly their daily production and pay. Many of the Italians were illiterate and unable to determine for themselves whether they were being cheated. Besides, the account books were not open to anyone other than the brokers. Compounding their problems, charcoal workers lived in unsanitary hovels in the surrounding forests. Adding to the tensions in the industry, the demand for charcoal went through periodic slumps, which generated upwards of 33 percent unemployment. Behind Strozzi's leadership and because of their large numbers, Italians led the workforce in its demand for higher wages. In 1880 when the company refused to raise wages, approximately two thousand workers went on strike. The number of strikers was in all likelihood an exaggeration by the strikers. Nevertheless, Italians accounted for more than 50 percent of the strikers. This conflict would become memorialized as the Italian Charcoal Burners' War, also known as the Fish Creek Massacre.[26]

In one incident, assuming the leadership in the strike, seventy-five Italians met at Tognini ranch. Tognini and his two partners steadfastly opposed the workers' demands. As a result, the strikers confiscated two thousand bushels of charcoal and destroyed them. In another incident, armed Italians attempted to stop a charcoal shipper by kidnapping him. They made threats to both teamsters and burners who refused to join their cause. To stop the loading and distribution of charcoal throughout the region, Italians formed "guerrilla-type" gangs in the hills to disrupt the delivery of charcoal. The governor called out the state militia, and the new president of the Charcoal Burners Protective Association, Angelo Del Bondio, was arrested. The local sheriff had already arrested Strozzi, who was in the county jail. Arrests continued until the local jail was "full to overflowing with Italians." New suspects had to be sent to the local armory.[27]

On August 18, 1879, matters came to a head at Fish Creek, where ninety to one hundred Italians and others confronted lawmen. Five Italian burners were shot and killed and six wounded. Accounts vary, depending on whether the lawmen or the strikers were recounting what sparked the shooting. Although the officers were charged with murder, the charges were eventually dropped. The matter of who exactly was responsible for the bloodshed, the lawmen or the Italians, was never resolved. Insisting that the police opened fire, Italians testified that they did not fire any shots. Many in Eureka actually sympathized with the immigrant workers. The *Gold Hill Daily News* and *Carson City Morning Appeal* were skeptical of official accounts and came out in articles on the side of the workers.[28]

With the end of the Charcoal Burners' War, the Italian community began a decline, a not-uncommon occurrence in western towns hit by labor unrest. While remnants of those ovens that the first Italians built remain, there are other reminders of the Italian presence in Eureka. The Colonnade Hotel, built in 1880 by the Italian Benevolent Society, and Celso Tatti's saloon where the Charcoal Burners Protective Association met remain standing on Monroe Street. Not far from Tatti's saloon stands the Tognini and Company Building. Nearby on O'Neil Avenue is St. Brendan's Catholic Church, built in 1874 and directed by Father D. Montiverde. The church was once the spiritual home of the Italian enclave. In the neglected town cemetery, there is a plaque that was erected in 1983 commemorating the deadly August incident and listing the names of the five Italian workers who died.[29]

Farming

The Charcoal Burners' War in Eureka did not stop Italians from continuing to settle in Nevada. They soon dominated Nevada agriculture. By the turn of the century, Italians, mainly from Tuscany, owned more than twenty-five farms. Initially, they were drawn to the high wages offered in Eureka's mines, especially in Lyon and White Pine Counties. Typically, these Italian miners saved their excess capital, bought land, and began farming. In 1866 Angelo Ferretto traveled to Virginia City to work in the area mines. He was soon able to buy land and quickly turn his investment into one of the Comstock's largest freight operations. This area became the breadbasket of the Comstock. Italians continued to settle in Dayton, Lyon County. Among them from Sicily, Antone Maestretti traveled to California in 1854 and shortly after moved to Nevada to work in the Virginia City and Gold Hill mines. He bought land near Austin and began farming and ranching. From his agricultural enterprise, he opened a successful mercantile business. Also from Sicily, Frank Bacigalupi arrived in California in

1854 and later settled in the Virginia City area in the 1860s. After working in the mines, he purchased land, began farming, and sold his vegetables in Virginia City.[30]

By 1910 Italians had established a foothold in agriculture throughout the state. In 1880 there were only three ranches owned by Italians along the Carson River near Dayton. But by 1900 Italians owned twenty-seven of the twenty-eight ranches and farms, producing fruits, vegetables, and meat for the growing Reno-Sparks area and for the smaller towns in surrounding counties. Before Italian farmers established their farms, vegetables and other agricultural products had to be trucked in at considerable expense from California. Because of their dominant role in farming, Alberto Pecorini wrote in a 1909 article that companies and railroads should take note of the Italians' contribution to the area and should "extend to the Italians the greatest and most sympathetic assistance and give them an opportunity to become prosperous in the shortest amount of time." Another commentator wrote that in the Reno area, "Many ranches are owned by Italians who are excellent gardeners, thrifty and make good citizens." Throughout Washoe County, where Reno is located, there were scores of successful Italian farmers. Among the surnames before 1940 were Garaventa, Ghiglieri, Avansino, Pecetti, Raffetto, Gardella, Raggio, and Piretto. Each of their narratives would fill pages. For the most part, Italian immigrants ran small vegetable and dairy farms with only enough acreage that could be worked by the family.[31]

A local historian observed that by 1917 in Truckee Meadows in Washoe County, "four-fifths of the land is now owned by Italians. Ten years ago every ranch around Dayton was owned and operated by Anglo-Saxons, but not one is now so operated in the whole section. The few remaining original owners have leased to Italians. The reason is not far to seek.... As a people the latter are content to begin on a small scale, live below our standard until their financial condition will warrant a home and an automobile." Another local observer pointed out that "different Italians have rented her five acre tract and always at the end of five years wanted to buy the place at a cash price." This was a typical immigrant strategy.[32] The locals' remarks could serve as a description of Italian achievement in farming in any western state.

In spite of the Italians' success in farming, because of its arid conditions, Nevada never became a major agricultural region. It produced moderate crops of peaches, apples, pears, and other fruits, as well as corn, wheat, barley, and rye. It supported a small number of dairy and cattle ranches. Nevada products were destined largely for local markets. But demand was balanced with supply and allowed those early Italian farmers to make a living. Out of the thirteen western states, it ranked only ahead of last-place Alaska in the number of farms, 3,163, and number of acres under production, 2,357,163, by 1920. Because of its climate and arid conditions, agriculture occupied only 3.4 percent of its land compared to nearly 39 percent of the land in nearby California and nearly 37 percent of the land in Colorado.[33]

Politics and Business

As a result of their early accomplishments, by the 1930s Italian immigrants were well represented in business and politics in the state. Decades before, one Reno businessman thought he could get away with calling local Italians "macaronies." But the outcry was so great that he felt compelled to apologize publicly to the Italian population. By the 1930s, their economic influence in the state had grown to such an extent that in 1937 Senator Patrick McCarran introduced a bill to end a long-standing land dispute over Native American land that resolved the issue in favor of five Italian immigrant investors.[34] In situations like this, at the expense of Native American rights, politicians in alliance with their business interests sided with immigrants because of what they saw as their economic value to the state. Such a radical shift in perception of immigrants, who were once perceived as the foreign and culturally subversive element in American society, was not uncommon in the West.

There were instances in Nevada when early Italian settlers shared a friendly relationship with the local Paiute. In Mendocino County, California, for example, Italian immigrants befriended and intermarried with the local Pomo people and lived on the reservation. As early as the 1860s, a small colony of Italians established farms on the outskirts of Reno near Pyramid Lake in Washoe County and sold vegetables in area mining towns. They shared a generally friendly relationship with the Paiute community. Relationships were strained at times, however, over water rights and land titles in later years.[35]

In the larger urban settlements, Italians were concentrated largely in the Reno–Virginia City–Carson City region, including Eureka. They also made their presence known in such place-names as Verdi in Washoe County, Italian Spring Canyon in Elko County, Italian Creek and Italian

Canyon in Lander County, and Paradise Valley in Humboldt County. Their influence in Paradise Valley resulted in at least twenty-three streets named after Italian immigrants. In Sparks, just four miles east of Reno in Washoe County, there are twelve streets named after Italians. In northeast Sparks in an area known as D'Andrea Ranch, there are twenty-four housing developments named after northern Italian villages with streets named after Italian cities, regions, and Renaissance artists. Also leaving a permanent record of his work, one of the chief architects in Paradise Valley was A. Pasquale. Pasquale's Mediterranean style can still be seen in the facades of several local businesses and the local Catholic church as well as the town's water tower.[36]

Late-Generation Revival

Nevada never ceased being a magnet for Italian immigration and late-generation migration. As Alan Balboni explains in *Beyond the Mafia: Italian Americans and the Development of Las Vegas* (1996), Italians came in great numbers to the adult Disneyland in the desert after World War II. While their development of the gaming industry after the war is outside the framework of this study, Balboni does a credible job of separating myth from historical reality. Francis Ford Coppola's film *The Godfather II* (1974) and Martin Scorsese's *Casino* (1995) contributed to the Italians' notoriety, if not mythology, in the development of the gaming industry. Italians were involved in the casino industry for good or for ill, from minor roles in casino ownership to more numerous positions as managers, floor walkers, and pit bosses. However, as Balboni explains, despite the myth surrounding Italian American ownership if not control of Nevada's casinos, only one Italian American, northern Italian immigrant Tony Cornero, built casinos in Las Vegas. His first venture began in the 1930s when he and his brother built the Meadows. When that proved unprofitable, in the 1930s he began operating gambling barges off the Southern California coast, which were ultimately shut down by the federal government as a national security risk when the war began. He returned to Las Vegas in 1954 and began building the Stardust, whose history plays a role in Scorsese's film. But in 1955 Cornero died before the casino was finished. In the 1940s and '50s a few Italian Americans did own and operate small casinos in the outlying areas surrounding Las Vegas. Otherwise, surrounding the gaming industry in Las Vegas, Italian businesses grew, including Italian ownership of restaurants, construction companies, hotels, and a plethora of other small businesses in the Las Vegas area. With the corporate takeover of the industry, Italian Americans remain active only at the lower ranks in the casinos.[37]

Although averaging only about 6 percent of the US population in 1960, Italian Americans were nearly 10 percent of Las Vegas's population, up from just 2 percent before 1940. The majority of these Italians were the result of secondary migration from eastern cities, not immigration from Italy. In 1990 Nevada counted 87,525 Italian Americans, 7.3 percent of the state's population. Today the Italian American population in Nevada stands at more than 132,000, 6.6 percent among the top-ten states in percentages in the United States.[38] The postwar rise in the number of Nevada's residents is consistent with other western states as new generations begin to identify with their roots.

In recent years, these late-generation Italian Americans established numerous organizations. Since the 1950s, Italian Americans have formed three chapters of the Order Sons of Italy, (Las Vegas, Reno, and Sparks), the Italian American Club established in 1960, and the Augustus Society established in 1983, as well as chapters of the National Italian American Bar Association and the National Italian American Foundation. In 1976 Italians began the Feast of Santa Maria in Dayton, about forty miles south of Reno near Virginia City. Since 1978 Las Vegas Italians have hosted the San Gennaro Feast and the Eldorado Great Italian Festival in Reno. In western Nevada County, in another example of the transnational development of their heritage in the West, Italian Americans have organized the annual Italian Film Festival. These organizations and festivals appeal to a cross-section of Italian American demographics and continue to attract new members. Although Nevada lost its three Italian newspapers before World War II, the area is now served by the Los Angeles–based *L'Italo-Americano*. Furthering their assimilation into Nevada society, as Balboni explains, while Italian Americans have won public office in Las Vegas, they did not do it on the Italian vote alone.[39] With their renewed group solidarity in American culture, Las Vegas Italians have contributed to the multicultural makeup of the Nevada social order.

CHAPTER 13

CALIFORNIA

Native Americans and the Land

Contrary to the simplistic construction of immigrant success, the immigrant narrative must be seriously qualified by the advantageous position in which all immigrants found themselves upon arrival in the West: a labor shortage, an extensive labor-contracting system, a profusion of jobs in diverse industries, a common immigrant economy, wages that outpaced the cost of living, and, above all, an abundance of cheap land. It cannot be ignored that the availability of cheap land came at the tragic expense of Native Americans. Certainly, this topic could have been treated in the introduction of each of the other chapters in this study. However, as Benjamin Madley's recent study recommends, California, as the western state that attracted the largest number of immigrants by 1920, is the appropriate place to address the subject.[1]

With the arrival of the Spanish-Russo-Mexican colonists in the years 1769–1846, approximately 60,000 California Native people died of disease by the 1840s. In Northern California, Mexican troops in 1837 executed 200 Sierra Miwok prisoners, and in 1841 or 1842 Captain Salvador Vallejo at Clear Lake attacked what was probably a Pomo village and massacred approximately 150 men, women, and children. When the Spanish-Russo-Mexican period ended, the original 310,000 Native Americans in California had been reduced by half, to approximately 150,000.[2]

When the United States took possession of California from Mexico in 1848, the results over the next three decades were equally devastating for Native people. The war of extermination during the Spanish-Russo-Mexican era continued under US rule. To the great detriment of California's Native population, by 1849 the gold rush began. In 1850 California's non-Native population was 92,597. By 1860 it had ballooned to 379,994 in just one decade. To make land available to this burgeoning population, by 1851 the California state legislature had established two militias, one compulsory and one volunteer. These became the official instruments of Native American removal. As the governor of California, Peter H. Burnett, said in 1851, "A war of extermination will continue to be waged between the races, until the Indian race becomes extinct." Supporting the governor, the popular press in California encouraged the state-sponsored genocide of Native Americans. Madley writes, "The number of California Indians killed by US Army soldiers, California militiamen, and vigilantes from 1850–1854 will likely never be known." As a result of official militia attacks and scores of vigilante attacks, by 1870 an additional 150,000 Native Americans perished, some by disease. Native American population by 1873 was reduced to approximately 30,000. By 1880 the census bureau listed 16,277 to 20,000 Native American residents of California.[3] In the nineteenth century, Helen Hunt Jackson advocated on behalf of Native American rights in *A Century of Dishonor: A Sketch of the United States Government's Dealings with Some of the Indian Tribes* (1881) and in her novel *Ramona* (1884), set in Southern California. Her exposure of the treatment of Native Americans was to no avail.

In the wake of Native American removal and extermination, the completion of the transcontinental railroad in 1869 brought tens of thousands of immigrants to California. By 1880 California's population increased to 864,694. By 1890 the foreign-born population would be more than 30 percent of the state's population. In 1920 California's foreign-born population stood at 757,625, approximately 21 percent of California's more than 3.5 million residents. At 88,502, Italian immigrants made up about 13 percent of the state's population. With cheap and even free homestead land available, California became the nation's second-largest agricultural producer behind Texas.[4]

Italians—Early Settlement

By the early 1850s, Italian Jesuits began migrating to California from other Jesuit missions in the West. They established missions and founded colleges, chief among them Santa Clara University and St. Ignatius College, which became the University of San Francisco. Before the arrival of the Jesuits, between 1781 and 1844, 44 Italians had settled in California, though census records do not exist. In the first official census in 1850–52, there were 229 Italians in the state, though that number might have been closer to 700. As the Italian population began to grow, Massimo d'Azeglio, the prime minister of what was at the time the Kingdom of Sardinia, took notice and opened a consulate in San Francisco to attend to the needs of Italian immigrants. King Victor Emmanuel II appointed Leonetto Cipriani as the first Sardinian consul of the area, thus making the Italian presence in the far-western state official. Cipriani was succeeded by Federico

Biesta. He became the vice president of the Italian Mutual Benefit Society, established the Italian Hospital Association, and started a business on Montgomery Street in San Francisco. In 1859 he established the first Italian newspaper in California, *L'Eco della Patria* (1859), and was the California correspondent for New York's *L'Eco d'Italia*.[5]

During his time as consul general, in 1856 Biesta identified a variety of Italian businesses in San Francisco and around the state in his consular report. One notable section outlined the auspicious beginnings of the California wine industry. He described the development of the "grape culture" in such towns as San Jose, Santa Clara, and Los Angeles, where "extensive vineyards were started three years ago [and were] beginning to bear abundantly, producing a wine of excellent quality." Biesta also listed approximately fourteen San Francisco Italian businesses: a hardware store, coffeehouse, import business, public bath, hotel, imitation-marble business, music store, and several pharmacies. By 1860 Italian immigrants had established a foothold in the northern towns of San Francisco, Sacramento, and San Jose and had settled in smaller communities in Mendocino and Sonoma Counties, north of San Francisco.[6]

Immigrants who followed the gold rush to California soon found that the quick riches proffered by gold fever were a chimera. However, the gold rush relocated thousands of Italians and introduced them to opportunities in the state, commercial and agricultural. Biesta's report reinforced the adage, "While the miners mined the mines, the Italians mined the miners." Many Italians became entrepreneurs and supplied the miners with necessary goods and services. Among the most successful, the San Francisco chocolate maker Domenico Ghirardelli, who came to California from Peru in 1849, began his life in the California Mother Lode, where he sold chocolate and other sweets to miners. Biesta reported that by 1851, Ghirardelli had already earned a fortune before a fire destroyed his commercial property. He rebounded and began manufacturing liqueurs and chocolates that became his famous San Francisco Ghirardelli Chocolate Company before he returned to his native village in northern Italy.[7]

Early in their settlement in California, Italians began to influence the direction of the American food industry. By 1880 the state was importing 300,000 gallons of olive oil, 4 million gallons of wine, 1,500 tons of dried figs, 500,000 gallons of brandy, and 140,000 cases of sparkling wine. By the end of the nineteenth century, California contained more irrigated small farms (ten to thirty acres) and large irrigated farms (approximately five hundred acres) than any other state in the West. In 1897 the Italian

Chamber of Commerce of San Francisco reported that there were 45,625 Italians living in California's fifty-six counties. The chamber counted 2,726 Italian-owned farms with an additional 837 Italian businesses worth $17,908,300. By 1916 another report estimated that Italians owned $200 million in real estate and $8 million in stocks and bonds and in 1914 had in savings accounts more than $34 million. By 1921 immigrants and their offspring owned 35,000 of California's approximately 100,000 farms. As Rolle pointed out, "In California the Italian westward migration flowered best."[8]

Mendocino County

By the late 1850s, a small number of Italian immigrants began to settle in remote Mendocino County, north of San Francisco. In 1850 the county had only about 55 residents, exclusive of its Native American population. By 1860 the county's population grew to 3,967 and nearly doubled to 7,545 by 1870.[9] The county offered settlers inexpensive farmland and opportunities in growing commercial centers such as Mendocino and Ukiah, the county seat.

Among the first Italians in Mendocino County by the 1860s were farmer Daniel Gobbi and businessman John Ginochio. Born in 1853, Gobbi left Italy as a youngster and settled in London. From there he made his way to America and in 1856 arrived in Mendocino, where he became a farmer and stock speculator. Italian American businessman Ginochio was born in El Dorado County but settled in Ukiah. Following Gobbi and Ginochio, in the 1870s Italians began to settle in Ukiah, the first important Italian community in the county. By 1900 Italians were joined by the Finns, the second-largest immigrant group behind the Italians, who numbered 1,414, about 6 percent of the total population of the county at 23,929.[10]

In Ukiah, Italians were greeted with the same stereotyping that they faced everywhere in America at the time. Newly arriving Italians worked day-labor jobs with other immigrants and Native Americans. The *Dispatch Democrat* described Italians and Finns as unpredictable and dangerous, the same terms that the local press used to describe Native Americans. Whenever Finns and Italians were arrested, the local papers were quick to depict the two groups as prone to violence, drunkenness, and lawlessness, especially Italians. The editor wrote, "The criminals, degenerates, illiterates and paupers pour into this country because they are a continued nuisance to their own land, are filling our charitable institutions, hospitals and jails and opening thousands of 'hell holes' in the United States. Both on account of their number and their character, we can hardly hope to assimilate them, and they should be restricted by legislation." Another local paper, the *Ukiah Republican Press*, agreed, calling immigrants "paupers" and "lunatics." As a result, in one newspaper account of an immigrant disturbance, the newspaper headline announced, "Italians on the Warpath." In another instance, the *Dispatch Democrat* called poor Emilio Rodoni, who lived in a cave and was involved in a barroom altercation, a "wild man." The *Ukiah Democrat* reported at the time that one young Italian "got too much dago-red and proceeded to whack old man Massoletti with a dull knife." In another instance, suspect Amerigo Baldocchi killed another Italian man and wounded another over a woman before he fled the county. The paper concluded that if he made it to the grape-growing region among other Italians, he would never be apprehended, although a short while later he was arrested near Yountville.[11]

Contributing to late-generation residents' xenophobic opinions of Italians was their close relationship with the local Pomo people. As newcomers they worked day labor with Native Americans on farms, occupied the same social and economic position, and formed personal relationships with their coworkers and their families. In 1890 there were 581 Native Americans in Mendocino County. By 1900 the Native American population had grown to about 1,353. Italians' relationship with Native Americans was similar to their relationship with African Americans in the Jim Crow South. One local resident, Joe Scaramella, reported that his father "didn't make the fine social distinctions." His father invited Native Americans home and served them food and the customary glass of wine, which was against the law. For obvious cultural reasons, Italians saw little harm in this. Likewise, saloon owners saw little harm in serving Native Americans liquor. But officers of the Indian Service viewed the Italians' cavalier attitude toward the law differently. Officers arrested saloon owner Ida Guidi often, and in 1908 they set up a sting operation and arrested Louis Baccaglio and Charles Guidi for selling liquor to the local Pomos. As they did in the South, Italians defied social convention and paid little attention to laws that conflicted with their customs. The *Ukiah Republican Press* wrote, "Italy has furnished more anarchists . . . than any other country."[12]

Further exacerbating locals' opinion of Italians, Italian men attended dances, and families were invited to celebrations on the rancherias (reservations). Italian families became friends with local Pomo families and attended Catholic Mass and even Protestant services with those living on the local rancherias. Eva Biaggi and her circle of immigrant women attended the Manchester rancheria Methodist Sunday school run by a local schoolteacher admired by both Native American and Italian children. In fact, Italians felt more at home at the rancheria Catholic churches in the Ukiah Valley than they did at the Irish- and German-dominated Catholic churches in town. One resident remarked that no "whites" ever came to their rancheria church, but Italian immigrants attended their services. Their children played together, and they forged strong social bonds while visiting each other's homes and sharing their cultural and culinary traditions. Italian men married Native American women and lived on the rancheria with their families. Some residents of the rancheria did complain about the presence of foreigners on their land. These Italian men were unaware of the threat that they posed to further expropriation of Native American land.[13]

The major employers in the county were the Union Lumber Company, Caspar Lumber, Pollard Lumber, and Glen Blair Lumber. Italians worked alongside Chinese, Japanese, and Mexican immigrants, who were paid between $2.00 to $2.50 a day, a relatively high wage for inexperienced labor in the West. Even so, the immigrant daily rate was lower than the union wage, which caused additional friction and fueled the general xenophobia in the county. Adding to the anti-immigrant sentiment, when threatened with a strike, management hired labor contractors to recruit Native Americans and immigrants from other regions to drive down wages and break the strike.[14]

There were also mines in the area, such as the Quick Silver Mine. However, with farming and business opportunities available to them, Italians were not drawn to work in the mines in the county, at least not in great numbers. In a unique development, years before Italians arrived in the county, lumber companies had clear-cut the surrounding hillsides and then abandoned them. Not wanting to undertake the costly and labor-intensive task of removing thousands of tree stumps, the lumber company sold the land to the early settlers, who pulled the stumps and cleared the land. With their experience in planting steep hillsides in Italy, they turned the otherwise useless land into productive farms. The farmers did not need irrigation in the county, which had an average rainfall that was nearly thirty-five inches a year.[15]

It did not take long for that intolerant view of Italians expressed in the local papers to change to one of praise for the Italian farmer, especially the grape farmer. Although earlier farmers had planted some vines, the local press credited Italians with the development and growth of the grape industry. The late-generation population suddenly saw a profitable future for "the culture of the vine" in the Ukiah Valley. Once calling the Italian immigrants wild and violent, they now suddenly described them as among "the most enterprising businessmen in the county." The local press even ran articles on how to plant vines on the hillsides. Hearing of Italians' success, Pietro Rossi from Andrea Sbarboro's Italian Swiss Colony winery in Asti, Sonoma County, in 1906 offered free cuttings to farmers who wanted to plant vineyards. As an incentive, Italian Swiss offered to buy all the grapes at fifteen dollars a ton. In February 1906, Rossi shipped one hundred thousand cuttings to the valley. Owing in part to Italian Swiss's own marketing strategy and growth, by June 1906 the price per ton had doubled to thirty dollars.[16]

The Italians who came to Mendocino County settled throughout the region wherever they could afford to buy land for farming and ranching. Coming from the farming and dairy regions of northern Italy, Italians established some of the largest and most successful dairy farms in the county. In 1912 Lorenzo Albonico partnered with Clemente Cittoni, both from Lombardy, to rent a two-hundred-acre ranch in Round Valley, northeast of the town of Mendocino, where they became two of the most successful dairymen in the county. Even if an Italian worker did not come with previous experience, ethnic networking provided leads to jobs in local dairies where they could learn the industry. Charles Galletti, from Ticino, arrived in California in 1891, worked as a dairyman, and by 1913 operated a more than three-hundred-acre dairy farm. Likewise, Augustus Sartori and Antonio Stornetta, both also from Ticino, became some of the county's most successful dairymen.[17]

There were numerous lumber companies providing well-paying jobs for the county's immigrant population. Among them, Romeo Incerti, born in Modena in 1873, arrived in Mendocino County in 1903, and within six years of working for both the Union and the Glen Blair lumber companies, he was able to finance the opening of a general store. With the influx of single men, the hotel business was among the most lucrative enterprises in the county. Between 1900 and 1915, no fewer than eight Italians opened hotels in Mendocino County. Like Incerti, nearly all worked in the lumber industry before investing in the hospitality industry. Among them was Francesco Persico, who owned the Italian Hotel in Willits and later built a forty-seven-room hotel, the New Italian. Three Italians opened hotels in

Fort Bragg: Pietro Berrettini owned the Lucca Hotel on Franklin Street, Amadeo del Grosso owned and operated the Pacific Hotel on Main Street, and Charles Pedretti built the Milano Hotel. Seeing yet another opportunity, after nearly twenty years in the dairy and creamery business, Charles Galletti partnered with his fellow Swiss Italian Antonio Stornetta and opened the Italian Hotel in Point Arena in 1913. Two other Swiss Italian entrepreneurs in 1914 opened the Swiss-American Hotel in Point Arena. Single, free-labor immigrants were able to move quickly from well-paying jobs to lucrative investments.[18]

Among these early Italian immigrant entrepreneurs, Andrew Rocca, born in Genoa in 1838, was perhaps the most successful. In 1853, at age fifteen, he left his hometown with two companions and set out for California. After years of working and careful investing, by 1899 he purchased the Quick Silver Mine, later renamed the Helen Mine, in Lake County, west of Mendocino County. Rocca built the Callayomi Lumber Mill, installed the water power needed to run the mill, and invested in dairy farming and land. He soon became the largest taxpayer in Mendocino County.[19]

By 1930 there would be only about 1,000 Italian immigrants in Mendocino County, down one-third from the beginning of the century. Contributing to the decline was that 60 percent of the Italians in the county returned to Italy.[20] Although their settlement was far from the densely populated Bay Area, those Mendocino Italians who remained in the county ultimately joined the larger network of Italians in their share of the ever-expanding immigrant economy and marketplace in California. As families prospered, the next generation moved on to higher education. As a result of those early enterprising Italian farmers and vintners, today Mendocino County is one of California's principal wine-producing regions with its own AVA (American Viticulture Area) designation.

Sonoma County

Like the small towns of Ukiah and Mendocino, in the 1870s the Bodega Township, which included the small village of Occidental in Sonoma County, had 1,407 people. By 1877 a narrow-gauge rail was built from Sausalito to a lumber mill near Occidental that opened the area to shipping, especially farm products and lumber. By the summer of 1877, three new lumber mills were operating near Occidental. In 1880 there were thirteen Italians in Bodega, but none in Occidental. Having arrived with the railroad, they initially found employment in Swiss Italian dairies, logging, and lumber mills. In the logging camps, immigrant workers lived in cabins with two or three other workers and in rare cases with their families.[21]

In a curious fact that contributed to the settlement of the county, Occidental was the beneficiary of the increased settlement of Italians in San Francisco. Many of the newly arriving Italians in San Francisco's North Beach community were influenced to settle outside the city in the surrounding countryside to avoid disrupting the labor pool and causing problems with the unions. By 1900 immigrants from Tuscany and Lombardy composed the majority of the 156 Italians in the area. In anticipation of the growing Catholic presence in the area, by 1903 the diocese built a church in Occidental. Adding to the number of Italians, Ermenegildo Gonnella, from Coreglia, Tuscany, encouraged 28 family members to immigrate to the county by 1907.[22]

Like those Italian farmers who saw an opportunity in Ukiah Valley's surrounding clear-cut hillsides, Occidental Italians also found an opportunity in the waste left by the lumber companies. By 1900 much of the surrounding timber had been cut. With the discarded trees left by the companies, Italians began making charcoal, which they were able to sell to local residents for home use. They also opened small mills, where they produced shingles, fence posts, and other wood products. When they had cleared the land of its logging remnants, they began family truck farms, where they grew fruits, vegetables, and hops that they sold locally. On their farms they also raised livestock from which they made their own preserved meats, cheese, and other products. They built their own wood-burning ovens for baking and cooking. In 1919 Occidental had three wineries, one owned by an Italian. All the wineries depended on Italian labor, both in the vineyards and in the wineries. During the hops harvesting season, the farms attracted hundreds of workers who made from $3 to $5 a day.[23]

By the 1920s, Occidental had a thriving enclave. Italian families from the surrounding farms came to town for supplies, while men visited the local saloons and pool halls. The Italians who did not own farms opened saloons, boardinghouses, hotels, restaurants, grocery stores, and other businesses in town. Owners of hotels hired their relatives, and restaurants served an American version of Italian cuisine. In 1891 Giovanni and Giovanna Gobetti purchased a building for $2,000 in gold from a local businessman, opened the Union Saloon, and ran both the saloon and the restaurant for more than thirty-five years. In 1925 they sold the Union Saloon to Carlo Panizzera, born in the northern Italian village of Brunico in 1869. Renamed the Union Hotel, it is still in the family after nearly a century.[24]

Residents soon formed a tight-knit community. The town sponsored dances and a Fourth of July celebration, the most popular event of the year. By 1930 there were 3,175 Italians in Sonoma County. Nearby Napa County had at the time 1,122. By the end of the 1930s, the small town of Occidental numbered about 400 Italians and Italian Americans out of 500 residents in the area. The town became known in the region as the Italian Village. Many of the original Italians became prominent citizens, joining civic organizations, even becoming Masons, which had once prohibited Catholics. As Paola Sensi-Isolani wrote, Italians in Occidental "managed to recreate their own Italian village, and their isolation made it easier for them to preserve their language and culture."[25] Occidental is an excellent example of how accommodating small western towns were for immigrant Italians. Italians were important in the development of commerce and innovators in agriculture, while at the same time they were able to transplant their traditional folkways in the small-town rural setting.

Early Settlers— Monterey and Santa Barbara Counties

Ahead of the mass immigration to California, the Trescony family played a major role in the development of California agriculture. As Hans Christian Palmer wrote, Alberto Trescony "was probably the most important of the early Italian pioneers" in California ranching and farming. Trescony arrived in California in the 1840s ahead of the gold rush and began selling equipment to miners. He then invested his profits in a variety of enterprises: merchandising, land investment, saloons, and hotels, including the Washington Hotel, the largest building and the only hotel in Monterey at the time. Taking his profits, he expanded his investments by purchasing parcels of land from families that were in foreclosure or in financial trouble. Turning his attention to ranching, by 1876 he had more than twenty-five thousand head of sheep in the Monterey area. By 1880 he owned nearly fourteen thousand acres in Monterey and Santa Clara Counties, where he had sheep and cattle ranches, ran a dairy farm, and raised grain.[26]

In 1876 when Alberto's son Julius took over his father's vast ranching and farming enterprises, he planted barley and other crops on the family's San Lucas Ranch in the Santa Ynez Valley in Santa Barbara County. The "Trescony Barley" label soon became one of the most famous brand names throughout the world. It remained a widely recognized label in California well into the 1930s.[27]

At the same time that Trescony had all but cornered the market in grain, California farmers were growing a wide variety of fruits, vegetables, and nuts. The introduction of railroad refrigeration cars in the region in 1877 opened the national market for California's farm products. Taking advantage of inexpensive land prices, Italians along with a plethora of other immigrants spread out across the state's interior counties. The fertile floodplains of the Sacramento and San Joaquin Rivers provided an opportunity for many incoming immigrants who settled in the state.[28]

Stockton and Enclave Businesses—San Joaquin County

By the 1880s, Italian immigrants had begun to farm around Stockton in San Joaquin County. In 1920 there were 3,454 Italian immigrants in the county with nearly half of them, 1,578, living in Stockton. There were other important Italian settlements in Northern California: Alameda, 726; Eureka, 728; Oakland, 5,094; Richmond, 863; Sacramento, 1,897; and San Jose, 3,497. San Francisco (a combined city-county designation in the census) had by far the largest settlement in the North, 23,924. By 1930 San Joaquin County's Italian immigrant population would grow again to 4,158 and Stockton's to 2,029, a little more than 13 percent of the European-born population of the county.[29]

Stockton was founded in 1849 by German immigrant farmer Charles Weber. By 1850 there were 27 Italians in the newly incorporated town of 3,644 residents. Italians enjoyed extraordinary success in both enclave businesses and farming in Stockton and the surrounding San Joaquin County. As the second-largest foreign-born group behind the Germans, the Italians, mainly from Liguria, owned hotels, boardinghouses, saloons, and merchandise stores. Among the early arrivals, Louis De Ferrari opened the Garibaldi House, Gabrielle Foppiano the Roma Hotel, V. Pellegrini the Europa Hotel, and P.M. Ricci the Hotel of Italy. Before the end of the century, Nicolas Sposati was co-owner of Stockton's first horse-drawn streetrail system. Domenico Ghirardelli opened his first biscuit and chocolate store in Stockton before moving his operation to San Francisco when his Stockton shop burned down. Another early Genovese, Giuseppe Di Pietri, opened a warehouse on the Stockton docks for the storage of agricultural products before he established the California Navigation and Improvement Company.[30]

Later settlers, largely northern Italians, opened businesses in the neighborhood around Wilson Way and Channel Street. Paul Troglia and a partner opened the Allies Pool Hall on South Center Street. Joseph Silva and his brother Emilio combined their resources and ran a grocery store, Silva & Bros., between 1890 and 1925 at the corner of Main and East Avenues. At the age of sixteen, Manlio Silva joined his brothers in Stockton in 1919, but only after he had graduated from the Conservatory of Chiavari. He opened a pharmacy and further burnished his image in town by becoming the music conductor and founding director of the Stockton Symphony in 1926.[31]

Others prospered as well in the Stockton Italian enclave. Giuseppe Paravagna and Paul Brichetto opened grocery stores in the vicinity of the nearby Ravenna & Co. pasta factory. Caesar Gaia, born in 1882 near Torino, came to California at the age of seventeen, worked on a ranch near Gilroy, and made his way to Stockton in 1914. He and partner Louis Delucchi bought the E. Fontana Ravioli Factory and then relocated it to East Market Street under the name Gaia & Delucchi's. Expanding their line, they sold other products to their surrounding Italian clientele.[32]

Genoa-born John Craviotto arrived in America in 1884. By 1899 he received his degree in pharmacy from the University of California–Berkeley and by 1904 completed his MD. However, after a career in medicine, in the 1920s he became president of the San Joaquin Marketing Association, the largest Italian American cooperative in California at the time. Founded in 1922 by Giacomo Tassano from Genoa, the association provided investment and advisory services for growers in San Joaquin County. Tassano was also a dried-fruit producer and past president of the Società Italiana dei Giardinieri established in 1902. The Marketing Association and the Società were important contributors to Italian solidarity and the exchange of social capital in the county. The Società originally served as a mutual-aid society that one resident explained was "formed basically to protect their own Italian culture.... The society was to keep the Italian community close." Offering health and death benefits at $250 per family, it recruited other Italians regardless of their region of birth. The strategy of solidarity and support worked. By 1920, the zenith of Italian settlement in Stockton, the business directories for the period reveal that Italian immigrants were well integrated into the business class, from jewelers, bookkeepers, and lab technicians to steamship agents and confectioners.[33]

Farming—San Joaquin County

Along with their success in business, Italians made their greatest contribution in agriculture. At the time that the Genovese merchants were colonizing Stockton's business district, an eclectic group of Italians began to settle the surrounding 4 million acres of unfarmed wetlands in the county. As one early settler, Mike Calosso, explained, "The Tuscanos and the Neapolitans farmed the wetlands, the Delta, and the Piedemontese [*sic*], Genovese, and Sicilians went east." According to Calosso, who farmed in the area and owned the Box Company, Italians composed 85 percent of the population just east of the wetlands in central Stockton. Many were members of the Società Italiana dei Giardinieri, which dominated the fruit and vegetable production and distribution in the area. From its humble beginnings as a mutual-aid society, the Società nearly doubled its membership from 2,417 to 4,453 by 1920. With a combined land value of over $7 million, its membership controlled more than 47 percent of the county's land. Three generations of the Calosso family have been members of the Società, which is now over one hundred years old.[34]

US-born Rodolfo Mussi was among those early settlers in the county. After working as a laborer, he began a small farm and married. He continued to buy land, and after thirty years of farming, he and his son farmed up to 6,500 acres that produced asparagus, grapes, and tomatoes. Among other Italians in the region, Joseph Solari immigrated to Stockton in 1887 and was among the first farmers to grow cherries. By the turn of the century, networking with other farmers, he and his offspring were responsible for starting the California Fruit Exchange in 1901, the San Joaquin Marketing Association in 1922, and the San Joaquin Cherry Growers in 1935. Four generations later, the Solari family still farms the area. A latecomer, Dino Cortopassi from northern Italy, in 1942 co-established Stanislaus Food Products, which sold tomato products. It is still in business today. Another latecomer, George Lagorio, in 1945 began growing tomatoes and then established a canning factory. In the postwar period, the Lagorio family expanded their enterprise to 10,000 acres and a variety of crops. Today the third and fourth generations of the family own and manage a number of food-related companies. Italian American, Stockton-born Frank Lucchetti joined other Italians in farming in the 1940s, planted cherries and peaches, and after World War II opened the Fruit Bowl, which his son took over after Frank retired.[35] Stockton provides a revealing example of not only enclave social and cultural capital but also the legacy that immigrants passed down to succeeding generations of Italian Americans.

Calaveras County

Calaveras County, east of Stockton, was also the home of Italian immigrants before and after the turn of the century. After their disappointment over not striking it rich in the goldfields, many miners stayed in Calaveras County to open businesses and to farm. Born in Genoa, Andrea Lagomarsino arrived in Northern California in 1857 and was among the few who did strike it rich mining gold in the Calaveras River. He invested his money in 160 acres of land and became a successful vegetable farmer. After gold-rush fever began to diminish, in the 1860s other Italians established farms and opened saloons and merchandise stores. By 1870 their ranks had expanded to ferryboat drivers, blacksmiths, barbers, and livery-stable proprietors. Entrepreneurs John Raggio and his brothers ran the largest stage line in the region. The Italian presence in farming increased from twenty-two in 1860 to forty-eight by 1870, and by 1900 seventy-three were in agriculture, as either owners or tenant farmers. By 1900 Italians were the largest foreign-born population in the county.[36]

The most remarkable story in Calaveras County is the life of Olivia Rolleri. Olivia was married to the enterprising Gerolamo Rolleri from Northern Italy. Shortly after his arrival in the United States before 1880, Gerolamo found work as a miner in the county. Whatever profits he earned he invested in land and began ranching and farming. He also ran Reynold's Ferry with his older brother and owned a grocery store. Unfortunately, Gerolamo died in 1888, leaving Olivia with eight children. With the family's considerable income from Gerolamo's investments, she bought the Calaveras Hotel in Angels Camp, a thriving quartz-mining center, and hired a Chinese cook, whom she trained to make Italian dishes. With the help of her grown children, she soon became the region's most successful hotelier. She then purchased a nearby ranch and opened a butcher shop and a saloon. By 1900 she had expanded her hotel to fifty rooms and two apartments, accommodating more than seventy-one residents. Almost 50 percent of her residents were Italian, while the remainder came from surrounding counties and states.[37] Rolleri is a further example of the vital role that entrepreneurial immigrant women played in settlements throughout the West.

Farming, Businesses, and the Professions—San Francisco and the Bay Area

Due west from San Joaquin County in the Bay Area, Italian settlement was complemented by numerous thriving Italian neighborhoods. Among those lesser-known neighborhoods are the Excelsior District, part of San Francisco's Outer Mission District, and the East Bay, specifically the north Oakland neighborhood of Temescal. The Italian presence was so great in the Excelsior District in 1898 that the diocese built the Italian National Catholic Church, Corpus Christi. When the 1906 earthquake hit San Francisco, the Excelsior District was relatively undamaged. As a result, many Italians moved from the damaged inner city to Excelsior. Just minutes south of the center of the city, the Mission District was also an immigrant center. In her novel *Miss Giardino* (1978), first-generation Italian American writer Dorothy Bryant chronicled the life of early Italian immigrants and the changes that occurred in the Mission District after World War II.[38]

Between 1900 and 1910, Oakland's Italian population, including the Temescal neighborhood, soared from 613 to 3,800. That number nearly doubled by 1930 to 6,350 Italian residents. Servicing the needs of this burgeoning Italian population, the surrounding area was home to numerous Italian truck farmers. The area soon became a Little Italy, composed of many Italian-owned and -operated businesses. G. B. Ratto opened three businesses, the Colombo Market, the G. B. Ratto & Co., and the International Grocers, Inc. Stefano Persoglio owned and operated the Grocery and Sausage Factory. The neighborhood was home to scores of bakeries, including a French-Italian bakery. There were as well numerous meat and poultry businesses supplied by the surrounding Italian farms. Italians also worked in area industries, especially with the outbreak of World War II. While some women worked in the local garment factories, others, such as Maria Ferro DeNurra from Liguria, worked as a seamstress at home. The Hutchinson Quarry, about ten miles north of Temescal, employed Italians from the neighborhood. Construction too was an important industry for Italians, whose companies were handed down to the next generation. As a result of the waste from the surrounding industries and construction companies, scavenger businesses developed that provided a few jobs for the first wave of unskilled Italian immigrants. Also active were social clubs and organizations in the neighborhood and Greater Oakland area.[39] As part of the larger Bay Area community of immigrants, the Italian neighborhood was a thriving cultural and business enclave with the usual exchange of social capital among its wage earners and the surrounding businesses.

By 1908 more than 1,200 Italian immigrants in the current areas of Bayview in Contra Costa County, Colma in San Mateo County, and Visitacion Valley of San Francisco owned or controlled more than eight thousand acres of vegetables. Further south in Santa Clara County, "Red" Lamantia and Joe Perrucci established drying yards to process cherries, apricots, and prunes. Several canning companies also opened in the county to process other crops. Santa Clara was soon declared the "fruit-canning capital of the world." Contadina Tomato Paste Cannery was among the first to can tomatoes. They were followed by Di Fiore Canning Company and Gangi Brothers Canning Company, which became the leaders in the industry in the county. Italians from all regions of Italy began to settle numerous other neighborhoods in the Bay Area and San Francisco: Washerwoman's Lagoon, Hayes Valley, Hunter's Point, Bernal Heights, and Telegraph Hill, known as Goat Hill.[40]

But overshadowing all Bay Area neighborhoods, San Francisco's North Beach has remained the iconic settlement of Italians in Northern California. Its families have been studied in depth, with revealing oral histories and studies that focus on the Italian family and customs. As early as the 1840s, Italian merchants began capitalizing on the growing opportunities in the port city. Nicola Larco had already established an import-export business by the 1850s. He purportedly owned three clipper ships, and by the time of the gold rush, his import-export business was booming before the economic slump of the 1870s forced him into bankruptcy. In the 1870s, Italians began to settle North Beach in growing numbers. By 1900 the Italian population in San Francisco reached 15,968, then rose in 1910 to 16,918, and by 1920 rose again to 23,924, the highest number in the state.[41] By 1920 Italians were the dominant immigrant group in San Francisco.

Included in the enclave was the usual range of other immigrants living in what became known as the Latin Quarter adjacent to North Beach. The Colombo Market was the center of the produce trade and was described "as the greatest vegetable market in the world." It was at the Colombo Market that Marco Fontana developed different canning processes to preserve overripe vegetables. After several failed businesses, his perseverance finally paid off. In 1868 he became part owner of San Francisco's largest cannery.[42] Although he was not the first to begin canning, his successful experiment would spawn an entire canning industry in California that employed thousands of immigrant men and women throughout the state.

Central to the canned- and fresh-produce trade were the Italian commission houses, produce brokers who bought produce from truck farmers for state and national distribution. As early as 1850, there were more than a dozen Italian immigrant distributors in San Francisco alone. Among the brokers was Antonio Galli, A. P. Giannini's stepfather, in whose commission house the young Giannini worked before going into banking. Italian partnerships included G. B. Levaggi and Paul Barbieri, Lelio Paulucci and Charles Casassa, and Bulletti and Selna, later bought out by the Zocchi and Giannini firm. Dissolving his partnership with Barbieri, Levaggi struck out on his own. After a trip in 1894 to his hometown, Lucca, he returned to San Francisco and established the Levaggi Import Company, which imported olive oil from Lucca. Wholesaling his oil to other firms on the Pacific Coast and selling his oil directly to Italian grocery stores throughout the United States, he became known as the king of olive oil. As Levaggi demonstrates, Italian business networking was local, national, and even international. Italian brokers, businesses, and farmers shared a close professional relationship. In addition to purchasing their produce, brokers often provided loans to area Italian farmers to cover expenses for the following year's crop. While at times exploiting the small Italian farmer, these commission houses were essential in opening markets to Italians beyond the local neighborhoods.[43]

In addition to their success in enclave businesses, Italians developed the full range of professional services and cultural associations. Notable among those early arrivals in the city was Sabaldano Rossi, who opened a pharmacy on Montgomery Street. His nephew Pietro Carlo Rossi came to work for him and soon after became Andrea Sbarboro's chief enologist. Professor Camillus E. Branchi, professor of neo-Latin literatures at the University of San Francisco, in addition to his other works, in 1913 translated the Koran into Italian. In 1852 San Francisco opened its first opera season, laying the foundation for what would become the San Francisco Opera Company, conducted in the 1920s by maestro Gaetano Merola from Naples. Italians in the neighborhood created as well mutual-aid societies, such as the Società di Mutuo Soccorso dei Cavalleggeri di Lucca, the Campania Garibaldi, the Società Piemontese, and the Sicilians' Società Meridionale. Among these societies was the Mutual Benevolent Society, now one of the oldest in the United States. In addition to providing aid to needy families, the societies also operated a job-placement service for newly arriving immigrants. To promote their business interests, by the 1890s Italians formed the Italian Chamber of Commerce of San Francisco. In the heart of the community in Washington Square was Sts. Peter and Paul Church, run by the Salesian order, which held religious classes for children and evening English and citizenship classes for adults.[44]

Adding to the Italians' sense of community, numerous Italian-language newspapers published both local news and news from Italy. They were important sources of advertising that gave Italian businesses a wider share of the immigrant market beyond the many enclaves in the Bay Area. Federico Biesta's *L'Eco della Patria*, established in 1859, was followed by Angelo Mangini's *La Cronaca*, established in 1860. They were joined in the 1870s by businessman Giovanni Fugazi's *La Scintilla Italiana*. Mangini would later purchase *L'Eco della Patria, La Scintilla Italiana*, and *La Voce del Popolo*, the organ of the Partito Nazionale Italiano di California. Remaining in print for forty-six years, from 1868 to 1943, *La Voce* became the most successful western Italian newspaper before World War II. A group of local Italians established the daily *L'Italia* in 1886, which ultimately bought out Mangini's *La Voce. L'Italia* continued publication until 1965. Among its notable editors was Italian novelist Paolo Pallavicini, who began as editor of *L'Italia* in 1908. Born in Milan and formerly with *Il Progresso Italo-Americano* in New York, Pallavicini wrote about the early San Francisco Italian community in one of his novels published in Milan. To fill the void left by *L'Italia*'s closure, in 1966 Vancouver-based Pierino Mori began publishing *L'Eco d'Italia*, which was purchased by *L'Italo Americano* of Los Angeles in 1980.[45] Beginning with Biesta's first paper, more than eight Italian-language newspapers serviced the North Beach and East Bay Italian communities before *L'Italo-Americano* absorbed the last of the original publications.

The Wine Industry—
From the Northern Valleys to Los Angeles

From the establishment of newspapers and business associations to fraternal and mutual-aid societies, Italians formed alliances to strengthen their cultural heritage and to protect their shared economic interests. In America their common interests overcame whatever differences had separated northern Italians from southern Italians. As Simone Cinotto wrote,

"The social and cultural capital that stemmed from the racial identity of these ethnic entrepreneurs allowed them to attract a nation-wide Italian American consumer base and develop their commercial networks."[46] The Italian dominance in winemaking in California was owing to their shared heritage and the role that wine consumption played in Italian cuisine and culture. When Prohibition was passed, Italians were responsible for keeping wineries such as Italian Swiss in Northern California and the Italian Vineyard Company in Southern California afloat through grape sales for the home winemaker. The notion that Italian wineries survived through the sale of sacramental wines alone to parishes cannot explain the survival of Italians' largest wineries. The exchange of social and cultural capital was fundamental to Italians' dominance in the wine industry.

In the early 1800s, the center of winemaking in California was not in the northern part of the state, but in Los Angeles around the Pueblo. During the early sixteenth century, Spanish Franciscans brought to California grape cuttings of the Criolla grape, a variety of *Vitis vinifera*, known by the generic name Mission grape. During the late 1600s, Jesuit Eusebio Francesco Chini (Kino), in addition to raising cattle, also planted vines and grain. Until the 1830s and the secularization of the missions by the Mexican government in 1833, the missions were the center of wine production in California.[47]

While Italians did not originate the wine industry in California, they did develop it into a major industry. By the 1830s, the number of vines and wineries in what is now downtown Los Angeles were so numerous that one street was named Calle de las Vinas, today known as Vine Street. Cattleman and Genovese immigrant Giovanni Battista Leandri, who arrived in California in 1827, was among the very first to produce wine in Los Angeles. In addition to owning a dry-goods business and a cattle ranch, he began making wine in the 1830s or early '40s. He and another Italian from Genoa, saloon owner Amadeo Sabici (Sabichi), played important roles in the development of early Los Angeles. Other wineries were owned by two Italian Dalmatians, Giovanni Cavacci and Giuseppe Gazza, and another by Antonio Pelanconi from Piedmont. By 1840 Los Angeles was producing sixty thousand gallons of wine a year, and by 1856 the area shipped seventy-two hundred cases of wine. In 1869 Los Angeles earned the distinction of being the wine center of the state. It had forty-three wineries and produced more than four million gallons of wine annually. By the turn of the century, Secondo Guasti was among the early Los Angeles vintners before he moved his operation east to the Cucamonga Valley.[48]

Even as urbanization began to change the rural landscape around the historic Plaza, Santo Cambianica from Lombardy established the San Antonio Winery in Lincoln Heights in 1917. He later relocated the winery to Lamar Street in downtown Los Angeles, where it remains today. He opened his winery at a time when Northern California was beginning to dominate the market. Ownership of the winery passed to his nephew Stefano Riboli, who had worked at the original Lincoln Heights location. Now more than a century old, the winery is currently owned and operated by Riboli's descendants. Without vineyards in Southern California, it owns ten vineyards in Paso Robles, Monterey, and Napa Valley.[49]

The Northern Valleys

Los Angeles's primacy in the industry would eventually be challenged and surpassed by Northern California wineries, located in a far more propitious climate for wine grapes. Their transformation of the industry continued in the northern part of the state. By the 1860s in Northern California, Italian wine growers in Amador County produced more than one thousand gallons of wine a year. In 1853 Andrea Arata from northern Italy was apparently the first Italian to plant grapes in Amador County. In 1857 Quirillo and Company founded the Italian Garden and Winery in South Fork, Mendocino County. In the same year, Giuseppe Migliavacca established the Migliavacca Winery in Napa Valley. By the 1890s, Migliavacca produced more than two hundred thousand gallons of wine a year. In spite of its reputation for producing bulk wine, over the years the Migliavacca Winery won gold medals at wine competitions in Paris. Joining these early winemakers, by the late 1860s Bartholomew Lagomarsino established a winery in Sonoma County. Notable among the early vintners, in the 1860s boardinghouse owner Angelo Marre settled in Amador County and began purchasing and planting vineyards. By the 1870s, he became the largest grape grower in the county. Challenging Marre's dominance, Giovanni Foppiano from Genoa arrived in Healdsburg in 1864 and opened Foppiano Vineyards. He survived Prohibition by selling his grapes to Italians in San Francisco and in the East. In 1933 the winery produced more than eighty-five thousand gallons of wine. With other labels under its logo, it remains in business today.[50]

On a much smaller scale, in the 1860s Thomas Pettinelli made the first sherry in Napa Valley. Joining him in the dessert-wine category, as early as 1877 in Amador County, the Ginocchio brothers used a technique for drying grapes, the "*passito* method," that made a unique port-like wine.

Their product would later be used by home winemakers when Prohibition banned commercial winemaking and bankrupted many of the state's small wineries. Several other early vintners made significant innovations that influenced the wine industry for decades. Frank Giannini was the first grower to plant the Italian Aleatico grape, and Julius Pagani planted a number of varietal grapes that became the basis of much of the bulk wine made throughout the state. Cleanliness was perhaps the most important aspect of commercial wine production. To lose fifty gallons of homemade wine was unfortunate. To lose a winery's entire fall production could result in financial ruin. In the 1880s, Anthony Caminetti became a pioneer in the elimination of unwanted bacteria that could either ruin or seriously compromise the quality of wine production. His scientific methods influenced the successful production of winemaking throughout California and ultimately the United States for decades.[51]

The labels of a small number of early Italian wineries remain on the market today. Chief among them is Louis M. Martini, who arrived in San Francisco in 1899 with his father. After going back to Italy to study winemaking, he returned to California in 1911 and by 1933 purchased the Eccleston farm, located in St. Helena, Napa County, and renamed it the Louis Martini Winery. An innovator, Martini is considered the first vintner in the Napa Valley to use mechanical refrigeration. Although now owned by E. & J. Gallo Wine Company, after more than one hundred years it is one of the Napa Valley's principal fine-wine producers. Sharing the centenary mark with Martini are the Seghesio Family Winery, established in 1902, and the Sebastiani Winery, established in 1904. Both wineries are still family owned. Adding to the list, by 1881 Giuseppe and Pietro Simi from Tuscany established the Simi Winery in Healdsburg. Although the family sold the winery in 1970, it remains a visible and widely distributed label in the California wine trade today.[52]

While climate and soil allowed for the production of better wines, Italian vintners in the northern valleys continued to produce bulk wines. In 1886 former San Francisco banker Andrea Sbarboro established the Italian Swiss Colony Winery in an area he named Asti, after one of the principal wine regions of Italy. Sbarboro arrived as a child in New York from Acero, Liguria, in the 1850s. He was lured to California by the gold rush as a teenager but did not succeed at striking it rich. He moved to San Francisco and by the 1870s established several successful bank and loan associations before investing in vineyards and winemaking. He intended to create "a profit-sharing agricultural cooperative of Italian immigrants with grape-growing and winemaking experience." He incorporated his plan in March 1881 under the name Italian Swiss Agricultural Association. After an extensive search from Arizona to Southern California, he decided on a site in Sonoma County. Sbarboro purchased the fifteen-hundred-acre Truett sheep ranch located on the Northwestern Pacific rail line, which would facilitate the shipment of his grapes and wine. The total cost of the land was $25,000, or about $17 an acre.[53]

Sbarboro had no trouble finding an experienced workforce for his winery since at the time Italians composed about 40 percent of the workers in the wine industry. He personally screened all his workers and hired more than one hundred seasonal workers, mostly Italians who lived in the area. However, when exposed to Sbarboro's innovative stock-option plan, his workers opted for weekly cash wages and their freedom to leave with their savings if another opportunity arose. He paid his workers between $1.25 and $1.50 a day, which included free lodging, well-balanced meals, and copious amounts of wine with dinner.[54]

By 1886 Italian Swiss had built a storage capacity of 14,650,000 gallons of wine and had more than forty-four hundred acres of vines under cultivation. For his newly planted vineyards, Sbarboro asked fellow Piedmontese Dr. G. Olino to choose new varietals compatible with the local climate and soil. On Olino's advice, Sbarboro imported cuttings from throughout Europe. Using imported and untested varietals in the California soil and climate was a risk, but it paid off for Sbarboro. He then recruited Carlo Rossi, who had a PhD in pharmacology from the University of Turin, to become his head enologist at Asti. As Anthony Caminetti had already demonstrated, the control of bacteria in wine during fermentation and storage was essential. Rossi introduced the use of sulfur dioxide, which reduced spoilage. By 1889 he was able to produce 130,000 gallons of a higher-quality wine than previous years' production. In 1901 Sbarboro merged with the California Wine Association, a move that allowed him to purchase new vineyards in Sonoma, Fresno, and Kings County. In 1920 Italian Swiss Colony Winery expanded to a new location in Madera and later to two other San Joaquin Valley locations in Kingsburg and Lemoore. With his expanded capacity, Sbarboro was among the first American vintners to distribute his wine nationally. In 1923 Italian Swiss dissolved and sold off its assets.[55]

Although among the largest wineries in California at the time, Italian Swiss would soon be challenged by new Italian-owned wineries. Chief among them was Raffaello Petri. Born in Tuscany, Petri arrived in San Francisco in the 1870s and established two successful businesses before teaming up with an experienced vintner, Dante Forresti. They bought a winery and vineyards in Escalon, San Joaquin County, and named it Petri Winery. With financial backing from the Bank of Italy, where Raffaello's son, Angelo, was a board member in 1936, Petri soon became the dominant winery in the state. Angelo networked with the Cella brothers, Dante Forresti, and Adolfo Podesta and formed the Alba Grape Products Company, which became the basis of the Petri wine empire. He purchased three other wineries, including Italian Swiss. In the post-Repeal period, Angelo pioneered in the use of brand-name recognition to sell his wines and became a leader in the distribution of bulk wine. Based in Sonoma County, his operation increased from 588,596 gallons in 1938 to more than 8 million gallons in 1951. For years Petri Wines competed with the Gallo brothers until the Gallos finally won the competition as the largest sellers of bulk wine in America.[56]

Chief among Italian winemakers in the 1930s and after, the Mondavi family entered the California wine market and changed the way wines were produced in the postwar era. Cesare Mondavi, the patriarch of the family, emigrated in 1906 from Le Marche and finally arrived in California in 1923. Between 1936 and 1943, the family purchased five wineries, including their last merger with Charles Krug that produced bulk wines at the time. Still under family ownership, Krug later began to produce vintage wines. After the death of his father, son Robert Mondavi left Krug to establish the Robert Mondavi Winery, today producing some of Napa Valley's best wines.[57]

The largest and commercially successful wineries are not the entire story of Napa and Sonoma Valley wineries. Sources list scores of other small Italian vintners who opened wineries in Northern California before World War II and who were later bought out by larger producers or had closed their doors before and after Prohibition. Names such as Capelli, DelCarlo, Gaddini, Lencione, Passalacqua, Pieroni, Sarzotti, and Sefani make up the list.[58] Over the decades, the immigrant network made it possible for Italians to maintain control of wineries and vineyards. The backstory of the larger vintners is the exchange of social and cultural capital that allowed them to merge their interests and to purchase many of the smaller wineries along the road to market dominance.

Italian Wineries and the Great Central Valley

In Fresno County in the San Joaquin Valley, Italians played a vital role in all aspects of agriculture, including vineyards and winemaking. Italians were among the first to settle Fresno County after the arrival of the railroad in 1872. In 1920 Italians numbered 2,694 in the county, third in European born. But before the influx of European and Asian immigrants to the valley, late-generation Americans from the Midwest and East had already established vineyards, orchards, and small wineries. The fertility of the valley's sandy loam was augmented by the limitless supply of water from more than a dozen rivers and their tributaries that flowed from the western watershed of the Sierra Nevada. Between 1850 and 1880, the privately owned Fresno Canal and Land Company that owned water rights from the Kings River constructed more than eight hundred miles of canals and other distribution channels in the valley. In addition to many artesian wells, the valley's subsurface contained water easily reached by wells. With water readily available, by 1878 early grape farmers had already planted more than twenty varieties of grapes. As one observer wrote, "Nowhere, either in America or Europe, have I seen such careful, thorough culture of the soil as in the orchards and vineyards of California.... California is... the land for small farmers." By 1882 early farmers in the valley had already established more than ten large vineyards and wineries totaling more than 4,000 acres.[59]

Among the earliest Italian vintners was Andrew Mattei, who became one of the valley's largest producers at the time. From Ticino, Switzerland, he arrived in California in 1874 at the age of eighteen and in 1887 settled in Fresno County, near the unincorporated area now known as Malaga, where he purchased 320 acres and planted his first vineyard. In 1915 at San Francisco's Panama Pacific Exposition, Mattei's products won twenty-two prizes, including a Medal of Honor. In 1919, with more than 1,200 acres of vines, he was ranked as one of the nation's largest grape growers, while his winery, producing one million gallons of wine a year, was among the largest family-owned wineries in the United States. His success did not go unnoticed in the industry. Eventually, a larger wine conglomerate purchased his holdings.[60]

Among Fresno's early bulk winemakers, the Cella brothers established Roma Winery just before Prohibition. Between Repeal and World War II, it became the state's largest winery, boasting a twelve-million-gallon capacity, before being bought out in 1944. In 1949 it was bought out again by the Seghesio family winery. Also important in valley wine history was the Cribari family that bought the old Las Palmas Vineyard, established in 1890 in Fresno. At one point, the Cribari Winery cultivated more than 10,000 acres of vineyards before the E. & J. Gallo Wine Company purchased Cribari in 1954. At the old Cribari site on Clovis Avenue, Gallo operates a ninety-five-million-gallon facility today.[61] Among these early Italians in the bulk wine industry was Giuseppe Franzia, who emigrated from Genoa in 1893. By 1915 he settled in the San Joaquin Valley, where he began commercial wine production. After selling the family winery in 1971, in 1973 three Franzia brothers established the JFJ Bronco Winery south of Modesto, near the small town of Ceres, where they continue to specialize in bulk wines.

Other notable but smaller valley wineries still in existence with their roots in Italian vinicultural history include what Leon Adams calls the "old fashioned" Nonini Winery in Fresno, family owned for more than eighty years. Although the stigma associated with the San Joaquin Valley as the state's bulk-wine capital persists, one of the first pioneers to produce a quality wine in the valley was Angelo Papagni at his Papagni Vineyards, established by his grandfather Demitrio Papagni in 1920. When Angelo assumed control of the Madera County winery, he was convinced that with the right techniques, he could produce a premium wine. After Papagni won international awards with his wines, one wine critic wrote that Papagni "has astonished the wine world and contradicted the opinions of experts," who once believed that quality wines could not be produced in the valley's hot climate.[62]

No history of wine production in the valley would be complete without the inclusion of what would become the dominant winery in the state and nation, the E. & J. Gallo Wine Company. The Gallo brothers were latecomers to the California wine industry. Modesto-born Ernest and Julio did not become involved in winemaking until after Prohibition. They began their careers brokering grapes as far as Chicago for their immigrant parents' Modesto vineyard in Stanislaus County. The Gallo brothers established their winery in 1933, a propitious moment for wineries and grape farmers in the valley. Because of Prohibition, the number of California wineries had dropped from approximately 700 to fewer than 140 by Repeal.[63] With just a few surviving wineries, Italian vintners, the Gallos foremost among them, capitalized on the ethnic network to purchase their wines and expand their markets.

By the 1940s, the Gallo brothers added numerous other labels to their wine corporation. In the post–World War II era, the E. & J. Gallo Wine Company expanded to more than sixty wine labels, a number that grows annually. They also began buying premium-wine labels and increased their investment in the premium-wine market by planting vineyards and opening wineries under the Gallo label in Sonoma, Napa, and Santa Ynez Valleys. At its original site in Modesto, the facility holds ninety-three million gallons on the 350-acre campus. The winery plans to expand its annual output to one billion bottles. *Forbes* estimates that in 2008 the Gallo empire was worth more than $1.3 billion, with more than 14,000 acres of vineyards under cultivation in California, from the San Joaquin Valley to Napa and Sonoma Counties.[64] With the deaths of the two brothers, the winery is now owned and operated by their descendants.

Kern County, at the southern end of the San Joaquin Valley, was as well the site of wine production before 1940. By 1920 there were only 657 Italians in Kern County. Among the major vintners in Kern County was one of the most powerful men in California agriculture, Giuseppe (Joseph) Di Giorgio, from Sicily. In 1919 he planted 5,600 acres of vineyards in Kern County and established a winery in Fresno County. A large part of his success was the contract he signed with his friend Andrea Sbarboro to provide Italian Swiss Colony with more than twenty-three thousand tons of grapes each year. But with a large and diversified agricultural operation, he never became a significant influence in the wine industry.[65]

Southern California

Among the giants in the wine industry before 1940 was Secondo Guasti's Italian Vineyard Company, located in the Cucamonga Valley in the unincorporated area of Guasti, San Bernardino County. Born in 1859 in Piedmont, he arrived in Los Angeles in early 1878 and in 1894 established a winery on Vine Street. By 1898 Guasti was harvesting about thirty-five hundred tons of grapes and selling more than four hundred thousand gallons of wine a year. Wanting to expand his winery, Guasti traveled east from Los Angeles to the Cucamonga Valley, where he purchased an initial 1,500 acres and within a decade expanded his vineyards to more than 5,000 acres. While he planted a number of varietals, zinfandel became his and the valley's signature grape. To fund his corporation, he organized approximately twenty to thirty Italian shareholders. Among those who helped finance his operations over the years was Italian American Joseph F. Sartori, president of the Security Savings Bank and Trust Company of Los Angeles.[66] Guasti had his banker just as the Northern and central California winemakers had Giannini as their source of investment capital and loans.

In 1919 a young Louis M. Martini, before he established his winery in Napa Valley, was Guasti's chief winemaker. At the height of the Italian Vineyard Company's production, it harvested twenty thousand tons of grapes each fall and had a storage capacity of three and a half million gallons of wine. Guasti hired a multinational immigrant seasonal labor force, while 250 Italians and Mexicans composed the permanent workers in the winery. In the wake of Repeal, by 1940 the Italian Vineyard Company shipped more than seven million gallons of wine and twenty-five thousand barrels of brandy. Women as well were employed in the bottling, labeling, and packaging departments of the winery.[67]

Overseeing everything from harvesting to production was a team of his northern Italian foremen, who were provided with single-family houses in the center of the winery on Pepper Tree Lane. To accommodate his seasonal workforce, Guasti hired fellow Piedmontese from New York Luigi Pozzo to build housing for seasonal workers and cottages for married couples in an area that was known as the Camp. In addition, Guasti built an elementary school, grocery store, and library. In 1924 he constructed the St. Secondo d'Asti Church, modeled after the church in his hometown. The bells for the church were forged in Rome. The church held an annual Grape Harvest Festival each year that began with the blessing of grapes. Shortly before his death in 1927, Guasti built a still-standing Spanish Revival villa for himself only steps from the existent winery and the St. Secondo Church.[68] While the winery, villa, church, and foremen's houses have been preserved, Pozzo's housing and cottages unfortunately did not survive.

As a result of his successful winery, Guasti extended his social capital to the surrounding community of Italian farmers. Many of the families followed Guasti's lead and planted zinfandel vines. In 1920 Italian immigrants (547) ranked third among the European born in San Bernardino County. Italian families settled in the surrounding towns of Etiwanda, Mira Loma, Ontario, and Cucamonga, known at the time as Grapeland. Many opened businesses or worked in the local Kaiser Steel Plant in Fontana. In 1919 the Cucamonga Valley had more than twenty thousand acres of vineyards, more than Sonoma County and double the number of acres of Napa County. The post-Repeal wineries in the area were owned by at least fifteen Italians. By the mid-1940s the valley hosted more than sixty wineries and approximately forty thousand acres of vines.[69]

Because of the national renown of the Italian Vineyard Company, all the boxes of grapes shipped east had to be labeled Cucamonga Grapes. Guasti was also instrumental in influencing his financial backer, Joseph Sartori, to extend generous loans to the valley's Italian farmers through the nearby Upland branch of the First National Bank, which had merged with Sartori's Security Savings Bank in the late 1920s. Not wanting to foreclose on any of the farmers, the local director always waited patiently each fall for repayment of the farmers' loans.[70]

With rising land values and housing development, nearly all of the original wineries are gone. Among the surviving Italian wineries from the era are the Filippi Winery, established in 1922, and the Galleano Winery, established in 1927. The Galleano Winery still harvests its grapes from the winery's original zinfandel vines, now approaching one hundred years old. San Diego County has the oldest winery in Southern California, the Bernardo Winery, established in 1889. All three wineries are still owned and operated by the original families.[71]

As the number of Southern California wineries declined, the Italian influence in the bulk- and premium-wine industry in the central and northern part of the state continued to grow. By 1965, Gallo, Petri, Di Giorgio, and Franzia wineries held more than 50 percent "of all wine storage cooperage in California." In fact, by 1965 if all Italian-owned wineries' capacities were added together, they held more than 65 percent of all storage in California. Many of the most successful wine producers were in some way related. Angelo Petri's son Louis married Giovanni Cella's daughter Fiore, while Ernest Gallo's sister married Joseph Franzia's sister, and Di Giorgio's Arvin operation was managed by Marco Fontana's grandson. Social and cultural capital played an essential role in Italian vintners' success. Regional origins were not a barrier: Franzia was from Genoa, Gallo from Piedmont, Petri from Tuscany, Fontana from Genoa, Di Gorgio from Sicily, and Cella from Bari. Italian American Giannini was friends with nearly all the major Northern and central California growers, while the financial benefits of Guasti's friendship with Joseph Sartori extended as well to all the small Italian valley growers, many of whom were from Sicily.[72]

The Fishing Industry—San Francisco

As Italians were assuming a major role in the development of California's wine industry, they were also having an equally important impact on the Pacific Coast fishing industry. From San Francisco to San Diego, Italians established fishing fleets alongside Chinese, Japanese, and Portuguese fishermen. Records indicate that as early as 1850, a small number of Italian fishermen in San Francisco established a mutual-aid society for fishermen and their families. With new arrivals and an expanding fleet, in 1864 Italians established the Società dei Pescatori. In 1867 there were 86 Italian fishermen out of a total of 353 in the San Francisco harbor area. At that time, there were about 1,000 Italian immigrants in the city. Although early in its settlement the Italian fishing community was fractured by regional differences, in time it began to organize and work together.[73]

As fishermen cooperated, the enclave economy worked for the benefit of all immigrants. The Chinese and Japanese began selling their catch to Italians, while the Chinese bought fish from the Italians to dry and export to China. By 1877 and with a growing number of new fishermen in their fleet, the Italians broadened the scope of their Società and changed its name to the Fishermen's Protective and Benevolent Association. In 1884 crab fishermen separated and established the Crab Fishermen's Protective Association. By 1887 crab fishermen were selling more than three hundred thousand crabs annually. Crab soon became the signature species on the wharf and still is today.[74]

As early as 1870, Italian fishermen in San Francisco were responsible for 90 percent of all fish consumed in the city. By 1885 San Francisco fishermen sold fifty thousand pounds a day and more on Friday to their Catholic customers. In 1888 fishermen at Fisherman's Wharf were hauling in more fish than all other Pacific fleets combined, from Seattle to San Diego. In 1900 California's catch was the second largest in the United States. Italians caught sea bass, rockfish, and several species of cod. Within the bay itself, they brought in shrimp, skate, chub, whiting, flounder, perch, sardines, and crabs. San Francisco led all other ports along the Pacific Coast in its catch of salmon and sardines, while the Southern California ports in San Pedro and San Diego focused on tuna and albacore. By 1905 San Francisco had more than four thousand fishermen. The industry had a capital investment of $3 million and an annual haul of twenty-five million pounds of fish valued at $2.5 million.[75]

In 1910 Fisherman's Wharf had more than seven hundred seaworthy fishing boats manned by twenty-five hundred men, the majority of whom were Italian. Initially, northern Italian fishermen constructed and used their traditional *felucca* and salina fishing boats. However, in 1915 Achille Paladini replaced Italians' traditional boats with steam-powered vessels that more efficiently dragged the *paranzella* net. His innovation had a dramatic impact on fishing in all California ports. Paladini employed seventy-five workers operating two trucks and five fishing boats. To store the ever-increasing catch by all the local fishermen, he was also among the first to use cold-storage warehouses. Because of his innovations and success in the industry, he was identified locally as the fish king. By 1930 there were thirty-five hundred Italian fishermen. The first group came largely from Genoa, but soon Sicilians from Palermo and the surrounding fishing villages of Isola delle Femmine, Sant'Elia, Santa Flavia, and Porticello would dominate the wharf. The Sicilians fished largely within the bay, while the Genovese made the long trip out to sea. In spite of the many other immigrant fishermen in San Francisco, the waterfront was labeled the Italian Harbor.[76]

The success of the fishing industry gave birth to a vigorous enclave economy in San Francisco as Italian businesses opened around the wharf area. By 1920 Italians composed 20 percent of the immigrant population in San Francisco. Members of the Alioto family were among the earliest Italians to establish businesses along the wharf. Born in Sant'Elia near Palermo, Ignazio Alioto came to San Francisco in 1902 and began working on the wharf with the International Fish Company. He also opened a shellfish stand on the wharf. From 1921 to 1932, he managed the fish department of F. E. Booth Company and became president of Consolidated Fisheries, with branches in Monterey, Eureka, and Pittsburg. Relative Joseph Alioto, also from Sant'Elia, came to America in 1897 and after 1908 was involved in a number of businesses: secretary of the West Coast Oyster Company, director of the wholesale Fish Dealers Association, North California Fish Co., and president of Golden Gate Macaroni Company. North California Fish operated nine large trawlers and several smaller fishing boats from Oregon, Eureka, and Fort Bragg to Pittsburg, Santa Cruz, and Monterey. His company's catch at its height averaged more than seventy tons of fish daily.[77]

Family relations and the fluid exchange of cultural and social capital provided a solid foundation for Italians' success and even dominance in the Bay Area fishing industry. Among the oldest restaurants on the wharf is Sabella & La Torre. Opened in 1927 by Luciano Sabella and his son,

Antone, under the name Sabella Restaurant, it would later become Sabella and La Torre after Antone sold his interest to his two brothers and two nephews, Toni and Louis La Torre. Today it is operated by the fourth generation. Salvatore Tarantino was a fish broker, while his son managed the Bell Smoked Fish Company. The younger Tarantino also established Tarantino's and the Franciscan restaurants. Mike Geraldi fished for more than twenty-five years before he became a successful restaurateur with the still-existent Fishermen's Grotto #9. The famous Di Maggio family opened a restaurant under the family name, still run today by the third and fourth generations of the family. In 1925 Nunzio Alioto, from Sant'Elia, opened Alioto's Restaurant. All were supplied with an abundance of fresh fish and crabs from their Italian compatriots. By 1917 immigrant Italians and their first-generation offspring in San Francisco were worth $200 million in real estate and $10 million in stocks and bonds, and they had more than $30 million in banks. By the end of the 1930s, Italians began to purchase canneries, and by 1949 Italian immigrants and Italian Americans owned half the canneries on the San Francisco wharf.[78]

As the fisheries industry grew, at the turn of the century Italian fishermen had begun to spread out along the California coast to establish other communities. Genovese fishermen moved south to Santa Cruz, while others settled near Martinez, Contra Costa County. Also in Contra Costa County, another community of special note is Black Diamond, known today as Pittsburg, where 90 percent of the two thousand residents were from Isola delle Femmine in northwestern Sicily. By 1910 in Pittsburg there were two hundred Sicilian fishing boats harvesting nearly 750 tons of salmon annually. The Sicilian community dominated the town's municipal offices and opened an Italian school and an Italian theater.[79]

Fishing and Canning—Monterey

By the 1880s, there were small Italian fishing communities on the central coast. By 1910 there were 696 Italians in Santa Barbara and 1,220 Italians in Santa Cruz. The numbers of Italians in both towns were a dramatic increase over their 1900 numbers. The relocation of Italian fishermen south along the coast was no doubt owing to the economic impact of the 1906 San Francisco earthquake, which also sent numerous Italian fishermen to southern ports. The number of Italians in both central-coast ports would drop dramatically by 1920, which suggests that many either returned north or relocated south.[80] Their catch would be surpassed by another central California port, Monterey, which rivaled all Pacific Coast ports in its catch of sardines.

At the beginning of the twentieth century, Italian fishermen from western Sicily settled in Monterey and joined the fleet, which by then included Chinese, Japanese, Portuguese, and Spanish fishermen. Italians began fishing with the *lampara* net, which increased their catch of sardines and contributed to the rise of sardine canneries. Surpassing San Francisco, Monterey soon became the Sardine Capital of the World. By 1920 there were approximately 900 Italians in Monterey, and in ten years that number rose to 1,657, the largest immigrant group in the town. As they began to expand their influence in the fishing industry by purchasing canneries, Italians extended their economic impact up and down the coast.[81]

In Monterey immigrant and first-generation women played a vital role in the seasonal canning industry. The Italian fishing community created a neighborhood along Franklin, Van Buren, Larkin, Watson, and Scott Streets, known variously as Garlic Hill or Spaghetti Hill, though the neighborhood was actually a mixture of Spanish, Mexican, Portuguese, Japanese, and German immigrants. Sicilians were the largest group, composing about one-third of the population. Italian women composed approximately 35 percent of the cannery workers. During their training week, women earned an hourly wage and thereafter worked piecework for about 30 cents per tray. By 1930 women averaged between $4.50 to $5.50 a day, depending on the hours and the species of fish they canned. Women who worked forty-eight to fifty-two weeks annually could earn upwards of $744 to $872 a year. However, because of the unpredictability of the catch, few women were able to work full-time.[82] But when a trawler did arrive in port and the cannery whistle blew, sometimes even in the middle of the night, they had to rush to the cannery. Depending on the size of the catch, they did not always know how many hours they would be away from their families. The women's skill as packers was a major component of the fishing industry in every port in California.

Working closely together in the canneries, women formed relationships with other immigrant families in the neighborhood. They lived adjacent to one another in the enclave where their children often played together. Although labor strife at times strained relationships among women in some of the state's canneries, in Monterey women created a "cannery culture," an "alliance" with other immigrant women workers. First-generation Toshiko Ueda, whose father was a sardine fisherman and a Cannery Row worker, said that she spent her youth playing among the fishing nets with her Italian and German friends. The Sicilian fishermen hired some of the newly arrived Japanese workers for their cannery and fishing operations. There was little competition between the two groups, since the Sicilians specialized in sardines while the Japanese fished for salmon and abalone. The Italian and Japanese neighborhoods were next to each other. One resident, Sally Ferrante Calabrese, recalled that when a Japanese worker wanted to buy a house, prohibited by local law, her father arranged the loan for him. Similarly, second-generation Japanese American Larry Oda reported that when his grandfather opened Cannery Row's first Japanese-owned cannery, Seapride, he was able to secure the purchase with the help of his non-Japanese business manager. When the Japanese were interned during World War II, Calabrese said, "We thought it was terrible.... They just took everything away from them. It was unfair." Another Italian immigrant, Baldassare Forestiere, who created Fresno's Underground Gardens, struck a similar note when he said, "How can I become a citizen of a country that imprisons its own people[?]"[83]

For good reason, there was solidarity between Japanese and Italian families in what they all felt was their collective vulnerability to governmental war policies. What Calabrese did not mention is that noncitizen Italian and German immigrants had to register as "enemy aliens," who were under strict curfews and travel restrictions. While the Japanese were evacuated and interned, noncitizen immigrant Germans and Italians (except those more than seventy years old) who lived in the coastal areas designated Military Zone 1 were evacuated and had to abandon their homes. Military Zone 1 stretched inland to the Pacific Slope, from the Canadian border to southern Arizona. Italians and interned Japanese also had to relinquish their fishing boats to the government. In 1942 there were 1,511 Italian national fishermen in California ports, 787 of whom were prohibited from fishing offshore. The US Navy requisitioned all tuna boats of more than ninety feet in length and dozens of purse seiners used for fishing for sardines. Those Italian fishermen who lost their boats had to find alternative work, many in seasonal agricultural work or canneries, in order to feed their families. In one case, Giuseppe Spadaro chartered a fishing boat from Seattle for the season until his own was returned. After Italy joined the Allies in 1943, when the government returned their boats, many Italian fishermen found that their boats were in an advanced state of disrepair and required expensive and sometimes prohibitive repairs.[84]

San Pedro

Joining Monterey, two of the largest Italian fishing communities were to the south in San Pedro and San Diego. In both the Long Beach and the San Pedro ports, the Italian fishing colonies were dominated by families from Sicily and the island of Ischia, southwest of Naples. In the beginning, they fished for sardines closer to shore while using the *paranzella* net before powerboats made offshore fishing, especially for tuna, possible. By the 1950s, these ports were at their peak with nearly seven hundred tuna boats crewed by five thousand men and with an annual catch of more than five million pounds of tuna.[85]

The California Fish Company, owned by Albert P. Halfhill and based in San Pedro, was among the first tuna-canning firms in California. As a result of his initial success, five new canneries opened in Southern California between 1911 and 1912. They provided a plethora of new jobs for the immigrant population. Although bluefin tuna was a highly sought-after catch for sportfishermen, the "chicken-white" flesh of the albacore was considered more palatable to the public. As a result, albacore fishing expanded rapidly in the San Pedro, Long Beach, Wilmington, and San Diego ports. Adding to the local canning industry's development, by 1919 the federal government opened a small experimental station in San Pedro, where it began experimenting with techniques to can various species of fish.[86]

The families from Ischia formed a tight-knit community in the enclave that provided immediate jobs in the fishing industry for arriving immigrants. As it was in the other California ports, chain migration, not labor contractors, was the major contributor drawing new arrivals. Men acquired jobs quickly on friends' and relatives' boats. Among the families that came from Ischia, Pasquale Di Meglio landed in San Pedro around 1903. He found work on a fishing boat and then soon was able to finance the purchase of his own boat. In those early days, Italians fished with the *lampara* before the trawlers upgraded their boats and their nets from the older cotton fibers to the new, more durable nylon nets. By 1925 another young man from Ischia, Raphael Galante, at the age of sixteen came to San Pedro to stay with relatives. Both the Di Meglio and the Galante families came from a long line of fishing families in Ischia. Raphael found work on Pasquale's boat and would later marry his daughter Lucia. From his father-in-law's boat, Raphael struck out on his own, bought his first of three fishing boats, and became one of San Pedro's most successful fishermen.[87]

Given San Pedro's proximity to San Diego, there was competition between the two ports. By 1914 the Japanese dominated the waters off both San Diego and San Pedro, where they were the largest fishing fleet. With forty-five trawlers and two hundred Japanese fishermen based nearby in San Diego, they were called the Japanese Monopoly. To protect their interests, they organized the Japanese Fishermen's Association of San Diego. To challenge the Japanese, canneries that also owned vessels formed the Tuna Exchange, an albacore wholesale agency designed to distribute evenly the annual catch to members in the San Pedro and San Diego ports.[88]

The competition among the various immigrant groups in Southern California never became acrimonious. Although Italians fished for tuna during the summer months, they continued to fish for sardines in waters where they faced little or no competition from the Japanese tuna fleet. In 1914 and 1915, the tuna industry in Southern California suffered a serious decline with the unexplained disappearance of the albacore. The shortage forced two canneries into bankruptcy and price wars within the industry. To compensate, plants merged, and the canning industry underwent reorganization in order to survive. At San Pedro's peak year in 1931, there were 134 Italians out of a fleet that included 603 Japanese, 459 Americans, 363 Yugoslavians, and 23 Portuguese. The Depression also caused a further decline in the San Pedro fishing industry. By 1933 there were just twenty-six tuna vessels based in San Pedro. Only four of those were Italian.[89]

Fishing and Canning—San Diego

Italian settlement in the San Diego port began as early as 1871 when several unnamed Italian fishermen arrived and began fishing for rock cod, which they salted to make the Italian staple *baccalà*. By 1886 these fishermen shipped five tons of *baccalà* to Italian enclaves throughout the United States. Adding to the fleet, in 1902 a small group of Genovese fishermen arrived. They were followed by other Italian fishermen who came principally from Liguria and Sicily. But the 1906 San Francisco earthquake served as a turning point for San Diego's wharf. Many San Francisco Italian fishermen migrated to the San Diego colony. Among those who joined the exodus from San Francisco's collapsed and fiery ruins was the Stagnaro family. In 1911 Stagnaro and his son began fishing with a thirty-two-foot power-driven trawler. Fishing for halibut in the waters off Point Loma, they laid nets made by Mrs. Stagnaro. Overall, Italians owned and operated about twenty of the vessels among the other Mexican, Japanese, and Portuguese fishermen. Between 1919 and 1921 San Diego fishermen brought in more than ninety-seven tons of fish. Between 1928 and 1931, forty-three new vessels entered the fleet in San Diego. In 1940 with ten trips out to sea, each crew member's take was nearly $3,000, a good salary at the time.[90] With limited competition from the depleted San Pedro port, the San Diego fleets flourished in spite of the Depression.

At the basis of the fishermen's success was the growing tuna- and sardine-canning industry at the wharf. Building on Albert Halfhill's success in San Pedro, the canning industry began in San Diego when in 1909 two investors opened a small cannery located on the bay at La Playa. However, the small cannery did not have an adequate supply of fish, especially sardines. With the introduction of the more efficient *lampara*, Italians were suddenly able to increase the size of their catch and improve the canning industry's profitability. By 1910 Italians dominated the sardine market in San Diego.[91]

As a result of the increased catch of both sardines and tuna, the Pacific Tuna Canning Company, San Diego's first large cannery and the second tuna-canning operation in Southern California, opened on F Street. It was followed by the opening of Premier Packing Company in 1912. These new canneries provided further opportunities for immigrant women. Photographic evidence of the Van Camp Cannery in San Diego in 1925 reveals the multicultural workforce of women, dressed in white ankle-length dresses with white head coverings and waterproof aprons. In addition to their cannery work, women also worked on the docks mending nets. There were more than a dozen other canneries that formed a cannery row along Laurel Street. "Packed in San Diego" became a globally recognized brand, and San Diego became the Tuna Capital of the World. In the 1930s, a new cannery row developed along Sixteenth and Twenty-Eighth Streets next to shipbuilding businesses, another industry that provided jobs in the enclave.[92]

In the wake of the unexpected disappearance of the albacore in 1914, the catch for bluefin and albacore suddenly increased and the market recovered. In 1917 the bluefin-tuna catch was 600,000 pounds. In 1918 the catch increased dramatically to 6,240,971 pounds and more than doubled in 1919 to 14,990,860 pounds. The value of the catch varied, but was calculated on approximately $80 per ton during this period.[93] The recovery gave the local economy renewed strength, in both the reorganized canning industry and the enclave businesses.

With a plethora of jobs available for the free-labor immigrant, by 1920 there were 935 Italian immigrants in San Diego. By 1930 that number grew to 1,027. During this period, Italians were about 6 percent of the total European-born population in San Diego. Among them, the Cutri family insured many of the fishing boats as well as provided property and personal insurance for crew members in case of injury or death. In 1912 Erminio De Rocco established the San Diego Macaroni Mfg. Company, winning a gold medal for its products in Rome in 1923. A community leader, he was an active member of at least ten Italian and community societies in San Diego, among them the Masons and the Order Sons of Italy. The Falco, Bernardini, and Zolezzi families opened merchandise and grocery stores in the enclave, which also had at least five other Italian-owned fish markets and wholesale fish-distribution businesses. Among them was entrepreneur Anthony Bregante, whose grandsons opened Anthony's Grotto on the wharf, which grew in the postwar period into a distribution business with nearly 600 employees and a payroll of more than $4 million.[94]

In 1925 the prosperous community funded and built the still extant Our Lady of the Rosary Catholic Church on Columbia Street. In an act of community solidarity, in 1943 fishermen formed a committee and pledged to donate 25 cents for every ton of fish they caught to relieve the church's debt.[95] The well-maintained church continues to serve the spiritual and community needs of the Catholic population in the neighborhood.

Italian American novelist Lawrence Madalena wrote about the struggles of those early Sicilian fishermen in San Diego in his novel *Confetti for Gino*, a Doubleday Book of the Month selection when it appeared in 1959. In his account of life in the Sicilian community, he depicts as well the conflict between the immigrant generation's values and the changes influencing the first generation of Italian Americans as they began to assimilate into American culture. In remembrance of the past, nearly all the ports along California's coast still hold annual festivals. San Pedro's and San Diego's festivals continue to this day and are among the oldest and the best known. Many of San Diego's historical markers along India Street remain in place and are identifiable.[96] To preserve the history of San Diego's fishing port, the city placed a sign overarching India Street that identifies the zone as San Diego's historic Little Italy, where Sicilian is still spoken in some of the neighborhood's Italian American restaurants.

Agriculture—The San Joaquin Valley

As the fishing industry was developing on California's coast, the San Joaquin Valley became the location of a vast agricultural industry. Native Americans had farmed the land in various locations throughout the West before European, Asians, and Mexicans arrived and developed the commercial farming industry. During the period from 1900 to 1940, California's population tripled, from 484,072 in 1900 to more than 1,623,580 in 1940. In the same period, the Italian foreign-born population in California grew almost fivefold, from 22,777 to 100,911. By 1900 there were more than 46,000 Italian immigrants and their offspring living in California's fifty-six counties. In 1920 California had more than 87,580 owner-operated farms, with only 25,141 operating as tenant farmers, a small percentage of tenant farms relative to other western states. Thus in the same year, California's total of more than 112,721 farms created a plethora of related jobs in the fruit and vegetable industry. In 1929 California had over 355,231 acres of vegetable farms and a harvest of more than $70 million a year.[97]

As California's immigrant population settled throughout the vast expanses of the San Joaquin Valley, Italians became a major force in the agricultural industry. The valley had an abundance of available water from at least six major rivers flowing from the Sierra Nevada, including numerous tributaries. With the Fresno Canal and Land Company's extensive canal system well established, the arid valley floor was ripe for agricultural development. With the arrival of the railroad in 1873 in Fresno, the center of the San Joaquin Valley, immigrants created a renaissance in California agriculture. As one historian wrote in the early 1880s, "It cannot be too strongly stated that California is, for small farmers, still an open and almost unexplored land. The best lands are still cheap; the best locations are by no means all taken up; the most profitable cultures have just fairly begun."[98] These words were prophetic.

As early as 1900, Italians owned more than 3 percent of the total number of the state's farms while composing just over 6 percent of the state's total foreign born. By 1911 Italian farmers' total farm output in all categories was more than $65 million, including their ownership of $200 million in real estate, $30 million in bank deposits, and $10 million in stocks and bonds. They produced $9 million in fresh and dried fruits, $7 million in potatoes and beans, $3 million in grains, and more than $5 million in other farm products. By 1929 Italian immigrants owned 60,000 acres of farmland, which was 27 percent of the vegetable and vineyard acreage in California, with 217,000 acres under cultivation. California ranked first among the states with $47 million in agricultural sales.[99] Italians' success in the agricultural industry not only provided jobs for immigrants but created a financial legacy for their late-generation offspring as well.

Merced County

Due south from Calaveras County is Merced County, with the small town of Merced as its county seat. Located at the northern edge of the San Joaquin Valley, Merced was a relatively unknown settlement of Italians before 1900. Many of the early Italian settlers, originally from Piedmont, came from the North Beach colony in San Francisco. By 1910 out of a total population of 15,148, there were 1,101 Italians in Merced County, approximately 7 percent of the county's overall population. By 1920 the total number of Italians in the county rose to 1,301 out of a total population of 24,578, or about 5 percent of the population. In 1900 there were only five recorded owned or leased farms in the county, but by 1910 that number grew to thirty-five Italian truck farms, including two Italian dairies. Among those early small but innovative farmers was Camillo Pregno, who is credited with starting the California tomato industry when he began growing tomatoes and showing other Merced farmers how to tie their vines on stakes. Networking through word of mouth, other Italians found jobs as day laborers on surrounding farms.[100]

Many others opened businesses. In 1910 there were about 200 Italians living in the town of Merced. By the 1920s, A. P. Giannini opened a Merced branch of the Bank of Italy that attracted 50 percent of the small town's Italians as depositors. Increasing their accumulation of capital, Italians owned and operated the traditional range of businesses aimed at the town's growing immigrant population. Women were employed in a variety of occupations, from clerks in Italian firms to stenographers and bookkeepers. Jane Garibaldi was a teacher in the local grammar school. Peter Allaria and Fred Lagomarsino opened a soft-drink company, and another Italian opened a Harley-Davidson dealership. The city had about ten grocery stores and several produce businesses, while other Italians were blacksmiths, bartenders, gardeners, shoemakers, and hotel owners. Notable among the hotel owners were partners Louisa Lord (who married an Englishman) and Rose Spagnoli, who owned and operated the Merced Rooms. Louis Perino, Steven Panasco, and Michael Schino ran hotels, as did Giuseppe and Emilio Varni, who owned the Europa Hotel. Louis Varni, along with Edward Cinquini, owned and operated the Merced Scavenger Company, a recycling business. The Varni family's second-generation offspring Steven Varni, who grew up in nearby Modesto, wrote about the vanishing influence of the north-valley Italian immigrant community in his poignant and illuminating novel, *The Inland Sea.*[101] Although little known, Merced was a flourishing Italian enclave that provided Italians with the full spectrum of opportunities, from unskilled and skilled labor to an educated professional class.

Fresno County, the Center of the San Joaquin Valley

With the extension of irrigation canals, farming on a large scale in the San Joaquin Valley became both feasible and profitable by the 1860s. Before the arrival of Italians, northern European immigrants and migrants from other parts of the United States had established small and large farms in the county. Counted among these early arrivals was wheat farmer A.Y. Easterby. By 1884 California dominated the national wheat market with a harvest of 57,420,188 bushels. In his novel *The Octopus* (1901), Frank Norris, while describing a vast valley landscape dominated by wheat production at the time, dramatizes the conflict between early wheat farmers and the railroad, which resulted in a shoot-out killing seven men in what is called the Mussel Slough Tragedy. However, by the 1880s farmers began planting row crops, vineyards, and orchards. M. Theo Kearney, Frederick C. Roeding, and J.C. Forkner planted, among other crops, nut and fruit orchards, especially fig groves, all of which provided thousands of jobs for arriving immigrants. Forkner became known as the valley's fig king. Workers earned about $1.25 to $1.50 a day, the average wage for day labor before World War I. While men did the heavy field work and pruned in the winter months, women worked in the late summer and early fall in the grape and fig harvests. Julie Otsuka wrote about immigrant Japanese women working as farm laborers in California, including their work in Fresno on the Kearney Ranch. At the time there were 5,732 Japanese in Fresno County. Among the Italian labor force, widowed Rosa Vatalaro and her daughters were among the immigrant women who worked at the Kearney Ranch after they left Utah and settled in the West Fresno immigrant community.[102]

As early as the 1870s, 26 percent of Italians in Fresno County were in agriculture, the highest percentage among immigrant groups. By 1920

Italians numbered 2,694 in the county and 1,119 in Fresno, 2.6 percent of the town's total population. At the time, Fresno County had more than 153 million vines producing more than two billion pounds of grapes for both wine and raisins and more than ten thousand tons of figs. By 1930 Italians represented about 17 percent of the total farms, a percentage that had remained fairly constant since the 1870s and higher than other immigrant groups in the state. In addition to vegetable farms, Italians were instrumental in establishing Fresno County's dominance in the raisin industry. This extraordinary production was the result of the many small valley farmers. Many of the descendants of the original farm families remain in farming in the valley. Mauro Simone landed in Fresno before World War I and began growing figs. The Simone Fruit Company is still being run by his grandson Mauro Simone. Among those remaining in Madera County, once a part of Fresno County, is the La Mattina family. Carlo La Mattina, born in Sicily in 1901, bought a farm in 1929. He and his wife, Barbara Virginia Di Filippo, who immigrated to the United States with her mother, Rosa Vatalaro, in 1911, operated their forty-acre farm until his son Leo assumed the ownership of the farm in 1972.[103]

In addition to the new crops that Italian farmers introduced in California, they also made significant innovations. Before 1920 Sicilian immigrant Robert Sorrenti and his Modesto-born wife, Janet, established a farm growing fruit in north Fresno County. Robert developed through his years of experience and experimentation a method for pruning his trees that allowed him to produce record crops. Word of his trees' productivity made it to a professor of agriculture at nearby Fresno State. Each year this professor brought students from the agricultural department to the Sorrenti farm for lessons from Robert on how to prune apricot and peach trees for maximum production and quality of fruit. The Sorrenti family was typical of so many immigrant valley farmers who grew, harvested, and processed their own fruit and nuts. The Sorrenti family ran its own cutting shed, sulfur houses, and dry yard to process its fruit. Today their son continues with the family's farming heritage with an almond orchard east of Fresno.[104]

Of all the valley towns they lived in, the immigrant residents of the southwest side of Fresno benefited perhaps the most from San Joaquin Valley agriculture. In the immigrant neighborhood known as the West Side, Italians played a vital role in the packing industry and enclave businesses. Three years before Fresno's incorporation in 1885, St. John's Catholic Church was established for a small number of Catholic families. The site of the parish was later moved, and a larger church was rebuilt on Mariposa Street. In 1903 it was renamed St. John's Cathedral. In 1915 Italian artist Luigi Brusatori adorned its interior with frescoes. However, its northern location was too far from the Catholic immigrant community in the West Side neighborhood, which had about 360 Catholic families at the time. By 1920 there were 1,190 Italians in the city of Fresno, third in European born. Besides Italians, the neighborhood was home to a variety of Catholic immigrants: Portuguese, Basques, Slavs, Mexicans, and Irish. In 1910 the Archdiocese of Los Angeles sent the Redemptorist Order of the St. Louis Province to the West Side to build the St. Alphonsus Church. The building project included a rectory, convent, and elementary school staffed by the Sisters of the Holy Cross. The nameplates identifying donors of the stained-glass windows in the church are the evidence of the Italian community's ability to help fund the new church. Parishioners created fifteen religious and social societies for adults and children, including societies for Italian and Mexican boys and girls. The church sponsored the annual St. Elia festival, the patron saint of the Maschitans, Albanian Italians from Basilicata, and the Our Lady of Guadalupe festival.[105]

The neighborhood was composed of family-owned two-bedroom, bungalow-style houses with ample yards. The neighborhood supported many Italian grocery stores, cafés, saloons, bakeries, and other businesses. After Prohibition in 1933 Antonio Faretta remodeled his grocery store that he built in 1913 and opened Faretta's café and bar on the corner of D and Fresno Streets. The numerous Italian grocery stores included Ochinero's on the corner of D and Stanislaus, Greco's on Walnut Street, Cetti's on C and Fresno, Contino's on A and Merced, the Naples Bakery on Merced and B, and Piemonte's grocery store on Fresno Street. There was a sizable settlement of Japanese immigrants in the neighborhood and a few blocks away a small community of German immigrants whose settlement was identified as German Town. Italians came mainly from Campania, Basilicata, Puglia, Calabria, and Sicily, with only a small number from the Piedmont region. Notable among the other immigrant groups in Fresno were the Armenians, whom Pulitzer Prize–winning dramatist William Saroyan wrote about in his many short stories, novels, and memoires set in Fresno. There was also a Chinatown where all the West Side residents shopped. By 1920 there were about 1,000 Chinese in Fresno County. Across the railroad tracks was Fulton Street, serving as the town's commercial center where families from the West Side and north Fresno's late-generation

Americans mingled and shopped. The shops were owned largely by late-generation northern Europeans and Jewish merchants. Decades later, the West Fresno neighborhood was memorialized in a novel, *La medaglia d'oro* (1993), written by a local priest, Father Flavio Trettel. Published in Italian in Florence, it chronicles the immigrant success story of the grandfather of the neighborhood's prominent Caglia family from the Basilicata region.[106]

Despite Trettel's idealized portrayal of the West Side, the neighborhood was not totally insulated from the racial problems that plagued America before World War II. Before the influx of immigrants, Native Americans, who numbered about 380 residents in Fresno County in 1920, had been removed and relegated to several "reservations" in the foothills surrounding Fresno and in other areas of the valley. In the same year, there were 508 African Americans in Fresno. Those early arriving African Americans were integrated throughout the immigrant neighborhood, including its schools. However, a new wave of African Americans came to the valley after World War I, many of whom settled in Fresno. As a result of new housing programs promoted in the 1930s by the Public Works Administration and later by the US Housing Administration, the federal government funded housing projects specifically for African Americans. These federal projects were often located near immigrant communities.[107] The only accurate way to describe the new public projects for African Americans located on the fringe of the West Side neighborhood is federally sanctioned segregation.

There was a plethora of agriculturally related industries that provided thousands of jobs for the local West Side immigrant residents. Residents were employed in the various local wineries and in the many packing sheds and dry yards that accompanied nearly every small farm harvesting and processing fruit. There were also neighborhood cottage industries. In the very midst of the West Side neighborhood on D Street in a shed in their backyard, the Piccolo family ran a vegetable canning business that employed neighborhood Italian women. In the 1930s, the family owned in partnership one of the many grocery stores on the West Side as well as a local saloon. Other small factories included Alfonso Borelli's Macaroni Manufacturing Company on Fresno and E Streets, which provided jobs as well to the local residents. Borelli passed the company on to his son, before it was finally bought out by a national brand.[108]

Before World War II and for at least two decades after, the agricultural industry provided something on a much larger scale that surpassed seasonal agricultural labor, small packing sheds, and even enclave businesses.

The neighborhood was surrounded by seven major national-brand packing companies: Del Monte, Bonners Packing Company, California Packing Corporation (Calpak/CPC, a subsidiary of Del Monte), Sun-Maid Raisins, Vagim Packing, Roeding Fig and Olive, and Rosenberg Bros., described at the time as the largest dried-fruit packinghouse in the world. It alone employed more than 2,000 workers with a weekly payroll of $40,000. Roeding, Vagim, and Bonners specialized in figs, while Sun-Maid Raisins processed, packed, and distributed raisins. Valley farmers provided the fruit for these national brands. By 1920 California's production of figs and raisins ranked first in the nation.[109] By the late 1930s, all the large plants became unionized, thus providing their workers, men and women, a higher wage and a rigid seniority system that protected their jobs.

The impetus behind the canning and packing industry in California had begun in the Colombo Market near San Francisco's North Beach, where Marco Fontana further developed the canning process. In 1889 Fontana established the California Fruit Packing Corporation, which by 1916 merged into the California Packing Corporation (CPC) under the Del Monte label. Thereafter, Fontana continued to expand his plants throughout the state. Fresno's CPC was a major link in the packing and canning industry.[110]

But not all canneries were corporate owned. There was room for family-owned canneries as well. As just one example, southern Italian Frank Felice owned the Hollister Canning Company and a 190-acre farm in Hollister, approximately one hundred miles west of Fresno. His cannery was part of a network of fruit and vegetable canneries that ran from Fresno to the central coast and north to San Francisco. Felice's cannery received its fruits and vegetables from his own farm as well as from Salinas Valley and San Joaquin Valley farmers. For his seasonal workers, Felice hired men and women from throughout the region, including Fresno. His cannery produced 250,000 cases a year and had a gross output of $500,000 annually. Women composed 90 percent of the cannery's workforce. A rare surviving photograph taken in the 1920s at the Hollister Canning Company shows the cannery's workforce of about 350 women from a variety of nationalities and a crew of about 50 men. The photograph is evidence of the important and essential role that women played in the agricultural industry. Among the other immigrant and African American women, Rosa Vatalaro and her daughters are featured prominently among the workers in the photograph. Her work at the Hollister cannery is an indication of what immigrant widows had to do in order to survive without their husbands.

Word of mouth from friends and relatives rather than labor agents was the usual means of locating such seasonal work in distant canneries for San Joaquin Valley workers, especially for women.[111]

By 1919 California had more than two hundred canneries employing more than 22,000 women. By 1922 the canneries produced 15,417,865 cases of fruits and 6,913,371 cases of vegetables. By the 1920s, adult women were earning 33.5 cents an hour, while minors earned 22 cents during their two-week training and 33.5 cents an hour thereafter.[112] Based on an eight-hour day and a six-day week, one cannery worker could earn the equivalent of more than $16 a week. Daughters working alongside their mothers could earn considerably more. As one example, Rosa Vatalaro, working alongside her daughters in the Hollister cannery, earned upwards of $65 a week for the season. These were unusually high wages for free-labor immigrant workers at the time, especially for women, though the work was only seasonal.

Kern County

South of Fresno County, Kern County was another major agricultural region in the valley. In addition to his winemaking and vineyards, Giuseppe Di Giorgio became the largest grower in the San Joaquin Valley. By 1919 Di Giorgio had established his Kern County farm in Arvin. He continued to expand, buying farms that ultimately totaled thousands of acres in Delano north of Arvin and throughout California and the United States. To lower his packaging costs, he purchased the Klamath Lumber Mills in Klamath Falls, Oregon. At the time of his death in 1951, the Delano farm alone was composed of fourteen square miles of vineyards, fruit trees, and vegetable crops. Di Giorgio was the largest grower of pears, plums, apricots, and grapes in the world. Although no longer under family control, the Di Giorgio Corporation is today a billion-dollar corporation.[113]

Just north of Bakersfield is the Giumarra Vineyards, one of the largest distributors of table grapes in the industry. From Ragusa, Sicily, Giuseppe Giumarra arrived in Los Angeles, where he opened a stall in the downtown Wholesale Produce Market on Seventh Street. In 1922 he partnered with his two brothers, John and George, and purchased a vineyard that became the home of their well-known label, GrapeKing. In 1946 the family established the twelve-million-gallon capacity Giumarra Vineyards winery. With more than eight thousand acres of vineyards, the Giumarra Fruit Company is still owned and operated by the third and fourth generations of the Giumarra family.[114]

In time, the majority of the family-owned canneries and small truck farms would be crowded out of the industry by corporate interests. As Carey McWilliams wrote in *Factories in the Fields* (1939) and John Steinbeck chronicled in *The Grapes of Wrath* (1939), by the 1930s agribusiness corporations began to absorb the small immigrant farmer. At the same time, post–World War II housing development in the valley, especially north of Fresno, raised land values, allowing the original farmers or their children to sell their property at a considerable profit. Whether future generations assumed ownership of the family farm or they sold the land, Italian immigrants' investment in the cheap valley land became a legacy for future generations.

While the percentage of foreign-born Italians was not large in California, they played a disproportionate role in the farming industry. They created the largest wineries and largest farms in the region. Moreover, with the railroads and a national produce brokerage system, they were able to extend their cultural and social capital beyond the enclave to the general population reliant on agricultural products.[115] As free labor, they worked as well in all the related industries, from field work to the countless jobs in packinghouses where in later years Italians became a force in the labor union movement. Opportunities created by the national market for farm products were complemented by secure union jobs guaranteeing seniority and better wages, advantages they shared with all other immigrants in the valley.

Los Angeles County

The San Joaquin Valley is separated from Southern California by the four-thousand-foot Tehachapi Mountains, a natural barrier that delineates the two regions. Before 1900 Los Angeles city residents were employed largely in industrial work, factories, and related businesses. Early Italian settlers owned hotels, restaurants, funeral parlors, saloons, grocery stores, and other small businesses located around the historic Plaza and north and east to Chinatown and Lincoln Heights. At the time, just to the south of the Plaza center, farms were still within the city's boundaries. They sold produce to the grocery stores, the Grand Central Market on South Broadway, and the Los Angeles Wholesale Produce Market, where distributors had their offices. As a result, the local enclave economy expanded in the first decades of the new century as growing regional and eastern markets became increasingly dependent on California fruits, vegetables, and canned fish. As they did throughout the state, Italians in the South also became involved in distribution businesses. When the Southern Pacific

Railroad arrived in Los Angeles in the late 1870s, markets throughout the United States suddenly became available to the region's agricultural industry.[116]

Sicilian Domenico Jebbia (also Gebbia) arrived in California in 1925 and soon after established the West Coast Banana Distributing Company in the Los Angeles Wholesale Produce Market. His company became the largest in the United States, which won him the title "banana king." In the 1920s, Jebbia was joined in the market by Luigi Visco's national distribution firm, L. M. Visco Company. Nicola Larco and later Luigi Lastreto also shipped produce and other goods to Mexico, Latin America, and Europe. Jebbia and Visco joined an already well-established ethnic network of fruit and vegetable distributors, which had grown sundry tentacles in the United States. Many of the client brokers in the East were Italian or at least part of the ethnic broker network that linked the East and the West. Such broker names as Anthony A. Bianco and the Italian and Jewish firm Tassini and Salisch, while located in the New York market, maintained direct personal and family connections with western farmers and distributors. Salisch's son was a fruit and vegetable broker in California.[117]

Notable among Los Angeles's other prominent entrepreneurs was civic and religious leader James Visceglia, born in Bari in 1896. Before he arrived in Los Angeles, he had earned a doctorate of economics and business administration from the University of Genoa. In 1928 he arrived with his wife in Los Angeles, where they opened a fruit and vegetable store. By the mid-1930s, he expanded his store to numerous other locations in Los Angeles. Active in civic and religious affairs, he wrote a column, "Cronica di San Pedro," in the 1960s for *L'Italo-Americano*, in Los Angeles, and later published the *National Chronicle*, a weekly paper dedicated to promoting Italian American culture and civic engagement.[118]

By the time Visceglia arrived in Los Angeles in the 1920s, there were 9,650 Italian immigrants in Los Angeles County, about 11 percent of the state's Italian immigrant population. While it was known as Little Italy, the Plaza district was a thriving immigrant commercial and residential zone. In his novels and short stories, John Fante captured better than any Los Angeles writer the heterogeneous nature of early Los Angeles. Although it was beginning to decline as a result of the development surrounding the Plaza, Los Angeles's wine industry was still present in 1920. In additional to Italian business owners in the Plaza area, there were also numerous professionals such as insurance agents, dentists, doctors, and pharmacists. Beyond the Plaza, Italians formed clusters throughout the downtown area, including Chinatown, Elysian Park, Lincoln Heights, and Boyle Heights. Besides the older Saint Vibiana and Our Lady Queen of the Angels Church, by 1893 the Catholic community in Lincoln Heights funded the building of Sacred Heart Church. The Italians' contribution to the construction of the church is documented in their names inscribed under the nave's windows. In 1904 the diocese built St. Peter's Italian Church, which burned in the 1920s in its original location and was rebuilt on North Broadway, where it continues to serve the Italian community in Los Angeles. The church's first pastor, Father Alessandro Bucci, served the parish for more than seventeen years. The growth and importance of the Italian community in Los Angeles were not lost on the Italian government. In the 1930s, to aid in the promotion of fascist propaganda within the Italian community, Mussolini established a consulate on North Spring and Second Streets.[119]

When his family moved to Los Angeles, Jo Pagano describes an idealized Lincoln Heights with its tidy single-family homes along sun-drenched, palm-lined streets. As a measure of Italians' success and settlement in Los Angeles, by 1900 nearly 50 percent of all Italian immigrants owned their own homes, while only 42 percent of the total city's population held title to their houses. Even in the poorest neighborhoods, 34 percent of Italian immigrants owned their personal residences. If home ownership is a sign of success, it appears that Los Angeles Italians were better off economically than most residents in Los Angeles.[120]

It did not take long for Italians to develop a sense of belonging and community in Los Angeles. In the 1890s, two Italian newspapers began publishing, the short-lived *La Voce del Popolo* (1890) and *L'Eco della Colonia* (1894). These papers joined more than sixty Italian-language newspapers being published by 1906 in the United States. In 1908 Gabriello Spini from Florence felt that the community needed a competing newspaper and established *L'Italo-Americano.* In 1924 his nephew Cleto Baroni became the associate editor and in 1933 became the owner and editor of the paper. More than one hundred years old, *L'Italo-Americano* is the oldest Italian newspaper in the United States.[121]

Italians also began to establish cultural, fraternal, religious, and mutual-aid societies. In 1920 an eclectic group of Italians formed the Società Garibaldina di Mutua Beneficenza. Other societies included the Dante Alighieri Society, Mazzini Club, St. Peter's Society, Società Vittorio Emanuele, Società Soccorso, Ex-Combattenti Italiani, Italian Relief Committee, Il Circolo Operaio Italiano, the Cycling Club of Los Angeles, and a fencing club, Club Schermistico. Other societies included the Società Bosconerese, the Pugliese Lodge of the Order Sons of Italy, the Giorgio Kastriota Club (which included Sicilians from the town of Piana dei Greci), and another Sicilian club, Contessa Entellina Society, composed of Albanese Italians from Corleone, Sicily. In 1924, in addition to his conducting the San Francisco Opera, conductor Gaetano Merola established the Los Angeles Grand Opera Company.[122] By 1930 Los Angeles had become a vibrant Italian immigrant business and cultural center rivaling all western immigrant enclaves.

Social and Cultural Capital— A.P. Giannini and the Bank of Italy

Underlying immigrants' success in their commercial and farming enterprises was the inestimable role of capital. Business associates, partners, friends, and family members made loans to each other to fund their enterprises, a form of capital that does not often appear on the record. The more visible role that capital played in Italians' farming and business enterprises came from major sources: banks, commission houses, and some mutual-aid societies. Chief among the banks at the time was A. P. Giannini's Bank of Italy. As Joseph Giovinco argues, Giannini brought "democracy" to banking, an industry that traditionally charged high interest rates and operated only for the wealthy. He established a bank for all immigrants, who had few resources or credit history, and made loans with flexible terms to his clients. In a revealing moment in José Antonio Villarreal's classic novel set in California in the 1930s, one of his Mexican immigrant characters calculates that, after buying twenty acres of land with his savings, for his farm equipment he could "borrow from the Bank of Italy."[123]

Giannini realized that to be successful, he had to take the Bank of Italy to the locations where the immigrant merchants, fishermen, and farmers lived. As a result, he created "one of the most important innovations to come out of California in the early twentieth century—the branch banking system." While several Italian banks preceded Giannini's in Northern California, none of these would have the success of Giannini's Bank of Italy, which later became the Bank of America.[124]

Born in San Jose in 1870 to Genovese immigrants, by the time he was thirty Giannini had amassed a fortune in his stepfather's produce company. Using $50,000 of his own money, he bought a saloon in the heart of North Beach, converted it to a bank, and opened the Bank of Italy on October 17, 1904. The new bank opened with a total capital worth of $300,000, including 160 stockholders representing a cross-section of

San Francisco's Italian community, from business owners to workers. His board of eleven directors was all Italian and served without compensation. Drawing on the area's Italian clientele, on the first day he had $8,780 in deposits and by December $109,413. In 1910 he had sufficient capital to expand his operation to a branch that targeted the San Jose Italian community.[125]

He established within the bank an Italian Department under the direction of the well-known San Franciscan Armando Pedrini. He was careful to hire agents who spoke the same dialect as their customers: Amadeo Ponzio was from Piedmont, Pietro Romeo from Sicily, F. P. Tommasini from Abruzzo, Raffaele Crisci from southern Italy, and Italian American Henry Nave, whose parents were from Genoa. These agents wrote loans for Italian workers, farmers, and small-business owners. But his vision extended beyond the northern enclaves. He advertised in community newspapers throughout the state. To implement his statewide advertising, his in-house agents, the hard-driving Pedrini and Robert Paganini from Sacramento, hired a phalanx of new "missionaries" to solicit business in all Italian communities from San Francisco to San Diego. Paganini explained, "It was not a question of shaking hands, staying a few moments and then go, but [one] must gain their confidence gradually by staying with them more than an hour sometimes and in many cases for lunch." Agents helped customers with many of their personal needs as well. As a result, the bank soon gained a reputation as an unofficial mutual-aid society.[126]

By 1919 Giannini had garnered 6 percent of all deposits in California. By 1925 he had attracted more than $3 million in new business and nearly five thousand new accounts. With the purchase of smaller local banks, by 1927 the Bank of Italy became the largest Italian bank in California. Because of his rapid success and aggressive marketing, his competitors called him a "dago huckster." Years later in his defense, Giannini said, "I could never understand it. They accused me of being undignified. I've always thought that if business was worth having, it was worth going after."[127]

The exchange of social capital was the basis of his success. His friends John Battista Cella, Angelo Petri, Carlo Rossi, and Louis M. Martini could obtain a loan from Giannini just by stopping by his office for a visit. Marco Fontana was on his board of directors. The success of his canning empire was no doubt in part owing to the loans he received from Giannini. By 1924 he had expanded his banking outreach to the San Joaquin Valley, where he provided a loan to Giuseppe Gallo for the purchase of a forty-acre vineyard in Stanislaus County, near Modesto. As Ernest Gallo said in an interview in 1994, "We needed cash to buy grapes and to build our inventory of wine. So we borrowed during the months of August, September, October, and November. As we sold the wine, money came in, and we paid back the bank. When it was harvest time again, we used our own money to buy grapes until we ran out. Then we borrowed again from the bank." By the 1930s, Giannini had more than one hundred branches from San Francisco and the San Joaquin Valley to Southern California. During the Depression when the wine industry faced collapse due to an oversupply of wine, Giannini organized the Central California Wineries, diverted surplus wine into vintage labels, and made brandy out of the surplus. When the war started and the government needed his supply of wine, the grape and wine industry, largely controlled by his Italian friends, made a quick recovery.[128]

By 1930 Italians held about 65 to 80 percent of the Bank of Italy's savings deposits and loans. In 1927 one bank survey reported that it had virtually all the business of Italians living in "Ventura, San Diego, and San Pedro." Within five years of establishing the Italian Department in these areas, the bank had forty thousand Italian depositors who held 20 percent of the total deposits. By 1930, 40 percent of the bank's more than one hundred thousand stockholders were Italian. Giannini was especially proud of the fact that many of these stockholders came from working-class families who trusted the bank's agents enough to purchase one to five shares in the bank.[129]

Little known and unappreciated about Giannini is that he had an equally aggressive policy to attract all immigrant entrepreneurs and farmers. As an Italian American, he had little connection to that Old World parochial tradition of *campanilismo.* Giannini established foreign departments and hired bilingual agents to attract business from Chinese, Yugoslavian, Mexican, Japanese, Greek, Spanish, and Portuguese communities throughout the state. Within a decade, the bank had over twenty thousand depositors and more than $7 million in Yugoslavian assets alone. Although there were Chinese banks in San Francisco's Chinatown, Giannini established a Chinese Department and hired a Chinese woman to run it. She then hired a group of Chinese agents fluent in Chinese dialects who canvassed not only North Beach but also Chinatowns from Sacramento and Stockton to Los Angeles. All immigrants, not just Italians, contributed to the Bank of Italy's success.[130]

His immigrant clients in California, however, were the ultimate beneficiaries of his banking policy. As the statistics illustrate, his empire was rooted in farming, fisheries, and agribusiness where immigrants, especially Italians, played major roles. By 1919 the Bank of Italy held loans of almost $75 million. More than 50 percent of these were to canneries, farmers, and fruit and vegetable packers. Included in that number were farm-equipment businesses and farm-tool suppliers. By 1930 he became the largest holder of irrigation-district bonds in California. The bank held loans on 12,147 California farms, 9 percent of the farm loans totaling more than $71 million. His loans covered the entire list of California crops. With 2,565 loans totaling $14,635,951, the San Joaquin Valley was first among all agricultural regions of the state.[131]

By 1930 he purchased banks in Oregon and Nevada and extended his investments to the East, where he purchased three New York banks and consolidated them under the name the Bank of America National Association. On November 3, 1930, Giannini's Bank of Italy became the Bank of America National Trust and Savings Association, with resources of more than $1 billion and savings deposits of more than $700 million. When Giannini died in 1949, his network of financial institutions had more than five hundred branches in four hundred towns and cities in California. Bank of America became by the end of World War II the largest privately owned bank in the world.[132]

However, Giannini and his agents apparently did not pursue African American communities with the same aggressiveness as they did immigrant communities. It is not known whether before 1930 the Bank of America ever gave loans to African Americans, many of whom lived within immigrant enclaves. Richard Rothstein demonstrates that with the establishment of the Federal Housing Administration in 1934, the federal government began a program of official segregation of African Americans. The FHA underwrote housing loans for African American housing projects, usually built on the fringes of immigrant communities. In the 1940s, the Bank of America funded the Federal Housing Administration's and Veterans Administration's other subdivisions that were designated as "whites only." These loans from Bank of America were accompanied by trust deeds that contained "restrictive covenants to prevent future sales to African Americans." The Bank of America, while a boon to immigrants everywhere, did not extend the same benefits of its loan policies to African Americans.[133]

Late-Generation Revival

As the Italian community dispersed to the outlying suburbs, the need for Italian societies diminished, and the majority of them disbanded. However, as the Christmas edition of *L'Italo-Americano* demonstrates each year in its advertising, Italian Americans in Southern California have established countless new Italian regional and cultural associations, far outnumbering those established by the immigrant generation before 1940. In 2004 the paper reverted to private ownership when philanthropist and publisher Robert Barbera purchased the newspaper. The paper is now under the editorship of Simone Schiavinato, among the new wave of post-1970s Italian immigrants.[134] With correspondents in the West and Italy, the bilingual paper covers a broad range of subjects, with articles on Italian immigration (both pre- and post–World War II), Italian history, Italian American events, book reviews, and contemporary Italian culture. Transnational in its scope, the paper also connects Italian American and Italian business interests.

Out of California's 1,450,000 residents who claim Italian ancestry, 4.3 percent, 568,000, live in Los Angeles. That number is up from 308,409 in 1990. As in other western states, it seems Italian American identity in California is on the rise, not decline. On the central coast, Italian Americans have established the Italian Cultural Heritage Foundation of Santa Barbara that includes a focus on Italian cinema. It also sponsors a Circolo Italiano club open to Italians and non-Italians. To commemorate the history of Italian immigration in Southern California, in 2016 Italians established the Italian American Museum of Los Angeles, administered by executive director Marianna Gatto. The museum is located in the Italian Hall, constructed in 1908, and was once the meeting place of numerous Italian organizations. The museum hosts an annual Taste of Italy Los Angeles Wine and Food Event in the historic Plaza area.[135]

In yet another resurgence of interest in the history of Italian immigrants in the Los Angeles area, in 2019 Italian Americans formed the Little Italy of Los Angeles Association in San Pedro. To commemorate families from Ischia and Sicily who settled San Pedro before 1940, the LILAA plans to promote Italian culture by sponsoring annual events and by developing Italian-oriented business in the once thriving fishing port. Identity remains as unpredictable in California as it does in any part of the West.[136] Suburban sprawl and the erasure of the old communities by development have not dampened late generations' interest in their Italian heritage, however diluted it may be by marriage and change in religious observance.

CHAPTER 14

SOCIAL AND CULTURAL CAPITAL

A. P. Giannini with his Bank of Italy accomplished on a statewide and national scale what all immigrants at the time were doing locally: networking and circulating capital within their respective enclaves before expanding beyond the boundaries of the neighborhood. At the base of the immigrant economy were entrepreneurs and common laborers, men and women. Not to be underestimated, however, is the importance of the labor-contracting system, with its national and international agents who located jobs for their respective immigrant groups. The labor contractors' negative image before World War II is largely justified. They often deceived their illiterate workers into signing indentured contracts and charged their workers exorbitant fees for services. In cooperation with mine owners, they were responsible for causing violence by recruiting workers to break strikes to undermine unionization and workers' demands for safer working conditions. Many of the tactics they employed "existed without any legal sanction whatsoever." Yet no matter the large incomes some agents earned, their gain was small compared with the total wages that contract- and free-labor immigrants produced in the West.[1] Ultimately, the exchange of social capital became the basis of all immigrants' success.

Also not to be ignored are the many state and private organizations in the West that not only actively recruited immigrants to come to their states but even provided housing and other services to the new settlers. Equally important were those companies that recruited immigrant labor and built entire communities, including schools and medical services for workers and their families. Once immigrants found jobs and established communities, chain migration played an important role in Italians' and other immigrants' decisions to come to the United States, especially to the distant regions of the West, where they had jobs waiting for them.

With savings derived from their wages or loans, institutional or personal from friends or family, immigrants were able to invest in farms and small businesses. Local markets such as the Denargo Market in Denver, the Pike Place Market in Seattle, Colombo Market in San Francisco, and Grand Central Market in Los Angeles were outlets for their produce.

Beyond local markets, there was a national network of immigrant communities for their products. California winemakers such as Sbarboro and Guasti sold their wine and, during Prohibition especially, survived by selling their grapes to Italians for home winemaking. This same network applies to all other farm products. The railroads that all immigrants built provided access to these national markets. Italians were major contributors to the fishing industry in Pacific ports, from Alaska to San Diego. Collectively, large and small, they contributed significantly to the development of the food industry, which, as Donna Gabaccia argues, was "central to American economic development."[2]

Certainly, along the road to their success, immigrants endured many hardships. They struggled against the xenophobia of the era and faced life-threatening conditions in mines, mills, and smelters. Many were lynched or lost their lives during labor strife. Scores of workers were maimed or killed in industrial accidents that left behind destitute families. Management treated them as though they were little more than expendable products in the labor market. Located in the remoteness of western towns, industries were able to escape government regulators' scrutiny. The recurring New Mexico, Utah, and Colorado mining disasters may have been brought to the attention of regulators, but the problems that caused the explosions were never adequately remedied.

Ultimately, workers in hazardous industries had the option of taking their savings from their high wages to find work in other occupations. As Gunther Peck demonstrates, although they may have initially been under contract with a labor agent, eventually immigrants became free agents in a market where wages outstripped the cost of living, and investment in a business or in land provided the legacy for future generations.[3] Immigrant mobility was the ever-present escape route to a better life in the West. Even though Sbarboro, Ghirardelli, Guasti, Di Giorgio, Gallo, Giannini, and Sartori are often cited as iconic examples of individual success, their success was still based on immigrant enclaves and the wider development of the immigrant network in the state and nation. Ultimately, the common worker, farmer, and enclave entrepreneur created an immigrant economy that was the basis of success of immigrants everywhere in the United States.

Unfortunately, African Americans and Native Americans have not had the same unrestricted movement and opportunities that all free-labor immigrants enjoyed in the West. When labor contracts expired or unionization mitigated labor agents' control of their working lives, immigrants became free labor with a plethora of opportunities in the West. Evidence indicates that Native Americans and African Americans were at times recruited by labor contractors to work in mills, mines, and other industries. However, when they completed their contracts with an agent or the job ended, Native Americans were largely restricted to returning to their reservations, which did not provide many job opportunities. Unlike immigrants, they could not relocate to the nearest immigrant enclave where friends or relatives had jobs waiting for them. African Americans were similarly restricted, not only by segregation restrictions in the United States but also by the personal dangers that they faced in certain states. While African Americans did establish dynamic business and cultural enclaves in America at the time, their achievements are made all the more remarkable when viewed against the restrictions and violence that they faced throughout the United States. The lack of job opportunities and the restriction of free-labor movement are major differences that separate the immigrant narrative from the African American and Native American experience in the West.

The immigrant economy and its component parts not only are indigenous aspects of immigrant history before 1940 but remain functional aspects of contemporary immigration. The enclave economy and the exchange of social and cultural capital are not historical artifacts that apply only to those immigrants who arrived in America before 1940. Although immigrants today face the same xenophobic attitudes that finally led to the Johnson-Reed Act of 1924, they are making the same inestimable contribution culturally and economically in the United States as did the generations of immigrants before 1940. As William Dean Howells said in his sagacious twist on the assimilation theme in immigrant history, "It is not for us to assimilate *them*, but for them to assimilate *us*."[4]

Howells was correct. Italians had a significant influence on American society in farming, labor relations, religion, cuisine, winemaking, and banking. But Italian immigrants were not alone in their influence and transformation of American society. Immigrant success was not achieved without a struggle. Immigrant lynchings and murderous attacks on Chinese workers certainly occurred, and their injustice cannot be diminished. These incidents remain indelible events within the Chinese American narrative, just as the lynchings of Italians, as well as other immigrants, remain important aspects of the struggle that all individual immigrant groups faced at the time. However, by separating out the African American narrative and the Native American narrative from the immigrant narrative, the lines of historical and social demarcation become clear. None of the immigrant groups before 1940 suffered what Native Americans and African Americans were forced to endure. Native Americans were massacred and segregated onto reservations, largely cut off from the benefits that immigrants enjoyed in the development of the West, especially jobs. Similarly, African Americans were segregated and lynched and did not have the same employment benefits that the masses of all immigrants had, mainly the extensive labor-contracting system. Jim Crow was not just limited to the South. I clarify as well the elements of the women's narrative, their contribution to the development of the West in spite of their unfortunate dehumanizing exploitation as prostitutes.

Distinguishing among the narratives does not form another line of division. Rather, it allows for a clearer view of each group's history and opens the pathway to a more constructive discourse over the social problems, racial and gender, that beleaguer contemporary society today. All immigrant groups have taken that same road to the suburbs, no matter their port of entry or the border they crossed. All late-generation Americans share in the history of the immigrant narrative, regardless of their distance from their forebears. As did immigrants before 1940, twenty-first-century immigrants and their offspring are also reshaping and renewing the ever-changing cultural and social landscape in American society today. A nation that closes its borders today risks its own future development, including the infusion of new and innovative ideas. Whatever the social problems that may attend contemporary immigration, my study demonstrates the invaluable contribution that immigrants are continuing to make today in the United States.

Notes

Introduction

1. Monroe Billington and Roger D. Hardaway, eds., *African Americans on the Western Frontier*, 1–6.

2. Michael Rogin, *Fathers & Children: Andrew Jackson and the Subjugation of the American Indian*; Benjamin Madley, *An American Genocide: The United States and the California Indian Catastrophe, 1846–1873*; Scott A. Merriman, "Alien Land Laws."

3. Khalil Gibran Muhammad, *The Condemnation of Blackness: Race, Crime, and the Making of Modern Urban America*; David M. Oshinsky, *"Worse than Slavery": Parchman Farm and the Ordeal of Jim Crow Justice*; Anne M. Butler, "Still in Chains: Black Women in Western Prisons, 1865–1910"; Richard Rothstein, *The Color of Law: A Forgotten History of How Our Government Segregated America*; Michelle Alexander, *The New Jim Crow: Mass Incarceration in the Age of Colorblindness.*

4. Gunther Peck, *Reinventing Free Labor: Padrones and Immigrant Workers in the North American West, 1880–1930*; Robert Campbell, "Blacks and the Coal Mines of Western Washington, 1888–1896."

5. John Higham, *Strangers in the Land: Patterns of American Nativism, 1860–1925*; Daniel Okrent, *The Guarded Gate: Bigotry, Eugenics, and the Law That Kept Two Generations of Jews, Italians, and Other European Immigrants Out of America*; Madison Grant, *The Decline of the Great Race; or, The Racial Basis of European History*, 209, 265–66; Okrent, *Guarded Gate*, 85; Ole Hanson, *Americanism versus Bolshevism*; Marcus Lee Hansen, *The Immigrant in American History*, 98; Christopher R. Browning, "The Fake Threat of Jewish Communism"; Amulya Shankar, "'Cosmopolitan' Is a Dog Whistle Word Once Used in Nazi Germany and Communist Russia."

6. See Vincent J. Cannato, *American Passage: The History of Ellis Island.*

7. Andrew F. Rolle, *The Immigrant Upraised: Italian Adventurers and Colonists in an Expanding America*; Oscar Handlin, *The Uprooted: The Epic Story of the Great Migration That Made the American People.*

8. Constantine M. Panunzio, *Immigration Crossroads*, 149; Okrent, *Guarded Gate*, 330, 344.

9. Donna Gabaccia, "Ethnicity in the Business World: Italians in American Food Industries," 4.

10. Rudolph J. Vecoli, "Are Italian Americans Just White Folks?"; Thomas Guglielmo, *White upon Arrival: Italians, Race, Color, and Power in Chicago, 1890–1945*; David Roediger, *Working toward Whiteness: How America's Immigrants Became White; The Strange Journey from Ellis Island to the Suburbs.*

11. Jacqueline Jones, *A Dreadful Deceit: The Myth of Race from the Colonial Era to Obama's America*; Cornel West, *Race Matters.*

12. Andrew Greeley, *Why Can't They Be Like Us? America's White Ethnic Groups*; Michael Novak, *The Rise of the Unmeltable Ethnics: Politics and Culture in the 1970s*;

Francis Fukuyama, *Identity: The Demand for Dignity and the Politics of Resentment*; Laura E. Ruberto and Joseph Sciorra, eds., *New Italian Migrations to the United States: Politics and History since 1945*, vols. 1–2.

13. Frank Shyong, "Together They Can Bank on It," *Los Angeles Times*, March 18, 2019.

Chapter 1. Texas

1. Christopher Thale, "Railroad Workers"; Valentine Belfiglio, *The Italian Experience in Texas* (1995), 5–13, 50; Belfiglio, *The Italian Experience in Texas: A Closer Look*, 91; Iorizzo, *The Italian-Americans*, 38–59.

2. Thale, "Railroad Workers."

3. Belfiglio, *Italian Experience in Texas* (1983), 1–16; Phylis Cancilla Martinelli, *Undermining Race: Ethnic Identities in Arizona Copper Camps, 1880–1920*, viii; Valentine Belfiglio, "Sicilian Immigrants in Jefferson County, Texas, 1890–1920: Their Folkways and Culture," 211–12; Valentine Belfiglio, "Italians in Small Town and Rural Texas," 33; Valentine Belfiglio, *Italian Experience in Texas* (1995), 56.

4. *Eleventh Census*, "Foreign Born," 8; *Fourteenth Census*, "Statistics of Population," 698; Elliott Robert Barkan, *From All Points: America's Immigrant West: 1870s–1952*, 468, 473; Richard L. Forstall, "Population of States and Counties of the United States: 1790 to 1990," 3; Peck, *Reinventing Free Labor*, 70–75, 102–3.

5. Belfiglio, "Sicilian Immigrants," 211–13; Paul E. Isaac, "Beaumont, Texas."

6. Diana Kleiner, "Jefferson County"; Belfiglio, "Sicilian Immigrants," 211–12; Beth Gallaspy, "Beaumont Texas," *Beaumont Enterprise*, January 4, 2004.

7. Donna Gabaccia, "Ethnicity in the Business World: Italians in American Food Industries," 4; Belfiglio, "Sicilian Immigrants," 212–13; Isaac Hourwich and US Immigration Commission, "The Immigrant and the Labor Market," 55; J. D. Gould, "European Inter-Continental Emigration, the Road Home: Return Migration from the U.S.A.," 73–112; Joseph Lopreato, *Italian Americans*, 15; Jerre Mangione and Ben Morreale, *La Storia: Five Centuries of the Italian American Experience*, 97–98.

8. Bonifacio Bolognani, *A Courageous People from the Dolomites: The Immigrants from Trentino on U.S.A. Trails*, 302; Gabaccia, "Ethnicity in the Business World," 4.

9. Belfiglio, *Italian Experience in Texas* (1995), 153–64; Stephen Harrigan, "Coppini the Great"; Paula Reynolds, "Western Boots with Italian Roots: The Lucchese Boot Company," *L'Italo-Americano*, December 22, 2016.

10. Belfiglio, "Sicilian Immigrants," 213; Filippo Salvatore, *Ancient Memories, Modern Identities*, 28–33; Herbert J. Gans, "The End of Late-Generation European Ethnicity in America?"; Belfiglio, "Sicilian Immigrants," 213.

11. Margaret Ann Hudson, *Dallas Quarterly*.

12. Hudson, *Dallas Quarterly*.

13. Hudson, *Dallas Quarterly*, 79–103, 99.

14. Belfiglio, *Italian Experience in Texas* (1983), 77–79; Belfiglio, *Italian Experience in Texas* (1995), 37, 65, 92–96, 141–43, 147–48; Leo Bielinski, "The Italian Presence in the Coal Camp of Thurber, Texas," 35; Frances M. Malpezzi and William C. Clements, *Italian American Folklore*, 226; Belfiglio, *Italian Experience in Texas* (1995), 111, 113; Bielinski, "Italian Presence," 35.

15. Bielinski, "Italian Presence," 34; Belfiglio, *Italian Experience in Texas* (1983), 79; Bielinski, "Italian Presence," 39, 33, 39.

16. Belfiglio, *Italian Experience in Texas* (1983), 136; Belfiglio, "Italians in Small Town and Rural Texas," 36; Eliot Lord, John J. D. Trenor, and Samuel J. Barrows, *The Italian in America*, 89–90.

17. Douglas Braudaway, *Del Rio: Queen City of the Rio Grande*, 30–36; Houston Tracy Jr., "A Sketch of the History of Del Rio"; Paula Reynolds, "Val Verde Winery: Francesco Qualia and Texas' Oldest Winery," 32.

18. Belfiglio, "Sicilian Immigrants," 39, 45, 211–12; Valentine Belfiglio, "Sicilian Houstonians," 39–42; "Catholic Churches in Houston (Harrison County) Texas," www.thecatholicdirectory.com.

19. Valentine Belfiglio, "The Nature and Impact of Italian Culture upon Galveston," 46; Vicki W. Shaffer, "The Great Flood in Texas Flood's Waters Rapidly Receding," http://txgenwebcounties.org/clay/newspapers/flood.html.

20. Belfiglio, "Italians in Small Town and Rural Texas," 38, 40–41; Belfiglio, "Nature and Impact of Italian Culture upon Galveston," 45–46.

21. Ira Condit, *Caprifigs and Caprification*, 1–6; Ira Condit, *Fig Culture in California*, 342–43, 369–71; Friendswood.

22. Belfiglio, "Sicilian Immigrants," 211–12.

23. Phylis Cancilla Martinelli, "Italian Immigrant Women in the Southwest," 330–31; Diane Raptosh, "Italian American Women on the Frontier: Sister Blandina Segale on the Santa Fe Trail"; Doris Weatherford, *Foreign and Female: Immigrant Women in America, 1840–1930*, 263–64; Laura E. Ruberto, *Gramsci, Migration, and the Representation of Women's Work in Italy and the U.S.*, 75; Belfiglio, "Italians in Small Town and Rural Texas," 46.

24. Belfiglio, "Italians in Small Town and Rural Texas," 33.

25. Belfiglio, "Italians in Small Town and Rural Texas," 32–34.

26. Hansen, *The Immigrant in American History*, 22–23; Belfiglio, "Italians in Small Town and Rural Texas," 33, 35–36; Lord, Trenor, and Barrows, *The Italian in America*, 89–90; *Twelfth Census*, "Statistics of the Population," 734, 798.

27. Donna Gabaccia, *Militants and Migrants: Rural Sicilians Become American Workers*, 81, 120, 124; Belfiglio, "Italians in Small Town and Rural Texas," 33; Lord, Trenor, and Barrows, *The Italian in America*, 89; Belfiglio, "Italians in Small Town and Rural Texas," 33–35.

28. Belfiglio, "Italians in Small Town and Rural Texas," 36–38.

29. Belfiglio, "Italians in Small Town and Rural Texas," 34–35; Robert Lowry, "The Families of Poggioreale," www.poggioreale.net/index.html; Scambray Family Papers, San Clemente, CA.

30. Belfiglio, "Italians in Small Town and Rural Texas," 37; Lord, Trenor, and Barrows, *The Italian in America*, 89.

31. Belfiglio, "Italians in Small Town and Rural Texas," 34; Valentine Belfiglio, "Public Policy and the Mexican Italians of El Paso, Texas (1880–1920)," 162–63, 166–67.

32. Mark Odintz, "Brazos County," https://tshonline.org/handbook/entries/brazos-county; *Agricultural Statistics*, 33–34, 70; Alwyn Barr, "Late Nineteenth Century Texas"; Lord, Trenor, and Barrows, *The Italian in America*, 89.

33. Odintz, "Brazos County"; William F. Holmes, "Colored Farmers' Alliance."

34. Odintz, "Brazos County"; George E. Cunningham, "The Italian: A Hindrance to White Solidarity in Louisiana, 1890–1898," 24–25.

35. Belfiglio, "Public Policy," 163; Thaddeus Russell, *A Renegade History of the United States*, 188; Scambray Family Papers, San Clemente, CA; Richard Gambino, *Blood of My Blood: The Dilemma of the Italian-Americans*, 193–222; Higham, *Strangers in the Land*, 178–86; Patricia Salvetti, *Corda e sapone: Storie di linciaggi degli italiani negli Stati Uniti*, 3–9, 11–38; Richard Gambino, *Vendetta*, 77–122.

36. Martinelli, *Undermining Race*, 122; Salvetti, *Corda e sapone*, 55–59; Norman Walker, "Tallulah's Shame"; Vincenza Scarpaci, "Walking the Color Line: Italian Immigrants in Rural Louisiana, 1880–1910," 63–64.

37. Cunningham, "The Italian," 31–32; Gambino, *Blood of My Blood*, 109; Salvetti, *Corda e sapone*, 49–55; Mangione and Morreale, *La Storia*, 200–213; Russell, *Renegade History*, 181–88; Clive Webb, "The Lynching of Sicilian Immigrants in the American South, 1886–1910," 61–62; Salvetti, *Corda e sapone*, 101–10.

38. Salvetti, *Corda e sapone*; Kenneth Gonzales-Day, *Lynching in the West, 1850–1935*; Charles H. Watson, "Need of Federal Legislation in Respect to Mob Violence in Cases of Lynching of Aliens."

39. Helen Hunt Jackson, *A Century of Dishonor: A Sketch of the United States Government's Dealings with Some of the Indian Tribes*; Linda Gordon, *The Second Coming of the KKK: The Ku Klux Klan of the 1920s and the American Political Tradition*, 139–61; Robert Alan Goldberg, *The Hooded Empire: The Ku Klux Klan in Colorado*, 10–11, 40–41, 60–64; Scambray Family Papers, San Clemente, CA; Filippo Sabetti, *Political Authority in a Sicilian Village*, 10–13.

40. Sabetti, *Political Authority*, 10–13.

41. Antonio Mangano, *Sons of Italy*, 71–80; John Alexander Williams, "Introduction: Regionalism and Ethnicity," 17–24; Belfiglio, "Sicilian Houstonians," 39–40; Malpezzi and Clements, *Italian American Folklore*, 238–45.

42. Greeley, *Why Can't They Be Like Us*; Novak, *Rise of the Unmeltable Ethnics.*

43. "Texas: Cities with the Highest Percentage of Italians in Texas," zipatlas.com/us/tx/city-comparison/percentage-italian-population.htm; Lowry, "The Families of Poggioreale"; Kenneth Scambray, "Poggioreale: Resurrecting the Campanile."

44. Ruberto and Sciorra, *New Italian Migrations*, 1:15–18; Frank J. Cavaioli, "Patterns of Italian Immigration to America," 9–11, 14.

45. Order 11, Order Sons of Italy; Isaac, "Beaumont, Texas"; Gallaspy, "Beaumont Texas"; Order 14, 16, Order Sons of Italy.

Chapter 2. New Mexico

1. Sr. Theresa Martin, SC, "Life Sketch of Sister Blandina Segale, 1850–1941"; Martinelli, "Italian Immigrant Women in the Southwest," 325; Andrew F. Rolle, *Immigrant Upraised*, 333–34; Sr. Blandina Segale, *At the End of the Santa Fe Trail*, 52; Raptosh, "Italian American Women on the Frontier."

2. Saint Francis, "The Cathedral Basilica of St. Francis of Assisi: Our Parish History," www.cbsfa.org/parish-life/about; Frederick G. Bohme, "Italians of New Mexico," 100; W.B. Sloan, "Bernalillo County," 236; Rolle, *Immigrant Upraised*, 234–36.

3. Nicholas P. Ciotola, "From Agriculturalists to Entrepreneurs: Economic Success

and Mobility among Albuquerque's Italian Immigrants, 1900–1930," 4–7; Italian Community of Albuquerque, www.abqarts.org/cultural/survey/italian-cs.htm, 2–3; Barkan, *From All Points*, 186, 464; Ciotola, "From Agriculturalists to Entrepreneurs," 4, 18; *Twelfth Census*, "Statistics of the Population," 734; *Fourteenth Census*, "Statistics of Population," 698.

4. Ciotola, "From Agriculturalists to Entrepreneurs," 4–7; Janet E. Worrall, "A Comparative Study of Hispanics and Italians in the Southwest."

5. Sloan, "Bernalillo County," 182, 17–103; Nicholas Armijo, "Nicholas Armijo," https://newmexicohistory.org/2015/07/09/nicholas-armijo/; Mariano S. Otero, "Bernalillo County, New Mexico," https://nmahgp.genealogyvillage.com/city/mariano_s_otero_bernalillo_county_new_mexico.html.

6. Ciotola, "From Agriculturalists to Entrepreneurs," 4, 8, 11–13; *Twelfth Census*, "Statistics of the Population," 734; *Fourteenth Census*, "Statistics of Population," 698.

7. Ciotola, "From Agriculturalists to Entrepreneurs," 21.

8. Ciotola, "From Agriculturalists to Entrepreneurs," 12–13; Bohme, "Italians of New Mexico," 108; Gabaccia, "Ethnicity in the Business World," 9–10.

9. Ruberto, *Gramsci, Migration, and the Representation of Women's Work*, 57–60; Ciotola, "From Agriculturalists to Entrepreneurs," 16.

10. Italian Community of Albuquerque, 4; Ciotola, "From Agriculturalists to Entrepreneurs," 12–13.

11. Ciotola, "From Agriculturalists to Entrepreneurs," 21; Andrew Sanchirico, "Small Business and Social Mobility among Italian Americans," 205; Bohme, "Italians of New Mexico," 108.

12. Ciotola, "From Agriculturalists to Entrepreneurs," 12; Italian Community of Albuquerque, 3; Bohme, "Italians of New Mexico," 108.

13. Ciotola, "From Agriculturalists to Entrepreneurs," 12–13.

14. Ciotola, "From Agriculturalists to Entrepreneurs," 14.

15. Ciotola, "From Agriculturalists to Entrepreneurs," 14–15.

16. Sanchirico, "Small Business," 207–8.

17. Sanchirico, "Small Business," 205; Ciotola, "Italian Immigrants in Albuquerque, 1880–1930: A Study in Western Distinctiveness," 45; Ciotola, "Italian Immigrants in Albuquerque," 45–46.

18. Ciotola, "From Agriculturalists to Entrepreneurs," 8–9, 20; Williams, "Introduction: Regionalism and Ethnicity," 15–26.

19. Jovina Cooks, "New Mexico's Italian Americans," July 26, 2013, https://jovinacooksitalian.com/2013/07/26/new-mexicos-italian-americans/; Rolle, *Immigrant Upraised*, 336; Panunzio, *Immigration Crossroads*, 131–54; Okrent, *Guarded Gate*, 330, 344; Aaron Goings, "Johnson, Albert (1869–1957)," September 3, 2008, historylink.org/File/8721; Cannato, *American Passage*, 337–49; Pietro Corsi, *Halifax: L'altra porta d'America*, 61–80.

20. Bohme, "Italians of New Mexico," 109–10; "Gaetano Palladino (1838–1906)," www.findagrave.com/memorial/64198847/gaetano-palladino.

21. *Agricultural Statistics*, 28–29; Ciotola, "From Agriculturalists to Entrepreneurs," 8.

22. Ciotola, "Italian Immigrants in Albuquerque," 3; Rebecca Harding Davis, *Life in the Iron Mills, and Other Stories*; Pietro Di Donato, *Christ in Concrete*; Pascal D'Angelo, *Son of Italy*, 97–126.

23. Jenni Lanham, "Carthage, NM, Mine Explosion, Dec. 1907."

24. New Mexico Legends, "The Ghosts of Dawson, New Mexico," www.legendsofamerica.com/nm-dawson.html; Fred Becchetti, "Home Again to Dawson," 7.

25. Becchetti, "Home Again to Dawson," 3–7.

26. Alessandro Trojani, "Dawson Tragedy," October 30, 2008, http://dawson.vps.it/index.php, 1; Becchetti, "Home Again to Dawson," 3–7.

27. Trojani, "Dawson Tragedy," 1–2; New Mexico Legends, "Ghosts of Dawson, New Mexico"; Tom Sharp, "Remembering the Dawson Mining Disaster," *New Mexican*, October 19, 2013.

28. Trojani, "Dawson Tragedy," 1–2; New Mexico Legends, "Ghosts of Dawson, New Mexico."

29. New Mexico Legends, "Ghosts of Dawson, New Mexico"; Vivian A. Andrews, "Dawson Cemetery," http://rootsweb.com-nma/coswsn.htm.

30. Prelinger Archives, "Dawson Mine Disaster," 1913, archive.org/details/0633_Gould_can_5263_Dawson_Mine_Disaster_11_01_00.

31. Prelinger Archives, "Dawson Mine Disaster"; New Mexico Legends, "Ghosts of Dawson, New Mexico."

32. Andrews, "Dawson Cemetery."

33. Andrews, "Dawson Cemetery"; Mark Di Vecchio, "Dawson, New Mexico," Dawson.vps.it/PDF/Dawson_site.pdf, 1–36; Andrews, "Dawson Cemetery"; Becchetti, "Home Again to Dawson," 6; Lanham, "Carthage, NM, Mine Explosion."

34. *Encyclopedia Britannica*, s.v. "Monongah Mining Disaster of 1907," https://britannica.com/Event/Monongah-mining-disaster-of-1907.

35. Trojani, "Dawson Tragedy," 1–2; Andrews, "Dawson Cemetery."

36. Order 11, Order Sons of Italy.

Chapter 3. Arizona

1. Rolle, *Immigrant Upraised*, 45–46, 189, 340–43; Bolognani, *Courageous People*, 387; William Boelhower, *Through a Glass Darkly: Ethnic Semiosis in American Literature*, 46–50.

2. Martinelli, "Italy in Phoenix," 319; Phylis Cancilla Martinelli, "Examining the Relationships of Italians and Mexicans in a 'Mexican Camp' and a 'White Man's Camp': Mexicans and Euro Latins in the Arizona Copper Industry, 1900–1930," 55, 56; Martinelli, *Undermining Race*, 172; *Fourteenth Census*, "Statistics of Population," 109.

3. Richard Nilsen, "Ambitions of a 'Modern' City Drove Phoenix Leaders in the 1920s," *Arizona Republic*, July 21, 2011.

4. Martinelli, "Examining the Relationships," 55; Rogin, *Fathers & Children*, 79.

5. Martinelli, "Italy in Phoenix," 319; Phylis Cancilla Martinelli, "Pioneer Paesani in Globe, Arizona," 153; Martinelli, *Undermining Race*, 124; Martinelli, "Examining the Relationships," 55, 57.

6. Martinelli, "Examining the Relationships," 59, 62.

7. Gerald Sherard, "Arizona Fatal Mining Accidents, 1912–1929," digital.denverlibrary.org/cdm/ref/collection/p16079coll16/id/449, 1–2; Gerald Sherard, "Colorado Mining Fatalities, 1884–1981," www.usmra.com/barrick/colorado.htm.

8. Martinelli, *Undermining Race*, 45.

9. Charles F. Gould, "Portland Italians, 1880–1920," 244; Keith C. Petersen,

Company Town: Potlatch, Idaho, and the Potlatch Lumber Company, 118–19; Martinelli, "Examining the Relationships," 56–64.

10. Martinelli, "Examining the Relationships," 56–64.

11. Nilsen, "Ambitions of a 'Modern' City"; Salvatore J. LaGumina, *WOP: A Documentary History of Anti-Italian Discrimination*, 6, 9, 21; Fuller, *With the Procession*, 96–97; Nilsen, "Ambitions of a 'Modern' City."

12. Parker Anderson, "A Brief History of the Ku Klux Klan in Prescott"; Gordon, *Second Coming of the KKK*, 106–7, 148, 182–89; Martinelli, "Examining the Relationships," 56, 58.

13. Martinelli, "Examining the Relationships," 56–63.

14. Martinelli, *Undermining Race*, 115–16; Bolognani, *Courageous People*, 301.

15. Martinelli, *Undermining Race*, 1–2, 47, 56–63, 125, 149–52; Martinelli, "Examining the Relationships," 60–62, 64.

16. Rolle, *Immigrant Upraised*, 240; Martinelli, *Undermining Race*, 86–88, 98; *Fourteenth Census*, "Statistics of Population," 698; Martinelli, "Italy in Phoenix," 321.

17. *Phoenix City Directory, 1899–1900*, 4; Martinelli, "Italy in Phoenix," 319–20, 324; Philip J. Mellinger, "Early Hartville and Sunrise: A Study of the Frontier and Immigration in Wyoming," 143; Alan Durning, "Rooming Houses: History's Affordable Quarters"; Paul Groth, *The History of Residential Hotels in the United States.*

18. Michael La Sorte, *La Merica: Images of Italian Greenhorn Experience*, 123; Ruberto, *Gramsci, Migration, and the Representation of Women's Work*, 119, 116–17.

19. Martinelli, "Italy in Phoenix," 321.

20. Martinelli, "Italy in Phoenix," 322; *Diffusione del cognome—Mappa dei Cognomi*, www.mappadeicognomi.it; Robert F. Foerster, *The Italian Emigration of Our Times*, 96; Elda Gentili Zappi, "Memory Gaps: The Risorgimento and the History of Women," 24; Samuel L. Baily and Franco Ramella, eds., *One Family, Two Worlds: An Italian Family's Correspondence across the Atlantic, 1901–1922*, 1–14.

21. Martinelli, "Italy in Phoenix," 322; *Phoenix City Directory*, 49, 107.

22. Martinelli, "Italy in Phoenix," 325; Donofrio-Zunkel Collection, Arizona Historical Society, Tucson.

23. "Italian Sweets: Itinerary," https://www.gourmetitalian.com/italian-candy-s/4.htm.

24. Joanna Dodder Nellans, "Exploring Carraro's Grotto," *Prescott Daily Courier*, September 7, 2011; Martinelli, "Italy in Phoenix," 328–29; Kenneth Scambray, "Creative Responses to the Italian Immigrant Experience in California: Baldassare Forestiere's Underground Gardens and Simon Rodia's Watts Towers"; Kenneth Scambray, "The Literary and Immigrant Contexts of Simon Rodia's Watts Towers," *Sabato Rodia's Towers in Watts*, 145–54.

25. Martinelli, "Italy in Phoenix," 319–21; Eliot, Trenor, and Barrows, *The Italian in America*, 88.

26. Joseph Gusfield, *Symbolic Crusade: Status Politics and the American Temperance Movement*, 3–8; Daniel Okrent, *Last Call: The Rise and Fall of Prohibition*, 44–47, 86–87; "Slumming and Black and Tan Saloons: Racial Intermingling and the Challenge of Color Lines," https://greenwichvillagehistory.wordpress.com/2011/11/04/slumming-and-black-and-tan-saloons-racial-intermingling-and-challenging-color-lines/; Okrent, *Last Call*, 27–28.

27. Okrent, *Last Call*, 29–30, 47.

28. Okrent, *Last Call*, 31–32; *Fourteenth Census*, "Distribution," 117.
29. Martinelli, "Italy in Phoenix," 322–24.
30. Martinelli, "Italy in Phoenix," 319, 324.
31. Martinelli, "Italy in Phoenix," 329–30; Cannato, *American Passage*, 98–106; Panunzio, *Immigration Crossroads*, 170–73; Okrent, *Guarded Gate*, 54, 97; Sanchirico, "Small Business," 203; Henry James, *The American Scene*, 95.
32. Martinelli, "Italy in Phoenix," 323.
33. Russell, *Renegade History*, 106–8; Nilsen, "Ambitions of a 'Modern' City."
34. Martinelli, "Italy in Phoenix," 324.
35. "The Visitors," *Chicago Packer*, February 6, 1915.
36. Martinelli, "Italy in Phoenix," 326; *Agricultural Statistics*, 17–18.
37. Bolognani, *Courageous People*, 387–90.
38. Barkan, *From All Points*, 473; Martinelli, "Italy in Phoenix," 330, 334.
39. Richard D. Alba, "Identity and Ethnicity among Italians and Other Americans of European Ancestry," 21–44; Gans, "End of Late-Generation European Ethnicity?"; John Mollenkopf, "Late Generation European Ethnicity Is Still with Us"; Martinelli, "Italy in Phoenix," 334; National Italian American Foundation, *Italian Americans in the U.S.: Statistics, 1990*, 2; Order 10, Order Sons of Italy.
40. Gans, "End of Late-Generation European Ethnicity?"; Rudolph J. Vecoli, "The Search for an Italian American Identity: Continuity and Change," 89–91.
41. Martinelli, "Italy in Phoenix," 334–36; Laura Battaglia-Mesrobian (former editor of *L'Italo-Americano*), telephone interview by the author, April 1, 2010.
42. Martinelli, "Italy in Phoenix," 336–37; Italian Association of Scottsdale, Arizona, italianassociation.org/.
43. Martinelli, "Italy in Phoenix," 338.

Chapter 4. Colorado

1. Giovanni Perilli, *Colorado and the Italians in Colorado* (1922), https://books.google.com/books?id=OHPNAAAAYAAJ, 159; Rolle, *Immigrant Upraised*, 169–71.
2. Rolle, *Immigrant Upraised*, 169–71.
3. Rolle, *Immigrant Upraised*, 171–72.
4. Martinelli, "Italian Immigrant Women," 328; Barkan, *From All Points*, 463–64; *Thirteenth Census*, "Country of Birth," 809, 813; Rolle, *Immigrant Upraised*, 169.
5. Janet E. Worrall, "Labor, Gender, and Generational Change in a Western City," 441; Humbert S. Nelli, *Italians in Chicago, 1880–1930: A Study in Ethnic Mobility*, xi; *Fourteenth Census*, "Statistics of Population," 149; Rolle, *Immigrant Upraised*, 172.
6. Segale, *End of the Santa Fe Trail*, 75; Raptosh, "Italian American Women," 96–99, 101; Sister M. Lilliana Owens, "Frances Xavier Cabrini, Foundress of the Queen of Heaven Institute," 139–40.
7. Owens, "Frances Xavier Cabrini," 139–46; Worrall, "Labor, Gender, and Generational Change," 443; Thomas G. Tancredo, "Cabrini Shrine, Golden, Colorado," http://memory.loc.gov/diglib/legacies/loc.afc.afc-legacies.200002783/.
8. Mangione and Morreale, *La Storia*, 327–29; Our Lady of Mount Carmel, ourladymountcarmel.com.
9. *Fourteenth Census*, "Composition and Characteristics," 149, 192; Karin Chapman, "Cultural Conflict in a Steel Town: Two Generations of Italian Women," 81; Rolle,

Immigrant Upraised, 174; Wade Broadhead, "History of Pueblo," https://Pueblo.org/history (see also *Colorado Encyclopedia*, https://coloradoencyclopedia.org/article/pueblo-county); Goldberg, *Hooded Empire*, 44, 61; Russell Frank, "Get on One End of the Rope and Pull Together: Italian-American Life and Work in Pueblo, Colorado," 145–47; Jeffrey DeHerrera, "Pueblo's East Side History: Pueblo City-County Library District, www.pueblolibrary.org/EastsideHistoryWall."

10. Silvio Manno, *Charcoal and Blood: Italian Immigrants in Eureka, Nevada, and the Fish Creek Massacre*, 24; Broadhead, "History of Pueblo"; Frank, "Get on One End," 145.

11. Frank, "Get on One End," 146–48.

12. Frank, "Get on One End," 145; Perilli, *Italians in Colorado*, 142–46.

13. Perilli, *Italians in Colorado*, 144–46; Joy Fisher, *1911 Colorado Business Directory, Trinidad, Las Animas County*; Perilli, *Italians in Colorado*, 50.

14. Philip E. Notarianni, "Italian Involvement in the 1903–04 Coal Miners' Strike in Southern Colorado and Utah," 47; Rolle, *Immigrant Upraised*, 177; Gabaccia, *Militants and Migrants*, 5–16; Laura E. Ruberto, "Grains of Truth: Rice, Labor, and Cultural Identity," 3–20; Rolle, *Immigrant Upraised*, 176–77.

15. Notarianni, "Italian Involvement," 47, 48–59; Rolle, *Immigrant Upraised*, 176–77.

16. Philip F. Notarianni, "Italianita in Utah: The Immigrant Experience," 311–12; Notarianni, "Italian Involvement," 50–57.

17. Rolle, *Immigrant Upraised*, 177–78.

18. Maria Susanna Garroni, "Coal Mine, Farm and Quarry Frontiers: The Different Americas of Italian Immigrant Women," 122, 124–25; Jennifer Guglielmo, *Living the Revolution: Italian Women's Resistance and Radicalism, 1880–1945*, 18–19; Anthony V. Riccio, *Farms, Factories, and Family: Italian American Women of Connecticut*, 37; Linda Reeder, *Widows in White: Migration and the Transformation of Rural Italian Women, Sicily, 1880–1920*, 4, 55–102; Mangione and Morreale, *La Storia*, 335.

19. Jo Pagano, *Golden Wedding*, 35–36.

20. Garroni, "Coal Mine, Farm and Quarry Frontiers," 119, 126.

21. Pagano, *Golden Wedding*, 13, 16–17; Kenneth Scambray, *Queen Calafia's Paradise: California and the Italian American Novel*, 33–50.

22. Gerald Sherard, "Colorado Mining Fatalities, 1884–1981," www.usmra.com/barrick/colorado.htm; Stu Beitler, "Tercio, CO, Mine Explosion Kills Twenty, Oct. 1904," www.gendisasters.com/colorado/5569/tercio-mine-explosion-kills-twenty-oct-1904; Linda Horton, "New Castle, CO. Vulcan Mine Explosion," December 1913, www.3.gendasters.com/Colorado/35522/Newcastle,-vulcan-mine-explosion,-dec-1913.

23. Gilpin County, "Rich History," www.co.gilpin.cous/departments/visitor_info/rich.history; Chapman, "Cultural Conflict," 81; Salvetti, *Corda e sapone*, 41–48, 94–95; Conrad Woodall, "The Italian Massacre at Walsenburg, Colorado, 1895," 297–317; Rolle, *Immigrant Upraised*, 174–75.

24. Salvetti, *Corda e sapone*, 41–48, 94–95; Rolle, *Immigrant Upraised*, 174–75.

25. Higham, *Strangers in the Land*, 288–89; Gordon, *Second Coming of the KKK*, 11–23; Goldberg, *Hooded Empire*, 40–41; Gordon, *Second Coming of the KKK*, 93–104; Goldberg, *Hooded Empire*, xiii; Higham, *Strangers in the Land*, 286–87; Gordon, *Second Coming of the KKK*, 106–7, 148, 182–9.

26. Goldberg, *Hooded Empire*, 10–11; Higham, *Strangers in the Land*, 288.

27. Goldberg, *Hooded Empire*, 31.

28. Goldberg, *Hooded Empire*, 60–64; Pagano, *Golden Wedding*, 50; Jo J. Meek (Jo Pagano's daughter), telephone interview by the author, July 19, 2013; Notarianni, "Italianita in Utah," 329.

29. Goldberg, *Hooded Empire*, 60–64; Frank, "Get on One End," 146; Goldberg, *Hooded Empire*, 63–64.

30. Goldberg, *Hooded Empire*, 77, 84–86.

31. John Fante, *Dago Red*; Scambray, *Queen Calafia's Paradise*, 132–33, 141–53, 196–97.

32. Panunzio, *Immigration Crossroads*, 131–54; Okrent, *Guarded Gate*, 330, 344; Goldberg, *Hooded Empire*, 181.

33. Worrall, "Labor, Gender, and Generational Change," 442–43; Janet E. Worrall, "Adjustment and Integration: The Italian Experience in Colorado," 178–79; Shelby Carr, "Hill's Black Hawk Smelter," https://coloradoencyclopedia.org/article/hills-black-hawk-smelter; Martinelli, "Italian Immigrant Women," 327.

34. Worrall, "Labor, Gender, and Generational Change," 442–43; Martinelli, "Italian Immigrant Women," 327; Our Lady of Mount Carmel, ourladymountcarmel.com; Isabel Wilkerson, *The Warmth of Another Sun: The Epic Story of America's Great Migration.*

35. Frank, "Get on One End," 151–53; Chapman, "Cultural Conflict," 81–82; *Italian-American Who's Who*, 195; Giovanni Schiavo, *Four Centuries of Italian-American History*, 393.

36. Perilli, *Italians in Colorado*, 28, 34–38, 47, 157, 192, back cover; "Italian-American Bank in Denver, CO," www.silogic.com/genealogy/; Perilli, *Italians in Colorado*, 36–37, 186–200.

37. Bolognani, *Courageous People*, 321–24; "Brothers Cutlery," https://bizstanding.com/search?bname=Brothers+Cutlery&location=Denver%2C+NY.

38. Bolognani, *Courageous People*, 321–24, 418; Mangione and Morreale, *La Storia*, 335–37; *Italian-American Who's Who*, 226.

39. Thomas Noel, "The Immigrant Saloon in Colorado," 201–12; Colleen O'Connor, "Patsy's Inn Closes after 95 Years of Italian Cuisine in Denver," *Denver Post*, August 23, 2016.

40. Noel, "Immigrant Saloon," 210–12.

41. Worrall, "Labor, Gender, and Generational Change," 441–42, 444–45, 461–62; Stuart Steers, "The Watermelon King"; Katie Rudolph, "Denver's Bygone Markets"; Giambrocco Food Services, www.giambroccofoods.com/.

42. *Agricultural Statistics*, 18–19; Perilli, *Italians in Colorado*, 138.

43. Worrall, "Labor, Gender, and Generational Change," 444; Sanchirico, "Small Business," 207; Worrall, "Labor, Gender, and Generational Change," 444, 447–48.

44. Worrall, "Labor, Gender, and Generational Change," 446–50, 452–54; Chapman, "Cultural Conflict," 83, 87; Worrall, "Labor, Gender, and Generational Change," 439–40, 443, 445–46, 448, 450–55, 467; Micaela Di Leonardo, "The Myth of the Urban Village: Women, Work, and Family among Italian-Americas," 277–80.

45. Worrall, "Labor, Gender, and Generational Change," 446–50, 452–54; Perilli, *Italians in Colorado*, 47, 192.

46. Maxine Seller, "The Education of the Immigrant Woman, 1900–1935," 243–47; Chapman, "Cultural Conflict," 82–83; Martinelli, "Italian Immigrant Women," 332.

47. Chapman, "Cultural Conflict," 81–82.

48. Chapman, "Cultural Conflict," 82–84; *Italian-American Who's Who*, 226, 195; Perilli, *Italians in Colorado*, 148; Linda K. Kerber and Jane De Hart Mathews, eds., *Women's America: Refocusing the Past*; Guglielmo, *Living the Revolution*, 176–215; Gabaccia, *Militants and Migrants*, 125, 140, 146, 153.

49. Garroni, "Coal Mine, Farm and Quarry Frontiers," 117; Martinelli, "Italian Immigrant Women," 327–28; Martinelli, "Italian Immigrant Women," *Italian Immigrant Women*, 327–38, 331–32, 333–34; Raptosh, "Italian American Women," 91–107; Perilli, *Italians in Colorado*, 36.

50. Chapman, "Cultural Conflict," 82; Noel, "Immigrant Saloon," 210; Schiavo, *Four Centuries of Italian-American History*, 413; Perilli, *Italians in Colorado*, 163; *Italian-American Who's Who*, 226; Chapman, "Cultural Conflict," 82.

51. National Italian American Foundation, *Italian Americans in the U.S.*, 2, 2000; Order 10, Order Sons of Italy.

52. Patricia Calhoun, "Colorado's War of the Words Continues over Columbus Day," October 3, 2018, www.westword.com/news/colorado-the-first-state-to-give-columbus-a-holiday-considers-abolishing-it-10844725; Colorado, "Order Sons of Italy," www.osia.org/about/chapters/colorado.org; "American-Italian Cultural Club," www.peakradar.com/organization/american-italian-cultural-club/; *Andiamo! Colorado's Italian Community Newspaper*, http://andiamocolorado.com/.

Chapter 5. Utah

1. Notarianni, "Italianita in Utah," 306; Philip F. Notarianni, "Italian Catholics among the Mormons: Maintaining Identity in Zion," 150–51; Peck, *Reinventing Free Labor*, 66–68.

2. Philip F. Notarianni, "Utah's Ellis Island: The Difficult Americanization of Carbon County," 179–82; *Eleventh Census*, "Foreign Born Population," 8; *Twelfth Census*, "Statistics of Population," 734; *Thirteenth Census*, "Statistics of Population," 581; Richard L. Jensen, "Immigration to Utah," www.uen.org/utah_history_encyclopedia/i/IMMIGRATION.shtml; "Resident Population," 2; Barkan, *From All Points*, 464; Walter Borla, "Italian Americans in Utah: Unlikely Immigrants," 20.

3. Yucheng Qin, "A Century-Old 'Puzzle': The Six Companies' Role in Chinese Labor Importation in the Nineteenth Century"; Peck, *Reinventing Free Labor*, 34, 51–56, 95.

4. Peck, *Reinventing Free Labor*, 28, 31, 34, 36, 51–56, 72; Notarianni, "Italianita in Utah," 314.

5. Peck, *Reinventing Free Labor*, 64–67, 228.

6. Notarianni, "Utah's Ellis Island," 181–82.

7. Ronald G. Watt, *History of Carbon County*, 2, 33–38, 73–74; *Italian-American Who's Who*, 356; "Pietro Ottavio 'P.O.' Silvagni," www.findagrave.com/memorial/52183266/pietro-ottavio-silvagni.

8. Philip F. Notarianni and Richard Raspa, "The Italian Community of Helper, Utah: Its Historic and Folkloric Past and Present," 23, 25.

9. "Joseph Barboglio Sr.," www.findagrave.com/memorial/39364429/joseph-barboglio; *Diffusione del cognome—Mappa dei Cognomi*, www.mappadeicognomi.it; Notarianni and Raspa, "Italian Community of Helper," 26–27.

10. Notarianni, "Italianita in Utah," 308, 321–22.

11. Notarianni, "Italianita in Utah," 320.

12. Notarianni and Raspa, "Italian Community of Helper," 26–27; Gordon, *Second Coming of the KKK*, 1–23.

13. Notarianni, "Italianita in Utah," 323–24; Notarianni, "Utah's Ellis Island," 192; Philip F. Notarianni, "The Italians in Utah," 18; Watson, "Need of Federal Legislation"; Guglielmo, *Living the Revolution*, 207–8.

14. Notarianni and Raspa, "Italian Community of Helper," 26–27, 32–33; Peck, *Reinventing Free Labor*, 131; Gabaccia, *Militants and Migrants*, 168–75.

15. Notarianni, "Italian Involvement," 52–56; Allan Kent Powell, *The Next Time We Strike: Labor in Utah's Coal Fields, 1900–1933*, 37–80.

16. Notarianni, "Italian Involvement," 52–56; Notarianni, "Utah's Ellis Island," 182; Notarianni and Raspa, "Italian Community of Helper," 25; Gabaccia, *Militants and Migrants*, 5–16.

17. Peck, *Reinventing Free Labor*, 211; Notarianni, "Utah's Ellis Island," 183, 187; Notarianni and Raspa, "Italian Community of Helper," 25.

18. Peck, *Reinventing Free Labor*, 211–12, 217, 219–23.

19. Kathy Hamaker, "Miners Killed in the Winter Quarter Mine Explosion," www.carbon-utgenweb.com/miners.html; Yvette D. Ison, "The Scofield Mine Disaster," https://historytogo.utah.gov/?s=scofield+mine+disaster.

20. Janeen Arnold Costa, "A Struggle for Survival and Identity: Families in the Aftermath of the Castle Gate Mine Disaster," 280; Michael Katsanevas, "The Emerging Social Worker and the Distribution of the Castle Gate Relief Fund"; Saline Hardee Fraser, "One Long Day"; Costa, "Struggle for Survival," 279.

21. Foerster, *Italian Emigration*, 83–84, 109; Scambray Family Papers, San Clemente, CA.

22. Notarianni, "The Italians in Utah," 9; Frank, "Get on One End," 71–75; Steve Siporin, "Folklife and Survival: The Italian-Americans of Carbon County, Utah," 86; Notarianni, "Italianita in Utah," 320.

23. Siporin, "Folklife and Survival," 81–82; Frank, "Get on One End," 75; Siporin, "Folklife and Survival," 86–87; Philip F. Notarianni, "Places of Origin: Calabresi in Carbon County, Utah," 69–73.

24. David A. Prevedel, *The Tyroleans: A Journey of Hope*, 67, 70–72; "Map of the Value of Farmland per Acre by State, 1910," https://accessgenealogy.com/america/map-value-farm-land-per-acre-state-1910.htm.

25. Prevedel, *Tyroleans*, 72–77, 80–83, 87, 94.

26. Prevedel, *Tyroleans*, 72–76, 81–83.

27. *Agricultural Statistics*, 34; Prevedel, *Tyroleans*, 96–97.

28. *Agricultural Statistics*, 34.

29. Barkan, *From All Points*, 478; "Rotisserie Inn," www.flickr.com/photos/boston_public_library/9361535212/in/photolist-fgfjgw; *Italian-American Who's Who*, 72, 323.

30. *Italian-American Who's Who*, 168, 233–34; "Death: Ernest F. Mariani," www.deseret.com/1993/7/10/19055478/death-ernest-f-mariani.

31. Prevedel, *Tyroleans*, 71; Ouida Blanthorn, *A History of Tooele County*, 170, 182; Saint Joseph Catholic Church, www.stjosephogden.org; Notarianni, "Italianita in Utah," 330–31; Notarianni, "The Italians in Utah," 21–22; Kristen Moulten, "St. Patrick

Parish: A Beacon for Immigrants," *Salt Lake Tribune*, March 12, 2010; "The Cathedral of the Madeleine," https://utcotm.org/; Prevedel, *Tyroleans*, 70–73.

32. Notarianni, "Italianita in Utah," 330–31; Notarianni, "The Italians in Utah," 24–25.

33. Notarianni, "Italianita in Utah," 330–31.

34. Stephen Fox, *The Unknown Internment: An Oral History of the Relocation of Italian Americans during World War II*, 25–27; Iris Origo, *A Chill in the Air: An Italian War Diary, 1939–1940*, 33; Adrian Lyttelton, "Under the Tuscan Gun," 42–43; Gloria Ricci Lothrop, "A Shadow on the Land: The Impact of Fascism on Los Angeles Italians."

35. National Italian American Foundation, *Italian Americans in the U.S.*, 4; Order 11, Order Sons of Italy.

Chapter 6. Wyoming

1. Barkan, *From All Points*, 464; *Twelfth Census*, "Statistics of the Population," 732, 734.

2. *Thirteenth Census*, "Statistics of the Population," 579; David Kathka, "The Italian Experience in Wyoming," 68; Barkan, *From All Points*, 464; Dwight A. Radford, "Ethnic Groups of Wyoming"; Kathka, "Italian Experience in Wyoming," 67–68; Paola A. Sensi-Isolani, "Tradition and Transition in a California Paese," 2; Radford, "Ethnic Groups of Wyoming."

3. Kathka, "Italian Experience in Wyoming," 68–69; Prevedel, *Tyroleans*, 32.

4. Bolognani, *Courageous People*, 64–65; Oreste Dito, *La storia Calabrese: E la dimora degli Ebrei in Calabria dal secolo V alla seconda metà del secolo XVI*, 285–304; Foerster, *Italian Emigration*, 324–25; Sensi-Isolani, "Tradition and Transition," 2; Iorizzo and Mondello, *The Italian-Americans*, 24–37; Mellinger, "Early Hartville and Sunrise," 68, 92.

5. Dee Garceau, *The Important Things of Life: Women, Work, and Family in Sweetwater County, Wyoming, 1880–1929*, 19.

6. Chris Propst, "Rock Springs, Wyoming," www.wyohistory.org/essays/rock-springs-wyoming; David A. Cookson, "The Basques in Wyoming," 95–96; Donald Hodgson and Vivien Hills, "Dream and Fulfillment: Germans in Wyoming," 39–40; Dean P. Talagan, "Faith, Hard Work, and Family: The Story of the Wyoming Hellenes," 161; Radford, "Ethnic Groups of Wyoming."

7. Garceau, *Important Things of Life*, 29; Kathka, "Italian Experience in Wyoming," 73; Mellinger, "Early Hartville and Sunrise," 82–83.

8. Bolognani, *Courageous People*, 255; Radford, "Ethnic Groups of Wyoming"; Kathka, "Italian Experience in Wyoming," 68; Bolognani, *Courageous People*, 255–56; Prevedel, *Tyroleans*, 32–33; *Fourteenth Census*, "Wyoming Introduction," 329; "Facts and Figures: Income and Prices, 1900–1999," https://usa.usembassy.de/etexts/his/e_prices1.htm; "Map of the Value of Farmland."

9. Kathka, "Italian Experience in Wyoming," 68, 70; Radford, "Ethnic Groups of Wyoming"; Bolognani, *Courageous People*, 259; Earl Stinneford, "Mines and Miners: The Eastern Europeans in Wyoming," 121; Bolognani, *Courageous People*, 259; Mellinger, "Early Hartville and Sunrise," 57, 73, 143; La Sorte, *La Merica*, 120.

10. Mellinger, "Early Hartville and Sunrise," 68, 92.

11. Peck, *Reinventing Free Labor*, 194–95; Mellinger, "Early Hartville and Sunrise," 56, 67–68; Peck, *Reinventing Free Labor*, 194–95.

12. Iorizzo and Mondello, *The Italian-Americans*, 136–37, 140; Peck, *Reinventing Free Labor*, 1–48, 93–99, 106–14; Foerster, *Italian Emigration*, 391; John C. Paige, "Country Squires and Laborers: British Immigrants in Wyoming," 8.

13. Iorizzo and Mondello, *The Italian-Americans*, 128, 137–40; Peck, *Reinventing Free Labor*, 21–22; Mellinger, "Early Hartville and Sunrise," 71; Kathka, "Italian Experience in Wyoming," 70; Peck, *Reinventing Free Labor*, 28, 34, 59, 66–67; John Koren, "The Padrone System and Padrone Banks"; Foerster, *Italian Emigration*, 39; Notarianni, "Italianita in Utah," 305; Peck, *Reinventing Free Labor*, 192–95.

14. Paige, "Country Squires and Laborers," 8–9; Garceau, *Important Things of Life*, 21.

15. Tom Rea, "Rock Springs Massacre," November 8, 2014, www.wyohistory.org/essays/rock-springs-massacre (see also "Thunder under the House: One Family and the Hanna Mine Disaster," November 8, 2014, www.wyohistory.org/encyclopedia/thunder-under-house-one-family-and-hanna-mine-disasters); Paige, "Country Squires and Laborers," 8–9; Garceau, *Important Things of Life*, 21; Rea, "Rock Springs Massacre"; Radford, "Ethnic Groups of Wyoming."

16. Rea, "Rock Springs Massacre"; Garceau, *Important Things of Life*, 21, 27.

17. Hodgson, "Dream and Fulfillment," 42; Paige, "Country Squires and Laborers," 21; Mellinger, "Early Hartville and Sunrise," 57; Kathka, "Italian Experience in Wyoming," 74; Propst, "Rock Springs, Wyoming."

18. Paige, "Country Squires and Laborers," 9; Kathka, "Italian Experience in Wyoming," 74–78; "Paul Mario Milatzo," www.findagrave.com/cgi-bin/fg.cgi?page=gr&GRid=24167158.

19. Kathka, "Italian Experience in Wyoming," 70–71; Peck, *Reinventing Free Labor*, 210.

20. Bolognani, *Courageous People*, 256; Kathka, "Italian Experience in Wyoming," 70–73; Garceau, *Important Things of Life*, 31.

21. Garceau, *Important Things of Life*, 29.

22. Gay Houchen Racina, "Hanna Cemetery," www.interment.net/data/us/wy/carbon/hanna/hanna.htm; C. R. Delamater, "Report: No. 1 Hanna Mine," https://usminedisasters.miningquiz.com/saxsewell/hanna_report_1908.pdf; Leathers, "List of Miners Killed in the March 28, 1908, Explosions of the Union Pacific Coal Company's No. 1 Mine in Hanna, Wyoming," www.hannabasinmuseum.com/list-of-miners-killed-in-the-march-28-1908-explosions.html; Stu Beitler, "Hanna, WY, Terrible Mine Explosion," www.gendisasters.com/wyoming/5568/hanna-wy-terrible-mine-explosion-june-1903; Leathers, "List of Miners Killed"; Racina, "Hanna Cemetery."

23. "Mining Disasters, Accidents, Cave Ins and Explosions," www.gendisasters.com/mainlist/mines/Wyoming.

24. Garceau, *Important Things of Life*, 31; Kathka, "Italian Experience in Wyoming," 79; "John Fred Dapra," www.findagrave.com/memorial/24501519/john-fred-dapra.

25. Garceau, *Important Things of Life*, 89–111.

26. Garceau, *Important Things of Life*, 45; Mangione and Morreale, *La Storia*, 335.

27. *Fourteenth Census*, "Wyoming, Introduction," 329; Garceau, *Important Things of Life*, 30; "Map of the Value of Farmland"; Garceau, *Important Things of Life*, 31; *Agricultural Statistics*, 36.

28. Garceau, *Important Things of Life*, 138; Kathka, "Italian Experience in Wyoming," 77; Bolognani, *Courageous People*, 260; Garceau, *Important Things of Life*, 26; Kathka, "Italian Experience in Wyoming," 76–77; Prevedel, *Tyroleans*, 34; Bolognani, *Courageous People*, 260; Kathka, "Italian Experience in Wyoming," 77.

29. *Italian-American Who's Who*, 44; Kathka, "Italian Experience in Wyoming," 75–77.

30. Prevedel, *Tyroleans*, 33–35; Garceau, *Important Things of Life*, 39, 74–114; La Sorte, *La Merica*, 121.

31. Mellinger, "Early Hartville and Sunrise," 76–77, 155, 173; Kathka, "Italian Experience in Wyoming," 73–75.

32. Kathka, "Italian Experience in Wyoming," 77–78; "Boschetto's European Market," homestead.com/Photo-Gallery.htm.

33. Propst, "Rock Springs, Wyoming."

34. Mellinger, "Early Hartville and Sunrise," 156–65.

35. Russell, *Renegade History*, 106–7.

36. Prevedel, *Tyroleans*, 61; Kathka, "Italian Experience in Wyoming," 78; Mellinger, "Early Hartville and Sunrise," 160; Kathka, "Italian Experience in Wyoming," 78; Okrent, *Last Call*, 197; Charles Walgreen, "Charles Walgreen," www.britannica.com/biography/Charles-R-Walgreen.

37. Prevedel, *Tyroleans*, 61.

38. Prevedel, *Tyroleans*, 64.

39. Mellinger, "Early Hartville and Sunrise," 156; Prevedel, *Tyroleans*, 61, 62.

40. Prevedel, *Tyroleans*, 61; Gordon, *Second Coming of the* KKK, 28–29.

41. Prevedel, *Tyroleans*, 64; Okrent, *Last Call*, 373.

42. Kathka, "Italian Experience in Wyoming," 75, 78; "Paul Mario Milatzo."

43. "DeBernardi, George Sr., Obituary," http://wygenweb.com/sweetwater/vitals/Obits1965.txt; Kathka, "Italian Experience in Wyoming," 78; Kathka, "Italian Experience in Wyoming," 78–79.

44. Bolognani, *Courageous People*, 257; Kathka, "Italian Experience in Wyoming," 78–79; Kim Ibach and William Howard Moore, "The Emerging Civil Rights Movement: The 1957 Wyoming Public Accommodations Statute as a Case Study."

45. Ibach and Moore, "Emerging Civil Rights Movement."

46. Kathka, "Italian Experience in Wyoming," 80; *Italian-American Who's Who*, 112.

47. Lawrence Kestenbaum, "The Political Graveyard: Politicians in Wyoming," politicalgraveyard.com/geo/WY/catholic.html; Prevedel, *Tyroleans*, 32–33; *Italian-American Who's Who*, 158, 225, 324; Kathka, "Italian Experience in Wyoming," 77.

48. Pasquale Verdicchio, *Bound by Distance: Rethinking Nationalism through the Italian Diaspora*, 90–135; Kathka, "Italian Experience in Wyoming," 84; Mellinger, "Early Hartville and Sunrise," 67; Kathka, "Italian Experience in Wyoming," 82, 84, 88.

49. Kathka, "Italian Experience in Wyoming," 82–84.

50. Kathka, "Italian Experience in Wyoming," 88–89.

51. Bolognani, *Courageous People*, 261; Racina, "Hanna Cemetery"; Order 11, Order Sons of Italy; *Historical Data Section: The Italian Hall Historic Structure Report;* "Wyoming: Cities with the Highest Percentages of Italians," zipatlas.com/us/wy/city-comparison/percentage-italian-population.htm; Gans, "End of Late-Generation European Ethnicity?"

Chapter 7. Idaho

1. Gordon, *Second Coming of the KKK*, 139; Laurie Mercier, "Confronting Race and Creating Community: Idaho's Ethnic History," 167; Boise County History, "Visit Boise County," www.boisecounty.us/visit_boise_county.aspx; Jacqueline Harvey et al., eds., "Immigration and Emigration," http://imnh.isu.edu/digitalatlas/geog/imem/imemfr.htm.

2. Richard Dean Scheuerman, "Multicultural Experiences in the Palouse Country: A Historical Narrative Investigating Ethnicity and Regional Immigration Patterns, 1860–1920," 68–69; Rolle, *Immigrant Upraised*, 196; Rodney Frey and Robert McCarl, "The Confluence of the Rivers: The Indigenous Tribes of Idaho," 13–18.

3. Rolle, *Immigrant Upraised*, 186; Frey, "Confluence of the Rivers," 32.

4. Leonard Arrington, *History of Idaho*, 1:159, 267; Frey, "Confluence of the Rivers," 27, 31.

5. Qin, "Century-Old 'Puzzle,'" 225, 228; Peck, *Reinventing Free Labor*, 51–56; Boise County History, "Visit Boise County"; Harvey, "Immigration and Emigration"; Mercier, "Confronting Race," 169, 171, 178–79; Scheuerman, "Multicultural Experiences," 77.

6. Harvey, "Immigration and Emigration"; Mercier, "Confronting Race," 186.

7. Mercier, "Confronting Race," 185–88; Arrington, *History of Idaho*, 2:270; Harvey, "Immigration and Emigration"; Barkan, *From All Points*, 464; *Thirteenth Census*, "Statistics of Population," 588, 590; Mercier, "Confronting Race," 171–74, 186; Arrington, *History of Idaho*, 2:266–67; *Fourteenth Census*, "Statistics of Population," 30, 240; Harvey, "Immigration and Emigration."

8. Mercier, "Confronting Race," 185–87; Gus Voltilini, interview by Russell Magnaghi, September 13, 1985, Washington State University Libraries, Digital Collections, wsu.edu/cdm/ref/collection/imis_3/id/1484.

9. Voltilini, interview by Magnaghi.

10. *Fourteenth Census*, "Number and Distribution," 11, Statistics of Population, 240; Arrington, *History of Idaho*, 2:276; Harvey, "Immigration and Emigration"; Mercier, "Confronting Race," 185–87.

11. Arrington, *History of Idaho*, 1:391, 2:5; Arthur Hart, "Prohibition Kept Boise Law Enforcement Officers Busy," *Idaho Statesman* (Boise), June 24, 2017.

12. Russell, *Renegade History*, 189.

13. Voltilini, interview by Magnaghi; Anthony Colaianni and John Colaianni, interview by unknown interviewer, August 22, 1985, Idaho State Historical Society, Pocatello, https://content.libraries.wsu.edu/digital/collection/imls_3/id/1487/rec/1; Mary Colaianni Lacy, interview by Russell Magnaghi, August 22, 1985, Idaho State Historical Society, Pocatello, https://content.libraries.wsu.edu/digital/collection/imls_3/id/1489/rec/1.

14. Mercier, "Confronting Race," 187.

15. Mercier, "Confronting Race," 187; A. Colaianni and J. Colaianni, interview; M. Colaianni Lacy, interview.

16. Rose Lamanna Naccarato, interview by Russell Magnaghi, September 14, 1985, Idaho State Historical Society, Pocatello, https://content.libraries.wsu.edu/digital/collection/imls_3/id/1491/rec/1; Charli Mills, "Ethnic Diversity of Idaho's Past: Italians of Elmira," January 22, 2016, https://goidaho.com/ethnic-diversity-of-idahos-past/;

Voltilini, interview by Magnaghi; Naccarato, interview; Mercier, "Confronting Race," 186.

17. Mercier, "Confronting Race," 186–87; *Fourteenth Census*, "Statistics of Population," 240; Scheuerman, "Multicultural Experiences," 79–82.

18. *Agricultural Statistics*, 21.

19. Potlatch Lumber Company Records, 1890–1949, University of Idaho Special Collections, Records, 1901–79, www.lib.uidaho.edu/special-collections/Manuscripts/mg193.htm; Scheuerman, "Multicultural Experiences," 78; Petersen, *Company Town*, 118–19; Scheuerman, "Multicultural Experiences," 78.

20. Potlatch Lumber Company Records, 1890–1949; Scheuerman, "Multicultural Experiences," 78; Petersen, *Company Town*, 118–19; *Fourteenth Census*, "Statistics of Population," 16.

21. Petersen, *Company Town*, 118–19.

22. Petersen, *Company Town*, 120–21, 143–44; Higham, *Strangers in the Land*, 234–63.

23. Petersen, *Company Town*, 119; Scheuerman, "Multicultural Experiences," 78–79, 82.

24. Cathedral of St. John the Evangelist, "St. John's Cathedral St. Alphonsus Hospital and St. Teresa's Academy: Monuments to Devotion and Zeal of Catholics of Idaho," *Idaho Statesman* (Boise), May 29, 1921; *Diffusione del cognome—Mappa dei Cognomi*, www.mappadeicognomi.it; *Fourteenth Census*, "Statistics of Population," 12, 13, 240; *Thirteenth Census*, "Statistics of Population," 592.

25. Barkan, *From All Points*, 464; Mercier, "Confronting Race," 188; Teri Ann Bengiveno et al., "Con le nostre mani: Italian Americans at Work in the East Bay," 1–9.

26. Scheuerman, "Multicultural Experiences," 82; *Fourteenth Census*, "Statistics of Population," 240; *Fifteenth Census*, "Statistics of Population," 428.

27. Order 13, Order Sons of Italy; "Idaho: Cities with the Highest Percentage of Italians in Idaho," http://zipatlas.com/us/id/city-comparison/percentage-italian-population.htm.

28. Grand Lodge, "Order Sons of Italy in America," www.glnw.org/; *Fourteenth Census*, "Statistics of Population," 16; "Idaho: Cities with the Highest Percentage of Italians in Idaho"; Ruberto and Sciorra, *New Italian Migrations*, 1:15–18.

Chapter 8. Montana

1. Rolle, "The Italian Moves Westward," 17; Rolle, *Immigrant Upraised*, 159, 185–86, 196–97.

2. Rolle, *Immigrant Upraised*, 185, 191–92, 186; Rolle, "The Italian Moves Westward," 18; Rolle, *Immigrant Upraised*, 195; Anthony Morvillo, *A Dictionary of the Numípu or the Nez Perce Language.*

3. Father Philip Rappagliosi, *Letters from the Rocky Mountain Indian Missions: Father Philip Rappagliosi;* Rev. Lawrence B. Palladino, SJ, *Indian and White in the Northwest: A History of Catholicity in Montana, 1831–1891*; Rolle, *Immigrant Upraised*, 190–91, 197; Lopreato, *Italian Americans*, 46–47.

4. Mary Murphy, *Mining Culture: Men, Women, and Leisure in Butte, 1914–41*, 10; Laurie Mercier, "Mexican Americans of the Yellowstone Valley," 222–24; Rolle, "The Italian Moves Westward," 21; *Fourteenth Census*, "Statistics of Population," 586.

5. Murphy, *Mining Culture*, 10; George Everett, "When Toil Meant Trouble: Butte's Labor Heritage," www.butteamerica.com/labor.htm; *Fourteenth Census*, "Statistics of Population," 586; Peck, *Reinventing Free Labor*, 54; Everett, "When Toil Meant Trouble"; Kara Rota, "Butte: Montana's Irish Mining Town," irishamerica .com/2010/08/montanas-mining-town; Facts and Figures: Income and Prices, 1900–1999," https://usa.usembassy.de/etexts/his/e_prices1.htm.

6. Murphy, *Mining Culture*, 9–10; Michael P. Malone et al., eds., *Montana: A History of Two Centuries*, 202; *Twelfth Census*, "Statistics of Population," 798; *Fourteenth Census*, "Statistics of Population," 586; Malone, *Montana*, 337–38; *Fourteenth Census*, "Statistics of Population," 585–86, 698; Barkan, *From All Points*, 462–65.

7. Everett, "When Toil Meant Trouble."

8. Malone, *Montana*, 209–11; Rota, "Butte"; Everett, "When Toil Meant Trouble."

9. Malone, *Montana*, 209–11; Rota, "Butte"; Everett, "When Toil Meant Trouble."

10. Everett, "When Toil Meant Trouble"; Rota, "Butte"; Everett, "When Toil Meant Trouble"; Murphy, *Mining Culture*, 18.

11. Murphy, *Mining Culture*, 16–17.

12. Everett, "When Toil Meant Trouble"; Murphy, *Mining Culture*, 18.

13. Everett, "When Toil Meant Trouble"; Murphy, *Mining Culture*, 16; Malone, *Montana*, 274; Stu Beitler, "Butte, MT, Speculator Mine Explosion, June 1917," https://gendisasters.com/montana/4352/butte.-mt-speculator-mine; James D. Harrington, "A Reexamination of the Granite Mountain–Speculator Fire," https://mhs.mt.gov/Portals/11/education/docs/CirGuides/Harrington%20Butte%201998.pdf; *Diffusione del cognome—Mappa dei Cognomi*, www.mappadeicognomi.it.

14. Everett, "When Toil Meant Trouble"; "Mining Disasters, Accidents, Cave Ins and Explosions," www.gendisasters.com/mainlist/mines/montana.

15. Richard Gibson, *Lost Butte, Montana*, 47–53; Richard Gibson, "Was Butte's Population Really 100,000 during Its Heyday?," *Montana Standard*, January 24, 2016.

16. Murphy, *Mining Culture*, 10, 106; Gibson, *Lost Butte, Montana*, 47–63; Tracy Thornton, "Little Italy," *Mountain Standard*, September 2, 2006.

17. Murphy, *Mining Culture*, 9–10; *Fourteenth Census*, "Statistics of Population," 586.

18. Patrick Sullivan, "Map of Butte," https://mhs.mt.gov/Portals/11/education/Mining%20Childhood/Patrick%20Sullivans%20ButteMap7%20(2).pdf; Thornton, "Little Italy"; Rota, "Butte"; Gibson, *Lost Butte, Montana*, 62–63.

19. Rolle, "The Italian Moves Westward," 21–22; Rolle, *Immigrant Upraised*, 199; Brian James Leech, *The City That Ate Itself: Butte, Montana and Its Expanding Berkeley Pit*, 69–70, 74, 81; Murphy, *Mining Culture*, 49–50; Thornton, "Little Italy"; Rolle, "The Italian Moves Westward," 21–22.

20. Rolle, "The Italian Moves Westward," 22–23; Rolle, *Immigrant Upraised*, 199; *Italian-American Who's Who*, 44.

21. "Sandstone Masonry and Historic Landmarks in Columbus, Montana," https://montanahistoriclandscape.com/2015/09/15/sandstone-masonry-and-historic-landmarks-in-columbus-montana/.

22. Ellen Baumler, "Butte's Red Light District: A Walking Tour," http://montanawomenshistory.org/wp-content/uploads/2013/06/ButteWalkingTour12_2013_Rev.pdf.

23. Baumler, "Butte's Red Light District"; Russell, *Renegade History*, 106–7.

24. Cannato, *American Passage*, 277–84.

25. Russell, *Renegade History*, 106; Peck, *Reinventing Free Labor*, 151; Baumler, "Butte's Red Light District."

26. Murphy, *Mining Culture*, 10, 74, 107, 150–62.

27. Rolle, *Immigrant Upraised*, 200; Rolle, "The Italian Moves Westward," 23; *Agricultural Statistics*, 27.

28. St. John's Catholic Church, Butte, secretary of the parish, interview with the author, August 14, 2019; Leech, *City That Ate Itself*, 4–7; Thornton, "Little Italy."

29. Thornton, "Little Italy."

30. National Italian American Foundation, *Italian Americans in the U.S.*, 4; Order 11, Order Sons of Italy.

Chapter 9. Alaska

1. Russell Magnaghi, "Italian Contribution to the Development of Alaska," 167–68; Rolle, *Immigrant Upraised*, 345–47.

2. Magnaghi, "Italian Contribution," 167–68; Rolle, *Immigrant Upraised*, 345–47.

3. Magnaghi, "Italian Contribution," 168–69; Joan M. Antonson and William S. Hanable, *Alaska's Heritage: Alaska's History and Cultural Studies*, chaps. 4–11.

4. Magnaghi, "Italian Contribution," 167–70.

5. Magnaghi, "Italian Contribution," 167–70.

6. Claus M. Naske and Herman Slotnick, *A History of the 49th State*, 187–88; Barkan, *From All Points*, 464, 466, 468; Magnaghi, "Italian Contribution," 170.

7. Chris Friday, *Organizing Asian-American Labor: The Pacific Coast Canned-Salmon Industry, 1870–1942*, 1–4; Shelley Sang-Hee Lee, *A New History of Asian America*, 71; Magnaghi, "Italian Contribution," 170–71, 177.

8. Magnaghi, "Italian Contribution," 170–71.

9. Antonson, *Alaska's Heritage*, chaps. 4–11; Naske, *History of the 49th State*, 90; Magnaghi, "Italian Contribution," 174–76.

10. Magnaghi, "Italian Contribution," 174–76.

11. Stanley Lebergott, "Wages and Working Conditions," www.econlib.org.library.Enc1; Magnaghi, "Italian Contribution," 175; Mangano, *Sons of Italy*, 11–14.

12. Magnaghi, "Italian Contribution," 171–72, 174; "Beatson Mine," https://dec.alaska.gov/spar/csp/sites/beatson-mine/; Gary Gillette, "Historic Structures Report: Jualpa Mine Camp of the Alaska Juneau Gold Mining Company," www.juenau.lib.ak.us/history/Jualpa_Mine/struct.pdf; "Images of Timber Mills, Alaska, 1910 Photographs," bing.com/images.

13. Foerster, *Italian Emigration*, 341; Magnaghi, "Italian Contribution," 172–74.

14. Foerster, *Italian Emigration*, 341; Magnaghi, "Italian Contribution," 172–74.

15. Magnaghi, "Italian Contribution," 173–74.

16. Gloria Ricci Lothrop, "California's Italians: A Promise Fulfilled," 236; William C. Richardson, "Fishermen of San Diego: The Italians," 84; Foerster, *Italian Emigration*, 341; Richardson, "Fishermen of San Diego," 84, 86.

17. Magnaghi, "Italian Contribution," 174.

18. Naske, *History of the 49th State*, 187; Antonson and Hanable, *Alaska's Heritage*, chaps. 4–16.

19. Antonson and Hanable, *Alaska's Heritage*, chaps. 4–16; Naske and Slotnick, *History of the 49th State*, 187; Magnaghi, "Italian Contribution," 173–74.

20. Naske and Slotnick, *History of the 49th State*, 187; Antonson and Hanable, *Alaska's Heritage*, chaps. 4–16.

21. Naske and Slotnick, *History of the 49th State*, 187; Antonson and Hanable, *Alaska's Heritage*, chaps. 4–17.

22. Naske and Slotnick, *History of the 49th State*, 88; Antonson and Hanable, *Alaska's Heritage*, chaps. 4–17.

23. Naske and Slotnick, *History of the 49th State*, 88; Antonson and Hanable, *Alaska's Heritage*, chaps. 4–17; Magnaghi, "Italian Contribution," 176; *Agricultural Statistics*, 17; "History of Alaska Homesteading," www.blm.gov/sites/blm.gov/files/documents/files/PublicRoom_Alaska_Homesteading_Brochure_2016.pdf.

24. Murray Lundberg, "The Matanuska Colony: The New Deal in Alaska," http://explorenorth.com/library/yafeatures/bl-matanuska.htm; Magnaghi, "Italian Contribution," 172, 176.

25. E. S. Harrison, *The Alaska Almanac*, 149, 160; Skagway Sleuth, "George Joseph Rapuzzi Jr."; Robert L. S. Spude, "Building the Gateway to the Klondike," www.nps.gov/parkhistory/online books/klgo/npd1/app1.htm; Magnaghi, "Italian Contribution," 176.

26. Cathedral of the Nativity of the Blessed Virgin Mary, juneaucathedral.org.

27. Magnaghi, "Italian Contribution," 170–71, 177–78.

28. Order 10, Order Sons of Italy.

Chapter 10. Washington

1. David L. Nicandri, *Italians in Washington State: Emigration, 1853–1924;* Barkan, *From All Points*, 473; *Thirteenth Census*, "Statistics of the Population," 594; *Fourteenth Census*, "Statistics of the Population," 1085–93; Barkan, *From All Points*, 466, 468; Nicandri, *Italians in Washington State*, 27–28.

2. Nicandri, *Italians in Washington State*, 8–10.

3. Rita Cipalla, "Father Luigi Rossi: Serving the Early Pioneer Communities in Puget Sound," *L'Italo-Americano*, 32; Nicandri, *Italians in Washington State*, 8–15; Rolle, *Immigrant Upraised*, 195.

4. Nicandri, *Italians in Washington State*, 8.

5. Nicandri, *Italians in Washington State*, 35; Rolle, *Immigrant Upraised*, 151–52; Nicandri, *Italians in Washington State*, 35–36.

6. Jens Lund, "Walla Walla Sweets: Onions and Ethnic Identity in an Italian Community in the Northwest," 113–29; Nicandri, *Italians in Washington State*, 29–31, 47; *Thirteenth Census*, "Statistics of Population," 594, 602; *Fourteenth Census*, "Statistics of Population," 698; Barkan, *From All Points*, 464.

7. Nicandri, *Italians in Washington State*, 25, 26; *Thirteenth Census*, "Statistics of Population," 594–99; *Fourteenth Census*, "Statistics of Population," 1085, 1093, 1098.

8. Nicandri, *Italians in Washington State*, 12, 36; Peck, *Reinventing Free Labor*, 71, 132, 136, 207.

9. Nicandri, *Italians in Washington State*, 64, 36–38.

10. Nicandri, *Italians in Washington State*, 34–35, 64; Weyerhaeuser Company, www.weyerhaeuser.com.

11. Robert Frost, *North of Boston*, 120; Nicandri, *Italians in Washington State*, 36–38, 64.

12. William Whitfield, ed., *History of Snohomish County, Washington*, 625, 670–71; Nicandri, *Italians in Washington State*, 64.

13. Robert Higgs, "Legally Induced Technical Regress in the Washington Salmon Fishery"; Sverre Arestad, "Norwegians in the Pacific Coast Fisheries," www.naha.stolaf.edu/pubs/nas/volume30/vol30_04.htm; Gig Harbor, "Preserving Gig Harbor's History for the Community," www.gigharborhistory.com/vessels.html; Katie Chase, "Skansie Shipbuilding Company," www.gigharborhistory.com/skansieshipbuilding company.html; Nicandri, *Italians in Washington State*, 63; *Report of the United States Commissioner of Fisheries for the Physical Year ended June 30, 1921*, 32–33.

14. Nicandri, *Italians in Washington State*, 34–35, 39; Alan J. Stein, "Black Diamond-Thumbnail History," www.historylink.org/index.cfm?DisplayPage=-output.cfm&file_id=460; Nicandri, *Italians in Washington State*, 27, 39–42; Stein, "Ravensdale Coal Mine Explosion Kills 31 Men on Nov. 16, 1915," www.historylink.org/index.cfm?DisplayPage =output.cfm&file_id=3576; William Kombol, "Coal Mining in an East Pierce County Area Known as Pittsburg (1889–1909), Spiketon (1910–1916), and Finally Morristown (1917–1927)," www.historylink.org/index.cfm?DisplayPage=output.cfm&file_id=8262; William Kombol, "Elk Coal: A Forgotten King County Coal Mining Town," www.historylink.org/index.cfm?Display Page=output.cfm&file_id=9419; Nicandri, *Italians in Washington State*, 27, 39–42; Stein, "Ravensdale Coal Mine Explosion," 2001; "Trappers, Hurriers, and Hewers: Working in a Coal Mine," https://thoroglove.wordpress.com/2015/03/12/trappers-hurriers-and-hewers-working-in-a-coal-mine/#:~:text=Trappers%2C%20Hurriers%2C%20and%20Hewers%3A%20Working%20in%20a%20Coal,to%20provide%20the%20fuel%20for%20the%20factory%20machinery.

15. Nicandri, *Italians in Washington State*, 27, 39–42; Stein, "Ravensdale Coal Mine Explosion"; Stein, "Black Diamond-Thumbnail History."

16. Stein, "Black Diamond-Thumbnail History."

17. David Wilma, "Worst Coal-Mine Disaster in Washington History Kills 45 Miners at Roslyn on May 10, 1892," www.historylink.org.

18. "Lawson Mine Disaster (November 6, 1910): Official Investigative Reports," www.historylink.org/File/9473; Stein, "Ravensdale Coal Mine Explosion."

19. "Mining Disasters, Cave Ins and Explosions," www.gendisasters.com/mainlist/mines/Washington; Kombol, "Coal Mining in an East Pierce County Area"; Frank Hammock with JoAnne Matsumura, "A Coal Miner's Story: Mike Babcanik's Week Trapped Underground (1914)," www.historylink.org/index.cfm?DisplayPage=Output.cfm&file_id=8698; "Franklin Mine Disaster," www.historylink.org/index.cfm?Display Page=Output.cfm&file_id=9165; Kombol, "Elk Coal," 2010.

20. Nicandri, *Italians in Washington State*, 34–35, 47; *Thirteenth Census*, "Statistics of Population," 596, 602; Barkan, *From All Points*, 464.

21. Nicandri, *Italians in Washington State*, 47, 64.

22. Nicandri, *Italians in Washington State*, 29–30, 34–35, 47; *Italian-American Who's Who*, 37, 90, 185.

23. *Italian-American Who's Who*, 203–4, 323.

24. Nicandri, *Italians in Washington State*, 54–55; *Italian-American Who's Who*, 37.

25. *Italian-American Who's Who*, 139; Nicandri, *Italians in Washington State*, 55; *Italian-American Who's Who*, 37; Rolle, *Immigrant Upraised*, 214.

26. Gloria Ricci Lothrop, "Unwelcome in Freedom's Land: The Impact of World War II on Italian Aliens in Southern California," 162–63; Matthew Frye Jacobson, *Special Sorrows: The Diasporic Imagination of Irish, Polish, and Jewish Immigrants in the United States*, 15; Verdicchio, *Bound by Distance*, 41–51.

27. Cipalla, "Father Luigi Rossi," 32; Oberto Sausage Company, "The Pepperoni-Powered American Dream," choosewashingtonstate.com.

28. Angelo Pellegrini, *Americans by Choice*, 95–96.

29. Susan Gilmore, "Marco Magnano Sr.," *Seattle Times*, November 20, 2009.

30. Mike Baker, "FBI Didn't Think Much of Washington's Gov. Rosellini, Files Show," *Seattle Times*, June 14, 2013; Walter Crowley, "Rosellini, Albert Dean: 1910–2011," www.historylink.org/File/5156; Payton Smith, *Rosellini: Immigrant Son and Progressive Governor;* Crowley, "Rosellini, Albert Dean"; Nicandri, *Italians in Washington State*, 62; Michael Ko, "Seattle Restaurant Legend Victor Rosellini Dies at 87," *Seattle Times*, January 11, 2003; Michael Hood, "Rosellini, Victor (1915–2003), Restaurateur and Epicure," https://historylink.org.

31. Blanton Owen, "The Melting Pot Works: Italians in Central Nevada"; Rita Cipalla, "America's First Saint Helps Ease the Way for Seattle's Italian Community"; Owen, "Melting Pot Works."

32. Nicandri, *Italians in Washington State*, 51; Our Lady of Mount Virgin-Seattle—Archdiocese of Seattle, www.seattlearchi-Diocese.org/Directory/ParishDetail.aspx?ID=74; "Blessed Sacrament Church," www.blessed-sacrament.org; Immaculate Conception, www.icseattle.org/; St. James Cathedral, stjames-cathedral.org.

33. "A Red Light History of Seattle," www.seattlemet.com.

34. Angelo Pellegrini, *American Dream: An Immigrant's Quest*; Handlin, *Uprooted*.

35. Nicandri, *Italians in Washington State*, 29–30; Pellegrini, *American Dream*, 7–8; Don Duncan et al., "Angelo Pellegrini Dies—UW Prof, Author, Gourmet," *Seattle Times*, November 3, 1991.

36. Pellegrini, *American Dream*, 17; Angelo Pellegrini, *Immigrant's Return*, 73; Pellegrini, *American Dream*, 17.

37. Nicandri, *Italians in Washington State*, 53–55.

38. Higham, *Strangers in the Land*, 237–38; Constantine M. Panunzio, *Soul of an Immigrant*, xi–xii; Constantine M. Panunzio, "Italian American Sociologist," https://snaccooperative.org/view/36352221.

39. Pellegrini, *Americans by Choice*, 153; Notarianni, "Italianita in Utah," 303–4.

40. Pellegrini, *Americans by Choice*, 77–126.

41. Pellegrini, *American Dream*, 17, 172, 188.

42. Nicandri, *Italians in Washington State*, 34; *Agricultural Statistics*, 35.

43. Caroline Tobin, *North Ranier Valley Historic Context Statement: City of Seattle Department of Neighborhoods*, 25; Nicandri, *Italians in Washington State*, 56–59.

44. Tobin, *North Ranier Valley*, 25; Nicandri, *Italians in Washington State*, 56–59.

45. Nicandri, *Italians in Washington State*, 57.

46. Rita Cipalla, "Joe Desimone: From Produce Farmer to Owner of Seattle's Pike Place Market."

47. Cipalla, "Joe Desimone," 8; Nicandri, *Italians in Washington State*, 57.

48. Cipalla, "Joe Desimone," 8.

49. Cipalla, "Joe Desimone," 8.

50. Tobin, *North Ranier Valley*, 7, 13–14, 24.

51. Tobin, *North Ranier Valley*, 7, 17, 22, 24, 29–30; Rita Cipalla, "Merlino Foods: Delivering Italian Products in Seattle for 120 Years," 28; Rita Cipalla, "Gai's Northwest Bakeries: A Seattle Institution and Baking Powerhouse for More than Fifty Years," 32; "Borracchini's Bakery: A Historic Seattle Bakery," www.nowcake.com/.

52. Nicandri, *Italians in Washington State*, 48–49, 53–55, 62; Tobin, *North Ranier Valley*, 17, 20–25.

53. Tobin, *North Ranier Valley*, 24–25; Nicandri, *Italians in Washington State*, 56–57, 61–62; *Italian-American Who's Who*, 61, 178; *Fourteenth Census*, "Statistics of Population," 1098.

54. Pellegrini, *American Dream*, 189–91; Angelo Pellegrini, *The Unprejudiced Palate*.

55. Luigi Ballerini, introduction to *Science in the Kitchen and the Art of Eating Well*, by Pellegrino Artusi, lviii; Leech, *City That Ate Itself*, 71; Donna Gabaccia, *We Are What We Eat: Ethnic Food and the Making of Americans*, 181–82; Malpezzi and Clements, *Italian American Folklore*, 229, 237–45; Hans Christian Palmer, "Italian Immigration," 220–22.

56. Malpezzi and Clements, *Italian American Folklore*, 222.

57. Michele Scicolone, foreword to *Science in the Kitchen*, by Artusi, xiii; Samuel Sharp, *Letters from Italy: Describing the Customs and Manners of That Country, in the Years 1765, and 1766*, 99–103; Gabaccia, *We Are What We Eat*, 150–51; Nicandri, *Italians in Washington State*, 62.

58. John Caldbick, "Census," www.historylink.org/File/9444; *Thirteenth Census*, "Statistics of Population," 600.

59. Nicandri, *Italians in Washington State*, 37; Nelson Wayne Durham, *History of the City of Spokane and Spokane County, Washington*, 686–87; Julie Sullivan, "Albi Would Love Fanning Statue Debate," *Spokesman-Review*, May 1, 1997.

60. Nicandri, *Italians in Washington State*, 37.

61. Aaron Goings, "Johnson, Albert (1869–1957)," September 3, 2008, historylink.org/File/8721; Okrent, *Guarded Gate*, 97–101; Hanson, *Americanism versus Bolshevism*, 18–113; Browning, "Fake Threat of Jewish Communism"; Shankar, "'Cosmopolitan' Is a Dog Whistle Word."

62. Nicandri, *Italians in Washington State*, 37.

63. Okrent, *Guarded Gate*, 72.

64. Catie M. Walker, *Wines of Walla Walla Valley: A Deep-Rooted History;* Schiavo, *Four Centuries*, 423–24.

65. C. Walker, *Wines of Walla Walla Valley;* Nicandri, *Italians in Washington State*, 59.

66. Lund, "Walla Walla Sweets," 114; Nicandri, *Italians in Washington State*, 59; Lund, "Walla Walla Sweets," 116, 119–21; *Thirteenth Census*, "Statistics of Population," 600; *Fourteenth Census*, "Statistics of the Population," 1098.

67. Nicandri, *Italians in Washington State*, 60; Lund, "Walla Walla Sweets," 119–21.

68. Lund, "Walla Walla Sweets," 119–21, 118.

69. Lund, "Walla Walla Sweets," 118–21, 125–29.

70. Lund, "Walla Walla Sweets," 116; Washington State, "State Facts—Washington State Wines," www.washingtonwine.org/wine/facts-and-stats/state-facts; *Agricultural*

Statistics, 18, 35; Washington State, "State Facts"; Walla Walla, "Best Walla Walla Wineries," www.winecountry.com/blog/best-walla-walla-wineries/.

71. COM.IT.ES., "San Francisco," http://comites-sf.org/associazioni.index.htm.

72. Rita Cipalla, "A Love of Onions Brings Two Cities Together," *L'Italo-Americano*, 13; Bolognani, *Courageous People*, 267; Seattle, "Local Italian Organizations—Festa Italiana Seattle!," www.festaseattle.com/localorgs.htm; Rita Cipalla, "Staying Connected in Times of Crisis—the Italian Way," 26.

73. Lund, "Walla Walla Sweets," 118; Cipalla, "Italian Immigrants: How they Helped Define the Wine Industry of Walla Walla," https://history.org/File/20607; Lund, "Walla Walla Sweets," 125–27.

Chapter 11. Oregon

1. Gordon, *Second Coming of the KKK*, 139–61, 170; David G. Savage, "State Jury Verdicts Must Be Unanimous," *Los Angeles Times*, April 21, 2020.

2. Rolle, *Immigrant Upraised*, 216–18.

3. Rolle, *Immigrant Upraised*, 216.

4. C. Gould, "Portland Italians, 1880–1920," 243.

5. *Eleventh Census of the U.S.*, "Foreign Born," 6; Gould, "Portland Italians, 1880–1920," 244, 246; Barkan, *From All Points*, 468, 473; *Thirteenth Census*, "Statistics of Population," 594; *Fourteenth Census*, "Number and Distribution," 7; *Fourteenth Census*, "Composition and Characteristics," 25; William Toll, "Ethnicity and Stability: The Italians and Jews of South Portland, 1900–1940," 165; Michelle Del Conte, "Italian Immigration to Portland, Oregon, 1900–1930," 79.

6. H.D. Scudder and E.B. Hurd, *Graphic Summary of Agricultural and Land Use in Oregon*, 13; Gould, "Portland Italians, 1880–1920," 247; Barkan, *From All Points*, 480; Del Conte, "Italian Immigration to Portland," 79; "Oregon History: Statehood," https://sos.oregon.gov/blue-book/Pages/facts/history/state-statehood.aspx; *Thirteenth Census*, "Statistics of Population," 602; *Fourteenth Census*, "Statistics of Population," 25, 33, 834.

7. Del Conte, "Italian Immigration to Portland," 60; Howard Zinn, *A People's History of the United States*, 349; Del Conte, "Italian Immigration to Portland," 121–25; Lopreato, *Italian Americans*, 15; Kenneth Scambray, *The North American Italian Renaissance: Italian Writing in America and Canada*, 81–84.

8. Reeder, *Widows in White*, 4, 55–102; Riccio, *Farms, Factories, and Family*, 33; Del Conte, "Italian Immigration to Portland," 121–22; Mangione and Morreale, *La Storia*, 92–93.

9. Toll, "Ethnicity and Stability," 167; Del Conte, "Italian Immigration to Portland," 73; Peck, *Reinventing Free Labor*, 51–53, 55–56; Toll, "Ethnicity and Stability," 167.

10. Gould, "Portland Italians, 1880–1920," 249; Del Conte, "Italian Immigration to Portland," 69; Toll, "Ethnicity and Stability," 169; Gould, "Portland Italians, 1880–1920," 250–53.

11. Del Conte, "Italian Immigration to Portland," 70; Gould, "Portland Italians, 1880–1920," 253; Bolognani, *Courageous People*, 302.

12. Linda Pacini Pitelka, "Indians and Italians: The Boundaries of Race and Ethnicity in Rural Northern California, 1890–1920," 68–69; Nicandri, *Italians in Washington*, 27, 64, 36–42.

13. Leonida Répaci, *Il Sud su un binario morto: A cura di Giuseppe Caridi*, 22; Del Conte, "Italian Immigration to Portland," 80, 87, 94.

14. Gould, "Portland Italians, 1880–1920," 249–50; Del Conte, "Italian Immigration to Portland," 69; Toll, "Ethnicity and Stability," 167; Del Conte, "Italian Immigration to Portland," 81; Toll, "Ethnicity and Stability," 166.

15. Gould, "Portland Italians, 1880–1920," 247–49.

16. Gould, "Portland Italians, 1880–1920," 247.

17. Gould, "Portland Italians, 1880–1920," 249; Del Conte, "Italian Immigration to Portland," 74; Gould, "Portland Italians, 1880–1920," 249; Del Conte, "Italian Immigration to Portland," 82, 108.

18. Kerry-Lynne Demarinis Brown, "St. Michael the Archangel," 11; Gould, "Portland Italians, 1880–1920," 255; Brown, "St. Michael the Archangel," 11; "St. Philip Neri Catholic Church," www.stphilipneripdx.org.

19. Del Conte, "Italian Immigration to Portland," 81–82; Toll, "Ethnicity and Stability," 166–67.

20. Del Conte, "Italian Immigration to Portland," 144–46; Mangione and Morreale, *La Storia*, 335–36; Del Conte, "Italian Immigration to Portland," 144–46, 153–55.

21. Mangano, *Sons of Italy*, 50, 71, 144–47, 168–69; Lord, Eliot, and Trenor, *The Italian in America*, 77; Gambino, *Blood of My Blood*, 14.

22. Gambino, *Blood of My Blood*, 14; Del Conte, "Italian Immigration to Portland," 128–33; Elizabeth Giovanna Messina, ed., introduction to *In Our Own Voices: Multidisciplinary Perspectives on Italian and Italian American Women*, xiii.

23. Gould, "Portland Italians, 1880–1920," 253–54.

24. *Thirteenth Census*, "Statistics of Population," 592; Toll, "Ethnicity and Stability," 166–67, 175; Higham, *Strangers in the Land*, 237–38.

25. Toll, "Ethnicity and Stability," 168–75, 186.

26. Toll, "Ethnicity and Stability," table 2, 174; Pino Aprile, *Terroni*, 244–77; Foerster, *Italian Emigration*, 458; Répaci, *Il Sud su un binario morto*, 71–72; Mangione and Morreale, *La Storia*, 99–101; Foerster, *Italian Emigration*, 515n1; Del Conte, "Italian Immigration to Portland," 83–85.

27. *Italian-American Who's Who*, 213, 139, 141, 101–2; Del Conte, "Italian Immigration to Portland," 86; Gould, "Portland Italians, 1880–1920," 254; *Diffusione del cognome—Mappa dei Cognomi*, www.mappadeicognomi.it; "Roberto Signer Corruccini," www.findagrave.com/memorial/144342070/roberto-signer-corruccini; Del Conte, "Italian Immigration to Portland," 94.

28. Scudder and Hurd, *Graphic Summary*, 8–9, 11–12.

29. Del Conte, "Italian Immigration to Portland," 69–70, 81; Gould, "Portland Italians, 1880–1920," 250–53.

30. *Agricultural Statistics*, 31; Del Conte, "Italian Immigration to Portland," 69, 94, 98.

31. Del Conte, "Italian Immigration to Portland," 96–101, 147–48; Gould, "Portland Italians, 1880–1920," 257.

32. Gould, "Portland Italians, 1880–1920," 259.

33. Gould, "Portland Italians, 1880–1920," 260; *Italian-American Who's Who*, 139.

34. *Italian-American Who's Who*, 140.

35. Lawrence DiStasi, "How World War II Iced Italian American Culture," 303–12; Lawrence DiStasi, *Branded: How Italian Immigrants Became "Enemies" during World*

War II, 275–90; Lawrence DiStasi, *"Una storia segreta": When Italians Were "Enemy Aliens"*; Fox, *Unknown Internment*, 100–124; Brown, "St. Michael the Archangel," 11.

36. "Festa Italiana Portland," http://festaitalianaportland.shutterfly.com/aboutus; Domenico Tupone, "Luca Vullo Presents *La voce del corpo* at the Italian Film Festival in Portland," 9; Ken Kane, "The Oregon Tuscans Turn 20," 9.

37. Order 14; "Portland Italians, 1880–1920," 260; Gans, *End of Late-Generation European Ethnicity*, 418–29.

Chapter 12. Nevada

1. Brian Frehner, "Ethnicity and Class: The Italian Charcoal Burners' War, 1875–1885," 46–47; *Fourteenth Census*, "Statistics of Population," 612; Barkan, *From All Points*, 466; *Fourteenth Census*, "Statistics of Population," 698; Barkan, *From All Points*, 473; Albin J. Cofone, "Themes in the Italian Settlement of Nevada," 120–22.

2. *Nevada Encyclopedia*, s.v. "Chinese Mining," www.onlinenevada.org/articles /chinese-and-mining; "Legends and Lore of Dayton's History," www.daytonnvhistory .org/history.htm; Andrew Gerthoffer, "Reno's Italian Americans," www.onlinenevada .Org/articles/renos-italian-americans; Albin J. Cofone, "Reno's Little Italy: Italian Entrepreneurship and Culture in Northern Nevada," 98; and Cofone, "Themes in the Italian Settlement," 118–22; *Thirteenth Census*, "Statistics of Population," 584; Rolle, *Immigrant Upraised*, 246–47.

3. Gerthoffer, "Reno's Italian Americans"; Cofone, "Reno's Little Italy," 98; Cofone, "Themes in the Italian Settlement," 118; *Thirteenth Census*, "Statistics of Population," 584.

4. Rolle, *Immigrant Upraised*, 146, 245–46; *Thirteenth Census*, "Statistics of Population," 584.

5. Rolle, *Immigrant Upraised*, 245–46: Peck, *Reinventing Free Labor*, 36, 215–17.

6. Cofone, "Themes in the Italian Settlement," 116–20; Bolognani, *Courageous People*, 302; Rolle, *Immigrant Upraised*, 244; Dennis Mack Smith, *Italy: A Modern History*, 69–71.

7. Cofone, "Reno's Little Italy," 98–99; *Reports of Cases Determined by the Supreme Court of the State of Nevada*, http://books.google.com/books?id=BNSOAQAAMAAJ, 142–47.

8. Frehner, "Ethnicity and Class," 48; *Diffusione del cognome Mappa dei Cognomi*, www.mappadeicognomi.it.

9. Cofone, "Themes in the Italian Settlement," 127.

10. Cofone, "Themes in the Italian Settlement," 117; Cofone, "Reno's Little Italy," 107; *Fourteenth Census*, "Statistics of Population," 615.

11. Samuel Crescenzo, obituary, *Reno Evening Gazette*, July 1, 1913; Cofone, "Reno's Little Italy," 99.

12. Cofone, "Reno's Little Italy," 99.

13. Cofone, "Reno's Little Italy," 99.

14. Cofone, "Reno's Little Italy," 100–101; LaGumina, *WOP*, 113–80.

15. Richard E. Lingenfelter and Karen Rix Gash, *The Newspapers of Nevada: A History and Bibliography, 1854–1979*, 195; Jerre Mangione, *Mount Allegro: A Memoir of Italian American Life*, 17–20; Cofone, "Reno's Little Italy," 107–8; Rolle, *Immigrant Upraised*, 246–47.

16. LaGumina, *WOP*, 163–80; Higham, *Strangers in the Land*, 178–82; Gordon, *Second Coming of the KKK*, 1–23; LaGumina, *WOP*, 217–26; Higham, *Strangers in the Land*, 180; Cofone, "Reno's Little Italy," 102, 107; Joseph Giovinco, "Democracy in Banking: The Bank of Italy and California's Italians."

17. La Sorte, *La Merica*, 158, 178; Cofone, "Reno's Little Italy," 103, 106.

18. Cofone, "Reno's Little Italy," 105–6, 110.

19. Manno, *Charcoal and Blood*, 23; Owen, "Melting Pot Works," 51; Phillip I. Earl, "Nevada's Italian War," 53; *Tenth Census*, "Statistics of Population," 401; Frehner, "Ethnicity and Class," 47–48; *Thirteenth Census*, "Statistics of Population," 582n1.

20. Manno, *Charcoal and Blood*, 18–19, 241.

21. Hansen, *Immigrant in American History*, 176, 184–86; Peck, *Reinventing Free Labor*, 94–96; LaGumina, *WOP*, 111–12.

22. Frehner, "Ethnicity and Class," 44, 47, 50, 58–59; Manno, *Charcoal and Blood*, 229.

23. *Diffusione del cognome;* Frehner, "Ethnicity and Class," 58; Manno, *Charcoal and Blood*, 34, 56, 122.

24. Saverio Strati, *Empty Hands*, 142–43; Owen, "Melting Pot Works," 49–50.

25. Frehner, "Ethnicity and Class," 43, 60; Manno, *Charcoal and Blood*, 23, 83; Earl, "Nevada's Italian War," 55–56; Peck, *Reinventing Free Labor*, 70.

26. Manno, *Charcoal and Blood*, 39, 73–74; Earl, "Nevada's Italian War," 54–55, 59; Manno, *Charcoal and Blood*, 98–99.

27. Earl, "Nevada's Italian War," 64–70; Manno, *Charcoal and Blood*, 106, 185–86.

28. Earl, "Nevada's Italian War," 68–83; Manno, *Charcoal and Blood*, 138–53, 164, 185–86.

29. Manno, *Charcoal and Blood*, 240–45.

30. Cofone, "Themes in the Italian Settlement," 123–24.

31. Cofone, "Themes in the Italian Settlement," 124–25; Gerthoffer, "Reno's Italian Americans"; Kathleen Coles et al., interview of Robert Capurro; Gerthoffer, "Reno's Italian Americans"; Cofone, "Themes in the Italian Settlement," 124–25.

32. Cofone, "Themes in the Italian Settlement," 124–25.

33. *Agricultural Statistics*, 27–28.

34. Cofone, "Themes in the Italian Settlement," 116–17.

35. Rolle, *Immigrant Upraised*, 246–48.

36. Cofone, "Themes in the Italian Settlement," 118; Cofone, "Reno's Little Italy," 106; Cofone, "Themes in the Italian Settlement," 117–18; Cofone, "Reno's Little Italy," 102–3; Alma Olsen, office administrator, St. Ann's Roman Catholic Church, Dayton, NV, telephone interview by the author, August 27, 2010; Rolle, *Immigrant Upraised*, 245.

37. Alan Balboni, "From the Little Italies of the East and California to a Boom Town in the Desert: Italian-American Migration to Las Vegas, 1947–1970," 20–21; Alan Balboni, *Beyond the Mafia: Italian Americans and the Development of Las Vegas*, 61–104; Gans, *End of Late-Generation European Ethnicity*, 418–29.

38. Balboni, "From the Little Italies," 19; National Italian American Federation, *Italian Americans in the U.S.*, 4; Order 11.

39. "Cover Story," *Reno Gazette-Journal*, October 4, 1998; Balboni, "From the Little Italies," 133.

Chapter 13. California

1. Madley, *American Genocide.*

2. Madley, *American Genocide*, 38–40.

3. "California Gold Rush Statistics," www.shmoop.com/california-gold-rush/statistics.html; Madley, *American Genocide*, 173–74, 3, 346–47.

4. "Resident Population of States in the United States, 1900–2000"; Barkan, *From All Points*, 464, 473; *Agricultural Statistics*, 18, 53; *Fourteenth Census*, "Statistics of Population," 109.

5. Rolle, *Immigrant Upraised*, 257–58; Palmer, "Italian Immigration," 104–7; Jennifer Jill Helzer, "The Italian Ethnic Substrate in Northern California: Cultural Transfer and Regional Identity," 31; Rolle, *Immigrant Upraised*, 254–55.

6. Ernest S. Falbo, "State of California in 1856: Federico Biesta's Report to the Sardinian Ministry of Foreign Affairs," 57–59, 64, 73; Sensi-Isolani, "Tradition and Transition," 58–59.

7. Palmer, "Italian Immigration," 133; Falbo, "State of California," 74; Helzer, "Italian Ethnic Substrate," 40.

8. Gabaccia, "Ethnicity in the Business World," 5; George L. Henderson, *California and the Fictions*, 17; Giovinco, "Democracy in Banking," 172; Lord, Trenor, and Barrows, *The Italian in America*, 144; Peter Belmonte, "Italians in Merced, California, 1900–1930," 148; Alan Olmstead and Paul Rhode, "The Evolution of California Agriculture, 1850–2000," 4; Rolle, *Immigrant Upraised*, 251.

9. *Ninth Census of the U.S.*, Compendium 28.

10. Pitelka, "Indians and Italians," 69, 67; *Thirteenth Census*, "Statistics of Population," 172.

11. Pitelka, "Indians and Italians," 67; Linda Pacini Pitelka, "Mendocino: Race Relations in a Northern California County, 1850–1949," 78–79; Pitelka, "Indians and Italians," 70; Pitelka, "Mendocino," 158–64; Amerigo Baldocchi, "The Murderer of Cinquini Is Captured near Yountville," 1907, Amerigo Baldocchi-Newspapers.com.

12. *Thirteenth Census*, "Statistics of Population," 166; Pitelka, "Indians and Italians," 70–71.

13. Pitelka, "Indians and Italians," 71–72.

14. Pitelka, "Indians and Italians," 68–69, 74.

15. Pitelka, "Indians and Italians," 68–69, 74; Aurelius Carpenter and Percy Millberry, *History of Mendocino and Lake Counties, California, with Biographical Sketches of the Leading Men and Women of the Counties Who Have Been Identified with Their Growth and Development from the Early Days to the Present*, 422, 899, 902; Pitelka, "Indians and Italians," 74; Carpenter and Millberry, *History of Mendocino*, 24.

16. Pitelka, "Indians and Italians," 74.

17. Carpenter and Millberry, *History of Mendocino*, 691, 900, 927, 750, 561.

18. Pitelka, "Mendocino," 100, 152; Carpenter and Millberry, *History of Mendocino*, 651, 901–2, 899; Peck, *Reinventing Free Labor*, 193.

19. Carpenter and Millberry, *History of Mendocino*, 423–27.

20. *Fifteenth Census*, "Statistics of Population," 267; Pitelka, "Mendocino," 155.

21. Sensi-Isolani, "Tradition and Transition," 58–60.

22. Sensi-Isolani, "Tradition and Transition," 59–60, 63–64, 66.

23. Sensi-Isolani, "Tradition and Transition," 60, 63–64.

24. Sensi-Isolani, "Tradition and Transition," 68; "Union Hotel History," www.union hotel.com/UH_History.asp.

25. Sensi-Isolani, "Tradition and Transition," 64–66; *Fifteenth Census*, "Statistics of Population," 267–68; Sensi-Isolani, "Tradition and Transition," 64–66, 68, 58.

26. Palmer, "Italian Immigration," 197–204, 207–10.

27. Palmer, "Italian Immigration," 197–204, 207–10.

28. Palmer, "Italian Immigration," 214; Sally M. Miller, "Changing Faces of the Central Valley: The Ethnic Presence," 175.

29. *Fourteenth Census*, "Statistics of Population," 124; *Fifteenth Census*, "Statistics of Population," 267.

30. Adele Maiello, "Italian Entrepreneurs in the Central Valley of California," 149–57.

31. Teri Ann Bengiveno, "California Italian American Project," www.aiha-wrc.org /CIAP/stockton/stockton.html; *Stockton Business Directory*, 242; *Stockton City and San Joaquin County Directory*.

32. Bengiveno, "California Italian American Project."

33. *Italian-American Who's Who*, 111, 370; Bengiveno, "California Italian American Project"; Register of the Silva (J.S.) & Bros. Grocery (Stockton, Calif.), https://oac.cd lib.org/findaid/ark:/13030/tf8f59n9rv/entire text/.

34. Bengiveno, "California Italian American Project"; Maiello, "Italian Entrepreneurs," 163–65; Sebastian Fichera, "Entrepreneurial Behavior in an Immigrant Colony: The Economic Experience of San Francisco's Italian Americans, 1850–1940," 337.

35. Bengiveno, "California Italian American Project."

36. Mary Alice Sanguinetti, "The Italians of Calaveras County," 38–43.

37. *Diffusione del cognome—Mappa dei Cognomi*, www.mappadeicognomi.it; "Gerolamo Rolleri," www.findagrave.com/memorial/25142152/gerolamo-rolleri; Sanguinetti, "Italians of Calaveras County," 43–44.

38. Phylis Cancilla Martinelli, "The Excelsior Villagers: A Study of an Italian American Neighborhood in Transition," 231–32; Scambray, *Queen Calafia's Paradise*, 85–100.

39. *Twelfth Census*, "Statistics of Population," 802; *Thirteenth Census*, "Statistics of Population," 180; *Fifteenth Census*, "Statistics of Population," 269; Bengiveno, Ruberto, and Rogers, *Con le nostre mani*, 1–9; Rick Malaspina, *Italian Oakland*, 16, 19, 20, 24–26.

40. Lothrop, "California's Italians," 242; Deanna Paoli Gumina, *The Italians of San Francisco, 1850–1930*, 1–3, 21–26, 19–42; Mangione and Morreale, *La Storia*, 194.

41. Gumina, *Italians of San Francisco*, 21–42; Mangione and Morreale, *La Storia*, 196; Micaela di Leonardo, *The Varieties of Ethnic Experience: Kinship, Class, and Gender among California Italian-Americans*; di Leonardo, "Myth of the Urban Village"; Micaela di Leonardo, "Five Families from the 1920s to the Present"; Fichera, "Entrepreneurial Behavior," 325; *Twelfth Census*, "Statistics of the Population," 802; *Thirteenth Census*, "Statistics of Population," 180; *Fourteenth Census*, "Statistics of Population," 123.

42. Gumina, *Italians of San Francisco*, 21, 101; Helzer, "Italian Ethnic Substrate," 141; Palmer, "Italian Immigration," 241–42.

43. Gumina, *Italians of San Francisco*, 97, 101; Gabaccia, "Ethnicity in the Business World," 9–10; "Giovanni Battista 'G. B.' Levaggi," www.findagrave.com/memorial/4440 2682/giovanni-battista-levaggi.

44. Lord, Trenor, and Barrows, *The Italian in America*, 144; Lothrop, "California's Italians," 257, 267; Gumina, *Italians of San Francisco*, 175; Richard Dillon, *North Beach: The Heart of San Francisco*, 52–81; *Italian-American Who's Who*, 58, 249; Gumina, *Italians of San Francisco*, 175.

45. Paolo Pallavicini, *Tutto il dolore, tutto l'amore*; Catherine Accardi, "Read All about It! 150 Years of San Francisco's Italian Newspapers"; *Italian-American Who's Who*, 281; Giovanni Fugazi, "San Francisco, Italy/Fugazi: Il papà della colonia," https://sanfranciscoitaly.com/post/51096847062/fugazi-il-pap%C3%A0-della-colonia; *La voce del popolo*, https://archive.org/details/lavocedelpopolo00asso/mode/1up.

46. Simone Cinotto, *Soft Soil, Black Grapes: The Birth of Italian Winemaking in California*, 3.

47. Rolle, *Immigrant Upraised*, 45–46; Dick Rosano, *Wine Heritage*: The Story of Italian American Vintners, 23–24.

48. Gabaccia, "Ethnicity in the Business World," 4; Palmer, "Italian Immigration," 187–88; Lothrop, "California's Italians," 243–44; Gloria Ricci Lothrop, "Italians of Los Angeles: An Historical Overview," 257–58.

49. Francesca Bezzone, "Ciao, Stefano: San Antonio Winery Says Goodbye to Its Founding Father, Stefano Giuseppe Riboli," 24–25; Rosano, *Wine Heritage*, 219; Simone Schiavinato, "Italian Tradition at the Heart of LA: The San Antonio Winery and the History of the Riboli Family."

50. Gabaccia, "Ethnicity in the Business World," 4–5; Helzer, "Italian Ethnic Substrate," 123; *Diffusione del cognome*; Rosano, *Wine Heritage*, 25, 32, 40; Thomas Pinney, *A History of Wine in America: From Prohibition to the Present*, 330–31; Rosano, *Wine Heritage*, 35.

51. Rosano, *Wine Heritage*, 35, 38, 61, 40.

52. Rosano, *Wine Heritage*, 184–85, 226–27, 223–24, 228.

53. Nickolas Marinelli, "Cavalier Andrea Sbarboro"; Deanna Paoli Gumina, "Andrea Sbarboro, Founder of the Italian Swiss Colony Wine Company," 1–4.

54. Sebastian Fichera, "California's Italian-American Wine Makers: A Business Trajectory," 330; Gumina, "Andrea Sbarboro," 3–4; Lord, Trenor, and Barrows, *The Italian in America*, 142.

55. Lothrop, "California's Italians," 244; Gumina, "Andrea Sbarboro," 1–4, 11; Lord, Trenor, and Barrows, *The Italian in America*, 138, 140, 141; Rosano, *Wine Heritage*, 24–25, 31–32, 39; Gumina, "Andrea Sbarboro," 5, 13; Leon Adams, *The Wines of America*, 391; Cinotto, *Soft Soil, Black Grapes*, 67; Gumina, "Andrea Sbarboro," 5, 14.

56. Fichera, "Wine Makers," 334; Palmer, "Italian Immigration," 289–90; Rosano, *Wine Heritage*, 210–11; Palmer, "Italian Immigration," 266, 289–90.

57. Rosano, *Wine Heritage*, 193–96; Jerry Hirsch, "Striving to Give Landmark Winery Bigger Place on Map," *Los Angeles Times*, May 5, 2008.

58. Rosano, *Wine Heritage*, 61.

59. *Fourteenth Census*, "Statistics of Population," 109; *History of Fresno County: California*, 213–16, 294; Fresno Irrigation, "History of the District," www.fresnoirrigation.com/index; *History of Fresno County*, 208, 205, 211, 213; Adams, *The Wines of America*, 393.

60. Paul E. Vandor, *History of Fresno County, California: With Biographical Sketches*, 1:937–38; Rosano, *Wine Heritage*, 54.

61. Fichera, "Wine Makers," 332; Adams, *The Wines of America*, 398; Palmer, "Italian Immigration," 288n125; Rosano, *Wine Heritage*, 44, 147–48, 226; Adams, *The Wines of America*, 396–97; John Cribari, telephone interview by the author, October 2005; Al Cribari, telephone interview by the author, October 2005.

62. Pinney, *History of Wine*, 331; Adams, *The Wines of America*, 390, 399; "Antonio Nonini Winery, Inc.," www.noniniwinery.com/history.html; James Jordan (Nonini), telephone interview by the author, March 5, 2008; Rosano, *Wine Heritage*, 201.

63. Rosano, *Wine Heritage*, 171; Fichera, "Wine Makers," 335–36.

64. Rosano, *Wine Heritage*, 171–73; Jerry Hirsch, "At 75, Wine Giant Gallo Is Refining Its Palate," *Los Angeles Times*, April 4, 2008; Rosano, *Wine Heritage*, 172–74.

65. Helzer, "Italian Ethnic Substrate," 54; *Fourteenth Census*, "Statistics of Population," 109; Palmer, "Italian Immigration," 238; Gabaccia, "Ethnicity in the Business World," 9–11.

66. Fichera, "Wine Makers," 330; Rosano, *Wine Heritage*, 39, 56; Lothrop, "California's Italians," 244–45, 248–49; Lothrop, "Italians of Los Angeles," 257–58; Pinney, *History of Wine*, 331; Cinotto, *Soft Soil, Black Grapes*, 5; Marcia Stumpf, *Growing Up in Guasti*, 3, 26; Mariann Gatto, *Los Angeles's Little Italy: Images of America*, 37–38; Gino Filippi, "Cucamonga Wine District," https://ginoffvine.wordpress.com/tag/rancho-cucamonga-wine-history; Joseph Francis Sartori, *Joseph Francis Sartori, 1858–1946*, 1–7, 41, 67, 96–98; Lothrop, "Italians of Los Angeles," 267; Fichera, "Wine Makers," 331.

67. Stumpf, *Growing Up in Guasti*, 38–40; Reno Morra, interview by the author, March 7, 2008; Cinotto, *Soft Soil, Black Grapes*, 5; Lothrop, "California's Italians," 244–45; Stumpf, *Growing Up in Guasti*, 6.

68. Morra, interview; Lothrop, "California's Italians," 249; Cinotto, *Soft Soil, Black Grapes*, 142; Sam Shiro, interview by the author, March 7, 2008; Morra, interview; Stumpf, *Growing Up in Guasti*, 58; Gatto, *Los Angeles's Little Italy*, 37.

69. *Fourteenth Census*, "Statistics of Population," 123–24; Filippi, "Cucamonga Wine District"; Mark Gutglueck, "The Cucamonga Wine Region," sbcsentinel.com/2015/03/the-cucamonga-wine-region/.

70. Shiro, interview; Morra, interview; Sartori, *Joseph Francis Sartori*, 115–16; Shiro, interview.

71. Filippi, "Cucamonga Wine District"; Galleano Winery, *The Historic Galleano Winery: Cucamonga Valley's Historic Landmark Winery*; Bernardo Winery, www.bernardowinery.com/about_us.htm.

72. Palmer, "Italian Immigration," 265, 294; Cinotto, *Soft Soil, Black Grapes*, 1–23, 193–97.

73. Dillon, *North Beach*, 4; *Fourteenth Census*, "Statistics of Population," 123–45; Fichera, "Entrepreneurial Behavior," 334–35.

74. Dillon, *North Beach*, 84–85, 89.

75. Dillon, *North Beach*, 84–85, 87, 91; Lothrop, "California's Italians," 236–37; Richardson, "Fishermen of San Diego," 84; Gumina, *Italians of San Francisco*, 95.

76. Palmer, "Italian Immigration," 183; Helzer, "Italian Ethnic Substrate," 1142–44; Mangione and Morreale, *La Storia*, 196; Lothrop, "California's Italians," 236–37; Richardson, "Fishermen of San Diego," 84; Gumina, *Italians of San Francisco*, 95; Dillon, *North Beach*, 84–85, 87, 91, 106–7; Helzer, "Italian Ethnic Substrate," 130.

77. Mangione and Morreale, *La Storia*, 195; *Italian-American Who's Who*, 17–18.

78. Sabella & La Torre, www.sabellalatorre.com; Dillon, *North Beach*, 84–85, 87, 91, 106–7; Richardson, "Fishermen of San Diego," 84; Lothrop, "California's Italians," 236–38.

79. Lothrop, "California's Italians," 236–37.

80. *Twelfth Census*, "Statistics of Population," 739; *Thirteenth Census*, "Statistics of Population," 124; *Fourteenth Census*, "Statistics of Population," 123.

81. Jonathan Kemp, "Chinese Start Monterey Fishing Industry," mchsmuseum.com /chinesefishing.html; "Cannery Row: Parade of Cultures," canneryrow.com/our-story /parade-of-cultures; Lothrop, "California's Italians," 237–38; Carol Lynn McKibben, *Beyond Cannery Row: Sicilian Women, Immigration, and Community in Monterey, California, 1915–99*, 17; *Fourteenth Census*, "Statistics of Population," 124; *Fifteenth Census*, "Statistics of Population," 270.

82. Richard Crawford, "San Diego Had Its Own Cannery Row," *San Diego Union-Tribune*, June 18, 2009; Arthur T. Sutherland, *Earnings and Hours in Pacific Coast Fish Canneries*, 19–25.

83. Ruberto, *Gramsci, Migration, and the Representation of Women's Work*, 116–17, 119; McKibben, *Beyond Cannery Row*, 17–18, 36–37, 39, 98–100; Charles Speroni, "California Fishermen's Festivals," 219–20; Teresa Watanabe, "They Stood Up," *Los Angeles Times*, September 10, 2017; Scambray, "Creative Responses," 67.

84. DiStasi, *Branded*, 125; Richardson, "Fishermen of San Diego," 90; DiStasi, *Branded*, 42–78; Lawrence DiStasi, "A Fish Story," 82; DiStasi, *Branded*, 43–194, 125, 259–61; DiStasi, "A Fish Story," 82–96; Rose D. Scherini, "When Italian Americans Were 'Enemy Aliens,'" 10–31; Fox, *Unknown Internment*, 58–87.

85. Lothrop, "California's Italians," 238–39.

86. Richardson, "Fishermen of San Diego," 86; August Felando and Harold Medina, "The Origins of California's High-Seas Tuna Fleet," 7–8; Lewis Radcliffe, *Fisheries Industry of the United States: Report of the Division of Statistics and Methods of the United States Fisheries for 1919*, books.google.com, 16–18.

87. Peck, *Reinventing Free Labor*, 126, 145–46; Nancy Vezzuto, daughter of Raphael Galante, interview by the author, October 25, 2017.

88. Richardson, "Fishermen of San Diego," 86; Felando and Medina, "High-Seas Tuna Fleet," 7–8.

89. Felando and Medina, "High-Seas Tuna Fleet," 1–7, 11, 26, 32n18.

90. Felando and Medina, "High-Seas Tuna Fleet," 13, 20; Richardson, "Fishermen of San Diego," 84–90; Felando and Medina, "High-Seas Tuna Fleet," 6–7, 13, 20.

91. Richardson, "Fishermen of San Diego," 86; Pasquale Verdicchio, "The Place of Identity: San Diego's Little Italy and Community as Archive," 12.

92. Richardson, "Fishermen of San Diego," 86; Felando and Medina, "High-Seas Tuna Fleet," 2, 3, 4, 8, 18, 29n2; Crawford, "San Diego Had Its Own Cannery Row"; Felando and Medina, "High-Seas Tuna Fleet," 22–25.

93. Felando and Medina, "High-Seas Tuna Fleet," 34n31.

94. *Fourteenth Census*, "Statistics of Population," 124; *Fifteenth Census*, "Statistics of Population," 269; Verdicchio, "Place of Identity," 11–13; *Italian-American Who's Who*, 138; Richardson, "Fishermen of San Diego," 84–89, 91–92.

95. Verdicchio, "Place of Identity," 11–13, 17–21.

96. Scambray, *Queen Calafia's Paradise*, 51–66; Verdicchio, "Place of Identity," 15; Speroni, "California Fishermen's Festivals," 213–31; Verdicchio, "Place of Identity," 11–13, 17–21.

97. *Fourteenth Census*, "Statistics of Population," 123–25; *Sixteenth Census*, "Statistics of Population," 43; Helzer, "Italian Ethnic Substrate," 42; *Agricultural Statistics*, 18; Palmer, "Italian Immigration," 136, 215–17; *Agricultural Statistics*, 18.

98. *History of Fresno County*, 208.

99. Lord, Trenor, and Barrows, *The Italian in America*, 144; *Agricultural Statistics*, 18; *Twelfth Census*, "Statistics of Population," 732, 734; Helzer, "Italian Ethnic Substrate," 141; Palmer, "Italian Immigration," 216, 219, 229–30; Lord, Trenor, and Barrows, *The Italian in America*, 144; Rolle, *Immigrant Upraised*, 272–73; *Fourteenth Census*, "Statistics of Population," 109.

100. *Thirteenth Census*, "Statics of Population," 172; *Fourteenth Census*, "Statistics of Population," 114, 124; Belmonte, "Italians in Merced," 148.

101. Belmonte, "Italians in Merced," 151–56; Scambray, *Queen Calafia's Paradise*, 101–15.

102. Karana Hattersley-Drayton, "Garden of Eden: An Historic Context for Fresno's Fig Garden," www.fresno.gov; Catherine M. Rehart, *The Valley's Legends and Legacies*, 7; *History of Fresno County*, 32, 88–93, 127–38, 210–12; *A Memorial and Biographical History of the Counties of Fresno, Tulare and Kern, California*, 87, 711, 740–41; Vandor, *History of Fresno County*, 1:256–57; Mark Arax and Rick Wartzman, *The King of California: J. G. Boswell and the Making of a Secret American Empire*, 76–78; Julie Otsuka, *Buddha in the Attic: A Novel*, 83; *Fifteenth Census*, "Statistics of Population," 266; Scambray Family Papers, San Clemente, CA.

103. Palmer, "Italian Immigration," 136; Vandor, *History of Fresno County*, 1:33; *Fourteenth Census*, "Statistics of Population," 109; Palmer, "Italian Immigration," 215–16; *Agricultural Statistics*, 18; Peter DeFendis, telephone interview by the author, March 24, 2008; Mauro Simone, telephone interview by the author, July 7, 2017; Eugene Sibley, "Carmelo 'Carl' La Mattina," www.findagrave.com/memorial/116379603/carmelo-la_mattina; Leo La Mattina, telephone interview by the author, May 31, 2020.

104. Jo Ann Sorrenti, telephone interview by the author, March 14, 2008.

105. Rehart, *Legends and Legacies*, 31; Lothrop, "California's Italians," 256; St. John's Cathedral, https://stjohnsfresno.org/parish-life/about; "Fresno History: Settlement of Fresno Delayed until the Arrival of Railroad," www.city-data.com/us-cities/The-West/Fresno-History.html#ixzz4btE1osXo; St. Alphonsus Church, "Story of St. Alphonsus Parish," Archives, Catholic Diocese of Fresno, 2; *Fourteenth Census*, "Statistics of Population," 123–45; National Archives; St. Alphonsus Church, "Story of St. Alphonsus Parish," 2–5; John E. Boydston, "A History of the Parish of St. Alphonsus," Archives, Catholic Diocese of Fresno, 5; Robert Scambray, telephone interviews by the author, 2004–8; Ann La Centra Backen, "Maschito, Italy: A Short History of the Maschitan People and Their Dialect," www.giura.com/LaCentra.htm; Stavro Skëndi, *The Albanian National Awakening, 1878–1912*; Mary Pecoraro Cawthon, "Ethnic Identity and Language: The Case of the Italo-Albanians," 51–61.

106. Woody Laughnan, "Faretta's: A Fresno Tradition Closes," *Fresno Bee*, September 8, 1980; "Faretta's," *Fresno Bee*, December 13, 1953; Terry Scambray, telephone interviews by the author, 2004–8; National Archives and Records Administration;

William Saroyan, *My Name Is Aram*; National Archives and Records Administration; DeFendis, interview; *Fifteenth Census*, "Statistics of Population," 266; Sally Caglia, daughter of Frank Caglia, interviews by the author, January–June 2007.

107. Paula Giese, "California Tribes: Main Access Map and Tribes Listing," www.strom.net/isk/maps/ca/California.html; *Fourteenth Census*, "Statistics of Population," 109, 118; National Archives and Records Administration; Scambray Family Papers, San Clemente, CA; Arax and Wartzman, *King of California*, 256–63; Rothstein, *Color of Law*, 17–38.

108. Sorrenti, interview; Marie Piccolo, daughter-in-law to Mario and Rosa Piccolo and wife of Jim, interview by the author, March 20, 2008; "The *Fresno Bee*," *Fresno Bee*, July 21, 1968.

109. Robert Scambray, interviews; Paula Lloyd, "Ask Me: Rosenberg Bros. Historic Building Still Stands in Fresno County," *Fresno Bee*, December 26, 2015; *Agricultural Statistics*, 18.

110. Fichera, "Entrepreneurial Behavior," 333–34; "Cannery Life," http://onlineexhibits.historysanjose.org/cannerylife/through-the-years/1917-1966/cal-pak/index.html; Palmer, "Italian Immigration," 243; Elizabeth Reis, "The AFL, IWW, and Bay Area Cannery Workers," 126; Salvatore J. LaGumina et al., eds., *The Italian American Experience: An Encyclopedia*, 4; Rolle, *Immigrant Upraised*, 274.

111. *Italian-American Who's Who*, 164; Scambray Family Papers, San Clemente, CA; Peck, *Reinventing Free Labor*, 117–57, 233.

112. Frank Murasky, *Second Biannual Report of the Industrial Welfare Commission of the State (California): 1916–1919*, 232; *Fourth Biannual Report of the Industrial Welfare Commission of the State (California): 1919–1922*, 133, 135, 138; Reis, "AFL, IWW, and Bay Area Cannery Workers," 129.

113. Wallace Morgan, *History of Kern County with Biographical Sketches*, 1335–41; Palmer, "Italian Immigration," 226; Gabaccia, "Ethnicity in the Business World," 9–11; Palmer, "Italian Immigration," 241, 234, 237–38; Adams, *The Wines of America*, 457; Di Giorgio Corp., "Company History," www.company-histories.com/Di-Giorgio-Corp-Company-History.html.

114. "The Giumarra Companies: Cultivating Clusters of Agricultural Activity," www.usbusinessexecutive.com/agriculture/case-studies/giumarra-companies-cultivating-clusters-agricultural-activity; Adams, *The Wines of America*, 456–57, 450; Jeff Nickell, "On Rich Soil: Kern County Families Provide Grapes Aplenty," *Bakersfield Independent*, June 30, 2012; Giumarra, "Giumarra Companies."

115. Palmer, "Italian Immigration," 298–305.

116. Rosalind Giardina Crosby, "The Italians of Los Angeles, 1900," 39–44, 46; Schiavo, *Four Centuries*, 452; Lothrop, "Italians of Los Angeles," 264; Janice M. Kresin, "Terminal Markets: The Center of the Produce Universe," www.thepacker.com/news/industry/terminal-markets-center-produce-universe.

117. Crosby, "Italians of Los Angeles," 46–47; Gatto, *Los Angeles's Little Italy*, 38; Francesca Bezzone, "Domenic Jebbia: The 'Banana King'"; Lothrop, "California's Italians," 242; Henderson, *California and the Fictions*, 76; "The Visitors," *Chicago Packer*, February 6, 1915; Lothrop, "Italians of Los Angeles," 263–64; "Cookie" Domenic Bianco, "Domenic 'Cookie' Bianco," www.producepedia.com/farmer/domenick

-cookie-bianco; Scambray Family Papers, San Clemente, CA; Gabaccia, *We Are What We Eat*, 88–92; Gabaccia, "Ethnicity in the Business World," 9.

118. James Visceglia, "James Visceglia Records, 1929–1978," https://cmsny.org/archives/cms_025/, 4; Schiavo, *Four Centuries*, 467.

119. *Fourteenth Census*, "Statistics of Population," 109; Scambray, *Queen Calafia's Paradise*, 45–46, 101–70; Lothrop, "California's Italians," 259; Lothrop, "Italians of Los Angeles," 249, 281–82; Crosby, "Italians of Los Angeles," 40–41; Gatto, *Los Angeles's Little Italy*, 81; Sacred Heart Church, Los Angeles, www.sacredheartchurchla.org; Crosby, "Italians of Los Angeles," 41–42; Gatto, *Los Angeles's Little Italy*, 44; Lothrop, "Shadow on the Land," 196; Lothrop, "Italians of Los Angeles," 268.

120. Pagano, *Golden Wedding;* Scambray, *Queen Calafia's Paradise*, 46; Crosby, "Italians of Los Angeles," 43.

121. Pietro Russo, "The Italian American Periodical Press, 1836–1980," 251; Gatto, *Los Angeles's Little Italy*, 87; Crosby, "Italians of Los Angeles," 41; Lothrop, "Italians of Los Angeles," 262.

122. Gatto, *Los Angeles's Little Italy*, 71–79; Crosby, "Italians of Los Angeles," 53; Lothrop, "California's Italians," 257; Lothrop, "Italians of Los Angeles," 260, 280; *Italian-American Who's Who*, 249.

123. José Antonio Villarreal, *Pocho*, 121.

124. Henderson, *California and the Fictions*, 61, 72–77; Fugazi, "San Francisco, Italy/Fugazi"; Giovinco, "Democracy in Banking," 173–74.

125. Henderson, *California and the Fictions*, 71; Giovinco, "Democracy in Banking," 177; Gumina, *Italians of San Francisco*, 101–2; *Fourteenth Census*, "Statistics of Population," 124; Giovinco, "Democracy in Banking," 181–83.

126. Giovinco, "Democracy in Banking," 182; Felice Bonadio, *A. P. Giannini: Banker of America*, 110, 113, 112.

127. Henderson, *California and the Fictions*, 71; Bonadio, *A. P. Giannini*, 109; Giovinco, "Democracy in Banking," 181–85; Fugazi, "San Francisco, Italy/Fugazi"; Giovinco, "Democracy in Banking," 173–74; Bonadio, *A. P. Giannini*, 109.

128. *Italian-American Who's Who*, 188; Bonadio, *A. P. Giannini*, 107; Fichera, "Entrepreneurial Behavior," 337–38; Giovinco, "Democracy in Banking," 173–74.

129. Bonadio, *A. P. Giannini*, 114–15.

130. Giovinco, "Democracy in Banking," 181–85.

131. Bonadio, *A. P. Giannini*, 108–9; Marquis James and Bessie Rowland James, *Biography of a Bank: The Story of Bank of America N.T. & S.A.*, 252–53.

132. *Italian-American Who's Who*, 188; Bonadio, *A. P. Giannini*, 26, 71–72, 116; James and James, *Biography of a Bank*, 252–53, 310–11; *Italian-American Who's Who*, 188; Bonadio, *A. P. Giannini*, 107–8.

133. Rothstein, *Color of Law*, 39–115; Russell, *Renegade History*, 186–87.

134. Ruberto and Sciorra, *New Italian Migrations*, 1:15–18.

135. Order 6–7, Order Sons of Italy; National Italian American Foundation, *Italian Americans in the U.S.*, 2; Italian Cultural Heritage Foundation of Santa Barbara, italianheritagesb.org; *Historical Data Section*, 33–35; Lothrop, "Italians of Los Angeles," 268.

136. Ann Potenza, "Celebrating Italian Heritage: By Birth or Adoption."

Chapter 14. Social and Cultural Capital

1. Peck, *Reinventing Free Labor*, 3, 7n16, 9, 16–31, 51–53, 55, 85–88, 191–236; Mangione and Morreale, *La Storia*, 105–6; Peck, *Reinventing Free Labor*, 9, 11, 191–225.

2. Gabaccia, "Ethnicity in the Business World," 1–19; Cinotto, *Soft Soil, Black Grapes*, 42; Gabaccia, "Ethnicity in the Business World," 2–3.

3. Peck, *Reinventing Free Labor.*

4. William Dean Howells, "A Paper Read at the Annual Meeting of the New York Society for Italian Immigrants," 28.

Bibliography

Accardi, Catherine. "Read All about It! 150 Years of San Francisco's Italian Newspapers." *L'Italo-Americano* (February 22, 2018): 26–27.

Adams, Leon. *The Wines of America*. 4th ed. New York: McGraw-Hill, 1990.

Agricultural Statistics. St. Louis: Hale, 1922.

Alba, Richard D. "Identity and Ethnicity among Italians and Other Americans of European Ancestry." In *The Columbus People: Perspectives in Italian Immigration to the Americas and Australia*, edited by Lydio F. Tomasi et al., 21–44. Flagg Place, Staten Island: Center for Migration Studies, 1994.

———. *Italian Americans: Into the Twilight of Ethnicity*. Englewood Cliffs, NJ: Prentice Hall, 1985.

Alexander, Michelle. *The New Jim Crow: Mass Incarceration in the Age of Colorblindness*. New York: New Press, 2011.

Anderson, Parker. "A Brief History of the Ku Klux Klan in Prescott." February 19, 2011. www.sharlot.org/library.

Antonson, Joan M., and William S. Hanable. *Alaska's Heritage: Alaska's History and Cultural Studies*. Anchorage: Alaska Historical Commission, 1984. www.akhistorycourse.org.

Aprile, Pino. *Terroni*. Milan: Edizioni Piemme, 2010.

Arax, Mark, and Rick Wartzman. *The King of California: J. G. Boswell and the Making of a Secret American Empire*. New York: PublicAffairs, 2003.

Arrington, Leonard. *History of Idaho*. 2 vols. Moscow: University of Idaho Press, 1994.

Baily, Samuel L., and Franco Ramella, eds. *One Family, Two Worlds: An Italian Family's Correspondence across the Atlantic, 1901–1922*. New Brunswick, NJ: Rutgers University Press, 1988.

Balboni, Alan. *Beyond the Mafia: Italian Americans and the Development of Las Vegas*. Reno: University of Nevada Press, 1996.

———. "From the Little Italies of the East and California to a Boom Town in the Desert: Italian-American Migration to Las Vegas, 1947–1970." In *To See the Past More Clearly: The Enrichment of the Italian Heritage, 1890–1990*, edited by Harral E. Landry, 19–32. Austin: Nortex Press, 1990.

Ballerini, Luigi. Introduction to *Science in the Kitchen and the Art of Eating Well*, by Pellegrino Artusi. Toronto: University of Toronto Press, 2011.

Barkan, Elliott Robert. *From All Points: America's Immigrant West, 1870s–1952*. Bloomington: Indiana University Press, 2007.

Barr, Alwyn. "Late Nineteenth Century Texas." Texas State Historical Society, June 15, 2010. https://tshaonline.org/handbook/online/articles/npl01.

Becchetti, Fred. "Home Again to Dawson." Special supp., *Raton Range* (September 2, 1988): 1–8. http://chuckspeed.com/Dawson/Dawson.html.

Belfiglio, Valentine. *The Italian Experience in Texas*. Austin: Eakin Press, 1983.

——. *The Italian Experience in Texas: A Closer Look.* Austin: Eakin Press, 1995.

——. "Italians in Small Town and Rural Texas." In *Italian Immigrants in Rural and Small Town America*, edited by Rudolph J. Vecoli, 31–49. Staten Island: American Italian Historical Association, 1987.

——. "The Nature and Impact of Italian Culture upon Galveston Island." *East Texas Historical Journal* 22 (March 1989): 44–54.

——. "Public Policy and the Mexican Italians of El Paso, Texas (1880–1920)." In *Italian Americans and Their Public and Private Life*, edited by Frank J. Cavaioli et al., 157–71. Staten Island: American Italian Historical Association, 1993.

——. "Sicilian Houstonians." In *Italian Americans in Transition*, edited by Joseph V. Scelsa et al., 39–46. Staten Island: American Italian Historical Association, 1990.

——. "Sicilian Immigrants in Jefferson County, Texas, 1890–1920: Their Folkways and Culture." In *To See the Past More Clearly: The Enrichment of the Italian Heritage, 1890–1900*, edited by Harral E. Landry, 211–15. Austin: Nortex Press, 1994.

Belmonte, Peter. "Italians in Merced, California, 1900–1930." In *Industry, Technology, Labor and the Italian American Communities*, edited by Mario Aste et al., 147–60. Staten Island: American Italian Historical Association, 1997.

Bengiveno, Teri Ann, Laura E. Ruberto, and Kathleen L. Rogers. "Con le nostre mani: Italian Americans at Work in the East Bay." In *Italian Immigrants Go West: The Impact of Locale on Ethnicity*, edited by Janet E. Worrall et al., 1–9. Cambridge, MA: American Italian Historical Association, 2003.

Bezzone, Francesca. "Ciao, Stefano: San Antonio Winery Says Goodbye to Its Founding Father, Stefano Giuseppe Riboli." *L'Italo-Americano* (July 25, 2019): 24.

——. "Domenic Jebbia: The 'Banana King.'" *L'Italo-Americano* (March 7, 2013).

Bielinski, Leo. "The Italian Presence in the Coal Camp of Thurber, Texas." *West Texas Historical Association Year Book* 80 (2004): 33–40.

Billington, Monroe, and Roger D. Hardaway, eds. *African Americans on the Western Frontier.* Niwot: University of Colorado Press, 1998.

Blanthorn, Ouida. *A History of Tooele County.* Salt Lake City: Utah State Historical Society, 1988.

Boelhower, William. *Through a Glass Darkly: Ethnic Semiosis in American Literature.* Oxford: Oxford University Press, 1984.

Bohme, Frederick G. "The Italians of New Mexico." *New Mexico Historical Review* 34, no. 2 (1959): 98–116.

Bolognani, Bonifacio. *A Courageous People from the Dolomites: The Immigrants from Trentino on U.S.A. Trails.* Trentino: TEMI, 1981.

Bonadio, Felice. *A. P. Giannini: Banker of America.* Berkeley: University of California Press, 1994.

Borla, Walter. "Italian Americans in Utah: Unlikely Immigrants." *Ambassador* (Winter 2003): 19–23.

Braudaway, Douglas. *Del Rio: Queen City of the Rio Grande.* Charleston, SC: Arcadia, 2002.

Brown, Kerry-Lynne Demarinis. "St. Michael the Archangel Catholic Church, the Italian National Parish of Portland." *L'Italo-Americano* (February 18, 2016): 11.

Browning, Christopher R. "The Fake Threat of Jewish Communism." Review of *A Specter Haunting Europe: The Myth of Judeo-Bolshevism*, by Paul Hanebrink. *New York Review of Books*, February 21, 2019, 14–15.

Bryant, Dorothy. *Miss Giardino.* Berkeley: Ata Books, 1978.

Bush, Mary Bucci. *Sweet Hope.* Toronto: Guernica, 2011.

Butler, Anne M. "Still in Chains: Black Women in Western Prisons, 1865–1910." In *African Americans on the Western Frontier*, edited by Monroe Lee Billington and Roger D. Hardaway, 181–97. Niwot: University of Colorado Press, 1998.

Campbell, Robert. "Blacks and the Coal Mines of Western Washington, 1888–1896." In *African Americans on the Western Frontier*, edited by Monroe Lee Billington and Roger D. Hardaway, 92–109. Niwot: University of Colorado Press, 1998.

Cannato, Vincent J. *American Passage: The History of Ellis Island.* New York: Harper, 2009.

Carpenter, Aurelius, and Percy Millberry. *History of Mendocino and Lake Counties, California, with Biographical Sketches of the Leading Men and Women of the Counties Who Have Been Identified with Their Growth and Development from the Early Days to the Present.* Los Angeles: Historic Record, 1914.

Cather, Willa. *Death Comes for the Archbishop.* New York: Alfred A. Knopf, 1927.

———. *My Antonia.* Boston: Houghton Mifflin, 1918.

Cavaioli, Frank J. "Patterns of Italian Immigration to America." In *Italian Americans in the Third Millennium: Social Histories and Cultural Representations*, edited by Paolo A. Giordano and Anthony Julian Tamburri, 1–18. New York: American Italian Historical Association, 2009.

Cawthon, Mary Pecoraro. "Ethnic Identity and Language: The Case of the Italo-Albanians." In *Italian Ethnics: Their Languages, Literature and Lives*, edited by Dominic Candeloro et al., 51–61. Staten Island: Italian American Historical Association, 1987.

Chapman, Karin. "Cultural Conflict in a Steel Town: Two Generations of Italian Women." In *Italian Immigrants Go West: The Impact of Locale on Ethnicity*, edited by Janet E. Worrall et al., 79–90. Cambridge, MA: American Italian Historical Association, 2003.

Cinotto, Simone. *Soft Soil, Black Grapes: The Birth of Italian Winemaking in California.* New York: New York University Press, 2012.

Ciotola, Nicholas P. "From Agriculturalists to Entrepreneurs: Economic Success and Mobility among Albuquerque's Italian Immigrants, 1900–1930." *New Mexico Historical Review* 74 (1999): 3–27.

———. "Italian Immigrants in Albuquerque, 1880–1930: A Study in Western Distinctiveness." *Journal of the West* 4 (Fall 2004): 41–48.

Cipalla, Rita. "America's First Saint Helps Ease the Way for Seattle's Italian Community." *L'Italo-Americano* (August 20, 2015): 12. www.italoamericano.org/story/2015-8-21/mother-cabrini.

———. "Father Luigi Rossi: Serving the Early Pioneer Communities in Puget Sound." *L'Italo-Americano* (July 3, 2017): 32–33.

———. "Gai's Northwest Bakeries: A Seattle Institution and Baking Powerhouse for More than Fifty Years." *L'Italo-Americano* (August 10, 2017): 32. www.italoamericano.org/story/2017-8-24/gai-bakeries.

———. "Joe Desimone: From Produce Farmer to Owner of Seattle's Pike Place Market." *L'Italo-Americano* (April 29, 2016): 9. https://italoamericano.org/desimone/.

———. "A Love of Onions Brings Two Cities Together." *L'Italo-Americano* (November 26, 2015): 13. www.italoamericano.org/story/2015/onion-cities.

———. "Merlino Foods: Delivering Italian Products in Seattle for 120 Years." *L'Italo-Americano* (October 31, 2019): 28. www.italoamericano.org/story/2019-11-6/Merlin Food-Seattle.

———. "Staying Connected in Times of Crisis—the Italian Way." *L'Italo-Americano* (April 2, 2020): 26. https://italoamericano.org/story/2020-4-9/ItalianClubs-Seattle.

Cofone, Albin J. "Reno's Little Italy: Italian Entrepreneurship and Culture in Northern Nevada." *Nevada Historical Society Quarterly* 26 (Summer 1983): 97–110.

———. "Themes in the Italian Settlement of Nevada." *Nevada Historical Society Quarterly* 25 (Summer 1982): 116–30.

Coles, Kathleen, et al. Interview of Robert Capurro. In *The Italian-American Experience in Northwestern Nevada, from Territorial Days to the Present*, 107–42. Reno: University of Nevada Oral History Program, 2006.

Condit, Ira. *Caprifigs and Caprification*. Bulletin no. 319. College of Agriculture: Agricultural Experimental Station, Berkeley, CA, 1920. https://ia800501.us.archive.org/9/items/caprifigs.

———. *Fig Culture in California*. California Agricultural Extension Service, College of Agriculture, Berkeley. Circular 77 (October 1933): 1–33. https://archive.org/details/figcultureincali77cond/mode/2up.

Cookson, David A. "The Basques in Wyoming." In *Peopling the High Plains: Wyoming's European Heritage*, edited by Gordon Olaf Hendrickson, 95–120. Cheyenne: Wyoming State Archives and Historical Department, 1977.

Corsi, Pietro. *Halifax: L'altra porta d'America*. Isernia: Cosmo Iannone, 2003.

Costa, Janeen Arnold. "A Struggle for Survival and Identity: Families in the Aftermath of the Castle Gate Mine Disaster." *Utah Historical Quarterly* 56 (1988): 279–92.

Crosby, Rosalind Giardina. "The Italians of Los Angeles, 1900." In *Struggle and Success: An Anthology of the Italian Immigrant Experience in California*, edited by Paola A. Sensi-Isolani and Phylis Cancilla Martinelli, 38–57. New York: Center for Migration Studies, 1993.

Cunningham, George E. "The Italian: A Hindrance to White Solidarity in Louisiana, 1890–1898." *Journal of Negro History* 50 (January 1965): 22–36.

D'Angelo, Pascal. *Son of Italy*. 1924. Reprint, Toronto: Guernica, 2003.

Davis, Rebecca Harding. *Life in the Iron Mills, and Other Stories*. New York: Feminist Press, 1972.

Del Conte, Michele. "Italian Immigration to Portland, Oregon, 1900–1930." PhD diss., Washington State University, 1995.

Di Donato, Pietro. *Christ in Concrete*. New York: Bobbs-Merrill, 1939.

di Leonardo, Micaela. "Five Families from the 1920s to the Present." In *Struggle and Success: An Anthology of the Italian Immigrant Experience in California*, edited by Paola A. Sensi-Isolani and Phylis Cancilla Martinelli, 175–97. New York: Center for Migration Studies, 1993.

———. "The Myth of the Urban Village: Women, Work, and Family among Italian-Americas." In *The Women's West*, edited by Susan Armitage and Elizabeth Jameson, 277–90. Norman: University of Oklahoma Press, 1987.

———. *The Varieties of Ethnic Experience: Kinship, Class, and Gender among California Italian-Americans*. Ithaca, NY: Cornell University Press, 1984.

Dillon, Richard. *North Beach: The Heart of San Francisco.* San Francisco: Presidio Press, 1985.

DiStasi, Lawrence. *Branded: How Italian Immigrants Became "Enemies" during World War II.* Bolinas: Sanniti, 2016.

———. "A Fish Story." In *Una storia segreta: The Secret History of Italian American Evacuation and Internment during World War II*, edited by Lawrence DiStasi, 63–96. Berkeley: Heyday Books, 2001.

———. "How World War II Iced Italian American Culture." In *Una storia segreta: The Secret History of Italian American Evacuation and Internment during World War II*, edited by Lawrence DiStasi, 303–12. Berkeley: Heyday Books, 2001.

———. *"Una storia segreta": When Italians Were "Enemy Aliens."* Project director, Lawrence DiStasi. 2020. https://unastoriasegreta.com/.

Dito, Oreste. *La storia Calabrese: E la dimora degli Ebrei in Calabria dal secolo V alla seconda metà del secolo XVI.* Cosenza: Edizioni Brenner, 1989.

Durham, Nelson Wayne. *History of the City of Spokane and Spokane County, Washington.* Vol. 2. Spokane: S. J. Clarke, 1912.

Durning, Alan. "Rooming Houses: History's Affordable Quarters." Sightline Institute, November 14, 2012. www.sightline.org/2012/11/14/rooming-houses-historys-affordable-quarters/.

Earl, Phillip I. "Nevada's Italian War." *Nevada Historical Society Quarterly* 12 (Summer 1969): 50–86.

Falbo, Ernest S. "State of California in 1856: Federico Biesta's Report to the Sardinian Ministry of Foreign Affairs." In *Fulfilling the Promise of California: An Anthology of Essays on the Italian American Experience in California*, edited by Gloria Ricci Lothrop, 57–81. Spokane: Arthur H. Clark, 2000.

Fante, John. *Dago Red.* New York: Viking Press, 1940.

Felando, August, and Harold Medina. "The Origins of California's High-Seas Tuna Fleet." *Journal of San Diego History* 58 (Winter–Spring 2012): 1–40.

Fichera, Sebastian. "California's Italian-American Wine Makers: A Business Trajectory." *Studi Emigrazione / Etudes Migrations* 37, no. 138 (2000): 329–51.

———. "Entrepreneurial Behavior in an Immigrant Colony: The Economic Experience of San Francisco's Italian Americans, 1850–1940." *Studi Emigrazione / Etudes Migrations* 32, no. 118 (1995): 321–45.

Fisher, Joy, transcriber. *1911 Colorado Business Directory, Trinidad, Las Animas County.* Denver: Gazetteer, 1911. http://files.usgwarchives.net/co/lasanimas/Directories/1911-trinidad.txt.

Foerster, Robert F. *The Italian Emigration of Our Times.* Cambridge, MA: Harvard University Press, 1919.

Forstall, Richard L. "Population of States and Counties of the United States: 1790 to 1990." US Bureau of the Census, Texas, 152–61. Washington, DC: US Bureau of the Census, 1996. www2.census.gov/library/publications/decennial/1990/population-of-states-and-counties-us-1790-1990/population-of-states-and-counties-of-the-united-states-1790-1990.pdf.

Fox, Stephen. *The Unknown Internment: An Oral History of the Relocation of Italian Americans during World War II.* Boston: Twayne, 1990.

Frank, Russell. "Get on One End of the Rope and Pull Together: Italian-American Life and Work in Pueblo, Colorado." In *Old Ties, New Attachments: Italian-American Folklife in the West*, edited by David A. Taylor and John Alexander Williams, 145–59. Washington, DC: Library of Congress, 1992.

Fraser, Saline Hardee. "One Long Day That Went on Forever." *Utah Historical Quarterly* 68, no. 4 (1980): 379–89.

Frehner, Brian. "Ethnicity and Class: The Italian Charcoal Burners' War, 1875–1885." *Nevada Historical Society Quarterly* 39 (Spring 1996): 43–62.

Frey, Rodney, and Robert McCarl. "The Confluence of the Rivers: The Indigenous Tribes of Idaho." In *Idaho's Place: A New History of the Gem State*, edited by Adam Sowards, 13–41. Seattle: University of Washington Press, 2014.

Friday, Chris. *Organizing Asian-American Labor*. Philadelphia: Temple University Press, 1994.

Frost, Robert. *North of Boston*. 2nd ed. New York: Henry Holt, 1915.

Fukuyama, Francis. *Identity: The Demand for Dignity and the Politics of Resentment*. New York: Farrar, Straus and Giroux, 2018.

Fuller, Henry Blake. *With the Procession*. New York: Harper and Brothers, 1895.

Gabaccia, Donna. "Ethnicity in the Business World: Italians in American Food Industries." *Italian American Review* 6, no. 2 (1997–98): 1–19.

———. *Militants and Migrants: Rural Sicilians Become American Workers*. New Brunswick, NJ: Rutgers University Press, 1988.

———. *We Are What We Eat: Ethnic Food and the Making of Americans*. Cambridge, MA: Harvard University Press, 2000.

Galleano Winery. *The Historic Galleano Winery: Cucamonga Valley's Historic Landmark Winery*. N.p.: n.p., 2006.

Gambino, Richard. *Blood of My Blood: The Dilemma of the Italian-Americans*. New York: Doubleday, 1974.

———. *Vendetta*. New York: Doubleday, 1977.

Gans, Herbert J. "The End of Late-Generation European Ethnicity in America?" *Ethnic and Racial Studies* 38 (February 2015): 418–29.

Garceau, Dee. *The Important Things of Life: Women, Work, and Family in Sweetwater County, Wyoming, 1880–1929*. Lincoln: University of Nebraska Press, 1997.

Garroni, Maria Susanna. "Coal Mine, Farm and Quarry Frontiers: The Different Americas of Italian Immigrant Women." *Storia Nordamericana* 5, no. 2 (1988): 115–36.

Gatto, Mariann. *Los Angeles's Little Italy: Images of America*. Charleston, SC: Arcadia, 2009.

Gibson, Richard. *Lost Butte, Montana*. Charleston, SC: History Press, 2012.

Giovinco, Joseph. "Democracy in Banking: The Bank of Italy and California's Italians." In *Fulfilling the Promise of California: An Anthology of Essays on the Italian American Experience in California*, edited by Gloria Ricci Lothrop, 169–88. Spokane: Arthur H. Clark, 2000.

Goldberg, Robert Alan. *The Hooded Empire: The Ku Klux Klan in Colorado*. Urbana: University of Illinois Press, 1981.

Gonzales-Day, Kenneth. *Lynching in the West, 1850–1935*. Durham, NC: Duke University Press, 2006.

Gordon, Linda. *The Second Coming of the KKK: The Ku Klux Klan of the 1920s and the American Political Tradition.* New York: Liveright, 2017.

Gould, Charles F. "Portland Italians, 1880–1920." *Oregon Historical Quarterly* 78, no. 3 (1976): 239–60.

Gould, J. D. "European Inter-continental Emigration, the Road Home: Return Migration from the U.S.A." *Journal of European Economic History* 1, no. 9 (1980): 41–112.

Grant, Madison. *The Decline of the Great Race; or, The Racial Basis of European History.* New York: Charles Scribner's Sons, 1916.

Greeley, Andrew. *Why Can't They Be Like Us? America's White Ethnic Groups.* New York: E. P. Dutton, 1971.

Groth, Paul. *The History of Residential Hotels in the United States.* Berkeley: University of California Press, 1994.

Guglielmo, Jennifer. *Living the Revolution: Italian Women's Resistance and Radicalism, 1880–1945.* Chapel Hill: University of North Carolina Press, 2010.

Guglielmo, Jennifer, and Salvatore Salerno, eds. *Are Italians White? How Race Is Made in America.* New York: Routledge, 2003.

Guglielmo, Thomas. *White upon Arrival: Italians, Race, Color, and Power in Chicago, 1890–1945.* Oxford: Oxford University Press, 2003.

Gumina, Deanna Paoli. "Andrea Sbarboro, Founder of the Italian Swiss Colony Wine Company." *Italian Americana* 2, no. 1 (1975): 1–17.

———. *The Italians of San Francisco, 1850–1930.* New York: Center for Migration Studies, 1978.

Gusfield, Joseph. *Symbolic Crusade: Status Politics and the American Temperance Movement.* 2nd ed. Urbana: University of Illinois Press, 1986.

Handlin, Oscar. *The Uprooted: The Epic Story of the Great Migration That Made the American People.* Boston: Little, Brown, 1951.

Hansen, Marcus Lee. *The Immigrant in American History.* New York: Harper and Row, 1940.

Hanson, Ole. *Americanism versus Bolshevism.* New York: Doubleday, Page, 1920.

Harrigan, Stephen. "Coppini the Great." *Texas Monthly*, October 1984. texasmonthly .com/articles/coppini-the-great/.

Harrison, E. S. *The Alaska Almanac.* Seattle: Harrison, 1909.

Helzer, Jennifer Jill. "The Italian Ethnic Substrate in Northern California: Cultural Transfer and Regional Identity." PhD diss., University of Texas at Austin, 1998.

Henderson, George L. *California and the Fictions of Capital.* Philadelphia: Temple University Press, 1998.

Higgs, Robert. "Legally Induced Technical Regress in the Washington Salmon Fishery." Independent Institute, June 30, 1982. www.independent.org/publications/article .asp?id=2453.

Higham, John. *Strangers in the Land: Patterns of American Nativism, 1860–1925.* 2nd ed. New Brunswick, NJ: Rutgers University Press, 1988.

Historical Data Section: The Italian Hall Historic Structure Report. Archives, El Pueblo de Los Angeles Historic Monuments. Los Angeles: Architectural Museum Services, 1989.

History of Fresno County: California. San Francisco: Wallace W. Elliot, 1892.

Hodgson, Donald, and Vivien Hills. "Dream and Fulfillment: Germans in Wyoming." In *Peopling the High Plains: Wyoming's European Heritage*, edited by Gordon Olaf Hendrickson, 35–65. Cheyenne: Wyoming State Archives and Historical Department, 1977.

Holmes, William F. "Colored Farmers' Alliance." Texas State Historical Association, June 10, 2010. https://tshaonline.org/handbook/online/articles/amaa01.

Hourwich, Isaac, and US Immigration Commission. "The Immigrant and the Labor Market." In *Immigration as a Factor in American History*, edited by Oscar Handlin, 53–59. New York: Prentice Hall, 1959.

Howells, William Dean. "A Paper Read at the Annual Meeting of the New York Society for Italian Immigrants." *Harper's Weekly*, April 10, 1909, 28.

Hudson, Margaret Ann, ed. *Dallas Quarterly. Texas State Business Directory* 38, no. 2 (1992): 79–103. https://dallasgenealogy.com/DGS_Docs/Quarterlies/1992/June/PDF/Dalas_Quarterly_XXXVIII_2_1992_06pdf.

Ibach, Kim, and William Howard Moore. "The Emerging Civil Rights Movement: The 1957 Wyoming Public Accommodations Statute as a Case Study." *Annals of Wyoming* 73 (Winter 2001): 2–13.

Iorizzo, Luciano J., and Salvatore Mondello. *The Italian-Americans*. New York: Twayne, 1971.

Isaac, Paul E. "Beaumont, Texas." Texas State Historical Association, 2010. https://tshaonline.org/handbook/online/articles/hdb02.

Italian-American Who's Who. Vol. 2. New York: Vigo Press, 1937.

Jackson, Helen Hunt. *A Century of Dishonor: A Sketch of the United States Government's Dealings with Some of the Indian Tribes*. New York: Harper & Brothers, 1881.

———. *Ramona*. New York: Little, Brown, 1884.

Jacobson, Matthew Frye. *Special Sorrows: The Diasporic Imagination of Irish, Polish, and Jewish Immigrants in the United States*. Cambridge, MA: Harvard University Press, 1995.

James, Henry. *The American Scene*. 1907. Reprint, New York: Penguin, 1994.

James, Marquis, and Bessie Rowland James. *Biography of a Bank: The Story of Bank of America N.T. & S.A.* New York: Harper & Brothers, 1954.

Jones, Jacqueline. *A Dreadful Deceit: The Myth of Race from the Colonial Era to Obama's America*. New York: Basic Books, 2013.

Kane, Ken. "The Oregon Tuscans Turn 20." *L'Italo-Americano* (April 28, 2016): 9.

Kathka, David. "The Italian Experience in Wyoming." In *Peopling the High Plains: Wyoming's European Heritage*, edited by Gordon Olaf Hendrickson, 67–94. Cheyenne: Wyoming State Archives and Historical Department, 1977.

Katsanevas, Michael. "The Emerging Social Worker and the Distribution of the Castle Gate Relief Fund." *Utah Historical Quarterly* 50 (Summer 1982): 241–54.

Kerber, Linda K., and Jane De Hart Mathews, eds. *Women's America: Refocusing the Past*. Oxford: Oxford University Press, 1982.

Kleiner, Diana. "Jefferson County." Texas State Historical Association, 2015. https://tshaonline.org/handbook/online/articles/hdb02.

Koren, John. "The Padrone System and Padrone Banks." Edited by Carroll D. Wright and Oren W. Weaver. *Bulletin of the Department of Labor*, no. 9 (March 1897):

113–29. https://fraser.stlouisfed.org/title/bulletin-united-states-bureau-labor-3943/march-1897-477561/padrone-system-padrone-banks-498100.

LaGumina, Salvatore J. *WOP: A Documentary History of Anti-Italian Discrimination.* Toronto: Guernica, 1999.

LaGumina, Salvatore J., et al., eds. *The Italian American Experience: An Encyclopedia.* New York: Garland, 2000.

Lanham, Jenni, transcriber. "Carthage, NM, Mine Explosion, Dec. 1907." *Dallas Morning News,* January 1, 1908. www.gendisasters.com/data1/nm/mines/carthage-mineexplosion1907.html.

La Sorte, Michael. *La Merica: Images of Italian Greenhorn Experience.* Philadelphia: Temple University Press, 1985.

Leech, Brian James. *The City That Ate Itself: Butte, Montana and Its Expanding Berkeley Pit.* Reno: University of Nevada Press, 2018.

Lingenfelter, Richard E., and Karen Rix Gash. *The Newspapers of Nevada: A History and Bibliography, 1854–1979.* Reno: University of Nevada Press, 1984.

Lopreato, Joseph. *Italian Americans.* New York: Random House, 1970.

Lord, Eliot, John J. D. Trenor, and Samuel J. Barrows. *The Italian in America.* New York: B. F. Buck, 1905.

Lothrop, Gloria Ricci. "California's Italians: A Promise Fulfilled." In *Fulfilling the Promise of California: An Anthology of Essays on the Italian American Experience in California,* edited by Gloria Ricci Lothrop, 233–73. Spokane: Arthur H. Clark, 2000.

———. "Italians of Los Angeles: An Historical Overview." *Southern California Quarterly* 85 (Fall 2003): 249–300.

———. "A Shadow on the Land: The Impact of Fascism on Los Angeles Italians." In *Fulfilling the Promise of California: An Anthology of Essays on the Italian American Experience in California,* edited by Gloria Ricci Lothrop, 189–214. Spokane: Arthur H. Clark, 2000.

———. "Unwelcome in Freedom's Land: The Impact of World War II on Italian Aliens in Southern California." In *Una storia segreta: The Secret History of Italian American Evacuation and Internment during World War II,* edited by Lawrence DiStasi, 161–94. Berkeley: Heyday Books, 2001.

Lund, Jens. "Walla Walla Sweets: Onions and Ethnic Identity in an Italian Community in the Northwest." In *Old Ties, New Attachments: Italian-American Folklife in the West,* edited by David A. Taylor and John Alexander Williams, 113–29. Washington, DC: Library of Congress, 1992.

Lyttelton, Adrian. "Under the Tuscan Gun." Review of *A Chill in the Air: An Italian War Diary, 1939–1940* and *War in Val d'Orcia: An Italian War Diary, 1943–1944,* both by Iris Origo. *New York Review of Books,* December 5, 2019, 42–43.

Madalena, Lawrence. *Confetti for Gino.* New York: Doubleday, 1959.

Madley, Benjamin. *An American Genocide: The United States and the California Indian Catastrophe, 1846–1873.* New Haven, CT: Yale University Press, 2016.

Magnaghi, Russell. "Italian Contribution to the Development of Alaska." *Italian Americana* 9, no. 2 (1991): 167–81.

Maiello, Adele. "Italian Entrepreneurs in the Central Valley of California." In *Italian Americans: A Retrospective on the Twentieth Century,* edited by Paola Alessandra

Sensi-Isolani and Anthony Julian Tamburri, 149–66. Chicago Heights: Italian American Historical Association, 2001.

Malaspina, Rick. *Italian Oakland.* Charleston, SC: Arcadia, 2011.

Malone, Michael P., et al., eds. *Montana: A History of Two Centuries.* Rev. ed. Seattle: University of Washington Press, 2003.

Malpezzi, Frances M., and William C. Clements. *Italian American Folklore.* Little Rock: August House, 1992.

Mangano, Antonio. *Sons of Italy.* New York: Missionary Education Movement of the United States and Canada, 1917.

Mangione, Jerre. *Mount Allegro: A Memoir of Italian American Life.* 1942. Reprint, Syracuse, NY: Syracuse University Press, 1998.

Mangione, Jerre, and Ben Morreale. *La Storia: Five Centuries of the Italian American Experience.* New York: HarperCollins, 1992.

Manno, Silvio. *Charcoal and Blood: Italian Immigrants in Eureka, Nevada, and the Fish Creek Massacre.* Reno: University of Nevada Press, 2016.

Marinelli, Nickolas. "Cavalier Andrea Sbarboro." *L'Italo-Americano* (May 27, 2011).

Martin, Sr. Theresa, SC. "Life Sketch of Sister Blandina Segale, 1850–1941." In *The Land Beyond: Italian Migrants in the Westward Movement*, edited by Gloria Ricci Lothrop, 291–98. San Marino: Patrons of Italian Culture, 2007.

Martinelli, Phylis Cancilla. "Examining the Relationships of Italians and Mexicans in a 'Mexican Camp' and a 'White Man's Camp': Mexicans and Euro Latins in the Arizona Copper Industry, 1900–1930." In *Italian Immigrants Go West: The Impact of Locale on Ethnicity*, edited by Janet E. Worrall et al., 55–65. Cambridge, MA: American Italian Historical Association, 2003.

———. "The Excelsior Villagers: A Study of an Italian American Neighborhood in Transition." In *Struggle and Success: An Anthology of the Italian Immigrant Experience in California*, edited by Paola A. Sensi-Isolani and Phylis Cancilla Martinelli, 231–38. New York: Center for Migration Studies, 1993.

———. "Italian Immigrant Women in the Southwest." In *Italian Immigrant Women in North America*, edited by Betty Boyd Caroli et al., 324–36. Toronto: Multicultural History Society of Ontario, 1978.

———. "Italy in Phoenix." *Journal of Arizona History* (Autumn 1977): 319–40.

———. "Pioneer Paesani in Globe, Arizona." In *Italian Immigrants in Rural and Small Town America*, edited by Rudolph J. Vecoli, 153–69. Staten Island: American Italian Historical Association, 1987.

———. *Undermining Race: Ethnic Identities in Arizona Copper Camps, 1880–1920.* Tucson: University of Arizona Press, 2009.

McKibben, Carol Lynn. *Beyond Cannery Row: Sicilian Women, Immigration, and Community in Monterey, California, 1915–99.* Urbana: University of Illinois Press, 2006.

McWilliams, Carey. *Factories in the Fields: The Story of Migratory Farm Labor in California.* New York: Little, Brown, 1939.

Mellinger, Philip J. "Early Hartville and Sunrise: A Study of the Frontier and Immigration in Wyoming." Master's thesis, Roosevelt University, 1969.

A Memorial and Biographical History of the Counties of Fresno, Tulare and Kern, California. Chicago: Lewis, 1892.

Mercier, Laurie. "Confronting Race and Creating Community: Idaho's Ethnic History." In *Idaho's Place: A New History of the Gem State*, edited by Adam Sowards, 167–97. Seattle: University of Washington Press, 2014.

———. "Mexican Americans of the Yellowstone Valley." In *Montana Legacy: Essays on History, People and Place*, edited by Harry W. Fritz, et al., 221–43. Helena: Montana Historical Society Press, 2002.

Merriman, Scott A. "Alien Land Laws." Immigration to the United States, 2016. www.imigrationtounitedstates.org/334-alien-land-laws.html.

Messina, Elizabeth Giovanna. Introduction to *In Our Own Voices: Multidisciplinary Perspectives on Italian and Italian American Women*, edited by Elizabeth Giovanna Messina, xi–xxviii. Boca Raton: Bordighera, 2003.

Micone, Marco. *Beyond the Ruins*. Toronto: Guernica, 1995.

Miller, Sally M. "Changing Faces of the Central Valley: The Ethnic Presence." *California History* 74, no. 2 (1995): 174–89.

Mollenkopf, John. "Late Generation European Ethnicity Is Still with Us." *Ethnic and Racial Studies* 37, no. 5 (2014): 795–98.

Morgan, Wallace. *History of Kern County with Biographical Sketches*. Los Angeles: Historical Record, 1914. https://archive.org/details/historyofkerncou01morg.

Morvillo, Anthony. *A Dictionary of the Numípu or the Nez Perce Language*. N.p.: St. Ignatius' Mission Print, 1895.

Muhammad, Khalil Gibran. *The Condemnation of Blackness: Race, Crime, and the Making of Modern Urban America*. Cambridge, MA: Harvard University Press, 2011.

Murasky, Frank. *First Biennial Report of the Industrial Welfare Commission of the State (California): 1913–1914*. Sacramento: State of California Printing Office, 1914.

———. *Fourth Biennial Report of the Industrial Welfare Commission of the State (California): 1919–1922*. Sacramento: State of California Printing Office, 1924.

———. *Second Biennial Report of the Industrial Welfare Commission of the State (California): 1916–1919*. Sacramento: State of California Printing Office, 1919.

Murphy, Mary. *Mining Culture: Men, Women, and Leisure in Butte, 1914–41*. Urbana: University of Illinois Press, 1997.

Napoli, Donna Jo. *Alligator Bayou*. New York: Wendy Lamb Books, 2009.

Naske, Claus M., and Herman Slotnick. *Alaska: A History of the 49th State*. Norman: University of Oklahoma Press, 1987.

National Archives and Records Administration. Chet Holifield Federal Bldg. Laguna Niguel, Calif. Microfilm Census Files, Fresno County, 1920 and 1930.

National Italian American Foundation. *Italian Americans in the U.S.: Statistics, 1990*. www.niaf.org/news/italian-american-statistics/.

Nelli, Humbert S. *Italians in Chicago, 1880–1930: A Study in Ethnic Mobility*. Oxford: Oxford University Press, 1970.

Nicandri, David L. *Italians in Washington State: Emigration, 1853–1924*. [Tacoma]: Washington State American Revolution Commission, 1978.

Noel, Thomas. "The Immigrant Saloon in Denver." *Colorado Magazine* 54 (Summer 1977): 201–19.

Norris, Frank. *The Octopus*. New York: Doubleday, Page, 1901.

Notarianni, Philip F. "Italian Catholics among the Mormons: Maintaining Identity in Zion." In *Italian Immigrants Go West: The Impact of Locale on Ethnicity*, edited by Janet E. Worrall et al., 149–57. Cambridge, MA: American Italian Historical Association, 2003.

———. "Italian Involvement in the 1903–04 Coal Miners' Strike in Southern Colorado and Utah." In *Pane e Lavoro: The Italian American Working Class*, edited by George E. Pozzetta, 47–65. Toronto: Multicultural History Society of Ontario, 1980.

———. "Italianita in Utah: The Immigrant Experience." In *The Peoples of Utah*, edited by Helen Z. Papanikolas, 303–31. Salt Lake City: Utah State Historical Society, 1976.

———. "The Italians in Utah." Italian Center of the West, 2009. www.italiancenterofthewest.com/histories/genhistory.htm.

———. "Places of Origin: Calabresi in Carbon County, Utah." In *Old Ties, New Attachments: Italian-American Folklife in the West*, edited by David A. Taylor and John Alexander Williams, 69–79. Washington, DC: Library of Congress, 1992.

———. "Utah's Ellis Island: The Difficult Americanization of Carbon County." *Utah Historical Quarterly* 47 (1979): 178–93.

Notarianni, Philip F., and Richard Raspa. "The Italian Community of Helper, Utah: Its Historic and Folkloric Past and Present." In *The Family and Community Life of Italian Americans*, edited by Richard N. Juliani, 23–33. Staten Island: Italian American Historical Association, 1983.

Novak, Michael. *The Rise of the Unmeltable Ethnics: Politics and Culture in the 1970s.* New York: Macmillan, 1971.

Odintz, Mark. "Brazos County." In Texas State Historical Association Handbook of Texas. March 10, 2016. https://www.tshaonline.org/handbook/entries/brazos-county.

Okrent, Daniel. *The Guarded Gate: Bigotry, Eugenics, and the Law That Kept Two Generations of Jews, Italians, and Other European Immigrants Out of America.* New York: Scribner, 2019.

———. *Last Call: The Rise and Fall of Prohibition.* New York: Scribner, 2011.

Olmstead, Alan, and Paul Rhode. "The Evolution of California Agriculture, 1850–2000." In *California Agriculture: Dimensions and Issues*, edited by Jerry Siebert. [Berkeley]: University of California Giannini Foundation of Agricultural Economics, Division of Agriculture and Natural Resources, 2003. Giannini.ucop.edu/CalAgbook.htm.

Order Sons of Italy in America. *A Profile of Today's Italian Americans: A Report Based on the Year 2000 Census Compiled by the Sons of Italy.* Washington, DC: OSIA. www.osia.org.

Origo, Iris. *A Chill in the Air: An Italian War Diary, 1939–1940.* New York: NYRB Classics, 2017.

———. *War in Val d'Orcia: An Italian War Diary, 1943–1944.* New York: NYRB Classics, 2017.

Oshinsky, David M. *"Worse than Slavery": Parchman Farm and the Ordeal of Jim Crow Justice.* New York: Simon & Schuster, 1996.

Otsuka, Julie. *The Buddha in the Attic: A Novel.* New York: Anchor Books, 2011.

Owen, Blanton. "The Melting Pot Works: Italians in Central Nevada." In *Old Ties, New Attachments: Italian-American Folklife in the West*, edited by David A. Taylor and John Alexander Williams, 49–67. Washington, DC: Library of Congress, 1992.

Owens, Sister M. Lilliana. "Frances Xavier Cabrini, Foundress of the Queen of Heaven Institute." In *The Land Beyond: Italian Migrants in the Westward Movement*, edited by Gloria Ricci Lothrop, 139–46. San Marino: Patrons of Italian Culture, 2007.

Pagano, Jo. *Golden Wedding.* New York: Random House, 1943.

Paige, John C. "Country Squires and Laborers: British Immigrants in Wyoming." In *Peopling the High Plains: Wyoming's European Heritage*, edited by Gordon Olaf Hendrickson, 1–33. Cheyenne: Wyoming State Archives and Historical Department, 1977.

Palladino, Rev. Lawrence B., SJ. *Indian and White in the Northwest: A History of Catholicity in Montana, 1831–1891.* Lancaster, PA: Wickersham, 1922.

Pallavicini, Paolo. *Tutto il dolore, tutto l'amore.* Milan: Sonzogno, 1937.

Palmer, Hans Christian. "Italian Immigration and the Development of California Agriculture." PhD diss., University of California, Berkeley, 1965.

Panunzio, Constantine M. *Immigration Crossroads.* 1927. Reprint, Englewood, NJ: Jerome S. Ozer, 1971.

———. *The Soul of an Immigrant.* New York: Macmillan, 1921.

Peck, Gunther. *Reinventing Free Labor: Padrones and Immigrant Workers in the North American West, 1880–1930.* Cambridge: Cambridge University Press, 2000.

Pellegrini, Angelo. *American Dream: An Immigrant's Quest.* San Francisco: North Point Press, 1986.

———. *Americans by Choice.* New York: Macmillan, 1956.

———. *Immigrant's Return.* New York: Macmillan, 1952.

———. *The Unprejudiced Palate.* New York: Macmillan, 1948.

Petersen, Keith C. *Company Town: Potlatch, Idaho, and the Potlatch Lumber Company.* Pullman: Washington State University Press, 1987.

Phoenix City Directory, 1899–1900. Arizona Memory Project. asmemory.aslibrary.gov/cdm/ref/collection/dir/id/2.

Pinney, Thomas. *A History of Wine in America: From Prohibition to the Present.* Berkeley: University of California Press, 1989.

Pitelka, Linda Pacini. "Indians and Italians: The Boundaries of Race and Ethnicity in Rural Northern California, 1890–1920." In *Italian Immigrants Go West: The Impact of Locale on Ethnicity*, edited by Janet E. Worrall et al., 66–78. Cambridge, MA: American Italian Historical Association, 2003.

———. "Mendocino: Race Relations in a Northern California County, 1850–1949." PhD diss., University of Massachusetts, 1994.

Potenza, Ann. "Celebrating Italian Heritage: By Birth or Adoption." *L'Italo-Americano* (October 3, 2019): 30.

Powell, Allan Kent. *The Next Time We Strike: Labor in Utah's Coal Fields, 1900–1933.* Logan: Utah State University Press, 1985.

Prevedel, David A. *The Tyroleans: A Journey of Hope.* Published by the author, 2010.

Qin, Yucheng. "A Century-Old 'Puzzle': The Six Companies' Role in Chinese Labor Importation in the Nineteenth Century." *Journal of American–East Asian Relations* 12 (Fall–Winter 2003): 225–54.

Radford, Dwight A. "Ethnic Groups of Wyoming." In *Red Book: American State, County, and Town Sources*, edited by Alice Eichholz. Provo, UT: Ancestry, 2004. https://wiki.rootsweb.com//wiki/index.php?title=Ethnic_Groups_of_Wyoming&_ga=2.263208068.961287628.1618252938-1441587867.1618252938.

Rappagliosi, Father Philip. *Letters from the Rocky Mountain Indian Missions: Father Philip Rappagliosi.* Edited by Robert Bigart. Translated from the Italian by Anthony

Mattina and Lisa Moore Nardini. Translated from the German by Ulrich Stengel. Lincoln: University of Nebraska Press, 2003.

Raptosh, Diane. "Italian American Women on the Frontier: Sister Blandina Segale on the Santa Fe Trail." In *Italian Ethnics: Their Languages, Literature and Lives*, edited by Dominic Candeloro et al., 91–107. Staten Island: Italian American Historical Association, 1990.

Reeder, Linda. *Widows in White: Migration and the Transformation of Rural Italian Women, Sicily, 1880–1920.* Toronto: University of Toronto Press, 2003.

Rehart, Catherine M. *The Valley's Legends and Legacies.* Sanger, CA: Quill Driver Books, 1996.

Reis, Elizabeth. "The AFL, the IWW and Bay Area Cannery Workers." In *Struggle and Success: An Anthology of the Italian Immigrant Experience in California*, edited by Paola A. Sensi-Isolani and Phylis Cancilla Martinelli, 124–45. New York: Center for Migration Studies, 1993.

Répaci, Leonida. *Il Sud su un binario morto: A cura di Giuseppe Caridi.* Catanzaro: Rubbettino Editore, 2000.

Report of the United States Commissioner of Fisheries for the Physical Year Ended June 30, 1921. Bureau of Fisheries, Document no. 900. US Bureau of Fisheries—1922. https://books.google.com/books?id=dVsaAQAAIAAJ.

"Resident Population of States in the United States, 1900–2000." State Census Counts: STATS. Indiana. www.stats.indiana.edu/populationPopTotals/historic_counts_states.asp.

Reynolds, Paula. "Val Verde Winery: Francesco Qualia and Texas' Oldest Winery." *L'Italo-Americano*, March 9, 2017, 32.

Riccio, Anthony V. *Farms, Factories, and Family: Italian American Women of Connecticut.* Albany: State University of New York Press, 2014.

Richardson, William C. "Fishermen of San Diego: The Italians." In *Struggle and Success: An Anthology of the Italian Immigrant Experience in California*, edited by Paola A. Sensi-Isolani and Phylis Cancilla Martinelli, 84–94. New York: Center for Migration Studies, 1993.

Roediger, David. *Working toward Whiteness: How America's Immigrants Became White; The Strange Journey from Ellis Island to the Suburbs.* New York: Basic Books, 2005.

Rogin, Michael. *Fathers & Children: Andrew Jackson and the Subjugation of the American Indian.* New York: Vintage, 1975.

Rolle, Andrew F. *The Immigrant Upraised: Italian Adventurers and Colonists in an Expanding America.* Norman: University of Oklahoma Press, 1968.

———. "The Italian Moves Westward." *Montana: The Magazine of Western History* 16 (January 1966): 13–24.

Rosano, Dick. *Wine Heritage: The Story of Italian American Vintners.* South San Francisco: Wine Appreciation Guild, 2000.

Rothstein, Richard. *The Color of Law: A Forgotten History of How Our Government Segregated America.* New York: Liveright, 2017.

Ruberto, Laura E. "Grains of Truth: Rice, Labor, and Cultural Identity." In *In Our Own Voices: Multidisciplinary Perspectives on Italian and Italian American Women*, edited by Elizabeth Giovanna Messina, 3–20. Boca Raton: Bordighera, 2003.

———. *Gramsci, Migration, and the Representation of Women's Work in Italy and the U.S.* Lanham, MD: Lexington Books, 2007.

Ruberto, Laura E., and Joseph Sciorra, eds. *New Italian Migrations to the United States: Politics and History since 1945.* 2 vols. Urbana: University of Illinois Press, 2017.

Rudolph, Katie. "Denver's Bygone Markets." Denver Public Library, September 3, 2013. https://history.denverlibrary.org/news/denvers-bygone-markets.

Russell, Thaddeus. *A Renegade History of the United States.* New York: Free Press, 2010.

Russo, Pietro. "The Italian American Periodical Press, 1836–1980." In *Italian Americans: New Perspectives in Italian Immigration and Ethnicity,* edited by Lydio F. Tomasi, 248–59. Staten Island: Center for Migration Studies, 1985.

Sabetti, Filippo. *Political Authority in a Sicilian Village.* Rutgers, NJ: Rutgers University Press, 1984.

Salvatore, Filippo. *Ancient Memories, Modern Identities.* Translated by Domenic Cusmano. Toronto: Guernica, 1999.

Salvetti, Patricia. *Corda e sapone: Storie di linciaggi degli italiani negli Stati Uniti.* Rome: Donzelli Editore, 2003.

Sanchirico, Andrew. "Small Business and Social Mobility among Italian Americans." In *Italian Ethnics: Their Languages, Literature and Lives,* edited by Dominic Candeloro et al., 201–14. Staten Island: American Italian Historical Association, 1990.

Sang-Hee Lee, Shelley. *A New History of Asian America.* New York: Rutledge, 2014.

Sanguinetti, Mary Alice. "The Italians of Calaveras County." In *Italian Immigrants Go West: The Impact of Locale on Ethnicity,* edited by Janet E. Worrall et al., 38–54. Cambridge, MA: American Italian Historical Association, 2003.

Saroyan, William. *The Human Comedy.* New York: Harcourt, Brace, 1943.

———. *Madness in the Family: Stories.* New York: New Directions, 1988.

———. *My Name Is Aram.* New York: Harcourt, Brace, 1927.

———. *Places Where I've Done Time.* New York: Praeger, 1972.

Sartori, Joseph Francis. *Joseph Francis Sartori, 1858–1946.* Los Angeles: Ward Ritchie Press, 1948.

Scambray, Kenneth. "Creative Responses to the Italian Immigrant Experience in California: Baldassare Forestiere's Underground Gardens and Simon Rodia's Watts Towers." *Italian American Review* 2 (Autumn–Winter 2011): 113–40. Republished in *Italian Folk: Vernacular Culture in Italian-American Lives,* edited by Joseph Sciorra, 63–82. New York: Fordham University Press.

———. "The Literary and Immigrant Contexts of Simon Rodia's Watts Towers." In *Sabato Rodia's Towers in Watts: Art, Migrations, Development,* edited by Luisa Del Giudice, 145–54. New York: Fordham University Press, 2014.

———. *The North American Italian Renaissance: Italian Writing in America and Canada.* Toronto: Guernica, 2000.

———. "Poggioreale: Resurrecting the Campanile." *Accenti* 30 (Winter 2014): 8–13.

———. *Queen Calafia's Paradise: California and the Italian American Novel.* Madison, NJ: Fairleigh Dickinson University Press, 2007.

Scarpaci, Vincenza. "Walking the Color Line: Italian Immigrants in Rural Louisiana, 1880–1910." In *Are Italians White? How Race Is Made in America,* edited by Jennifer Guglielmo and Salvatore Salerno, 60–76. New York: Routledge, 2003.

Scherini, Rose D. "When Italian Americans Were 'Enemy Aliens.'" In *Una storia segreta: The Secret History of Italian American Evacuation and Internment during World War II*, edited by Lawrence DiStasi, 10–31. Berkeley: Heyday Books, 2001.

Scheuerman, Richard Dean. "Multicultural Experiences in the Palouse Country: A Historical Narrative Investigating Ethnicity and Regional Immigration Patterns, 1860–1920." PhD diss., Gonzaga University, 1992.

Schiavinato, Simone. "Italian Tradition at the Heart of LA: The San Antonio Winery and the History of the Riboli Family." *L'Italo-Americano* (October 31, 2019): 26.

Schiavo, Giovanni. *Four Centuries of Italian-American History*. New York: Vigo Press, 1952.

Scicolone, Michele. Foreword to *Science in the Kitchen and the Art of Eating Well*, by Pellegrino Artusi. Toronto: University of Toronto Press, 2011.

Scudder, H. D., and E. B. Hurd. *Graphic Summary of Agricultural and Land Use in Oregon*. Agricultural Experimental Station and Bureau of Agricultural Economics, US Department of Agriculture. Station Circular 114. Corvallis: Oregon State Agricultural College, 1935. https://ir.library.oregonstate.edu/downloads/fq977v871.

Segale, Sr. Blandina. *At the End of the Santa Fe Trail*. Milwaukee: Bruce, 1948.

Seller, Maxine. "The Education of the Immigrant Woman, 1900–1935." In *Women's America: Refocusing the Past*, edited by Linda K. Kerber and Jane De Hart Mathews, 242–56. Oxford: Oxford University Press, 1982.

Sensi-Isolani, Paola A. "Tradition and Transition in a California Paese." In *Struggle and Success: An Anthology of the Italian Immigrant Experience in California*, edited by Paola A. Sensi-Isolani and Phylis Cancilla Martinelli, 58–75. New York: Center for Migration Studies, 1993.

Shaffer, Vicki W. *St. Louis (MO) Republic*. "The Great Flood in Texas: Flood's Waters Rapidly Receding," July 19, 1899. Transcribed from the original newspaper, which belonged to Wm. Thomas Wilson, Bellevue, Clay Co., Texas. txgenwebcounties.org/clay/newspapers/flood.html.

Shankar, Amulya. "'Cosmopolitan' Is a Dog Whistle Word Once Used in Nazi Germany and Communist Russia." Public Radio International's *The World*, August 3, 2017.

Sharp, Samuel. *Letters from Italy: Describing the Customs and Manners of That Country, in the Years 1765, and 1766*. 1766. Reprint, Chestnut Hill, MA: Adamant Media, 2005.

Sinclair, Upton. *The Jungle*. New York: Doubleday, Jabber, 1906.

Siporin, Steve. "Folklife and Survival: The Italian-Americans of Carbon County, Utah." In *Old Ties, New Attachments: Italian-American Folklife in the West*, edited by David A. Taylor and John Alexander Williams, 80–93. Washington, DC: Library of Congress, 1992.

Skagway Sleuth. "George Joseph Rapuzzi Jr." *Skagway Stories*, June 10, 2010. www.skagwaystories.org/?s=rapuzzi+.

Skëndi, Stavro. *The Albanian National Awakening, 1878–1912*. Princeton, NJ: Princeton University Press, 1967.

Sloan, W. B. "Bernalillo County." In *Business Directory of New Mexico and Gazetteer of the Territory, 1882*. Santa Fe: New Mexico Printing, 1882.

Smith, Dennis Mack. *Italy: A Modern History*. Ann Arbor: University of Michigan Press, 1969.

Smith, Payton. *Rosellini: Immigrant Son and Progressive Governor.* Seattle: University of Washington Press, 1997.

Speroni, Charles. "California Fishermen's Festivals." In *The Land Beyond: Italian Migrants in the Westward Movement,* edited by Gloria Ricci Lothrop, 213–31. San Marino: Patrons of Italian Culture, 2007.

Steers, Stuart. "The Watermelon King." *Westword,* October 10, 2002. www.westword.com/news/the-watermelon-king-5071740.

Steinbeck, John. *The Grapes of Wrath.* New York: Viking Press, 1939.

Stinneford, Earl. "Mines and Miners: The Eastern Europeans in Wyoming." In *Peopling the High Plains: Wyoming's European Heritage,* edited by Gordon Olaf Hendrickson, 121–48. Cheyenne: Wyoming State Archives and Historical Department, 1977.

Stockton Business Directory. San Joaquin County: California Online Historical Directories, 1859; San Francisco: Herrick & Hoogs, 1859.

Stockton City and San Joaquin County Directory. Sacramento: Polk-Husted Directory, 1920.

Stoddard, [Theodore] Lothrop. *The Rising Tide of Color against White World-Supremacy.* New York: Charles Scribner's Sons, 1920.

Strati, Saverio. *Empty Hands.* Translated by Peter Moule. London: Abelard-Schuman, 1963.

Stumpf, Marcia. *Growing Up in Guasti.* Rev. ed. Published by the author, 2000.

Sutherland, Arthur T. *Earnings and Hours in Pacific Coast Fish Canneries.* Women's Bureau Bulletin, no. 186. Washington, DC: US Government Printing Office, 1941. https://fraser.stlouisfed.org/title/earnings-hours-pacific-coast-fish-canneries-5459.

Talagan, Dean P. "Faith, Hard Work, and Family: The Story of the Wyoming Hellenes." In *Peopling the High Plains: Wyoming's European Heritage,* edited by Gordon Olaf Hendrickson, 149–68. Cheyenne: Wyoming State Archives and Historical Department, 1977.

Thale, Christopher. "Railroad Workers." In *Encyclopedia of Chicago.* Chicago Historical Society: Newberry Library, 2005. www.encyclopedia.chicagohistory.org/pages/1038.html.

Tobin, Caroline. *North Rainier Valley Historic Context Statement: City of Seattle Department of Neighborhoods.* Seattle: Rainier Valley Historical Society, 2004.

Toll, William. "Ethnicity and Stability: The Italians and Jews of South Portland, 1900–1940." *Pacific Historical Review* 54, no. 3 (1985): 161–89.

Tracy, Houston, Jr. "A Sketch of the History of Del Rio." USGenWeb Project Archives, 2000. usgwarchives.net/tx/valverde/valvertoc.htm.

Trettel, Flavio. *La medaglia d'oro.* Trento: Reverdito Edizioni, 1993.

Tupone, Domenico. "Luca Vullo Presents *La voce del corpo* at the Italian Film Festival in Portland." *L'Italo-Americano* (April 28, 2016): 9. www.italoamericano.org.

United States Census, 1870–1940. Washington, DC: US Census Printing Office. See individual citations in text for cities, counties, and states cited by years, 1870–1940.

Vandor, Paul E. *History of Fresno County, California: With Biographical Sketches.* Vols. 1–2. Los Angeles: Historical Record, 1919.

Varni, Stephen. *The Inland Sea.* New York: William Morrow, 2001.

Vecoli, Rudolph J. "Are Italian Americans Just White Folks?" *Italian Americana* 13, no. 2 (1995): 149–65.

———. "The Search for an Italian American Identity: Continuity and Change." In *Italian Americans: New Perspectives in Italian Immigration and Ethnicity*, edited by Lydio F. Tomasi, 88–112. Staten Island: Center for Migration Studies, 1985.

Verdicchio, Pasquale. *Bound by Distance: Rethinking Nationalism through the Italian Diaspora*. Madison, NJ: Fairleigh Dickinson University Press, 1997.

———. "The Place of Identity: San Diego's Little Italy and Community as Archive." In *Italian Immigrants Go West: The Impact of Locale on Ethnicity*, edited by Janet E. Worrall et al., 10–24. Cambridge, MA: American Italian Historical Association, 2003.

Villarreal, José Antonio. *Pocho*. New York: Doubleday, 1970.

Walker, Catie M. *Wines of Walla Walla Valley: A Deep-Rooted History*. Charleston, SC: American Palate, 2014.

Walker, Norman. "Tallulah's Shame." *Harper's Weekly*, August 1899, 79.

Watson, Charles H. "Need of Federal Legislation in Respect to Mob Violence in Cases of Lynching of Aliens." *Yale Law Journal* 25, no. 7 (1916): 561–81.

Watt, Ronald G. *History of Carbon County*. Utah Centennial County History Series. Salt Lake City: Utah Historical Society, 1997.

Weatherford, Doris. *Foreign and Female: Immigrant Women in America, 1840–1930*. Rev. ed. New York: Facts on File, 1995.

Webb, Clive. "The Lynching of Sicilian Immigrants in the American South, 1886–1910." *American Nineteenth Century History* 3 (Spring 2002): 45–76.

West, Cornel. *Race Matters*. Boston: Beacon Press, 1993.

Whitfield, William, ed. *History of Snohomish County, Washington*. Vol. 2. Chicago: Pioneer Historical, 1926.

Wilkerson, Isabel. *The Warmth of Another Sun: The Epic Story of America's Great Migration*. New York: Random House, 2010.

Williams, John Alexander. "Introduction: Regionalism and Ethnicity." In *Old Ties, New Attachments: Italian-American Folklife in the West*, edited by David A. Taylor and John Alexander Williams, 14–27. Washington, DC: Library of Congress, 1992.

Woodall, Conrad. "The Italian Massacre at Walsenburg, Colorado, 1895." In *Italian Ethnics: Their Languages, Literature and Lives*, edited by Dominic Candeloro et al., 297–317. Staten Island: Italian American Historical Association, 1990.

Worrall, Janet E. "Adjustment and Integration: The Italian Experience in Colorado." In *The Land Beyond: Italian Migrants in the Westward Movement*, edited by Gloria Ricci Lothrop, 173–86. San Marino: Patrons of Italian Culture, 2007.

———. "A Comparative Study of Hispanics and Italians in the Southwest." In *Italian Americans: A Retrospective on the Twentieth Century*, edited by Paola Alessandra Sensi-Isolani and Anthony Julian Tamburri, 110–26. Chicago Heights: Italian American Historical Association, 2001.

———. "Labor, Gender, and Generational Change in a Western City." *Western Historical Quarterly* 32, no. (2001): 437–67.

Zappi, Elda Gentili. "Memory Gaps: The Risorgimento and the History of Women." In *In Our Own Voices: Multidisciplinary Perspectives on Italian and Italian American Women*, edited by Elizabeth Giovanna Messina, 21–36. Boca Raton: Bordighera, 2003.

Zinn, Howard. *A People's History of the United States*. 35th ed. New York: Harper Perennial, 2015.

Index

About the Author

Kenneth Scambray is the author of *A Varied Harvest: The Life and Works of Henry Blake Fuller, The North American Italian Renaissance: Italian Writing in America and Canada, Surface Roots: Short Stories*, and *Queen Calafia's Paradise: California and the Italian American Novel*. Since 1978 he has served as the book and film critic for *L'Italo-Americano*. He is professor emeritus of English at the University of La Verne.